PRAISE FOR
Ghosts of Vesuvius

"Compelling. . . . Bold. . . . Compulsive reading."   —*New Scientist*

"A stunning and magical alchemy of science, philosophy, bible study, and brilliantly detailed on-the-scene reporting, Pellegrino's book moves effortlessly from the sweeping grandeur of infinite time and space to the briefest moment in the lives of ordinary men."
                              —*Publishers Weekly* (starred review)

"Natural history as written by Walt Whitman, or, better yet, by Gertrude Stein. . . . Clear, concise, and persuasive."
                              —*Pittsburgh Post-Gazette*

"First quality writing."   —*Houston Post*

"Fascinating. . . . Full of insights into science and history."
                              —*Portland Oregonian*

"[A]n engrossing, challenging read."   —*Kirkus Reviews*

Lewis Abernathy, Mir-2

About the Author

CHARLES PELLEGRINO has been known to work simultaneously in entomology, forensic physics, paleogenetics, preliminary design of advanced rocket systems, astrobiology, and marine archaeology. The author of eighteen books of fiction and nonfiction, including *Return to Sodom and Gomorrah*, *Unearthing Atlantis*, *Dust*, *Ghosts of the Titanic*, and the *New York Times* bestseller *Her Name, Titanic: The Untold Story of the Sinking and Finding of the Unsinkable Ship*, he is the scientist whose dinosaur-cloning recipe inspired Michael Crichton's bestselling novel *Jurassic Park*. Dr. Pellegrino lives in New York City.

GHOSTS OF VESUVIUS

A NEW LOOK AT
THE LAST DAYS OF POMPEII,
HOW THE TOWERS FELL,
AND OTHER STRANGE
CONNECTIONS

CHARLES PELLEGRINO

HARPER ● PERENNIAL

NEW YORK ● LONDON ● TORONTO ● SYDNEY

IN HONOR OF TWO LITERARY FATHERS,

WHO WENT EXPLORING ON THE SAME DAY,

IN MAY OF 2002:

WALTER LORD AND STEPHEN JAY GOULD.

AND WITH A SPECIAL THANK-YOU TO

"PADDY" BROWN, WHO KNOWS WHY.

HARPER ⬤ PERENNIAL

A hardcover edition of this book was published in 2004 by William Morrow, an imprint of HarperCollins Publishers.

HarperCollins books may be purchased for educational, business, or sales promotional use. For information please write: Special Markets Department, HarperCollins Publishers, 10 East 53rd Street, New York, NY 10022.

First Harper Perennial edition published 2005.

Designed by Gretchen Achilles

The Library of Congress has catalogued the hardcover edition as follows:

Pellegrino, Charles R.
    Ghosts of Vesuvius : a new look at the last days of Pompeii, how the towers fell, and other strange connections / Charles Pellegrino.— 1st ed.
        p. cm.
    ISBN 0-380-97310-3
    1. Vesuvius (Italy)—Eruption, 79. 2. Pompeii (Extinct city). 3. Excavations (Archaeology)—Italy—Pompeii (Extinct city). I. Title.

DG70.P7P44 2004
937'.7—dc22   2003071055

ISBN-10: 0-06-075100-2 (pbk.)
ISBN-13: 978-0-06-075100-5 (pbk.)

06 07 08 09 ❖/RRD 10 9 8 7 6 5 4 3 2

CONTENTS

Will not we fear, though the earth be removed, and though the mountains be carried into the midst of the sea; though the waters thereof roar and be troubled, though the mountains shake with the swelling thereof. Selah . . . [T]he earth melted . . . Selah . . .

PSALM 46

PART I

A WALK THROUGH
TIME AND SPACE

IN THE BEGINNING

And it came to pass on the third day in the morning, that there were thunders and lightnings, and a thick cloud upon the mount, and the voice of the trumpet exceeding loud; so that all the people that were in the camp trembled. And Moses brought forth the people out of the camp to meet with God; and they stood at the nether part of the mount. And Mount Si'nai was altogether on a smoke, because the LORD had descended upon it in fire: and the smoke thereof ascended as the smoke of a furnace, and the whole mount quaked greatly.

EXODUS 19:16–18 *(ca. 1630 B.C.)*

Let none be deceived by the fictions poets tell
That Aetna is the home of a god.

THE VOLCANO AETNA

(from a poem by Lucius Junior, as referenced by Seneca, A.D. 63–79)

Volcanoes.

Call them Alpha and Omega.

The beginning and the end.

Somewhere very far back in my ancestry, and in yours, they were the source of water and ice, the creators of proteins and porphyrin molecules. Somewhere near 4 billion B.C., volcanoes became the cause of every breath we take. They are the foundations of life, the fountains of Eden. The rocks tell us so.

By the measure of human life spans, our civilization is very old, but the water and the carbon that run in our veins are the exhalations and regurgitations of Earth itself; and our Earth is older than life itself. And our universe—most certainly nothing more (or less) than the most recent episode in an infinite and possibly identical series of "Big Bangs" and "Cosmic Crunches"—is older still . . . far, far older than Earth itself.

Even before the first atom of silicon existed, long before the most basic components of lava and volcanic dust were born, our universe was a fascinatingly violent and beautiful womb. And most of all, when we come to think about our beginnings at all, even the dust teaches us that our universe was a *strange* womb, as viewed from the perspective of anything larger than a proton.

When the wizards of CERN and Fermilab smash protons and antiprotons together, they are working the same sort of magic on atomic nuclei that a child might inflict upon a watch: smashing it open with a hammer to learn from its pieces what makes the watch work. Seen up close, a proton is nothing more (or less) than forces—gyrating, interconnected bends in space-time called, for human convenience, quarks and gluons. The very basis of matter arose from defects in what would otherwise have been perfectly flat space-time geometry; as if the substance of our existence burst forth from mere geometric flaws, from submicroscopic cracks in the universe; as if all matter is in fact as close to nothing as anything can be and still manage to think of itself as being something—which, in fact, it is.

From this discovery, from this simple observation, scientists have begun to pen a new story of Genesis—

(*And the earth was without form, and void; and darkness was upon the face of the deep*)—

And when we peer into the darkness and the void, when we peer as deeply as our primitive tools allow, we descend into a realm of the "jiffy"—which defines the travel time of light across the diameter of a proton, or one billion-trillionth of a second. Within this space, far below the realm of everyday human experience, invisible lines of force—lines of interconnected quarks and gluons—stretch out of nothingness, contracting, gyrating, and creating the spherical field of an equally transparent proton.

If one is permitted to imagine a single proton in a single atom of silicon, containing fourteen each of protons and neutrons, and if we then allow ourselves to pull back the view ever so slightly, we behold a bundle of twenty-eight colorless spheres with gyrating interiors—the nucleus of the most abundant element on this planet.

Pull back farther still, and the silicon nucleus recedes completely from view, through an expanse of space so vast that by the time we retreat to the outermost electron shell, the nucleus is, when scaled against that spherical, ghostly shell, no larger than a New York City bus scaled against the sphere of Earth. And this, too, is a ghostly and empty, yet forceful realm. To continue drawing backward reveals the outermost shells of atoms interlinked by electrons—which manifest, self-contradictorily and simultaneously and almost everywhere at once, as waves and particles . . . Bound electron shell to electron shell, silicon and oxygen form an array of molecules arranged in rows—silicon bound to oxygen . . . silicon and oxygen . . . silicon and oxygen, row after parallel row—a crystalline array in a chip of volcanic rock. And as our retreat from the proton propels us from the quantum universe into the universe of the very large, we can no longer see individual molecules. With increasing distance, the first hints of color begin to enter the world.

The wavelengths of visible light are far smaller than a grain of sand or a fleck of crystalline basalt and far larger than the diameter of an atom of silicon or oxygen—so only now do we begin to see the brownish black hue of a nugget of once-molten rock collected by my daughter, Amber, not far from midtown Manhattan.

All is exactly as the Greek naturalist Democritus and his student Epicurus had said it would be, nearly 2,400 years ago. Scientists of the future, they predicted, would come inevitably to believe in nothing, for nothing existed in this universe except atoms and empty space—

(And the earth was without form, and void . . .)

And perhaps nothing itself really is everywhere in that ten-to-the-eightieth power of protons spread throughout the visible universe, but only because our understanding of nothing is everything—

(And Democritus said, in fragment 125: *By convention there is color, by convention sweetness, by convention bitterness; but in reality there are [only] atoms and space.*)

And so, here I sit inside the *Mir-2* submersible, an awed and all too often seasick human being, some 2.5 miles (4 kilometers) below the open Atlantic, in a sunless and strangely peaceful abyss. Here we sit, you and I, on the very edge of creation. Outside the viewport, 40 million years of silt lie under our feet, 40 million years of bacterial and proteanaceous snow, 40 million years of African dust storms billowing out to sea, of nematode worms and silt-dwelling monsters leaving their chitin and their bones behind. All the dust and carbon residuum of those vanished ages is piled about us in a deep-ocean snowfield more than a mile thick. And beneath the snow, the ground is a lake of solidified glass. The very foundations of all the oceans are volcanic glass. Hundreds of miles eastward, out there in the cold and the dark, the lava fields are so new that there has been no time for the dust of the earth to settle upon them.

There is a place with hundreds of smoking volcanic cathedrals, obsidian bright and Bible black. Near one of them, armies of crabs forage in a bacterial garden. In such places, life itself must have had one of its many starts.

I know of a world in which water emerges four times hotter than steam, but the overlying miles of ocean press down with such force as to forbid the water to boil, though it emerges hot enough to glow.

I know of a deep-ocean vent where the ground is littered with the shells of limpets and mussels, preyed upon constantly by sulfur-dwelling snails.

I know the place where a large shrimp—red, black, and brown—ventured too near to the top of a black smoker and, injured by volcanic water, sought shelter in a semitransparent flower that turned out to be some hitherto unknown animal with needlelike teeth, each made, apparently, of glass.

I know where fields of hydrothermal vents protrude through the bed of the Atlantic like clusters of organ pipes—and all around and beneath the volcanic pipes, the world is a feeding frenzy, curiously slow and stately, but a feeding frenzy nonetheless. I have named the place "Hell's Kitchen."

We have come a long way from the realm of the jiffy to the scale of volcanic vents and submarines. This is the scale we know best: our own. Yet here, inside the little steel shell of *Mir-2,* I carry with me my little girl's chip of volcanic rock from the world above: Amber's chip of time. The stone is barely larger than a thumbnail, yet it is an anthology of the universe.

IN THE BEGINNING, there was hydrogen—and not very much of anything else. Even today, there are 9,200 more atoms of hydrogen spread throughout the universe than there are atoms of carbon or silicon. As we look around, our spectrographs and telescopes reveal, in the dust of exploded suns, that the iron running through our veins, the oxygen in our lungs, and the silicon upon which we stand came about, as it were, from fusion-based waste products in the hearts of dying stars. We can track the universal accumulation rates of the heavy elements backward along the stream of time and see that 7 billion years ago the formation of rocky, Earth-like worlds was unlikely, 9 billion years ago exceedingly improbable, and 11 to 12 billion years ago next of kin to impossible.

There was a time, inevitable and far, far in our past, when our remotest ancestors were mere hydrogen nuclei—protons. Hydrogen, the simplest atom, consists of a single proton and a single electron held together by their opposite charges, by their lines of electromagnetic force. When infinitely curved and infinitely dense space-time had unraveled into a universe that, though newly born, was by our standards already ancient, an entire system of stars and Jupiter-like brown dwarfs could be scoured for all the elements heavier than helium, and we would have failed to find enough material from which to fashion a single, fist-sized rock.

In the beginning, there was little except the strong and the weak forces, gravitation, and electromagnetism—little except the miracle of a universe in which energy was running down slowly, unavoidably, into matter: a miracle in which submicroscopic cracks in the universe gave way to frozen energy—which was, stated another way, matter.

In the beginning, there was little except hydrogen and helium, with a trace of lithium here and there; but from the lights in the heavens, you might have guessed that these were enough, and almost never would the universe be quite so simple again. Life was inevitable. The lights in the heavens—the stars—would have told you so.

Some 5 billion years later, the lives and deaths of stars had fused hydrogen nuclei into helium nuclei, helium into carbon, oxygen, neon, magnesium, silicon, and iron. The collapse of stars into supernovae had produced, and then scattered, an entire spectrum of elements both heavier and lighter than iron. Some of those elements were injected into our solar system almost at the moment of its formation, to judge from a careful reading of radioactive decay products in the Allende meteorite, sometimes called the "Genesis Stone." This oldest of all known crumbs from the early solar system resided above a volcanic zone inside one of the asteroid parent bodies 4.6 billion years ago. (Most of the present-day asteroids and meteorite samples originated inside globes of rock and ice up to 500 miles wide—which were subsequently ground down in collisions with other asteroids, through the same process that has cratered every inch of the Moon.)

Blobs of magnesium 26, the daughter decay product of the very short-lived aluminum 26, reveal that ancient and highly radioactive isotopes, freshly manufactured in a supernova explosion, were stirred into the matrix of Allende just prior to or during its creation. Diamonds were also stirred in—uncountable trillions of microdiamonds forged in the outermost reaches of a giant red star's atmosphere. The oldest known diamonds on Earth are only a few molecule layers thick, so small and so numerous that anyone who has worked with the Genesis Stone presently exhales diamonds with every breath, and will continue to do so for the rest of their lives.

The phrase *carbonaceous chondrite*, which defines a very rare stony meteorite, carbon-rich, with traces of indigenous water, is also used to describe the Genesis Stone, Allende. Hollow spaces within Allende are sometimes clustered with crystals of pyrrhotite (Fe_7S_8), a form of "fool's gold." The Orguel and Murchison carbonaceous chondrites (named, like Allende, after the towns upon which they fell) are similarly filled with veins of pyrrhotite, identical in every way to veins found in rocks sampled from volcanic chimneys on the floor of the Atlantic. Salt veins and chemically produced proteins, along with precursors to chlorophyll and

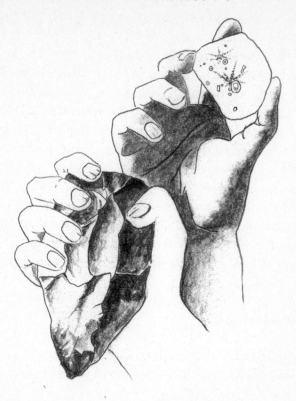

A *Homo erectus* hand ax (*bottom*), found far below the oldest ruins of Egypt's Karnak, dates back almost to a half-million years B.C. People have been drawing rocks from the earth and reshaping them to human needs ever since. The Genesis Stone (*top*), the oldest rock that human hands have ever held, fell in Allende, Mexico, in A.D. 1969. Certain rare products of radioactive decay reveal that isotopes of carbon and aluminum were injected by a supernova explosion into our solar system just prior to the formation of Earth's mantle. It has taken the carbon atoms that run in our veins 4.6 billion years to discover that they (some of them, at least) are 4.6 billion years old.

hemoglobin (complex organic molecules called porphyrins, different from any porphyrins known on Earth), tell us that somewhere between the molten cores and the outer surfaces of the asteroid parent bodies there existed, for a half-billion years or so (until the nickel-iron cores froze), warm, wet zones in which the early solar system, in diverse places, was trying to make life.

From atoms and empty space . . .

From the dust of the stars . . .

From such beginnings, it is possible to believe that the phenomenon we call life is but the most likely outcome of some very common elements, if stirred together and kept warm enough and wet enough for long enough. From such beginnings, it is possible to believe that someone, somewhere over the far side of the galactic core, is gazing skyward tonight, in our direction, and asking the same questions we ask.

What was it that astronomer Carl Sagan had said? "We are star stuff. Simply that: cosmic debris."

We are the dust of the universe, trying to understand where it is going and whence it came—sometimes through theology, sometimes through science, sometimes through a combination of both.

We are the dust of the universe, trying to understand itself.

(Where did I come from?)

Volcanoes.

The holy grails of our existence. The beginning and the end.

By 4.5 billion B.C., give or take 100 million years, the hydrothermals must already have been dreaming.

From energy running down into matter, from the ash of cracked and cooling space-time, dust had begot stars and stars had begot heavy nuclei. Dust had begot dust—which gathered into chambers of magma and water.

When planetesimals and planets began to form, though the Sun itself was still hundreds of thousands or perhaps even millions of years from igniting, the solar system was far from cold. The heat of accretion, and the decay of aluminum 26 and its radioactive brethren, guaranteed that Jupiter's moons Europa and Ganymede, Saturn's moons Enceladus and Titan, Neptune's moon Triton—and a half-dozen places just like them—were molten inside. They collected at their cores those relatively rare atoms of nickel, iron, platinum, gold, and uranium. Lighter elements, including silicon and aluminum, tended to bubble up from the cores and collect in the mantles of the infant worlds. Water, of course, being lighter than the rocks, was squeezed up to the surface and became the major constituent of the protoplanetary crusts. Somewhere below Titan's or Triton's self-sealing (and insulating) icy shells, and above their seething hot mantles, existed a zone in which oceans and hydrothermal oases could form, sustained by long-term volcanic activity. Jupiter's moons Europa and Ganymede are examples of this.

Oceans, of course, are the key to life. Oceans, yes, and volcanic dust. As above, near Jupiter, so below, on Earth.

Rocks collected from the Moon have provided glimpses of what happened next. The daughter decay products of radioactive elements have dated the last extensive heating and melting (as indicated by the oldest rocks found on the lunar surface) to about 4.2 billion years ago, suggesting that the Moon's crust had cooled and rigidified by the time Allende reached an age of 400 million years. The oldest Moon rocks were also baked dry by the solar wind, confirming that the Sun had ignited by that time, probably long before that time. By 3.9 billion years ago, the great storm of meteoritic bombardment (the last stage of planetary rock collecting) was subsiding, but asteroids were still occasionally puncturing the skin on the Moon's Earth-facing side. Between 3.8 and 3.3 billion B.C., basaltic lava welled up from the mantle and slowly filled the wounds, forming the dark lunar maria, or "seas." Then, as radioactive elements continued to decay and their abundance dwindled, internal heating faltered and failed to keep pace with cooling at the surface. The crust solidified to a depth of more than 600 miles (more than 1,000 kilometers)—scabbed over and became impenetrable to ascending lava. By 3.2 billion B.C. (the age of the youngest known Moon rocks), the Moon, as a geologic entity, was dead; we view it today much as it looked then.

If the Moon was hot very early in its history, Earth, with its greater volume and relatively smaller ratio of surface area, must have been hotter still, especially in its birth stages, when even Allende, Murchison, and Orgueil were young.

At first glance, the dryness of Earth and the Moon, when compared against the Genesis Stone and Ganymede, is a puzzle. As much as 60 percent water, by weight, and almost as large as Mars, Ganymede resembles a giant orbiting snowbank. Pieces of the Allende and Murchison meteorites, when first recovered, weighed in with up to 10 percent water composition, meaning that they came from someplace two thousand times wetter than the earth itself. Unless Earth formed from rocks some-how different from rocks in the outer solar system, Allende, Murchison, and Ganymede suggest that our planet, in its birth stages, was a far, far wetter place than it is today.

Jupiter's Ganymede and its sister moon Europa display surface markings suggestive of thick, icy crusts sheltering subsurface seas whose volcanic zones are kept active to this day by a never-ending pulse of tidal friction between the ice worlds themselves and their tiny, not fully formed star (the so-called "gas giant," Jupiter). They are, in effect, a solar system orbiting within our solar system. The same can be said of Ence-ladus and Titan at Saturn, and Triton at Neptune. With so many throws of the hydrothermal dice, the probability of extraterrestrial life in our own solar system (including, just maybe, complex creatures resembling fish and crabs and not just bacterial mats) rises so high as to approach a biochemical and statistical certainty.

That's how my high-school friend Jesse Stoff and I were coming to view the surrounding light-hours in 1973, while *Pioneer 10* sped toward the outer planets and *Voyager 2* was being prepared for service in his-tory's most extreme game of gravitational billiards (also known as the "Grand Tour" of the outer planets). We were, after all, living on Long Island, home of the Grumman Lunar Module. There were a lot of "space cadets" walking around Long Island in those days. Jesse and I were two of them. We spent our summers teaching science at the 4-H camp, walking through cornfields, and obsessing on carbonaceous meteorites. If exploring strange frontiers can be called addictive, we were mainlining asteroids, Jovian moons, and Allende diamonds.

Jesse had proposed that Jupiter's innermost moon, Io, might be molten inside, due to tidal flexing (on account of being caught in the middle of a gravitational tug-of-war between Jupiter on one side, Europa and Ganymede on the other)—molten, and perhaps overlain by a thin layer of water, with a layer of ice above the water. In reality, the tidal effects turned out to be more extreme than even Jesse had guessed: The *Voyagers* revealed that Io was molten from the core all the way to the surface. Its entire skin was lava. Volcanoes—the whole thing. If one were to hope for icebound seas, one had to look a bit farther away from Jupiter, to the moons next door.

And, of course, even then thoughts of seas on (or rather in) Europa or Ganymede went hand in hand with thoughts of life gathering around those hidden volcanoes. On the question of life, Jesse was a believer. I was a doubter—which was just as well for us, because neither Jesse nor I had ever learned anything new from people who simply looked at our work and nodded in agreement. In the sciences, "I like it" was (and still is) the most progress-killing of all known phrases.

In those days, chlorophyll in green plants was "known" to be the molecule that sustained life on this planet. I "knew," therefore, that life in a subsurface sea could not possibly endure unless, for example, the ice was thin enough here and there to let sunlight penetrate to near-surface green algae. "On what else," I asked Jesse, "could a food chain be based?"

In those days, he had no answer. "Volcanoes there are," I had said, and warm wet zones, too, in great abundance, from Jupiter's Europa to Neptune's Triton and perhaps even as near as Mars. "Volcanic water and volcanic dust there may be," I emphasized. "Dust. But until or unless we find a food chain—no allergens."

Then, one day early in 1979, Jesse handed me a stack of papers and said, "Here's your damned food chain!" He had written to Woods Hole Oceanographic Institution, where a team led by Robert Ballard had just announced the discovery of deep-ocean hydrothermal vents. Oases had sprung up around the volcanic springs of the deep, revealing an ecology based upon a process called "chemosynthesis," which was powered by sulfides instead of sunlight. That quickly, Woods Hole had thrown open a biological window on the entire universe. That quickly, what has since come to be called "the Europa theory" was tenable. On the heels of this discovery, astrobiologists Claire Edwin Folsome and Cyril Ponnamperuma became the first to propose that abundant heat and ever-expanding mineral deposits near deep-ocean volcanic vents were, almost from the day of Earth's formation, a source of life's origins. It could have begun, here on Earth, almost on Day One.

When I met him in Sri Lanka in 1989, Cyril Ponnamperuma reminded me that the men who penned the Old Testament had declared, "From dust we came, and to dust we shall return. Dust to dust, the beginning and the end." The imagery was always haunting and evocative, but late in the twentieth century it became even more so to a small group of scientists, perhaps because we were beginning to learn that the old psalms were not without a certain poetic truth—

(Psalm 90: *To you, a thousand years are but a single day. Before the mountains were born, before the earth and the world came to birth, you were God. You can turn a man back to dust by saying, "Back to what you were!"*)

But who among us could really believe that we arose from the dust of the stars, or from the dust of the earth?

Who, in those days or in time-present, could believe in such things?

Who but a believer in miracles, or a believer in science?

According to Cyril, if we really wanted to track life on Earth back to the start, "We had better be prepared to think a little more kindly of dust and clay." Rocks from the hydrothermal vents were formed from crystals of magnetite (Fe_3O_4), stacks of magnesium sulfate ($MgSO_4$), and sheets of pyrrhotite (Fe_7S_8). As now, 4.6 billion years ago the total surface area accessible to water and organic compounds percolating through the mineral grains was enormous, providing excellent substrates for the capture and concentration of prebiological molecules. Furthermore, the abundance of negative and positive charges carried by the minerals could have allowed them, with a little assistance from volcanically heated water, not merely to bind and concentrate charged organic molecules but also to act as primitive catalytic centers, accelerating the formation of chemical bonds—nudging atoms of carbon, forcefully and with statistical inevitability, in the direction of biochemistry.

As such, the phenomenon we call life—or at least the very first steps in life's direction—would appear to have been pulled from a curiously simple bag of tricks.

There is, perhaps, no stronger example of the probable ease with which those first steps were taken than the one produced during the Second World War. For years, the German military had been synthesizing hydrocarbon fuels to power its tanks, trucks, and planes. With burning rubbish serving as a heat source, mixtures of methane (CH_4) and other simple organic gases were passed at high temperature over bentonite (a type of clay) and iron ore (which catalyzed the formation of chemical bonds) in huge pressure cookers. One of the great inefficiencies of this process was the synthesis of unanticipated and unwanted by-products that had to be filtered out and continually clogged and overran the filters. The "clots" and "plugs" turned out to be made of arginine (and other amino acids, sometimes clumping into globs of randomly assembled protein), purines, fatty acids, and the occasional porphyrin molecule. Had it occurred to Germany's syn-fuel scientists that they were probably simulating reactions between lava, dust, and a "primordial broth" somewhere on Earth, somewhere near 4.6 billion B.C., they could easily have gone to Sweden and claimed their Nobel Prize in chemistry. This is exactly what two American scientists did ten years later, with a much smaller and simpler version of the same apparatus.

Some Germans complain to this day about a "stolen" prize; but the Stanley Miller–Harold Urey Nobel was neither stolen nor undeserved. The Miller-Urey breakthrough lay in looking at what everyone else had been looking at for years (and disposing of as "garbage"), and thinking what no one else had thought.

Near 4.6 billion B.C., Earth's hydrothermals, and Europa's and Ganymede's, must have been performing a variation on Nazi Germany's syn-fuel theme. Earth, it turns out, was not unusual in being able to take those first steps in the direction of life (as revealed by clots of amino acids, purines, and the occasional porphyrin molecule in the Murchison and Orgueil meteorites, and to a lesser degree in Allende—all chemically distinct from any possible earthly contaminants). What makes Earth unusual is that the first steps toward life came perilously close to being cut short.

Remember? Earth and the Moon, compared against the icy interiors of Allende and Murchison, compared against Europa and Ganymede, are as dry as a pair of old bones. If, for comparison's sake, you were to hold a polished brass sphere about the size of a basketball in your hands and puff just a single breath onto it, the amount of water vapor condensed onto its surface would be proportionally deeper than all of Earth's oceans combined. At Jupiter and beyond, we have seen worlds whose mantles are mostly ice and whose crusts erupt lava made of water instead of rock.

Earth, in its birth stages, (and its more far-flung cousin, Mars) must have been very much the same: a sphere of molten rock overlying a core into which most of its heavy metals were descending. Lighter materials, including water and hydrogen-bearing carbon compounds, were moving in the opposite direction, toward the surface, where they stole away with some of Earth's heat and collected into a world-encircling ocean, overlain by an icy shell that, if left undisturbed, would have grown hundreds of miles thick.

If Cyril Ponnamperuma and Claire Folsome are right about hydrothermal vents being a cradle—if not *the* cradle—of life, then the ancient, snowball Earth, left on its own, would have produced the raw materials of natural selection and biocomputation even in the absence of a sun.

But this was not to be. Somewhere between 4.5 and 4.6 billion years ago, while Earth continued to sweep up meteorites and other bits of solar driftwood, increasing slowly in girth and mass, the Sun reached *critical* mass, at which point a half million miles (820,000 kilometers) of overlying gas pressed down with a force sufficient to squeeze hydrogen nuclei (now stripped of their electrons) into such small volumes, and to accelerate them to such high velocities, that when protons struck, they stuck together and began to form helium nuclei. The process by which four protons became two each of protons and neutrons, produced a nucleus lighter than the sum of its parts. A little bit of its mass—1 percent—disappeared from the universe. With each fusion, 1 percent of matter—1 percent of frozen energy—went back to being energy again . . . an enormous amount of energy . . .

We know from very close study of our own star—the Sun—that the energy produced at the core takes about a million years to reach the surface. So, for a million years after the Sun began to pulse with fusion's surge, the solar system must have remained relatively dark.

From observations of very young stars in various stages of formation, we know that the arrival of hydrogen-fusion burning's first pulse, at the surface, blasts an enormous amount of gas away from the star and its immediate surroundings. The blast is called a "T-Tauri Wind." Such a storm must have raged across the surfaces of both Earth and the Moon by 4.5 billion B.C. Any primordial atmospheres were stripped away—in the case of the smaller world, beyond recall; in the case of the larger, nearly so. Ice converted to gas and trailed out beyond the orbits of Mars and Jupiter in great shimmering veils. At the onset of the Sun's T-Tauri phase, Earth and the Moon might best be described as a pair of giant comets. Mars, too, must have sent forth cometary veils, though its outer shell of ice and dust had a greater chance (albeit only a slightly greater chance) of surviving.

All the water and hydrogen we have on Earth today—a puff of condensed breath against a basketball's worth—percolated up from within our world *after* the storm passed, and was contributed to fractionally, between then and now, by comets and meteorites.

By the time the solar storm passed, all the organic compounds produced by hydrothermal vents *before* the storm, all the prebiological molecules, were condensing into a thin crust of drying mudflats and shales. The surface of Earth thus became an anvil under the Sun, or a crucible in which the chemicals of life (if not the remnants of life itself) were concentrated into powder and clay. Like condensed milk, the substance of evolution awaited only the application of water, awaited only the cooling of the Sun to a point at which the planet could once again maintain a gravitational hold on its hydrogen—awaited, then, only the continued venting of the hydrothermals.

Molecular biologist Sidney Fox has already provided a laboratory analogy of what could have happened when the hydrothermals held sway once again. He creates microspherules and microtubes of protein by first stirring amino acids (the building blocks of protein) into water, then evaporating the water by pouring it over hot volcanic rocks. Finally, he splashes water over the dried mixture, and the resulting runoff is full of protein microspheres, or "protocells."

Life from nonlife. You could probably start the process in your own kitchen, if you wanted to. It's that easy. Claire Folsome demonstrated that you need only assemble carbon, hydrogen, nitrogen, and oxygen in one place, in almost any combination, then apply heat, shock waves, X rays, or ultraviolet radiation—almost any form of energy input—and, invariably, within twenty hours or so, you will have incited the formation of carbon compounds ranging from simple amino acids to complex microstructures resembling spheroids, rods, and hollow tubes with tantalizing, septa-like divisions—built, all of them, out of randomly assembled proteins.

Folsome's spheres, rods, and divisions teach us two things: (1) multi-cellularity was there at the beginning, even before cells themselves existed, and (2) the structures we associate with cells are mere stability shapes in nature, dictated by physics and not by biology. They could easily have been here from the very start. And yet, such experiments involve only small volumes over very short periods of time—

(To you, a thousand years are but a single day. Before the mountains were born, before the earth and the world came to birth . . .)

The earth, our cradle, has had billions of years and entire oceans to work with. And in the basements of the oceans resides a system of volcanic vents that, even to this day, weaves a lengthy path, somewhat like the seam on a baseball, over more than 40,000 miles (65,600 kilometers) of seafloor.

Carl Sagan once tried to convey time's vastness by compressing the entire history since the Big Bang (approximately 13.7 billion years) into a single year—with Earth forming between August 15 and September 10, dinosaurs arriving just ahead of Christmas Eve, and human civilization occupying the last few seconds of December 31. By Sagan's measure, we have just entered the New Year, equipped with brains and seeking to understand how we were born. Our bodies ripple with energy-releasing-and-capturing molecules that conduct symphonies written on DNA and performed by protein. The music might have begun, at one time or another, on an Earth laid bare—baked dry and scoured airless, under the fires of an infant Sun. It begins to look as if the composer in our lives was Earth itself, in whose volcanic exhalations and regurgitations the dust of the stars was forged into the substance of the first living cells. And it becomes possible for us to believe that the poets and the myth-makers, while often at odds with the likes of Democritus and Epicurus, were right about this much: Though in one sense we have grown like mold on a rotting apple, in another sense this particular apple did not simply provide a surface upon which we took root; rather, like a parent, Earth gave us life.

2

THE GODS THEMSELVES

Call it mother, if you will—but Earth is not a doting parent.

ISAAC ASIMOV

Big Bang theory?
You've got to be kidding.

GOD *(seen on a billboard near Brookhaven National Laboratory,*

with no fine print or sponsoring organization indicated)

Volcanoes, those forges of God known to the Hindus as being next of kin only to Siva the Destroyer, are at once paradoxical preservers. If Fox, Folsome, and Ponnamperuma are correct about hydrothermal vents as modern-day windows on a route to the origin of life on Earth, then the vents—the vents themselves—are our remotest earthly forebears. With such credit, or blame, we can equate volcanoes with all three members of the Hindu Triad—with Brahma the Creator, Siva the Destroyer, and Vishnu the Preserver.

The last two, Destroyer and Preserver, are rarely more apparent than when one stands in Pompeii or Herculaneum, two cities that died so they may live forever.

The same white-hot ash that sears and encases paper, flesh, and wood, hardens those very same substances against the forces of dissolution. The more a piece of wood or bone is singed, the less it will decay. Carbonized—turned, as it were, into charcoal—it cannot decay at all. In the 95-million-year-old amber forests of northern New Jersey, just across the river from Manhattan, I have pulled ashen flowers and seeds out of the earth. They appear to have aged barely a day since they last bloomed alongside the minisaurs and underfoot of the dinosaurs, barely a day since a forest fire converted them to ash.

In Pompeii's sister city, Herculaneum, I have seen carbonized scrolls recovered from the Villa of the Papyri—a whole library of scrolls. At first sight, they are blacker than sackcloth and their words are lost to the ages; but under polarized light, and with a little enhancement from an ordinary photoshop program, computer imaging can separate burned black ink from burned black paper and, for the first time in nearly two thousand years, Epicurus and his students can speak to us clearly, in their own words.

(Then listen, Democritus. . . . Death, therefore, the most awful of evils, is nothing to us, seeing that when we are, death is not come, and when death is come, we are not.)

A whole library, coming only now into view—its books, its frescoes, its sculptures becoming open windows on beliefs about life and suffering, about love and death among humans and their imagined overlords: Poseidon, god of the sea, took for his lot a volcanic island; he begot children by a mortal woman and settled them under the mountain. Prometheus was a Titan born in human form. When Zeus, god of all gods, hid fire from humankind, Prometheus stole it by trickery and brought enlightenment to man. For this offense, Zeus chained Prometheus to a rock and every day sent an eagle to peck out his liver, which grew back to its full size every night, so he might be tortured in this very same manner again, again, again.

The idea of a suffering servant, paying for his love of humanity, was already ancient by the time the first Christians, Gnostics, and Jewish reformers settled in and around Herculaneum. Prometheus was predated by Isis and Osiris, two deities popular in Roman literature and borrowed from Egypt. Osiris brought agriculture to civilization and was murdered by a fallen divinity named Seth—murdered by his own blood, his own brother. Osiris was best known for his subsequent restoration, or resurrection, as the ruler of that region of the afterworld to which the souls of the just would venture, and find eternal life, after death.

Long before the burning of the two cities, and long afterward, there existed a theme—distinctly Greek, and Egyptian, and tragic—in which one who was too caring, too enlightened, or too pure would be made to suffer for all humanity.

"Pigeradamas appointed a son, Seth, to the second eternal realm, along with a second star, Oroiel." So begins codex 2, chapter 5, verse 14, of the Nag Hammadi texts, unearthed near Alexandria in 1945 (ominously, some theologians say, in the year of the first atomic bomb). Dating from the decades after the burning of Pompeii and Herculaneum in the west and the destruction of Jerusalem in the east, the Nag Hammadi texts, or "Nile River gospels," are curiously apocalyptic and include ancient Hebrew themes mixed with Roman, Greek, and Egyptian deities. And these are mixed with something new. In codex 2, a messianic figure reveals to "John" that Adam, the first human, suffered the tortures of Prometheus and Osiris:

"They said . . . [b]reathe some of your spirit into the face of Adam, and then the body will arise. . . . The body moved, and became powerful. And it was enlightened. At once the rest of the powers became jealous, although Adam had come into being through all of them, and they had given this power to this human[.] Yet Adam was more intelligent than the creators, and the first ruler. When they realized that Adam was enlightened, and could think more clearly than they, and was free of evil, they took and threw Adam into the lowest part of the whole material realm [John, codex 2, chapter 10] . . . They devised a plan with the whole throng of rulers and angels. They took fire, earth, and water, and combined them with the four fiery winds. . . . Thus Adam became a mortal human being, the first to descend and become estranged [John, codex 2, chapter 11] . . . The human beings were made to drink the waters of forgetfulness [water of the river Lathe in the underworld] . . . so that they would not know [whence] they had come [John, codex 2, chapter 13] . . . These things were communicated to John as a mystery, and afterward the Savior disappeared at once. Then John went to the other disciples and reported what the Savior had told him. Jesus (the Savior) amen."

Much as the oldest rocks give us glimpses of what the first steps toward the origin of life might have looked like, these oldest Christian-like texts (sometimes paralleling the canonical New Testament books, at other times rivaling them) are a window on the birth stages of the creation tales, apocalyptic prophecies, and teachings about time and redemption that would prevail more than three centuries later, after the fall of Rome. In Nag Hammadi codex 1, chapter 3, the Savior tells James, "Consider how long the world has existed before you—and how long it will last after you. Then you will discover that your life lasts but a single day, and your suffering is but a single hour . . . So disdain death, but care about life. Remember my cross and my death, and you will live."

Present-day Jesuits can be heard to remark, "Man's concept of God evolved as man evolved." Near the border of the first and second centuries A.D., suffering and death, and triumph over misfortune in an unjust universe, were already evolving into a prevailing theme. This view of life was, of course, descendant from an older, Graeco-Roman and Egyptian theme, with a new element added.

(*And the Lord said* [to James the Just, in Nag Hammadi codex 1, chapter 3], *Will you not forsake the love of flesh and the fear of suffering? Do you not know? You have not been insulted, you have not been accused falsely, you have not yet been thrown into prison, you have not yet been condemned unjustly, you have not yet been crucified without reason, and you have not yet been buried in the ground, as I was by the evil one.*)

Osiris . . . Prometheus . . . Adam . . . Jesus. An old story: persecution, descent, and resurrection—a story that was itself undergoing resurrection and only then on the verge of coming into sharp focus during that August of A.D. 79, when the twin cities and most of their inhabitants were buried in the ground by a strange and hitherto unrecognized evil.

Beginnings.

Secret origins.

Shadowy and sometimes strange, beginnings have always been the very substance and core of archaeology . . . of paleontology . . . of astronomy.

The Nag Hammadi books reveal to us that at an early stage, at least one of Christianity's first branches, or a parallel faith much like Christianity, was incorporating legends from multiple colliding cultures into what are now called the Gnostic gospels (known on Vatican Hill as the "heretical" gospels). Despite the new (and eventually ruling) faith's early-first-millennium purges against Jews and Gnostics—in what the church's founding prophet called "brother against brother," and what the prophet of codex 2, saying 16, called "father against son and son against father"—in centuries to come, the Roman Catholic Church would include in its Bible the ancient Hebrew stories of man's origins and struggles, while mostly (but never entirely) rejecting the Egyptian, Roman, and Indus Valley legends.

The Christian Bible, even in its earliest stages, became distinctly apocalyptic. The few historical records that survive from those days teach us that the Christian and Gnostic books were indeed born in a conflict of father against son, against the contrasts of riot and reason, visionary dreamers and apocalyptic visionaries.

The Nag Hammadi library was created in the decades during which Rome's destruction of Jerusalem, and Mount Vesuvius's destruction of Pompeii and Herculaneum, were still fresh in memory. The names of the twin cities, especially, must have been as universally horrifying in the late first and early second centuries as the names Hiroshima and Nagasaki were to people living in the late twentieth and early twenty-first centuries. Yet for all the horror, for all that was spoken about and written, only those documents most extensively reproduced had a chance of surviving. Only four letters describe the eruption and mention Pompeii and Herculaneum by name, but hundreds, probably thousands, of written accounts are long turned to dust. Without Pliny the Younger and Dio Cassius, it would seem to most of us today that the cities simply vanished without mention.

Writing to the historian Cornelius Tacitus between A.D. 103 and 107, Pliny the Younger, in his opening sentences, suggests that the catastrophe was so memorable, even legendary, that he hoped his late uncle's reputation would live on by mere association with Pompeii's name: "It is true that [Pliny the Elder] perished in a catastrophe which destroyed the loveliest regions of the earth, a fate shared by whole cities and their people, and one so memorable that it is likely to make his name live forever."

Of his own escape from the eruption—"though my mind shrinks

from remembering"—Pliny the Younger wrote, "When we left at Misenum . . . [w]e saw the sea sucked away and apparently forced back by the earthquake: at any rate it receded from the shore so that quantities of sea creatures were left stranded [and dying] on dry sand. On the landward side [eastward, across the Bay of Naples] a fearful black cloud was rent by forked and quivering bursts of flame, and parted to reveal great tongues of fire, like flashes of lightning magnified in size . . . Soon afterwards the cloud sank down to earth and covered the sea . . . spreading over the earth like a flood . . . [D]arkness fell, not the dark of a moonless or cloudy night, but as if a lamp had been put out in a closed room . . . Many besought the aid of the gods, but still more imagined there were no gods left, and that the universe was plunged into eternal darkness forevermore . . . [When] genuine daylight [returned,] the sun [was] but yellowish as it is during an eclipse. We were terrified to see everything changed, buried in deep ashes like snowdrifts . . . Fear predominated, for the earthquakes went on . . . Darkness . . . fire . . . sparks . . . (and hot) ashes falling . . . [And] the belief that the whole world was dying with me and I with it."

"And all was consumed in the flames, all covered with the gray ash," added the Roman poet Martial, "and the gods themselves would not that they had such power."

Nearly two hundred years later, in the time of Bishop Eusebius of Caesarea, in Roman Palestine, the apocalyptic verses of Matthew, Luke, and the Revelation of John the Divine were taking their final form, laced with visions of fiery death and the sun as black as sackcloth, as if in eclipse:

"And Jesus said unto them [in Matthew, chapter 24]—There shall not be left here one stone upon another, that shall not be thrown down—And except those days shall be shortened, there should no flesh be saved: but for the elect's sake those days shall be shortened . . . For as the lightning cometh out of the east, and shineth even unto the west—of those days shall the sun be darkened, and the moon shall not give her light, and the stars shall fall from heaven, and the powers of the heavens shall be shaken . . . And great earthquakes shall be in diverse places [according to Luke, chapter 21], and famines, and pestilences; and fearful sights and great signs shall there be from heaven—the sea and the waves roaring; men's hearts filling them for fear, and for looking after those things which are coming on the earth . . . [Nicodemus] came to Jesus by night, and said unto him, Rabbi [for even in A.D. 300, in fully evolved texts, Christians called their founding prophet "Rabbi"], we know that thou art a teacher come from God . . . And Jesus answered . . . [In Revelation, chapters 8 and 9] the angel took the censer, and filled it with fire of the altar, and cast it into the earth: and there were voices, and thunderings, and lightnings, and an earthquake . . . and there followed hail and fire mingled with blood, and they were cast upon the earth: and a third part of the trees was burnt up. And the second angel sounded, and as it were a great mountain burning with fire was cast into the sea: and the third part of the sea became blood; and the third part of the creatures which were in the sea, and had life, died . . . And he opened the bottomless pit; and there arose a smoke out of the pit, as the smoke of a great furnace; and the sun and the air were darkened by reason of the smoke of the pit . . . And thus I saw the [three] horses [of apocalypse] in the vision . . . By these three was the third part of men killed, by the fire, and by the smoke, and by the brimstone."

No one knows for sure whether or not recollections of Vesuvius made their way into the New Testament, here and there projected forward in time and converted into the language of prophecy and apocalypse.

No biblical scribe ever said plainly that the burning of entire cities gave early Christians a taste for apocalypse. Though it is easy to see parallels between Pliny the Younger, Luke, and John—easier still to connect them to volcanic death—no one knows. Truly no one. But this is the way of science and discovery. If you cannot bear the unknown, if pushing half-blind toward an always mutable image of truth becomes not a celebration of the mysterious but rather a fear of bumping around in the dark, coupled with a refusal to utter the words "I don't know," then go back to brightly lit rooms, never question what is written in the science books (including this one), and do not make science your profession. "I don't know" is the best place for a scientist to be.

Saint Thomas, the doubter who (according to Scripture) insisted on putting his own fingers in his resurrected Messiah's wounds before believing, made "I don't know" his creed. According to some Jesuit scholars, Thomas was the first scientist of the Christian era. And, though Jesus is said to have remarked that those with faith—those who believed without seeing—were more blessed than Thomas, the biblical scribes never did damn Thomas for his questions.

(Pompeii as a source of apocalyptic visions?)

If you have not shaken your head today, slowly, from side to side, and said, "I don't know," or "Gee, what *is* that?" then you probably have not had a very interesting day.

(Pompeii and Herculaneum?)

We don't know.

So, let's wonder, you and I. Let's wonder about time and about evolving religions—

("Man's concept of God evolved as man evolved.")—

Let's look a little more closely at Pliny the Younger and John the Prophet, at Thomas and Dio Cassius, and at Pompeii.

PLINY THE YOUNGER wrote his firsthand eyewitness account about twenty-five years after the eruption. His was, in most respects, a scientific observational account, with tantalizing echoes arising in writings attributed to Matthew, Luke, and John: Fire and brimstone going up into the sky, like the smoke of a giant furnace, the Sun and the Moon blotted out, part of a mountain cast into the sea, in flames . . . the fire and the lightning coming out of the east . . . the burning of trees, the death of sea creatures . . . earthquake . . . a darkness born of smoke spreading over the earth like a great flood tide . . . the smoke rising from a bottomless pit in the earth.

By A.D. 300, two centuries beyond Pliny's account, Bishop Eusebius was assembling material for his ten books of church history, *Historia ecclesiastica*. By this time, the books of Matthew, Luke, and John probably existed in something very close to their familiar, canonical form. Living about 70 years before Eusebius, and almost 130 years after Pliny the Younger, Dio Cassius, when he wrote about the A.D. 79 eruption, imagined demonic giants from the Roman creation myths, sent by divine will against Pompeii and Herculaneum. In the century following Pliny, not only had the eruption acquired a legendary quality, but the destruction of

Pompeii and Herculaneum was evidently swelling to mythical proportions as well. Along the path to cautionary tale, in the manner of Sodom and Gomorrah, the event acquired impressive embellishments. In his *Epitome*, or "History of Rome," Dio did not describe the gods as being merely "besought" by those fleeing the eruption (as Pliny had told it); rather, he wrote of their direct involvement, in allowing the Titans, or "Giants," to rise in revolt against the people and their temples—to rise, curiously, to the sound of trumpets, as had John's seven angels—

(Revelation 8:2—*And I saw the seven angels which stood before God; and to them were given seven trumpets*)—

And each of the angels, or giants, as it cast thunderings and lightnings and smoke and great quakings upon the Vesuvian landscape—and pestilence and fire—sounded the last trump.

"This is what befell," wrote Dio, about A.D. 230: "Numbers of huge men quite surpassing any human stature—such creatures, in fact, as the Giants are pictured to have been—appeared, now, on the mountain, now in the surrounding country, and again in the cities, wandering over the earth day and night and also flitting through the air. . . . There were frequent rumblings, some of them subterranean, that resembled thunder, and some on the surface, that sounded like bellowings; the sea also joined in the roar and the sky reechoed it.

"Then suddenly a portentous crash was heard, as if the mountains were tumbling in ruins; and the first huge stones were hurled aloft, rising as high as the very summits, then came a great quantity of fire and endless smoke, so that the whole atmosphere was obscured and the sun was entirely hidden, as if eclipsed. Thus day was turned into night and light into darkness. Some thought that the Giants were rising again in revolt (for at this time also many of their forms could be discerned in the smoke and, moreover, a sound of trumpets was heard), while others believed that the whole universe was being resolved into chaos and fire. Therefore they fled, some from the houses into the streets, others from outside into the houses, now from the sea to the land and now from the land to the sea; for in their excitement they regarded any place where they were not [presently], as safer than where they were.

"While this was [happening], an inconceivable quantity of ashes was blown out, which covered both sea and land and filled all the air. It wrought much injury of various kinds, as chance befell, to men and farms and cattle, and in particular it destroyed all fish and birds.

"Furthermore, it buried two entire cities, Herculaneum and Pompeii, the latter place while its populace was seated in the theatre. Indeed, the amount of dust, taken altogether, was so great that some of it reached . . . Rome, filling the air overhead and darkening the sun. There, too, no little fear was occasioned, that lasted for several days, since the people did not know and could not imagine what had happened, but like those close at hand, believed that the whole world was being turned upside down, that the sun was disappearing into the earth and that the earth was being lifted into the sky. These ashes now did the Romans no great harm at the time, though they later brought a terrible pestilence upon them."

(Of those days shall the sun be darkened, and famines, and pestilences.)
And Dio described a second conflagration.

(And fearful sights and great signs shall there be from heaven . . . for I am a jealous God.)

"In the following year," Dio recorded, a second conflagration, above ground, "spread over very large sections of Rome while [Emperor] Titus was absent in Campania [at Pompeii] attending to the catastrophe that had befallen that region. It consumed the Temple of Serapis, the Temple of Isis [wife-goddess of Osiris], the Saepta, the Temple of Neptune, the Baths of Agrippa, the Pantheon, the Diribitorium, the Theatre of Balbus, the stage building of Pompey's theatre, the Octavian buildings together with their books, and the Temple of Jupiter Capitolinus with its surrounding temples. Hence the disaster seemed not of human but of divine origin."

And so it came to pass that the destruction of so many Roman and Egyptian gods, during and after the Vesuvian upheaval, resounded loudly in the mind of at least one Roman writer, a century and a half after the eruption.

Nearer the actual time of Vesuvius, the Nag Hammadi's Book of John echoes interest in this same issue of multiple competing deities. Church historian Eusebius placed the "heretic" writings of the Gnostics (in book 4 of his *Church History*) after the Christian "illumination" that began in Emperor Hadrian's eighteenth year, A.D. 135, or fifty-six years after Pompeii. At that time, the "schools of detestable heresy," according to Eusebius, were preexisting and already well established from Egypt to Syria—which brings the initial spread of Gnostic scripture very close to the Vesuvian apocalypse, if not rendering the scribes and the volcano exact contemporaries.

The disciple John, according to his Nag Hammadi Revelation, sees a jealous God (one of several deities) who can, with his angels, bring power to kingdoms or destroy them. In codex 2, chapter 7, he dares to confront his followers with a question absent from all biblical texts, a question that makes both Dio's fear (of an unmentioned deity) and Eusebius's anger (at anyone who would pen heretical questions) understandable. According to John, the power that was in the "Creator" (which "the great maker" had taken from his Mother) produced the world by accident: "And when he saw creation all around, and the throng of angels that had come forth from him, he said to them, 'I am a jealous God, and there is no other God besides me.' But by making this announcement, he suggested to the angels with him that there is another God. For if there were no other God, of whom would he be jealous?"

Dio was clearly thinking along such lines himself—jealousy and wrath from above—when he listed the temples destroyed and named their gods, then concluded that the disasters seemed to be of divine origin.

ONLY AT THE END of the twentieth and the beginning of the twenty-first centuries did the true nature and extent of the Vesuvius eruption become apparent. More than a hundred years earlier, most of the homes in central Pompeii were found to be abandoned, and it was presumed that the populace had escaped. But outside the city gates, under present-day homes, vineyards, and garbage dumps, more than ten thousand human skeletons are now known to lie within the earth's fossil record. Ten thousand—perhaps twenty thousand and more—no matter which way they ran, were cut down by the volcanic death cloud.

At the boatyard of Herculaneum, a man on horseback was vaporized to the bone in less than two-tenths of a second. Before the nerves could even begin to transmit pain, they had ceased to exist; and as he and the horse fell, the volume of water released from their tongues and their eyes and their internal organs flashed jets of vapor into the air—where, being immeasurably cooler than the surrounding atmosphere, the jets caused the ash to condense, to crystallize instantly into clumps of fluff—adding a strange, mineral snowfall to the terrestrial din. Their tongues were charcoal and their blood had become lava snow before their bones could fall to the ground.

"There is but a little time before what you can see will pass away," wrote the chroniclers of Thomas's Gnostic prophecies. According to codex 2, chapters 6 and 7: "Some of those who rush into this madness do not realize they are foolish, but think they are wise. They are drawn to the beauty of the body, as if it would not perish. Their minds turn to themselves, their thoughts are on their own pursuits, but the fire will consume them . . . What sows and what is sown will pass away in fire, in fire and in water, and will be hidden in dark tombs. The angel Tartarouchos [guardian of a sunless abyss below Hades] will take up fiery lashes, and chase them with fiery whips that spew forth sparks into the faces of those being pursued. If they run toward the west, they find fire. If they turn south, they find it there, too. If they turn north, erupting fire threatens them again. They cannot find the way to the east, either, to run there and be safe . . . on the Day of Judgment."

In later writings, collected, edited, and eventually adopted by the church, there was agreement with the "heretics" on at least one point: Whenever cities were destroyed and the unburied dead lay in the streets, there was always a reason for it. Judgment: the destruction was always associated with Egypt or Sodom, or with some prophesied future destruction of Babylon and Jerusalem (which had a record of cyclic destructions throughout history and would presumably continue the cycle deep into futurity). In a just universe, according to the scribes, the victims must have been villains because they became victims, must have become victims because they were villains.

In present-day vernacular, the scribes would have put their lesson thus: "Be good. Or you'll be sorry."

And so they recorded, after a mountain left more than ten thousand either vaporized or bleeding under the stars . . . and in the streets: "I looked, and beheld a pale horse: and his name that sat upon him was Death, and Hell followed with him . . . And I beheld when he had opened the sixth seal, and, lo, there was a great earthquake; and the sun became black as sackcloth of hair, and the moon became as blood [Revelation 6] . . . And their dead bodies shall lie in the street of the great city, which spiritually is called Sodom and Egypt . . . And the same hour was there a great earthquake, and the tenth part of the city fell, and in the earthquake were slain of men seven thousand [Revelation 11] . . .

"Alas, alas, that great city, that was clothed in fine linen, and people, and scarlet, and decked with gold, and precious stones, and pearls . . . And every shipmaster, and all the company in ships, and sailors, and as many as trade by sea, stood afar off, and cried when they saw the smoke of her burning . . . Alas, alas Babylon . . . for in one hour is she made desolate . . . And the light of a candle shall shine no more at all in thee; and the voice of the bridegroom and the bride shall be heard no more at all in thee: for thy merchants were the great men of the earth; for by thy sorceries [heretical temples] were all nations deceived [Revelation 18]."

Alas, Babylon. The city referred to by name in the eighteenth chapter of Revelation was located 300 miles (450 kilometers) from its nearest sea, the Persian Gulf. The city is also referred to "spiritually" as Sodom and Egypt and "prophetically" as Jerusalem.

Interestingly, Pliny the Younger (who worshiped what the Christians regarded as abominations—false idols and false gods—in blasphemous temples) recorded, in his letters to Tacitus, eyewitness accounts of Pompeii and Herculaneum from ships at sea. His uncle, Pliny the Elder, happened to be an admiral stationed at Misenum, a city west of Pompeii and Vesuvius, some 25 miles (41 kilometers) across the Bay of Naples. During the early afternoon of August 24, A.D. 79, Vesuvius ejected ash more than 10 miles into the heavens, and the younger Pliny recorded that the great weight of the cloud caused it to occasionally collapse groundward under its own mass, then to spread out over the earth.

The elder Pliny gave orders for the fleet to be launched eastward on a mission of rescue—"hurrying," Pliny the Younger wrote, "to the place which everyone else was leaving, steering his course straight for the danger zone. He was entirely fearless, describing each new movement and phase of the portent to be noted down exactly as he observed them."

The admiral had actually brought his secretary along, to take dictation of his scientific observations of the event. Ashes were falling upon the ships as they drew near the doomed cities, hot enough to threaten ignition of sails and clothing. Their passage east was eventually blocked by a sea of floating, gas-filled pumice stone, and all they could do was watch from afar as the larger city, Pompeii, was blotted out by black clouds and erupting firestorms. Others wailed and wanted to turn back, but Pliny the Elder allayed the fears of his companions: "When the helmsman advised this [turning back] he refused, telling him that 'Fortune favors the brave.' "

When at last the surge cloud reached them, it choked Pliny the Elder—and Pliny alone—to death, as if something in the cloud had been seeking him, specifically. Afterward he became (in a manner of speaking) a permanent resident of the twin cities.

When Bishop Eusebius of Caesarea penned his church history some 220 years later, he knew of and was impressed by the Plinys. In book 3, *Missions and Persecutions,* he recorded that during the reign of Trajan, in A.D. 112, Pliny the Younger wrote to the emperor expressing some small misgivings about condemning Christians to death. There were, he had discovered, more of them in his territory than originally anticipated, and they seemed to him, upon closer inspection, "mostly harmless."

According to Eusebius, "Pliny the Younger, one of the most distinguished governors[,] . . . after condemning certain Christians and reducing their rank [in the province of Bithynia] was alarmed at their number. Not knowing what to do in the future, he wrote to Emperor Trajan that he found nothing wicked in their behavior, other than their unwillingness to worship idols. He further informed [Trajan] that the Christians rose at dawn, sang hymns to Christ as a god, and upheld their teachings by forbidding murder, adultery, fraud, robbery, and the like. In response Trajan sent [an order] that Christians were not to be hunted but were to be punished if found."

Since the church clearly looked favorably upon Pliny the Younger, his writings were less likely to be burned or purged by the bishops as

Rome's Christians grew in strength and stature. Indeed, the newly evolving church became one of the key places where Pliny's descriptions of two cities going up like the smoke of a furnace were preserved and recopied . . . and recited. This was a time during which Bishop Eusebius noted that "Symeon found fulfillment in martyrdom" (about A.D. 110, during Trajan's reign). This was a time of messianic Judaism and apocalyptic belief, a time in which Christianity was in some quarters indistinguishable from a Jewish reformist movement—as when, according to Eusebius, "[a] certain Jew named Justus, one of the vast number of the circumcision who believed in Christ by that time, succeeded to the bishop's throne in Jerusalem." This was, above all, a time in which— with the horrors of Pompeii and Herculaneum vividly described in library scrolls and still fresh in memory and urban myth—the apocalyptic books were beginning to take form.

(And every shipmaster, and all the company in ships, shall bewail her, and lament for her, when they see the smoke of her burning)—

In chapters and verses that shifted abruptly from prophecy to past tense, and back again to prophecy, the book of Revelation was moving quickly toward its final draft—

(And [the shipmasters of chapter 18] *shall stand afar off for the fear of her torment, weeping and wailing . . . And they* [did] *cast dust upon their heads, and cried—Alas, alas, that great city, wherein were made rich all that had ships in the sea by reason of her costliness! For in one hour is she made desolate.)*

Again, we cannot yet know that in biblical visions of Armageddon we truly are seeing ghost images of cities that actually did die in the century of the first Christians. We do not have all the science, all the artifacts, all the ancient texts. If in fact the peculiar horrors unique to volcanic death strengthened or shaped an already messianic faith's sense of apocalypse and made its followers believe all the more devoutly in the wrath of the heavens and a coming battle between good and evil, then *if* remains the key word.

We may never know for sure, but this should not discourage us from looking with wonder upon the possibilities, and trying to explore them. If some fragment of text still lies buried within the earth, waiting to speak clear—waiting to cement Vesuvius and apocalypse—its discovery will scarcely be cause for shock or even surprise; for this will not be the first time that the uneasy marriage between continental plates has spawned visions of brimstone and hellfire and sent ripples through the history of life.

Time and again, the uneasy earth has both nurtured and destroyed—has, at random, opened up new pathways to life and cut those paths short.

It is possible to believe that had not the isle of Thera produced the most powerful explosion in human memory, in the very center of Minoan civilization, there should have been moon landings by the time of Augustus, and the Savior about whom John and the Gnostics were writing could have become the world's first television evangelist.

It is possible to believe, looking backward and backward along the stream of time, that the dinosaurs might never have risen to dominance if not for a volcanic catastrophe that paved an area the size of India in lava more than a mile thick, about 250 million years ago.

It is possible to believe that neither we nor the dinosaurs would ever have been, if not for the seething hell within the earth, if not for volcanoes.

Backward and backward along the stream of time, along the line through infinity—

"If species lived forever and everything remained the same throughout all of geological history, we would have no science of paleontology and I might have become a fireman after all," said paleontologist Stephen Jay Gould. He was paleontology's poet, and it is ironic that as a child, in Mrs. Bogart's class at PS 26, "Stevie" really did want to grow up to be a fireman; for at the end of his life he went to Manhattan's Ground Zero—from "Day One," bringing bottled water and supplies and hot apple pies to the firemen in the crater. He helped in every way that he could, until the fumes did their work, and crashed his already cancer-weakened immune system.

In the spring of 2002, the New York City Fire Department's bagpipers played "Amazing Grace" at Stephen Jay Gould's memorial service, symbolizing the loss of a brother who had died a fireman's death. In the end, little Stevie really did grow up to be a fireman after all.

He sleeps now, within the earth, beside Pliny, the apatosaurs, his fossil *Pikaia,* and our remote Precambrian ancestors. "For some reason," Gould once said, "we are powerfully drawn to the subject of beginnings. We yearn to know about origins and we readily construct myths when we do not have data. Most of us know that the Great Seal of the United States pictures an eagle holding a ribbon reading *e pluribus unum.* Fewer would recognize the motto on the other side (check it out on the back of a dollar bill): *annuit coeptis*—'He smiles on our beginnings.' "

3

TIME GATE: THE COEVOLUTION OF VOLCANOES AND LIFE

Dear Steve: Looks like we both burned our lungs out a bit, this year. Forever klutzes, both of us. Frank Lombardi told me how you broke T. rex's teeth; whereas I only stumbled and broke his toes, when we both studied under him at A.M.N.H. Frank said that some believe it took an asteroid to kill the dinosaurs—but it took you and me to [really] finish the job. If you're there, Steve, give my best to T. rex—and have a good romp with him.

TO STEPHEN JAY GOULD (1941–2002):
"PALEONTOLOGIST, POET, TEACHER,
GROUND ZERO RELIEF WORKER"
(from a friend's farewell, penned in the Family Room Book,
1 Liberty Plaza, Ground Zero, New York City)

In a house on the main shopping street of Pompeii, a pair of human skeletons lies. And on the wall beside them, on a brightly colored fresco, this image is displayed: Flowers and songbirds living in a green world on the slopes of a mountain. And by aid of PCR, and electron microprobe, and computer, DNA from the bones teaches us that the skeletons were father and son. In August of A.D. 79, the pair climbed atop a knee-deep drift of volcanic dust that had snowed down from the mount and flowed indoors—flowed from the very same mountain depicted upon the wall. The boy, aged about fourteen years, is lying on his back upon the drift. His jaw hangs open at an angle suggestive of a last conscious moment spent gaping like a fish, and trying to swallow air. His head is turned to one side, as if to fix his gaze forever upon his father's outstretched left hand. They died, apparently, at the same instant, their fingers gently entwined. In the Vesuvian ash, among bones shut out from starlight and from sunlight for close on two thousand years, I have gazed into the eyeless sockets of a skull that never lived to see a pocket-computer-assisted scientist, never lived to see flying machines above the mount or space station *Alpha* speeding beneath the stars. And though the empire of Rome stretches far and away, like a civilization completely alien to us, the bones speak still of our common humanity, speak still, from their last second of life, of love and mutual tenderness.

THE ROLE PLAYED by the observer in archaeological research—or in any sort of scientific information gathering—is often called reductionism: exploring the details in a chip of bone or stone, then the details within the details, until one descends through the smallest bits of molecular structure, through sodium or hydrogen into the realm of immortal electrons and ageless quarks . . . until, at last, through these same tiny cracks, we are looking out upon the entire universe. Or so we say.

Sometimes, working in this way, we fail to see the leaves for the carbon atoms, fail to see the forest for the trees. Or so our detractors say.

But it's all connected. Even a leaf in the palm of your hand is hitched to everything else in the world, to every field of science. Even the skeletal hand of a father reaching out to his son, in a house on Pompeii's main street, can be an anthology of the universe. Or so we say.

We are—again—simply the dust of the universe, trying to understand itself.

In the house on "Main Street," molecular biologists Marilena Cipollaro and Antonio Cascio have identified DNA from a total of thirteen skeletons. They have determined that all thirteen "were, at the molecular level, strongly bonded." Put another way, they were family. Like the boy and his father, the other members of the household had climbed atop a carpet of warm Vesuvian ash, as it poured in through broken wood shutters, and deepened. When the end came, they were all lying on the ash, as people might lie atop a bed of snow. Some of the skeletons are craning their necks upward, as if toward the imagined safety of cleaner air; they died, all of them, by inhaling something that instantly seared their lungs in the same part of a second.

Looking beyond DNA linkages, beyond molecular biology, Cipollaro sees hints of how they came to be preserved. "One of these people was a young pregnant woman at the end of her term," Cipollaro reads from the bones. "She was very close to giving birth." And so they stayed, hoping against hope that the ever-worsening crisis would simply abate. "One decides to stay because one lover is sick," Cipollaro believes. "And they cannot flee, because they all want to remain together."

In this house, family policy was simple and clear-cut: No one gets left behind.

The comedian and social critic George Carlin considered the uncounted thousands of human fossils under and around Mount Vesuvius, whenever he heard the late-twentieth-century mantra "Save the Earth." He thought long and hard about the fossil Pompeiians. To Carlin, the idea that humans were stewards of the planet was at worst hubris, at best hilarious. Stephen Jay Gould, Michael Rampino, and all the other "rock hounds" had taught him that asteroids periodically punched holes through the planetary crust, wiping out dinosaurs and giant oysters and stirring up tsunamis tall enough to shove clouds out of their way as they swept inland . . . And yet the earth still remained blue and green. North America had been overgrown alternately by sheets of lava and sheets of ice taller than skyscrapers, and according to the latest evidence from *Apollo* rock samples, the Moon might have formed about 100 million years after Earth collided with a planet the size of Mars. If this was true, then the Moon was simply what fell together from the collision's splash-off. Earth was still here, and would always be here, Carlin decided. Earth had been here for 4.6 billion years without us. Earth was in no particular danger and was not about to go anywhere, according to Carlin and Gould—"but maybe *we* were."

If one really wanted to know how well the planet was holding up, Carlin observed, "just ask those people in Pompeii."

"THE PESSIMISTIC BIBLICAL BOOK of *Ecclesiastes* finds almost everything to be void and empty of meaning," wrote Isaac Asimov, in response to my "peculiar hobby" of tracing the chain of cause and effect backward through time, often by powers of two. This was in 1982. The biblical scholar, biochemist, astronomer, science fiction writer, and famed agnostic pointed out that the prophet was speaking of human vanity. Ecclesiastes opens: "Vanity of vanities, saith the preacher [the son of David], vanity of vanities, all is vanity. What profit hath a man of all his labor which he taketh under the sun? One generation passeth away, and another generation cometh: but the earth abideth forever."

"But Earth abideth not," Asimov declared. "With all due respect to biblical authority, this is wrong." He acknowledged that if our civilization is, in time, reduced to the mere substance of archaeology—with not even archaeologists surviving in its future—then it may indeed turn out to be true that everything is pointless and empty of meaning, and that human beings get nothing in return for the labor of centuries. "But it is not true," he said, "that the Earth abideth forever. The implication is that it is eternal and changeless—the mere scenery and props, the backdrop against which the drama of humanity is played—but it isn't."

Even in biblical terms, there were contradictions; nothing abided forever, not even the earth, and least of all we human beings. The first book of the Bible, Genesis, described Earth's creation; and the last book of the Bible, Revelation, described Earth's end, and the end of all the stars, rolling up into heaven like spots on a painted scroll. Between the beginning and the end, the biblical scribes saw a gap of about six thousand years, covering the history of life.

If we narrow history down to the time frames of the Bible, to the time frames of human life spans or the rise and fall of nations, "[t]hen," observed Asimov, "the Earth would indeed appear to be changeless. There are earthquakes and volcanic eruptions, but these are pinpricks, comparatively. They pass and the Earth abideth, so that we can use, as a favorite cliché for great age, 'as old as the hills.' That is not bad, for the hills are far older than the history of civilization."

Asimov thought that Carl Sagan's cosmic calendar (with all of existence scaled against a single year, and humans occupying only the last few seconds) was a good start at understanding the time frames of dinosaurs and pyramids, or Mount Vesuvius and the Bay of Naples. But to those of us who spent more time than anyone else on Earth thinking about time, there were, alas, drawbacks: "Speed up time in that fashion," said Asimov, "and there is nothing changeless about the Earth. It heaves and shifts like a living thing. Continents break up, move about, reunite, break up again . . . Trilobites and dinosaurs come and go (the former disappearing before 'Christmas,' the latter, right afterward) . . . Vast mountain ranges are heaved up and worn down . . . It is an ever-changing vista full of drama and excitement . . . But in that fast-moving perspective, the works of humanity—and humanity itself—are obscured and lost."

In the "time gate" approach (in my telling of world history—backward), Asimov believed science had at last found a solution to this dilemma: a thought experiment in which a slow perspective revealed human change against a changeless Earth, while a fast perspective revealed a changing Earth with all human works lost. It was, to him, a meeting place between science and poetry: "We move backward in increasing steps—first one year, then two years, then four—doubling each time. We begin by watching the works of humanity slowly peel away. [. . .] Then, more rapidly, and then, faster and faster, the Earth begins to change, and the very stars in the sky begin to drift and then to race."

And at every step, as we pause to observe the changes and the scientific clues that reveal them, our descent into the past becomes at first a walk through human history, then a strange overview of archaeology, of evolutionary development, of geology, of astronomy, and of everything else our species has chosen to touch. In this manner, tracing the connections between man and mountain backward through time, we follow the coevolution of humans and volcanoes down through the origins of Vesuvius, through the rise of dinosaurs, and into the Big Bang. The chapter ahead is a constantly accelerating plunge into the giddying depths of time itself. At journey's end, if I have succeeded in some small measure of what I have set out to accomplish, neither of us will be able to step away without a truer, more intuitive sense of time, and our place in it. When you step away, the story of how Vesuvius and its inhabitants came to be will no longer seem a mere tour of dates and archaeological oddities. The years A.D. 79, and 1628 B.C., and a quarter million B.C. will be much more than numbers recited. And we will be ready then, you and I, to approach the buried cities with the most important archaeological tool of all: a deeper and more tangible feel for time than we have ever possessed before.

It is only fair to warn you, before you read any further, that Earth truly abideth not, and that the hunt for beginnings may truly be a tale with no ending.

But it does have a definite beginning:

Once upon a time, there were only 6 billion of us upon the planet. The year was A.D. 1997. On any given day, nearly a dozen of us might be seen living outside of Earth altogether, aboard the *Mir* space station and the American space shuttle. A half-dozen could be seen, on any given day, dwelling more than two miles down on the beds of the oceans, inside the submersibles *Alvin, Nautile, Mir-1,* and *Mir-2.* Everywhere humans went, they created rooms or chambers heated to just the right temperature, until finally a once-obscure tropical mammal had managed to spread itself from pole to pole, onto the high seas, deep under them, and high above them. It was also the only animal known to store information externally, outside of its own brain. All the works of civilization, from road maps of ancient Pompeii to the complete works of Josephus, were already stored in computers and were becoming available on the ever-expanding Internet. Therein lay the first vestiges of a living, global membrane of human thought.

A.D. 1996

In this year, there are nearly 100 million fewer of us than shall exist just a year later, yet the mass of human flesh upon the planet weighs in at just 450 million tons. Squeezed head to head, shoulder to shoulder, we humans would form a cube barely more than a mile (1.6 kilometers) on a side, barely more than four times the height of the Empire State Building or the Twin Towers. And if one were to shove that cube off the edge of the continent and into the Atlantic, it would fail to raise the height of the world's oceans by the width of a human eyelash. Against such seeming insignificance, the works of humanity—our farm belts and our city lights—are plainly visible from the surface of the Moon through even the most modest pair of binoculars.

A.D. 1994

Already, one can easily notice the human population diminishing backward through time. The cube of flesh has lost nearly one-twelfth of its height. A half-billion fewer people have brought it down by the depth of a forty-story building. Still . . . at 5.5 billion, if all the people in the world were to build, for themselves, a single metropolis with the population density of Manhattan (including the open spaces of Central Park), the entire city would occupy a space slightly smaller than the state of Texas. And with the proper, least destructive land and water management strategies, the city could be sustained by a farm no larger than the continental United States, by an ocean no broader than the Atlantic, and by a solar power grid (embedded in roadways) requiring no greater land mass than the shoulders of the world's highways.

A.D. 1990

As the human biomap project begins, the world population reaches 5 billion. Moving backward from a population of 6 billion, the human cube, still a mile high, has nevertheless shaved off slightly more than the height of the Washington Monument.

A.D. 1982

Twelve pairs of human footprints mark the Moon. Beyond lunar orbit, robotic spacecraft have landed on Mars and Venus and flown past the rings of Jupiter and Saturn.

A.D. 1966

Computerized storage of films, music, and literature does not exist yet, outside of the science fiction stories of Isaac Asimov and Arthur C. Clarke. Libraries (personal and public), audiotape, and film are presently the only means of storing information outside the human brain.

A.D. 1934

The human cube has shrunk by the height of the Empire State Building. There are 1.7 billion of us, living within a civilization reeling from global economic collapse; during which Emperor Hirohito and his war-lords begin to plan the enslavement of China; during which Joseph Stalin eliminates more than a million real and imagined enemies in Russia; during which Italy's Benito Mussolini travels from Rome to ally himself with a rejected and angry bar-brawling artist who once pro-fessed that all he ever wanted to do was paint. Ahead of Mussolini's visit, the artist has been released early from prison on account of having "turned his life around" and put his jail time to good use by writing a book titled *Mein Kampf*. Most Americans look on with a sense of dread at the growing commotion in the east, for memories are still fresh with visions of World War I. In 1934, they still call it "the war to end all wars." The number will come later, naturally. In the major art institu-tions of Paris and Berlin, looking back from the twenty-first century, administrators shall be heard to remark, "The next time a loud and wild-eyed young man shows up at the admissions office and insists that we help him to spend the rest of his life learning how to paint landscapes—let him in!"

A.D. 1874

Exploration of the Antarctic coast is in its first decade. Ulysses S. Grant has begun his second term as America's eighteenth president; Mark

Twain is thirty-nine years old; Charles Darwin, aged sixty-five, has been living a semireclusive existence following the publication of his *Origin of Species* some fourteen years before. Grant, Twain, and Darwin: They are three of only 1 billion. Between 1874 and 1936, the height and width of the human cube differ by only one-tenth of a mile, or one city block (about 160 meters). A super-city, accommodating the entire cube at a population density comparable to Manhattan's five boroughs in the early twenty-first century, would encompass less than one-sixth the area of Texas, less than one-third the surface area of Italy or England. At this time, advances in medical and scientific understanding, more so than ventures of colonization and conquest, are beginning to account for increases in the human population. Although almost every family on Earth still knows the death of at least one child, and though many children still grow up with the tragedy of a father who died from a simple finger cut or bruise, the discovery of extensive indoor plumbing (complete with such luxuries as faucets and garden sprinkler systems), supported by sophisticated, clean-water technology—dating back 1,800 years to the ruins of Herculaneum—are met with a mixture of astonishment and embarrassment by the "modern world." At this time, the ancient Chinese and Roman germ theories of disease are finally being rediscovered and applied, twenty-four years after the American president Zachary Taylor died in office after eating "bad" cherries and washing them down with "stale," unpasteurized milk. During the next century, the pasteurization of milk, the refrigeration of food, the purification of drinking water, and the reintroduction of Herculaneum-style underground sewage systems will contribute more to the lengthening of human life spans and the swelling of the world's population density than all of science's combined medical advances.

With a total global human population of 1 billion, the world's largest cities have shrunk beyond recognition. In midtown Manhattan, Times Square and Hell's Kitchen are mostly farmland. Country homes stand north of Canal Street. Mulberry Street is where one finds the tastiest mulberries in town. There are tall pines on Pine Street, cedars on Cedar, apple trees on Orchard, and cherry trees on Cherry Street. George Washington had spent a presidency at Number 3 Cherry Street, the site of America's first White House in America's first capital city.

Number 3 Cherry Street is fated to disappear without a trace, under the northwest foundation of the Brooklyn Bridge.

Throughout the world, the "years without a summer" that followed the eruption of Tambora in 1815 are legendary after nearly two generations. Indonesia's Tambora explosion (which deposited ash layers in the ice of the North and South Poles) had visited July frosts and snow flurries upon New England. From Maine to Times Square, farmers were forced to abandon their lands and migrate into America's western territories. Volcanic sulfur had enveloped the stratosphere from pole to pole, intercepting enough solar radiation to simultaneously heat the outermost reaches of the atmosphere and plunge temperatures on the earth below. From California to Italy and China, the volcanic winter was felt and recorded. In Europe, the false winter ruined the honeymoon of a young poet and his eighteen-year-old bride, driving them indoors from the shores of Lake Geneva. Between hours of marital bliss, while "confined for days," the bride wrote of "the uncongenial summer," during which she took up a challenge "to make-up a ghost story." The bride's name was Mary Shelley, and the story she wrote was titled *Frankenstein*.

A.D. 1750

At a population of 760 million, the human cube is reduced to one-eighth its early-twenty-first-century volume, and one-half its height. A half-mile on a side (800 meters), it stands barely more than twice as tall as the Empire State Building.

North and south, the range of human habitation and exploration has become restricted at high latitudes, leaving the north polar regions unexplored and the Antarctic continent undiscovered. In terms of longitude, much of what, in this year, is known as the "New World" or the "Western Frontier" belongs to Russia, France, and Spain, while England owns what will one day become the eastern United States. Twenty-six years earlier, in 1724, Czar Peter the Great had sent Vitus Bering eastward across Siberia to the superpeninsula of Kamchatka. There, he supervised the construction of ships, named the Bering Strait, and sailed across it, claiming the Aleutian Islands and Alaska as he went. Russian explorers became the first to map the coasts of British Columbia, Washington State, Oregon, and northern California. Near San Francisco, Russian settlers ran into Spanish explorers heading north, producing history's first Mexican standoff. This tie will not be broken until Napoleon, scrounging for money to finance his wars, persuades France to sell to the United States all the land between the Mississippi River and the Rocky Mountains—1803's Louisiana Purchase—which will set the stage for America's expansion west. The economy-ravaging winter in the summer of 1816 (which will force-feed the westward expansion) is, in 1750, still latent in the earth, still latent under the Tambora volcano, still waiting to teach human beings not just that civilization is weak and inef-

The last major ice advance within our still-ongoing Ice Age began seventy-five thousand years ago and ended ten thousand years ago. Oscillations within the ice sheets are recorded by tree rings, fossil pollen grains, and the skeletons of microscopic oceanic plankton called foraminifera. The postglacial climatic optimum, when average temperatures were 1 to 3 degrees Centigrade (2 to 5 degrees Fahrenheit) warmer than they are now, reached a peak between 3520 and 2020 B.C. and lasted into the time of Vesuvius and Pompeii. The "Little Ice Age," raging from the death of Columbus through Washington at Valley Forge, force-fed Europe's textile industry . . . which rendered the Draper family (producers of draperies) almost instantly wealthy . . . which gave them the spare time they needed to produce *The Draper Catalogue of Stars* . . . which is why we have names for the stars of the Big Dipper.

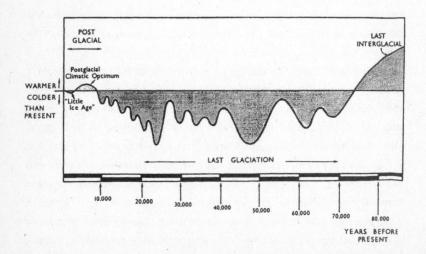

fective when pitted against the geologic pressures lying underfoot, but that humanity's cherished parade of history may in fact be governed by those underlying volcanic forces.

Catherine the Great is twenty years old in 1750, and George Washington is eighteen. In Manhattan, the land north of Fourteenth Street is mostly forest. There are still farmhouses where Liberty Street meets Church Street, where the World Trade Center will one day stand and fall. Trinity Church and Saint Paul's Chapel are the tallest reigning structures in a city that will bear the name of the tribespeople who once lived there: the Manhattans.

The cleft that runs knee-deep with every high tide has already been named Water Street. On another street, down which a stream of cool, clean water flows, Dutch girls line up on warm days to wash their clothes, and because the street is so often lined with young women, the people have named it Maiden Lane. No one will ever know how South Street got its name. It has always been east. Nearby, during the Revolutionary War, Washington's troops will attempt to build a wall to keep the British out, but New Yorkers will complicate Washington's plan by continually stealing the lumber. The wall never quite holds up, but they will name the place Wall Street anyway.

The pillars being fashioned for Saint Paul's Chapel and many of the new American buildings have a distinctly Roman appearance. Indeed, many of the American principles about to be written into law, including an inevitably disastrous continuation of slavery, are derived directly from still existing and recently republished copies of the Roman republic's laws. One reason for the public fascination with, and glorification of, ancient Rome (including anything written in Latin) is the recent discovery of two cities, perfectly preserved under Mount Vesuvius, with all their gold and ivory and amber treasures intact. Pompeii and Herculaneum had long ago faded into legend, and then, after the burning of libraries by Christians and Muslims, faded altogether from memory . . . until now.

At this time, libraries and printing presses are humanity's most efficient means of external information storage. In Philadelphia, Benjamin Franklin, who has been declared "the most dangerous man in America" (by King George III), has opened the Philadelphia Public Library and championed the reemergence of the experimental method in science.

He publishes the nation's first "girlie magazine" and, between experiments with lightning, steam pumps, and making music from wet glass, obsesses on the works of the Epicurean philosophers and Democritus—which he translates from Latin and republishes.

Thirty-three years hence, as an elder statesman and ambassador to the court of King Louis XVI, Benjamin Franklin will publish an observation on the global effects of Iceland's Laki eruption of 1783. In another year that (like 1816) sees no spring season and almost no summer at all, Franklin notes that as far away as France, the volcanic haze—"quite unlike ordinary fog"—so attenuates the Sun's rays that he is barely able, on an otherwise cloudless day, to ignite a piece of dark brown paper with the concentrated beam of a magnifying glass. By reducing the amount of solar radiation reaching the ground, the scientist correctly proposes, volcanic veils can bring about false winters and hold sway over climate, national economies, and perhaps even history.

A.D. 1500

The world population has reached 500 million. The human cube stands at 90 percent of its A.D. 1750 height—still about a half-mile (720 meters) on a side. This is the time of the Renaissance, with voyages of discovery setting off from Europe and Ming dynasty China. Printing presses proliferate, reproducing instructions for the manufacture of gun powder, cannons, and handguns. Michelangelo is twenty-five years old and Leonardo da Vinci has published his first drawings of submarines, parachutes, and armored "tanks"—glimpses of the world to come. In Italy, Venice has emerged as the strongest financial power in the Mediterranean. At this time, Christians are still shunning cats (on account of alleged feline associations, as "familiars," with witches and Satanists), but the church no longer advocates the wholesale slaughter of cats. During the recently ended Dark Age (which had followed in the wake of Rome's collapse), bonfires of cats had wrought a kind of feline vengeance upon Europe by assisting the proliferation of rats—which were recognized, too late, as carriers of the Black Plague.

A.D. 1000

The world population is stable at 300 million. At a height of approximately 2,330 feet (660 meters), the human cube is also stable at about two Empire State Building lengths. A supercity of Manhattan's density could hold the entire population in an area about the size of Sicily or Crete, and could sustain it with a land surface area not much larger than Spain or Texas, and with a sea no larger than the Mediterranean or the Gulf of Mexico.

Most of western civilization's surviving books are kept in the libraries of Córdoba, Spain, by Islamic and Jewish scholars. China, too, is a huge outpost of libraries, medical schools, and systems of plumbing and sanitation. With entire subcontinents between them, Spain and China are the technological masters of the world, though the former will be overrun by the Crusades and the latter, despite perfection of the magnetic compass and voyages of discovery reaching as far away as Africa and Alaska, will, under a series of unifying dynasties, become so stable that it draws mysteriously within itself. The nation-state henceforth becomes increasingly bound by tradition, and exists in a self-imposed isolation that will not be broken until the last decade of the twentieth century. As a result, one will be able to visit China in A.D. 1987 and witness essentially the same culture and architecture that exists in A.D. 1000, and which existed in 1000 B.C. If one wonders what would have happened had the culture of ancient Egypt survived intact into the electronic age, China circa 1987 gives an answer—ever so briefly, before Shanghai and Beijing, in less than a decade, begin to resemble every other city on Earth.

A.D. 1000 is the time of both the "Dark Age" and the twilight before the "Little Ice Age." Between Córdoba and China, civilization (what is left of it) might be described mostly as troglodytes who wander along Roman roads that lead nowhere and pitch tents under Roman pillars and in the shadows of crumbling Egyptian temples. The troglodytes find survival itself difficult enough, without having to be reminded that everything grand in their world—the Acropolis, Karnak, the Colosseum—signifies a fossil of something once mighty gone extinct. Had a man like Benjamin Franklin or Leonardo da Vinci appeared in this time and this place and started acting like Franklin or da Vinci, he would more likely than not have been martyred as a saint or burned as a witch, or both. A man named Gutenberg will come frighteningly close to this very fate, for printing the Bible, in 1455.

During the long night of barbarism, both Sun and Earth seem to have been conspiring against civilization. The annual growth rings of both living and fossil trees record, over more than seven thousand years, several anomalies in production of carbon 14, a radioactive variant of the carbon atom. This substance is produced exclusively from the exposure of nitrogen 14 to high-speed particles in the upper atmosphere, most of them consisting of hydrogen and helium nuclei flung from the solar atmosphere by magnetic storms (sunspots). One of the largest dips in carbon 14 production corresponds to a period from A.D. 1645 through 1715, during which European and Chinese astrologers record a near-total absence of sunspots. This is precisely the coldest period of the "Little Ice Age," which begins near A.D. 1300 and abates after 1850. Evidently, the solar constant is not so constant as humans would like to believe.

Just ahead of the Little Ice Age, in A.D. 1259, a Tambora-class volcanic eruption deposits a vein of sulfur in the ice of both poles and spreads microscopic glass beads across vast regions of the Pacific Ocean. Though no specific volcano is (by the early twenty-first century) identified as a prime suspect, trees from Turkey to California record frost scars during the summers that follow, after which the world returns, until 1300, to its pre–Little Ice Age warmth. For a while—for a generation or two—the Sun appears to carry on at its own stellar scale, as if to drive home the lesson that earthly impactors on climate, whether of volcanic or human origin, are merely blips superimposed upon the activity cycles of a star.

But even a lowly blip has the power to prove human innovation ineffective, to remind us time and time again that we are of nature, not above it.

The worst blip of the first millennium seems to precede, by a very tiny margin, the coming of the Dark Age: By A.D. 535, Christianity had been a state religion for two centuries, and what then remained of the Roman Empire ruled from Constantinople in Turkey. Another sulfur event, also Tambora-class, left its imprint in North and South Polar ice. This occurred near the tail end of an approximately six-thousand-year period of global warming, to which the civilizations of the world had become keenly adapted. Then, one day, into their world came a great calamity.

Classical Greece and Imperial Rome had lived through milder winters and longer, wetter growing seasons than would be experienced even during the warming trend of the late twentieth and early twenty-first centuries. But even this—so the philosophers say and so the earth instructs—could not last forever. Under Emperor Justinian, about A.D. 535, according to dendrochronologist ("chronicler of tree rings") Mike Bailey, trees began to record stunted, freeze-scarred rings—and even years of skipped ring growth. The years A.D. 536, 539, 541, and 542 were especially bad, marked by missed summers, from Constantinople to Ireland, from California to Chile.

Throughout much of the Eastern Roman Empire, the populace appears to have dispersed from a farming and city-dwelling existence into nomadic fort building. In Turkey alone, at least 5 million people (accounting for nearly 2 percent of the world's population) simply went missing—or, like nomads, became archaeologically invisible. As the Eastern Empire fell, so fell the world. The end came so swiftly that only its earliest stages produced written documents, and even these were bound to be scarce. Then, inevitably, predictably, the record simply broke off.

Historian David Keys, searching through archives ranging from the Vatican to China's Bamboo Annals, has discovered a half-dozen firsthand eyewitness accounts dating from the last days of the Eastern Empire and the first days of the volcanic sulfur event. In A.D. 535, an Italian monk reported that "rain had poured red, as if tainted by blood. Cold gripped summer," and there followed drought, famine, rationing, and plague. In China, the seasons "came in disorder," after yellow dust fell like snow upon the land. When famine and then plague struck Constantinople, about A.D. 542, the city census-keepers recorded ten thousand dead in a single week. They stopped keeping records after the body count reached two hundred thousand, noting that the stench of death and decay was becoming too much to bear, and the city must henceforth be abandoned.

Writing in Italy, a man named Casidorus wanted historians of the future to know how, in the year A.D. 536, the end began: "We had a darkened Sun; and summer without heat . . . and the reaper [of crops] fears new frosts."

Writing in Constantinople in A.D. 536, the Syrian bishop John echoed (or, rather, anticipated) Benjamin Franklin's theory of volcano weather: "There was a sign from the Sun, the like of which had never been seen or reported before. The Sun became dark and its darkness lasted for eighteen months. Each day it shone for about four hours, and still this light was only a feeble shadow. Everyone declared that the Sun would never recover its full light again."

The last days of the Eastern Roman Empire (sometimes called Byzantium) had marked, for better or for worse, a level of technology and social organization that would not be seen again until the Renaissance, almost a millennium away. At the end of his life, Casidorus must have envied those who had died in the generation preceding, for they at least had perished ignorant of civilization's eclipse, never sensing the rout of Byzantium. To see it all unfolding, and to know exactly how it would end—what could be more horrible?

A.D. ZERO

The world population has reached (and for a thousand years will never far exceed) 300 million; the human cube stands two Empire State Buildings tall—just as it will in A.D. 1000. In Alexandria and throughout Egypt, the populace supports more than 6 million cats. Bred smaller, now, than their forebears, cats were first domesticated more than two thousand years earlier from a Nile variety of wildcat. To outside observers in Rome, it is sometimes difficult to discern who has gained mastery over and domesticated whom, for the Egyptians now pamper and worship cats as gods. (And two thousand years hence, some will claim, "cats have not forgotten this.")

In Rome, Augustus Caesar has been emperor (or supreme dictator) for twenty-seven years, and will rule for fourteen more. He stands on the transition between the Roman republic and hereditary monarchy. In addition to rebuilding Rome into a capital city, he has redesigned the astrological calendar, and while doing so renamed the month Sextilis "August," after himself.

Vesuvius, at this time, is still an "extinct" volcano. Pompeii is a thriving port. Its sister city, Herculaneum, has an unusually large population of freed slaves, who have managed to raise their town to even greater prosperity than Pompeii. As human nature was bound to dictate, the once-owned slaves have themselves become slave owners. Long ago, the city's formerly enslaved founding fathers chose as their local patron god the once-enslaved Hercules—who, according to Roman scripture, was born human, performed superhuman tasks, or "labors," died as a human, was buried, resurrected, and ascended to heaven as a god. In honor of the resurrected man-god, the settlers had named their city Herculaneum.

On crisp, cloudless nights in decades past, Vesuvian astrologers drew imaginary lines in the sky and created the large northern constellation Hercules, whose kneeling figure points the way to Ursa Major. It is not quite the same Ursa Major, or "Big Dipper," that people of the early twenty-first century will know; for up there, in the frontiers of the night, Alkaid (the star at the very tip of the Dipper's handle) has shifted almost 184 seconds of arc southeast of its A.D. 2010 position. One can almost see the difference, if one happens to have a good pair of binoculars: the shift is equivalent to the head of a pin held out at arm's length.

Against time frames dozens of times greater than human life spans,

Stars of the Big Dipper

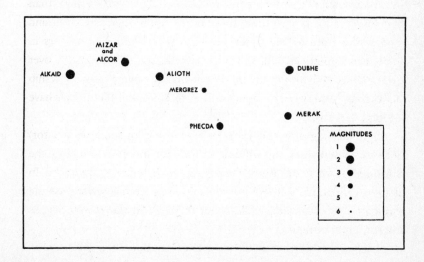

not even the eternal constellations are immutable, or truly eternal. The stars of the Big Dipper, all by themselves, reveal much about humanity's status in time and space.

Alkaid (also called Eta Ursae Majoris) is a giant white star that shines 630 times more fiercely than our Sun. A star such as this is so massive that in far less than a quarter-billion years it is fated to fuse so much of its hydrogen and helium into unfusable iron that its nuclear fires will falter, triggering a catastrophic collapse and detonation known as a supernova. Once the explosion begins, the star will incinerate, out to a radius of nearly 200 light-years, whatever life it touches. We view this giant, Alkaid, far, far younger than Earth, from a distance of 210 light-years. (As scaled by a tape measure spooled out at 186,000 miles per second, the Sun, our nearest star, is 8 light-minutes from Earth.) Alkaid is approaching us at a velocity of 6.5 miles (10.5 kilometers) per second, meaning that the distance between Earth and Alkaid decreases by 25.5 light-days (nearly a light-month) between Emperor Augustus and President George Walker Bush. In 6 million years, the stellar time bomb will be almost upon us (and 6 million years after that, Alkaid, if it still exists, will once again be 210 light-years away).

The next star in the Dipper's handle is actually two double stars called Mizar and Alcor. Mizar B is itself a family of double stars in orbit around a double star. The family also contains at least one Jupiter-like brown dwarf, probably with its own system of Europa-like "moons"—in effect, solar systems, within solar systems, within solar systems (or, if you will, the heavenly realization of the prophet Daniel's "wheels within wheels"). Water and hydrocarbon chemistry there may be—perhaps even an early stage of life—but to a near certainty, Mizar, Alcor, and all the other stars of the so-called Ursa Major Stream are without Earth-like planets sprouting forests and grassy fields, for a specific and interesting reason.

Mizar and Alcor, coursing away from Earth at 5.5 miles (8.9 kilometers) per second, or 28 light-years per million years, are moving in parallel with as many as one hundred other stars. This moving group of stars (the Ursa Major Stream) includes all of the Big Dipper stars between the Dipper's "lip" (the double star Dubhe) and the tip of its handle (Alkaid)—and extends as far as Sirius, "the Dog Star."

If the middle of the Big Dipper is pictured as moving ahead of our solar system, then Sirius is creeping up behind us. These traveling companions occupy a volume of space that surrounds the Sun. They are moving southeast across our sky, toward the eastern portion of Sagittarius, at an average velocity of 9 miles (14.5 kilometers) per second. The Ursa Major Stream does indeed resemble a stream of stars that overtook us and is washing past us.

Tantalizing clues provided by the spectral signatures of iron and other elements in the atmospheres of the stream stars suggest that many of them (but not Sirius, which has an orbiting white dwarf that may be several billion years older than our Sun) were born very late in our galaxy's history. They are, in terms of heavy element abundance, identical to stars of the Pleiades cluster and appear therefore to be about the same age as the Pleiades stellar nursery. Born late during the reign of Earth's dinosaurs, the central stars of the Big Dipper are all in their infancy. On the outskirts of Mizar, where at least one doublet star orbits closer than the Sun and Mercury, basking in each other's fires, exchanging matter, and evolving in strange ways, the first volcanically rifted seas might now be forming under the ice of a rough world—a likeness of Earth, Europa, or Ganymede some 4.5 billion years ago.

That the stream of stars is still recognizable as a stream is, itself, testimony of its relative youth. Traveling families of stars also provide testimony of common origin. We have learned from the oldest known nuggets of matter in our solar system (pieces of the Genesis Stone, the meteorite Allende) that the collapse of gas and dust into the Sun and planets was coincident with—and probably triggered by—the outracing shock bubble of an exploding star, a supernova.

Much as our species has been made puny against the power of volcanoes, geology diminishes under the frightful majesty of the stars.

Looking outward from our solar system, we can observe expanding spheres of supernova ejecta. At their periphery, collapsing nebulae studded with associations or clusters of very young stars are a common sight. ("Young," in a galaxy more than 13 billion years old, is a relative term—just as "slow," when measured by miles per second in a galaxy 150,000 light-years wide, is relative. Thus, even at supernova shock-bubble speeds of 640 miles per second, no motion at all can be detected, from hundreds or thousands of light-years away, without the aid of spectrographs.) Rafted along on a spherical shell of "slowly" expanding hydrogen and helium, newly formed stars—mixed with a few older ones caught up in the wave front—travel on a parallel trajectory pointing away from the explosion center.

In "only" a few million years, some of the moving group's most massive members will swell to red giantism, become supernovae in their own right, and scatter traveling companions in odd directions. Others will be swung off course by close encounters with passing stars until, after not much more than 250 million years, moving groups should dissipate and no longer be recognizable as, say, the Ursa Major Stream.

The Sun, too, was born in the wake of a supernova. Somewhere out there, riding the night at immense distances, are stars and planets born in the same place on almost the same day. Like our own solar system, they are very old, now—among the oldest worlds around. Like Mizar and Alcor, Mergrez and Merak, the Sun once had traveling companions of its own, but it is impossible to identify any of these with certainty because, though Earth may have a twin, their paths diverged long, long ago.

(All that is, is transitory . . .)

Stars scatter. Human lives and human empires exist for an instant and then disappear. We are not the measure of all things, but we are a good starting point against which all things can be measured.

Stars of the Big Dipper, as they appear in 2000 B.C.

2000 B.C.

To the 150 million to 250 million human beings now populating Earth, the stars of the Big Dipper look very much the same as they will in the twenty-first century A.D. From this time, as viewed by ground-based observers, Alkaid has shifted the length of a small garden ant held out at arm's length. In actuality, it has covered more than 1.5 light-months.

The Great Pyramid at Giza is practically new in 2000 B.C.—a mere six centuries old. All gleaming white and sharp-edged, its peak cased in brilliant gold plate, the monument stands hard and silent over the commotion of a thriving and wealthy port. This is the time of Egypt's Isis and Osiris cults, and its first libraries. Religious song-stories, mathematical tables, detailed instructions for surgically removing a diseased kidney and cleaning the wound with alcohol and germicidal powders—all such knowledge is being stored external of human memory and given away, mind to mind, to anyone who can read hieroglyphic and cunei-form texts.

Elsewhere in the world, under a climate that is milder than it will be in the early twenty-first century A.D.—warmer by about 2 to 6 degrees Fahrenheit (1 to 3 degrees Centigrade)—Chinese civilization is flowering. In texts that will be easily datable (on account of a record of solar and lunar eclipses in the margins), scribes accurately calculate the circumference of Earth and the Moon and provide details of complex surgical procedures that make use of antibiotics, cultured and harvested from green mold (penicillin) on bread.

Rome does not yet exist. The forebears of empire are intensely provincial, clustering into villages of no more than seven hundred inhabitants, surrounded by their own local farms. One Bronze Age town resembles Venice on a microscopic scale. But in 1750 B.C., flash-frozen by searing ash and mud, Italy's first Venice will become its first Pompeii, above which inhabitants of the second Pompeii will plant grape vineyards. All wooden structures in the town are simultaneously buried in ash and seared out of existence, while the hollow spaces they leave behind are filled with volcanic mud—which transforms the "hollows" into fossil casts one story deep.

Outside one home, a pig's bones survive inside a cast of its body.

Nearby, someone had raised a wooden cage, chest-high, on stilts, apparently to keep its contents—several pregnant goats—beyond reach of the village's dogs. When the end comes, a kiln is preserved with a half-fired pot inside; someone drops a hat decorated with the teeth of a wild boar; and not very far from the hat, a young couple enters the fossil record, leaving their skeletons near a doorway, posed in the disquieting attitude of instantaneous death. A farmer will discover their village in A.D. 2001, while trying to bury his cat.

About a century after a Vesuvian Venice becomes a prehistoric Pompeii, the volcanic isle of Thera intervenes in human plans, and alters the path of civilization. While Tambora (in A.D. 1815) and the terminal Roman eruption of the mid-sixth century A.D. have a power to bring chaos to the world's climate, they exert their influence from very far away, in the Pacific. The eruption of autumn, 1628 B.C., occurs dead in the center of the first European empire.

Left on their own (but fated to such utter erasure that no one shall ever know what they had come to call themselves), the "Minoans," once their civilization had begun to evolve, should have continued evolving. Between 2000 B.C. and 1700 B.C., they have become the world's first naval power and, according to records left behind by Eighteenth Dynasty Egyptians (who called these people "Keftiu"), they exert their power economically and diplomatically, from the Sea of Galilee to Greece, from Crete to Upper and Lower Egypt. They build an entire town in Avaris, Egypt, without defensive walls or fortifications of any kind, and every room in Avaris is adorned with works of strangely impressionistic art, some of it anticipating Picasso by more than three millennia.

More than 1,500 years before Imperial Rome, the Minoans build dams and aqueducts to rival Imperial Rome. On Thera and on Crete, the buildings are multi-storied, with pipes in the walls. There are showers, baths, flush toilets, and central heating. A handful of ships from this period (and from the era of Greek civilization that shall take over in centuries to come) contain pieces of the so-called "Antikithera devices"—another of history's great what-ifs. One remarkably complete mechanism will be discovered in a shipwreck believed to have originated somewhere between Crete and Rhodes, sometime prior to 700 B.C.: a bronze case enclosing thirty-nine gears arranged in layers—that is, differential gearshifts allowing two shafts to transmit motion at differing rates of rotation, just like the multiple gearshifts of automobile transmissions or the first analog computers of the twentieth century A.D. The one Antikithera mechanism that survives intact, completely encased in coral, displays on its face a scale of measurements for the positions of the Sun and Moon in what archaeologists of the future will identify as the Greek zodiac. By turning the gears, three dials can be made to chart eclipses and predict lunar phases for every day of the year—past, present, and future. Antikithera (which is eventually displayed in the Athens Museum) not only appears to be but is in fact the world's first known analog computer.

Greek legend will speak of Daedalus and his son Icarus trying to escape King Minos by flying on man-made wings from Crete to Thera; and in an Egyptian tomb dating from the time of Thera, a toy bird in the shape of a glider (destined for the Cairo Museum) displays knowledge of Wright brothers–era wing design—and identical replicas will indeed glide for great distances when thrown.

By A.D. Zero, civilization might well reach the Moon and Mars; by A.D. 1500, the nearer stars and beyond. By A.D. 2000, something very much like *Star Trek,* instead of being forward-looking fiction, might be ancient history if not for the volcanic explosion of Thera. At nature's random whim, as the mountain dictates, Minoan civilization will cede to the Greeks, who will act as both preservers and destroyers of Minoan technology (much as the Greeks, in their own turn, will cede to Roman power, the paradoxical destroyer and preserver of Greek-Minoan knowledge). As the rocks measure time, the maritime empire whose focus is Crete—only 70 miles (about 100 kilometers) from Thera—dies abruptly and at its zenith. Even as human lives measure time, the end begins with startling rapidity, but the tribulation then stretches out with agonizing sloth, through years of earthquake and Pompeii-class eruptions, culminating in an empire-encompassing spasm of human sacrifice.

"There have been, and there will be again, many destructions of mankind arising out of many causes," says the Egyptian priest of Neith (about 590 B.C.) to Plato's ancestor Solon, in accordance with Plato's *Critias* (347 B.C.). "You have no antiquity of history, and no history of antiquity . . . you do not know that there formerly dwelt in your land the fairest and noblest race of men which ever lived, and that you [Greece and Crete] and your whole city [Athens] are descended from a seed or remnant of them which survived."

Plato will also write about the priest's records of pestilence "streaming from heaven," upon Egypt and upon all civilizations, and of sacred bulls being tied with nooses, having their throats slit upon the altar, and their blood collected in sacred golden cups. He calls the bull worshipers "Atlanteans," and ends his *Timaeus* dialogue with the bull-worshiping "invaders" defeated by mainland Greeks, amid "violent earthquakes and floods," and a single day and night of misfortune in which an island disappears.

On the isles of Thera and Crete, during the decade leading up to the fall of Minoan civilization, people are continually rebuilding earthquake-ravaged palaces and homes. On the southern shore of Thera (today called Santorini), somewhere between 1635 and 1630 B.C., a Pompeii-class surge cloud—or death cloud—incinerates the western half of a major port city, claiming an estimated minimum of ten thousand lives. No one will ever know for certain how many Theran towns are felled by the eruption, because it is only a prelude. In the autumn of 1628 B.C. most of the island simply disappears in a volcanic conflagration against which all previous earthquakes, floods, and volcano-driven death clouds are minor disturbances by comparison. Thera's false winter is recorded in China and triggers a rebellion against Emperor Chieh. If an exploding island can produce such havoc as far away as China, it cannot help but go down into the legends and religious histories of the civilizations that immediately surround it.

The final Thera calamity converts some 40 to 50 cubic miles (160 to 200 cubic kilometers) of rock into ash and vapor. This is approximately equivalent to the energy release of twenty-four thousand one-megaton hydrogen bombs, or the estimated potential energy output of an early-twenty-first-century-A.D. global nuclear war. The A.D. 79 eruption of Vesuvius will register 24 megatons, or one-thousandth the force of Thera.

Near the end, a Minoan civilization that (according to wall murals and Egyptian records) had previously sacrificed only bulls, regresses deeply into superstition and fear—and, as a Minoan Dark Age approaches, the people offer the ultimate sacrifice, evidently in an effort to stop the eruptions and to forestall Judgment Day. Futile effort . . . There are descriptions in *Theogony* (lines 630–719) and in the Bible (Genesis and Exodus) of whole cities turned instantly to dust and being swallowed by waves—Sodom, Argos, and some Eighteenth Dynasty pharaoh's army. This much is certain: No one taking in air and still in his right mind wants to be anywhere downwind of, or around, or on the Mediterranean the day Thera explodes.

On the isle of Crete, the mountaintop Shrine of Akames preserves one of the final and apparently desperate Minoan ceremonies—the world's only instance of a human sacrifice simultaneously interrupted and (in an archaeological sense) flash-frozen. In the immediate aftermath of the killing, the ground heaves and brings down the entire shrine, after which the temple is never rebuilt or even invaded by sappers in search of sacred cups shaped in gold. The thick layers of volcanic ash deposited across eastern Crete testify that the last, post-Thera Minoans have more immediate, strictly survival-based concerns on their minds.

Three skeletons, instantly buried and preserved, lie within the temple walls. The priest has fallen backward, attempting to shield his head from exterior walls coming suddenly indoors, and from slabs of roofing. The priestess, having dropped a cup of blood, seeks escape in a corner, behind a sacred pillar, where her skeleton is crushed, facedown. On the altar, a young man, aged about seventeen years, is tied exactly in the manner of a sacred bull, as depicted in Minoan art. His throat has been slit, and the history written on his globin genes bears witness that it is his blood within the priestess's cup. It is a tragic and gruesome final portrait of a once-powerful and strangely modern civilization—as if the legend of Atlantis, as penned by Plato, is the history of the Minoans.

6000 B.C.

Prehistory.

No ruler, no place, has a name that will live on. There is no writing; only oral history. Song-stories pass down from generation to generation and will continue to do so even after writing and printing have become widespread, because some of the hymns and stories will, by then, be sacred. Many of the Bible's eight books, and most of its prayers, shall be preserved in this way for dozens of centuries, before being committed to

EVENT	DATE	TYPE	ENERGY IN KILOTONS, MEGATONS
WORLD TRADE CENTER	A.D. 2001	COLLAPSE COLUMN(S)	1.6 KILOTONS
HIROSHIMA	A.D. 1945	FISSION BOMB	10–24 KILOTONS
MOUNT PELÉE, MARTINIQUE	A.D. 1902	VOLCANIC EXPLOSION	15–20 KILOTONS
MOUNT SAINT HELENS	A.D. 1980	VOLCANIC EXPLOSION	10 MEGATONS
TUNGUSKA, SIBERIA	A.D. 1908	COMETARY IMPACT (SMALL)	10–15 MEGATONS
POMPEII	A.D. 79	VOLCANIC COLLAPSE COLUMN(S)	24 MEGATONS
KRAKATOA, INDONESIA	A.D. 1883	VOLCANIC EXPLOSION	240 MEGATONS
TAMBORA, INDONESIA	A.D. 1815	VOLCANIC EXPLOSION	20,000 MEGATONS
TERMINAL BYZANTINE EVENT	A.D. 535	VOLCANIC, PACIFIC	*THERA*-CLASS ERUPTION
THERA	1628 B.C.	VOLCANIC EXPLOSION	24,000 MEGATONS

The Nomenclature of Destruction: Some of the better-known explosive events of the past four thousand years form the basis of a simple scale of megatonnage, broken into three classes, *Hiroshima*, *Pompeii*, and *Thera*. Within the limits of error for estimating total kilotonnage and megatonnage (tons of TNT), each measure is approximately one thousand times stronger than the one preceding. One *Pompeii* is one thousand times stronger than *Hiroshima*; 1 *Thera* equals 1,000 *Pompeiis*. Under this nomenclature, Tambora and the terminal Byzantine event, though actually slightly weaker than *Thera* (0.83 *Thera* in the case of Tambora), can both be ranked as Thera-class eruptions. The Krakatoa explosion weighs in at 10 *Pompeiis*, whereas the Tunguska and Mount Saint Helens events are roughly half as strong as Pompeii. The Mount Pelée eruption of 1902 (which obliterated the city of Saint-Pierre) was approximately equivalent to 1 *Hiroshima*. The two collapse columns of the World Trade Center directed a combined force of 1.6 kilotons into the volcanic bedrock of Manhattan, approximately equivalent to one-tenth of a *Hiroshima*. At the high end of the scale, 1 *Thera* is easier said, and understood, than 24,000 megatons (approximately equivalent to one global nuclear war). The terminal Cretaceous impact of a Manhattan Island–sized asteroid, near Mexico, about 64.4 million B.C., released 1,347 million megatons, or slightly more than 56,000 *Theras*. One *Thera* is a civilization-killer; 56,000 of them are a major extinction event. Although different types of explosive events are represented here, they provide a familiar and instructive (though admittedly a rough) scale against which all explosive events can be gauged. (Megatonnage figures for volcanoes and asteroids are courtesy of Charles Sheffield and Eugene Shoemaker.)

writing in the time of King David. In these days, brains do all the storing of all information external to one's own DNA.

There are fewer than 30 million people in the world. The cube of human bodies, shoulder to shoulder, head to toe, stands somewhere between the height of the Washington Monument and the Empire State Building. The entire cube, spread across a super-city with a population density approximating New York, would occupy an area equivalent to Manhattan's five boroughs, or an area some 15% smaller than the early-twenty-first-century city of Tokyo.

East of Manhattan, New England's first Asian settlers have erected small towns across Long Island, where office-block and skyscraper-sized boulders of ice have only recently (during the last two thousand years) melted into deep, kettle-shaped ponds. Much farther east, and forty years hence, in 5960 B.C. (according to a calendar written in tree rings and volcanic dust), Mount Vesuvius will suddenly alter its shape, and the shape of the entire landscape, with a force exceeding 4 *Pompeiis*. The mount will repeat this action in 3580 B.C., ranking both eruptions among the largest in Europe.

The Big Dipper in 6000 B.C.

In 6000 B.C., the small tribal settlements living on the shores of Vesuvius are indistinguishable, in their basic appearance, from camps now being established across the Atlantic by the Manhattan, Rockaway, and Massapequa tribes. People in Thailand are cultivating beans and manufacturing wood-fired pottery. Agricultural and pottery industries have sprung up in Japan and China, across Iraq, Turkey, and up the Nile into Africa, through a Sahara that is mostly braided streams, grassland, and hippopotamus-supporting swamps. In Catal Huyuk, Turkey, one agricultural community has grown to support more than five thousand inhabitants—the largest concentration of humans anywhere on Earth, the world's first city. In the center of the city is a temple. Like the Minoans who will come after them, these people are bull worshipers.

Far, far east of Turkey and Italy, and south, seafaring people have settled Australia, Micronesia, and New Zealand—the stars, their only means of navigation. Compared against how they will appear eight thousand years hence, the constellations are becoming slightly but noticeably distorted. The handle of the Big Dipper is straightening out with each step backward in time, and its lip has lengthened. The Atlantic, meanwhile, has decreased its width. The same volcanic seam that produces hydrothermal vents on the mid-Atlantic is slowly nudging Europe and North America apart—at an average rate of just under an inch (actually, 2.1 centimeters) per year. This brings a certain amount of calamity—albeit an extremely slow-motion calamity, from a human point of view—to an innocent bystander named *Anguilla anguilla*.

Forcing European anguillid eels to swim an extra inch each year to their spawning grounds may not seem particularly dramatic. It may not, perhaps, because it is a distance only barely equivalent to the length that human fingernails grow each year. Even across an entire human lifetime, even across 160 human lifetimes, or eight millennia, the distance added seems of but trifling consequence: 560 feet, or little more than the length of three football fields (not quite 200 meters). But multiplied over a million years, over more than twenty thousand human lifetimes, it adds up to just over 13 miles (or 21 kilometers). Multiplied over *millions* of years, continents adrift at the rate of human fingernail growth can easily split one eel species in two.

Adult eels, leaving their European streams and heading west, toward spawning grounds in the Sargasso Sea, must pass over the mid-Atlantic Ridge, where two giant, volcanic slabs of Earth's crust are being pushed apart. The European eels are known by the genus and species names, *Anguilla anguilla*. On the American side of the continental spreading center, where the distance between the mainland and the Sargasso Sea remains essentially unchanged, a related species, called *Anguilla rostrata*, leaves the Hudson and Delaware Rivers and heads east. Both American and European eels migrate to and spawn in the Sargasso Sea; but they mate at different times, and the European species has larger, more efficient muscles (the better to swim a greater distance than the American species). The American eels take several months to reach the Sargasso Sea. Only their offspring return, and the "round trip" requires a year. The European eels travel three times as far (1,700 miles each way): The adults need a full year to reach the spawning grounds, and three years for their offspring to complete the return trip.

When the Atlantic Ocean was hundreds of miles narrower and the western spawning ground was nearer the middle, American and European eels were, doubtless, a single interbreeding species with a common spawning center. A consequence of gradually increasing the migration time on one side of the ocean was to throw breeding times into disharmony, leading to segregation, on a behavioral level, of the eastern and western populations. Think upon this, if ever you find yourself inside a deep-diving *Mir* submersible on the bed of the Atlantic: Seventy million years of volcanic rock lie underfoot and 20 million years of disrupted migration lie overhead, opening a new window on the origin of species, albeit one of Earth history's slowest and most drawn-out examples.

14,000 B.C.

At a maximum of 11 million, the world human population would form a cube forty stories tall, about the height of the Washington Monument. At this time, the population of all our ancestors is most probably below 8 million. Ice sheets more than 2 miles thick cover Europe and much of North America. According to Alan Wilson's "DNA clock," the history

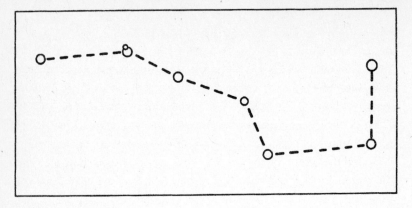

The Big Dipper in 14,000 B.C.

written in the varied genes of Native Americans suggest that at least fifteen different influxes of people have occurred by this time, exclusively (or almost exclusively) from the direction of China, and most likely by boats following icebound shores eastward. Skilled, seafaring people have also, by this time, crossed the Exmouth Trench to Australia, where a kangaroo species as tall as *Tyrannosaurus rex* evades pack-hunting marsupial lions—which, in their own turn, evade a Komodo dragon–like monitor lizard 40 feet (13 meters) long.

Although Australian fauna are no longer entirely familiar to us, anguillid eels and the Big Dipper are still recognizable. Vesuvius is not. In a catastrophic collapse that must have dwarfed the 5960 B.C. eruption (exceeding, therefore, 4 *Pompeiis*), most of a mountain disappeared into the earth and a crater lake formed in its place. Soon, a new volcanic cone begins to rise from the center of the lake. Vesuvius is a perpetual planetary hot spot, standing on a zone where the African continental plate is driving Italy into western Europe like a giant nail, at 1 inch (2.5 centimeters) per year. The nail, as it hammers north, pushes up the Alps and renders the Bay of Naples, geologically speaking, only slightly more stable than a jar of nitroglycerin, on a train, moving at high speed, along a rickety track. Had the cave painters and elephant hunters of 14,000 B.C. known the story of the rocks, they and their progeny would have shunned the hot spot for all time.

30,000 B.C.

With continent-sized ice sheets tying water up in glaciers, simultaneously dropping sea levels and altering rain patterns, forests now grow on
what will become Egypt's deserts, the bottom of the Java Sea, and the
floor of the Bay of Naples. Mount Vesuvius is crowned by a large
caldera "only" two thousand years old. The eruption of 32,000 B.C. has
collapsed the mouth of the volcano, once again extinguishing all life in
the region. By now, pine forests have sprung up on the mineral-rich volcanic soil. Trees rim the shore of a mountaintop glacial lake, where animals find shelter near steaming mineral pools and hot spring oases in the
middle of an ice age.

Two major tribes (or races) of human beings exist at this time: the
thick-boned Neanderthals and the more thinly boned, anatomically
modern tribes. Much like anguillid eels, they represent two branches of
a divided ancestry (stemming back, probably, to a race known as *Homo
erectus*). Their combined world population is probably below 8 million.
Both are toolmakers, and both have demonstrated an ability to build and
navigate boats into Australia, across 62 miles (100 kilometers) of the
Exmouth Trench: First the Neanderthals arrived, then the "gracile,"
thin-boned people followed. And everywhere the gracile people followed, the Neanderthals began dwindling toward extinction, sometimes
leaving their de-fleshed and partially cooked bones in someone's camp-

The Big Dipper in 30,000 B.C.

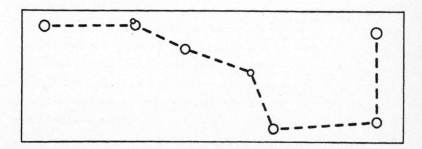

fires. There are, in these days, only a few million people wandering the earth; but with each passing century, fewer and fewer of the bones entering the fossil record are of Neanderthal origin.

Down here in the cellars of time, with the Neanderthal race dwindling toward extinction, humanity's first global war appears to be drawing to a close.

64,000 B.C.

Earth is in the grip of a long series of ice ages, stretching back over more than 2 million years. Although temperatures are cooler than they will be in the twenty-first century A.D., "only" fifteen thousand years earlier the planet had been considerably warmer (and again, subtle changes in fossil trees hint at fluctuations in the production of carbon isotopes, pointing toward an inconstant Sun).

In 64,000 B.C., the planet seems on the verge of another warm, "interglacial" period. At the mouths of rivers, ancient sediments record that the Mississippi, the Tiber, and the Thames have been discharging more than 4,000 cubic miles (16,000 cubic kilometers) of glacial-melt water in a single year; and in just one Northern Hemisphere summer, the world's oceans can sometimes rise 2 inches (5 centimeters). But such warmth is just a minor respite in the midst of a major glacial advance.

The Big Dipper in 64,000 B.C.

About 72,000 B.C., the volcanic cone of Toba, in northwest Sumatra, exploded, and marked the beginning of the last glacial age. The ash fell westward across Singapore and the Arabian Sea, piling several inches deep in Sri Lanka. Layered on top of whatever changes Earth's inconstant Sun might force upon the climate, Toba—like the Theran and terminal Byzantine calamities still lying dormant within continental slabs—was more than able to plunge the planetary temperature curve, perhaps even to meddle in human evolution. Toba sent between 250 and 500 cubic miles (between 1,000 and 2,000 cubic kilometers) of rock and rock-turned-ash into the heavens, equivalent to somewhere between 5 and 10 *Theras*.

After Toba, temperatures plunged, and continued plunging, for close on four thousand years. Only now, near 64,000 B.C., do we begin to see a warming trend; but like the one that begins near 10,000 B.C., it is only transitory, only a blush within surges of ice. Sixty-six thousand years hence, a distant descendant of the thin-boned people—NASA's Michael Rampino—will see a cause-and-effect relationship between Toba and the ice.

In 64,000 B.C., the Neanderthal tribes, numbering (a very roughly estimated) 7 million people, are leaving bones and tools in the fossil record. From western Europe to central Asia, from Afghanistan to southern China, the robust-boned people flourish. In Africa and in southeast Asia, outnumbered globally between seven and ten to one, the thin-boned humans (called the "gracile" *Homo sapiens*) have been depositing their own bones and stones in the fossil record. The gracile peoples' stone tools, at this time, are cruder than those found among Neanderthal fossils—inferior in both design and function.

As the blush ends and as walls of ice continue to march down from the north, robust and gracile tribes will be driven and confined (again) to progressively narrower pastures and hunting grounds near the equator: geographic compression, force-fed by climate. Over the course of a few thousand years, both gracile and Neanderthal tools will become more sophisticated, as if to record for us an Ice Age arms race, with gracile tools evolving suddenly toward the beautiful and deadly Clovis point, and the Neanderthal tribes extinguished. Here, too, in this Cain and Abel–esque ancestry, one begins to see hints of cause and effect. If a

Toba-induced (or Toba-amplified) human bottleneck really does have its beginnings near 72,000 B.C., then this is neither the last nor the first time that the parade of life marching across this planet is either orchestrated or diverted by volcano weather.

130,000 B.C.

Ursa Major more resembles a mutated chevron than a Dipper. This is the time of a warm interglacial period—which renders Earth itself unfamiliar. West Antarctica's mountains are discharging melting ice seaward, and the shores near Mount Eribus support scrub brush and grasses. Mount Vesuvius is building a new volcanic cone, in the midst of a tropical paradise with tides now rising 20 feet (6 meters) above their year 2000 flood level. Local lakes and streams support populations of elephants, hippos, and herds of giraffe.

The Sargasso Sea is 1.24 miles (2 kilometers) nearer to Europe, which scarcely makes a difference to migrating eels. They have long ago divided into two species.

Deep in the trenches of the Pleistocene epoch, the human brain is the newest and brightest thing around. Only dolphins, some of the great apes, and perhaps one or two extinct and unknown saurian species have

The Big Dipper in 130,000 B.C.

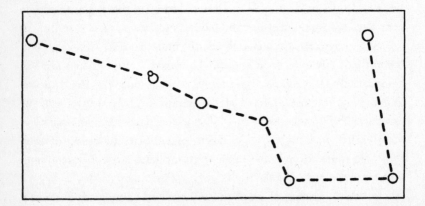

ever come close to storing such vast quantities of information beyond the limits of one's own DNA, in nerve tissue, then connecting that information together to enhance survival. The new creatures—an inevitable outcome of evolutionary arms races and extinction lotteries—are extraordinarily adaptable. If an expansion of the diet is required, it is genetically more complex to add 40 yards to the human digestive system for, say, the more efficient breakdown of cellulose in green plants, than to discover fire. By this time, the gracile humans and their forebears have been controlling fire for more than a quarter-million years. Cooking is the equivalent of evolving a supplementary digestive system and throwing open the doors to whole new sources of nutrition. In time, such adaptability will lead humans where no other creatures can survive: into the vacuum of space and onto the Martian ice caps.

Yet in 130,000 B.C., intelligent life is a mere blemish upon the planet. In the Americas there are no traces of humankind at all. Over most of the tropical wilderness that will become Africa, Europe, and Asia, only in a few isolated locales can the elephant hunters be seen gathering into lairs of fifty or more people. Near the Nile Delta, members of one small tribe are planting the wooden supports for dome-shaped reed huts in the fossil record. Their midden heaps and campfires shall preserve the bones of hippopotamus brought down with flint-tipped spears. Broken spear points, too, go into Egypt's midden heaps, and oyster shells, and the skulls of creatures flayed to the bone with oyster shells. Some of those creatures are human.

The most adaptable minds to awaken on Earth evoke images of tribe chasing tribe with weapons of wood and flint over deposits of copper, oil, and uranium. The combined population of all those human tribes—both gracile and robust—probably numbers fewer than a million people, possibly only a few tens of thousands, or even thousands. But copper, with its promise of better, more easily mass-produced spears; oil, with its promise of rapid global transport; and uranium, with its own brand of promise and peril, set no limits on what human brains can do and shall encourage the blemish to spread from the cellars of deep time—to spread from pole to pole, growing from a few thousand individuals to the multiple billions.

A careful reading of DNA in the bones of Neanderthals suggests that they were a very separate people from the tribe of our grandmothers' grandmothers' grandmothers. Fossil campsites, fossil seeds, and scraps of dog bone add depth to the story.

The bones of northern European dogs found near Neanderthal campsites suggest that animal domestication had begun before the thin-boned humans—our people—radiated out of Africa and began casting their own DNA into nature's library of blood, bones, and stones. The first signs of agriculture, along the shores of Africa's Nile River, point to hit-and-miss nomadic wheat growers who (near the end of the Neanderthal age) simply scattered their seeds in marked locations, departed, and came back to the same camp season after season. If one is permitted to speculate upon these clues, knowing from archaeological hindsight that everywhere our thin-boned ancestors went, the flame of Neanderthal civilization was snuffed out, then it is possible to sense an echo through time, in the biblical tale of Cain and Abel.

Abel, the herdsman (the legendary domesticator of animals), was favored by his God; and out of jealousy, Cain, the farmer, killed Abel. Can it be that the killing of the Neanderthal lived on in human memory? Can it be that this memory, grotesque and vague—the stubborn substance of legends—entered the book of Genesis as a story of how murder first entered the world?

Can this be true?

260,000 B.C.

This is the time of *Homo erectus*. Near Karnak and across the Nile, in what will become Egypt's Valley of the Kings, these people, whose bones are even more robust than the Neanderthal's, have been leaving flint spears and hand axes in the archaeological record since about 500,000 B.C.. They have also been participating in well-organized hunts, in which brush fires, set in strategic locations, drive migrating herds of deer, horses, and elephants over cliffs and into swamps. The leg bones, after being cooked in campfires, are often cracked open for their marrow, then arranged, oddly, in rows.

The *Homo erectus* tribes have spread from Africa to Asia. They proba-

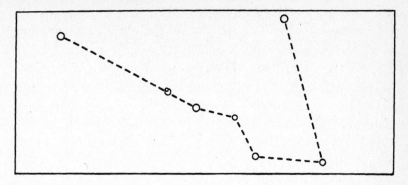

The Big Dipper in 260,000 B.C.

bly number a million or fewer individuals. The Neanderthal and thin-boned branches of the human tree are still latent in the loins of at least two separate *Homo erectus* tribes—reminding us that ours is not a straight and narrow ancestry (or so-called evolutionary ladder). Instead, the city builders will find themselves located at the tip of a branching pattern that knows no end (in which, perhaps, the humans shall eventually clear the decks for their own artificially created descendants, much as dinosaurs once cleared the decks for humanity's mammalian forebears). For a moment, however, *Homo erectus* holds dominion over the earth.

The territory around Vesuvius looks much as Yellowstone National Park will look in the twenty-first century A.D. The oldest Vesuvian rocks date from about this time. The region is once again an oasis of hot springs in the center of the coldest part of the ice ages. The fields will still be venting sulfur and steam a quarter million years hence, when the contemporaries of Josephus and the Plinys will know them as the Plegraean Fields, and will draw from them the inspiration for images of Hades. Nearly 2,000 years after the time of the Plinys, other *Homo erectus* descendants will begin studying the impacts of asteroids and comets on the history of life; and they will discover that volcanic upheavals can be even worse, and more frequent. Near a quarter-million B.C. as the Vesuvian hot spot begins to make its presence felt, the world between Misenum and Stabiae is a dry land interspersed with terraced hot pools and erupting geysers. One day, the entire region drops into the earth like an

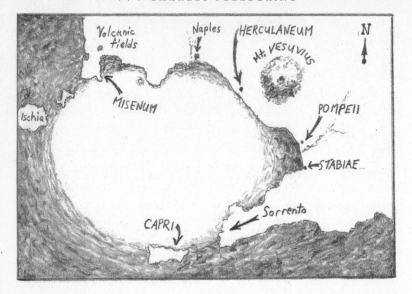

About 250,000 B.C., with a force exceeding 5 *Theras* (exceeding 120,000 megatons), the land between Misenum and Capri explodes. More than a quarter-million years later, the Bay of Naples is a flooded blast zone, with the isle of Ischia, Misenum, Sorrento, and the isle of Capri (where Emperor Augustus built history's first known museum of dinosaur skeletons) marking the perimeter of the blast. The hot baths of Ischia, the Phlegrean Fields, and Mount Vesuvius are the mere smouldering remnants of a volcanic giant.

express elevator, with a mega-tsunami generating force exceeding 5 *Theras*. Misenum, Puteoli, Herculaneum, Pompeii, and Stabiae will all be built along the rim of a water-filled crater—which people will one day name the Bay of Naples.

Presently, the stars of the Big Dipper resemble a giant spade, stretched out over twice as much sky as they will cover by A.D. 2000. The Bay of Naples will, in the fullness of time, prove itself even more malleable than the stars. Between A.D. 1982 and 1985 alone, 80 square kilometers (31 square miles) of the region will be raised nearly 2 meters (6 feet) into the air. This will not discourage *Homo erectus* descendants of A.D. 2004 from planting new vineyards and erecting new hotels on the flanks of Vesuvius.

522,000 B.C.

The Vesuvian hot zone does not exist as yet, nor do the vast ice sheets of the Mindel glacial period, now only in its birth stages.

Homo erectus still holds sway. The land around what will one day be reshaped as the Bay of Naples is heavily forested, and the people here occasionally damage their prized flint tools and abandon them to the archaeological record. Hundreds of miles away in the northeast, in Terra Amata, France, people are building dome-shaped tents from saplings, wooden poles, and animal hides. In mudflats nearby, their fossilizing footprints are preserving impressions of animal-hide footwear. They have invented animal-skin coats and scarves, and have begun to move away from the European subtropics into regions of more rigorous climate, including Russia and Tibet, where, inevitably, they will encounter other *Homo erectus* tribes radiating out of Asia. Though Mount Vesuvius is yet to be born, their world is not without a certain amount of geologic drama.

According to the rate at which certain argon isotopes decay in once-molten glass, the small asteroid that struck the continental shelf, off the west coast of Australia, fell from the sky in 800,000 B.C. give or take thirty thousand years. It struck with a minimum force of 10 *Theras*. Almost simul-

The Big Dipper in 522,000 B.C.

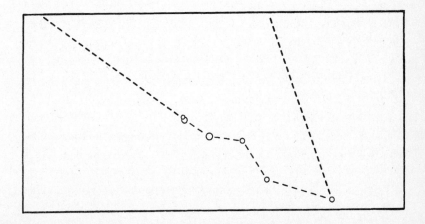

taneously, a volcano in the center of New Zealand's North Island exploded, leaving behind a crater 20 miles (32 kilometers) in diameter—which would one day be named Lake Taupo. This eruption was equivalent to between 5 and 10 *Theras*. The North American eruption of 620,000 B.C.—whose smoldering remnant *Homo erectus* descendants would one day name Yellowstone National Park—expelled between 500 and 625 cubic miles (2,000 to 2,500 cubic kilometers) of volcanic ejecta toward the stratosphere. The Yellowstone explosion was measurable between 10 and 13 *Theras*.

These were Pleistocene times, with glacial advances either amplified or hindered by the amount of volcanic (and occasionally asteroidal) dust lingering in the upper atmosphere. In China, the descendants of *Homo erectus* would one day conjure a curse disguised to sound, on first hearing, like a blessing: "May you live in interesting times." For our remotest human forebears, the Pleistocene epoch was the ultimate realization of the curse.

1,046,000 B.C.

In Africa, Ghana Crater and Ivory Coast impact glass speaks of a 5- to 10-*Thera* asteroid impact between 1.25 and 1.35 million B.C.—the precise geologic "moment" in which two "humanoids" named *Australopithecus boisei* and *Homo habilis* (by *Homo erectus* descendants) ceased contributing bones to the fossil record. About this same moment (about 1.3 million B.C.), Yellowstone National Park exploded on schedule, in a cycle of roughly 620,000 years. This time, it had expelled approximately 70 cubic miles (280 cubic kilometers) of rock and dust, with a force almost equivalent to 2 *Theras*.

History teaches us that we, as a species and as a civilization, may owe nearly as much to random celestial trapshoots as to volcanic throws of the dice.

(Watch the skies . . . watch the ground.)

Homo erectus, an apparent descendant of an Asian lineage of *Homo habilis*, has only recently populated Africa and inherited the earth. A winner in the planetary extinction lottery, the *Homo erectus* tribes have already left their distinctive flint tools in the ground, from Kenya and the Ivory Coast to China and Java.

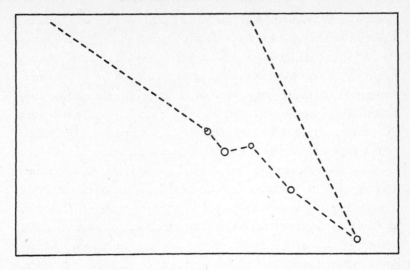

The Big Dipper in 1,046,000 B.C.

In caves across Africa and China, pack-hunting cats are occasionally trapping themselves and leaving their bones behind for tomorrow's paleontologists. Many of them are larger than the lions of futurity, and these carnivorous rodent descendants have spread across every habitable continent except Australia.

About 1 million B.C., one of Africa's "bone caves" is evidently a lair for big cats, where human bones are gnawed and mined for their nutrient-rich marrow. One of the older cubs, contributing its favorite plaything to the fossil record, treats the skull of a *Homo erectus* youth much as a human child of the twenty-first century A.D. might treat a teething ring. From such beginnings . . . the tiger on my couch. I cannot escape the notion that (much as I love her) my cat Europa is *still* sizing me up as food.

2.1 MILLION B.C.

The period between 2.2 and 2.1 million years B.C. is marked by a 9-*Thera* event at Yellowstone—which ejects approximately 625 cubic miles (or

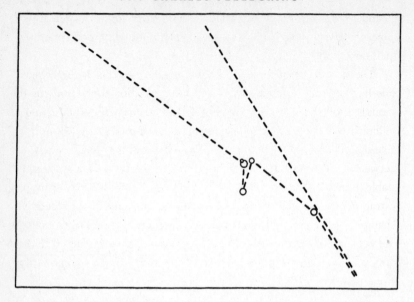

The Big Dipper in 2.1 million B.C.

2,500 cubic kilometers) of debris. To what degree 9 *Theras* act as pruning shears against the tree of human lineages is anybody's guess.

We stand at the beginning of the Pleistocene epoch, in which ice ages come and go in cycles of roughly ninety thousand years. Humanity's family tree is, at this point in time, a rather luxuriant family bush. *Homo erectus*, a slightly larger-brained variant of the *Homo habilis* lineage, has only recently or is only now about to branch off from either *Homo habilis* or some closely related (and still undiscovered) tribe. Though the Wood Age probably extends at least 2 million years deeper into the past, the first crude Stone Age tools (belonging apparently to the *Homo habilis* people) have already appeared from China to Egypt.

The *Homo habilis* tribes currently share the world, and especially Africa, with at least three (and probably more) anatomically distinct tribes of australopithecine man-apes. These include the leaf-eating *Australopithecus robustus* and the omnivorous *A. boisei* and *A. africanus*.

Of all the variants now extant, only *Homo erectus* will hold sway, apparently all alone upon the earth, for close on a million years, until the

Neanderthals and thin-boned tribes radiate from some isolated fringe zone of *Homo erectus* habitation, and become founding populations in their own right.

The first thing one notices about *Homo erectus* skulls is that, placed side by side, they exhibit surprisingly little variation over hundreds of thousands of years. The differences between *Homo erectus* skulls dating a million years apart will, by the time they are extinct, prove less noticeable than the difference between *Homo erectus* and the Neanderthals, or between the Neanderthals and the thin-boned tribes. This apparently stable branch of the human bush, as it moves on into futurity, spans an extraordinary interval of time, revealing no evidence of a cumulative change of gene content, frequency, or expression taking place (indeed, the variation of the thin-boned people into multiple races, each with distinctive bone structures, from 100,000 B.C. onward, will look like explosive diversification by comparison).

There will be, and there are, no major morphologic excursions in *Homo erectus*—merely a thicker brow ridge here, a subtle variation of tooth structure there, and not much else—as if a substantial stretch of human history were to be characterized not by change, but by stasis, by equilibrium.

Two *Homo erectus* descendants—Niles Eldredge and Stephen Jay Gould—would begin to wonder 2.1 million years hence if what is really required for widespread change might be the buildup of a genetic potential at the periphery of a widely spread and still-spreading population, where the environment is harshest and the species might scarcely be hanging on to survival. Its DNA programming pushed to the limit, something new might emerge, stronger and perhaps a little meaner as well—sweeping outward (and eventually homeward) over the whole ancestral population and becoming a new central population, until its own periphery generate something new. The Gould and Eldredge view of life would, in time, cast all the DNA programs of all the earth as naturally occurring computer programs operating against each other (and occasionally leapfrogging over each other) in a biological arms race of ever-increasing complexity.

The abrupt appearance (punctuation) and subsequent stability of *Homo erectus* (equilibrium), followed by the abrupt appearance of *Homo sapiens neanderthalensis* and *Homo sapiens sapiens* (punctuation), followed by the rapid diversification of "our people" (more punctuation), is consistent with Eldredge and Gould's "punctuated equilibrium" theory—which describes the origin of species as sudden spurts of genetic change, often followed by long periods of stasis.

By this measure, changes in the human bush—and in every other branching lineage—become relativistic, in the manner of Einstein's theory of "special relativity," by which two observers moving at different velocities, relative to each other, view the same phenomena differently.

We began our journey (relative to our present velocity of twenty thousand centuries per step) falling backward through historical time frames, then through archaeological frames, and now we are accelerating through biological and geological frames, in which a millennium seems dwarfed by a human pulse beat. On a scale of the year-by-year experience of human lifetimes, gradual change in a population will have real meaning only if the rate of change is punctuational. At our present, backward velocity, the long equilibrium of *Homo erectus's* population has real meaning even if the rate of change is gradual or nonexistent. The theory of punctuated equilibrium places branching events in discrete pockets of time and space, and forces us to think about regulatory genes, spreading and/or self-competing populations, and the genetic code's ability to mimic the projection (and selection) of probability curves, so that biocomputation and DNA itself (and not humanity itself) become the true masters of Earth.[1]

Gould and Eldredge's view of life focuses attention on *how* species diverge into new forms. Their focus on modes of change (as revealed through the fossil record's brand of time-lapse photography) emerges as punctuated equilibrium's most lasting contribution to our understanding of the past, and our anticipation of the future.

Soon, in just one more back-step, it will become difficult to discern, among multiple species of man-apes, the lineage that will raise Pompeii

---

[1] Given this biological edict, DNA does not work in our best interests; meaning that if we are not wise, and if we fail to pay attention, we shall become merely one of the many temporary masks that DNA will wear. If DNA is indeed engaged in a global biological arms race with itself, it matters little whether a snippet of genetic code resided in a human or a worm, or in an infectious yeast cell. The basic DNA program will run just as well, either way.

and Herculaneum from wood and iron. Soon it will become impossible to draw a clear line of ancestry to the people who shall one day deposit their bones in the shadow of Vesuvius.

4.2 MILLION B.C.

Presently, these are Pliocene times. The region that will become the Bay of Naples stands on high ground, overlooking a Mediterranean Sea that has been dammed by a collision between the African and European plates, producing a dry canyon more than 2 miles deep. All of Italy, located more than 40 miles (60 kilometers) south of its twenty-first century A.D. position, is being carried north, like a parcel on a conveyor belt, by the same magma-driven spasms that have dammed the Strait of Gibraltar and caused the Mediterranean to dry out. Except for occasional volcanic upheavals, and the sudden releases of constantly building pressure through earthquakes, the descendants of australopithecine man-apes will be unable to notice, without the aid of laser-assisted measuring devices, that the Mediter-

The Big Dipper in 4.2 million B.C.

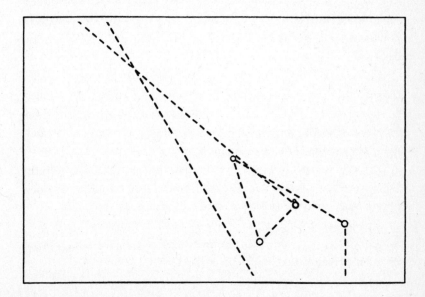

ranean grows narrower with each passing year. So slowly does the change occur, by the measure of human years, that they (and their ancestors) cannot notice it happening, even as it happens before their eyes.

As the Mediterranean narrows, spawning new volcanic hot zones on the Aegean and Tyrrhenian plains, the Atlantic simultaneously widens. European eel migrations are nearly 50 miles (82 kilometers) shorter than they will be in the third millennium A.D. Anyone who has ever wondered how the Atlantic Ocean began, need only track the narrowing back to the time of the dinosaurs. Track back far enough, and the crack in the earth looks just like the Red Sea, about the time the descendants of australopithecines invent flying machines and television networks, about the time *National Geographic* photographer Row Findley looks down from a helicopter upon the aftermath of an explosive force smaller than one two-thousandth of a *Thera*, less than 0.5 *Pompeii*. Findley will be staggered by what he sees, in the wake of the A.D. 1980 Mount Saint Helens surge clouds: "We detected no evidence of life," Findley will say. "We hovered over a half-buried car and tried to blow away ash with the rotors. But it boiled up menacingly. Fully two days had passed since the mountain exploded, but the ash was still very hot. I felt a growing appreciation for all of us living on a planetary crust so frighteningly afloat atop such terrible heats and pressures. Never again, it came to me then and remains with me to this day, would I regain my former complacency about this world we live on."

8.4 MILLION B.C.

Among scraps of stone and bone, we can no longer recognize ourselves at all. There are no protohumans, only protochimpanzees (or protoaustralopithecines), and they exist in such small numbers that only rarely do they leave traces of themselves among fragments of orangutan jaw and among other, unidentifiable apes. The protochimpanzees are not necessarily possessors of the largest and most efficient brains on Earth. Dolphins and whales, at this point in time, may be even more capable of storing information external of their own DNA.

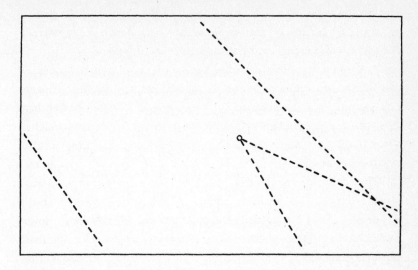

The Big Dipper in 8.4 million B.C.

Here, at the close of the Miocene epoch, the migration of European anguillid eels is shorter by 3 percent (80 miles). Though significant, this is not enough of a change to bring the European and American migrants to the Sargasso Sea at the same time. Though sharing the same breeding ground, they have been mating during different seasons since at least the Oligocene epoch, and they are therefore living as two genetically isolated species.

In the heavens, the constellations have become far less familiar than either eels or protochimps. All of them are gone beyond recall. Alkaid, the star at the tip of the Big Dipper's handle, has shifted more than halfway around the circle of the sky.

Up to this point in our descent, the temperature of the universe has remained constant at an almost uniform 2.8 degrees Kelvin (2.8 degrees Centigrade above *zero degrees Kelvin*, or *absolute zero* [−273.15 degrees C, or −459.67 degrees F]). Cold, empty space is neither entirely cold nor truly empty. The average density of the universe (at least beyond the 150,000-light-year diameter of our galaxy, out to a radius of our present back-step: 8.4 million light-years) is two hydrogen atoms per 10 cubic meters, or 10^{-30} the density of water. Equipped with radio telescopes, protochimp descendants will discover that when they look 8.4 million light-years into space, the light reaching them then (in futurity) is presently 8.4 million years to Earth. As they look progressively deeper into space, they are also looking progressively backward into time. Imperceptibly, at first, the density and temperature of the universe begin to creep upward, as if all of substance, all of space-time geometry, is evolving into a stupendous explosion viewed in reverse—which, as a matter of fact, it is.

16.8 MILLION B.C.

Thickened by contraction, during our acceleration into deep time, the background of microwave radiation emanating from every direction in space has risen by 0.02 degrees Centigrade. The density of the universe is now three hydrogen atoms per 10 cubic meters of space, an increase of 30 percent.

During this warmest part of the Miocene epoch, pine forests line the Antarctic coast. Subtropical forests have spread into northern Alaska. And Italy—now a large island attached to the African continental plate—is thickly carpeted with jungle vegetation. In the forests of the night, the ancestral cats are virtually indistinguishable from their rodent prey. In Pakistan they live among relatives of the creatures they will one day domesticate: the ramapithecine and sivapithecine apes. Both apen branches will be named, by their distant future cousins, after members of the Hindu triad: Rama, the reincarnation of Vishnu, and Siva, the Destroyer.

At this time, the forests belong to the apes, but a great dying, a kind of evolutionary bottleneck, has been written in the sky. About 14.8 million B.C. (give or take about seven hundred thousand years, according to radiometric dates scratched into molten glass), an asteroid carves out Germany's Reis Basin, 15 miles (24 kilometers) wide. Its total kinetic energy is in the range of 20 *Theras* and probably considerably higher. Streamers of molten rock are steam catapulted into space, where they form a deadly, suborbital arc aimed at Czechoslovakia. From southern

Germany spreads a giant black curtain laced with sheets of lightning and made heavy with hot, descending ash. All downblast and horizontal velocities, the surge clouds run like tidal waves over the ground, faster than airplanes, slashing down forests as they move. Far above, dozens of cubic miles of ultrafine dust are lofted to the edge of space and begin to form a global shroud. The sky's transparency changes. In the waters near Christchurch, New Zealand, the lush subtropical assemblage of early Miocene marine organisms is replaced abruptly by a less diversified, cold-water fauna. Carbon and oxygen isotope changes etched into their shells suggest that the rate of change is greatest between 14.8 and 14.0 million B.C. Ice sheets might (or might not) already be driving across the Antarctic when the asteroid arrives, and the arrival might (or might

Nature's extinction lottery. Arrows (*top*) represent asteroid and comet impacts that punched holes in Earth with diameters of 10 kilometers or more. Beneath the arrows, a dotted line traces the Southern Hemisphere's paleotemperature curve. Scaled against climate and impacts, generic curves representing (a) dinosaurs, (b) reef corals, and (c) planktonic foraminifera suggest that some organisms, including reef corals and planktonic foraminifera (but not dinosaurs), disappeared at the "instant" the late Cretaceous impact signature was recorded in stone. Some, including reef corals and dinosaurs, had begun to decline during the worldwide climatic deterioration that preceded the arrival of the Mexico impactor, the North Sea impactor, and a simultaneous volcanic upheaval in India. (Data compiled by N. D. Newell and C. R. Pellegrino.)

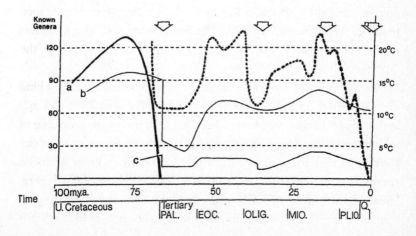

not) worsen a global cooling already under way. Giant crabs vanish from the shores of New Zealand; and in both hemispheres, tropical rain forests that have for hundreds of thousands of years encircled the margins of what were, in the previous epoch, regions of polar climate, are once again constricting toward the equator.

The fair-weather branching and diversification of apes is nearing its end. The sivapithecines and their brethren are about to be compressed by advancing ice into stiff competition, into a new round of biological arms races, force-fed by shrinking habitats and diminishing food sources.

In the immediate aftermath of the Reis Basin explosion, before the dust cloud has time to spread, the noise alone is strong enough to deafen. Across Europe and into Asia, apes shall live their remaining years with a maddening ringing in their ears. They are the lucky ones.

33.6 MILLION B.C.

Protocats and protodogs live together in the forests of Sahara. One protofeline lineage has returned from the land to the sea—and in time the descendants of protomonkeys (there are, as yet, no apes) will name the "sea cats" seals. The ancestors of cows are also branching into seafaring lineages: one living like hippos in the rivers of Sahara, the other wandering into the deeper waters of northern Egypt to become the ancestral cetaceans (the great-grandparents of dolphins and whales).

In the Atlantic, now narrowed by hundreds of miles, two separate eel species have become one.

Between 33.8 and 35 million B.C., the earth is stricken by two asteroid impacts, each spreading beads of microscopic glass and heavy, platinum-group metals across the Caribbean floor. Each qualifies, minimally, as a 10-*Thera* event.

This pair of glass-forming events appears to mark the transition from early to middle Oligocene time. The cooling trend that marked the end of the Eocene epoch's global tropics—with average winter temperatures all over Earth dropping by almost 10 degrees Centigrade (34 degrees Fahrenheit)—is still in effect when the multi-*Thera* impacts occur. The distribution of forests and animals changes globally, and in the seas, the microscopic shells of five radiolarian species stop entering the fossil record. What this means is that the sudden disappearance of shelled marine protozoans (which were previously ubiquitous in the oceans of both hemispheres) becomes a signal to distant, future sapience, that terrestrial and oceanic ecosystems have been rocked from the bottom up—again.

67.0 MILLION B.C.

As in middle Miocene times and throughout Eocene time, average global temperatures are 20 degrees Centigrade higher than they will be in the twenty-first century A.D. This is the end of the Upper Cretaceous period, the age of the last dinosaurs. First the positions of the stars and now the positions and shapes of entire continents are twisting beyond recall. At the South Pole, Australia and Antarctica are joined solidly into a single supercontinent—but Earth is so warm that even during the six-month polar night, dinosaurs have, for millions of years, been thriving in Antarctic forests. The Atlantic Ocean is narrower by more than half, and the gulf between Europe and Africa has become an ocean in its own right.

The place on Earth that will become Italy, Vesuvius, and the Bay of Naples lies mostly underwater, offshore of northern Africa. In that place, in its northern reaches, clams and cockles dwell on muddy undersea plains, forming fossil beds that will one day be thrust into sunlight and thin air—on the high Alps. Presently, mosasaurs, icthyosaurs, and plesiosaurs swim above them.

Across the shrunken Atlantic, what will one day become the bedrock on which Manhattan's skyscrapers are anchored is bleeding out of the earth from seven live volcanoes. In what shall become eastern Montana, flowering plants and broad-leaved evergreens are slowly being replaced by conifer trees more tolerant of cold winters. Northern Alaska (now even nearer the North Pole than it will be in the third millennium A.D.) is recording similar shifts from temperate and subtropical forests to cold-weather flora; dinosaurs are retreating from the margin

Ever since the "Cambrian explosion," near 600 million B.C., the history of life was headed toward the storage of increasing quantities of information outside of DNA and inside nerve tissue. By 65 million B.C., the ornithomimids (the ostrich dinosaurs) were evolving large brains and manipulative limbs, or hands. If not for global deterioration of the climate, a pair of asteroid impacts, and a simultaneous volcanic catastrophe in India, the "ossies," or something very much like them, might have built the first cities, discovered the age of the universe, and laid the foundations for ascents to the nearer stars. Nature did not "select against" the dinosaurs so much as plow over them without even noticing. Those who say we humans must be wise and be caretakers of the earth, or nature will take revenge against us, are missing a far more frightening, far more sobering point: Nature does not notice us. Nature does not care.

of the pole, and sedimentary rocks from the region are beginning to preserve ice-rafted sands. Polar ice caps, it seems, are on the verge of forming.

Antarctica's "dinosaurs of the night" are retreating into Australia, in the direction of the shrinking tropics. All over the world, the story is the same: After more than 100 million years of equable climate, something is happening. A census of North America's horned dinosaurs (as will be compiled in the twenty-first century A.D., by the descendants of ratlike marsupial insect eaters) will reveal that the rhinolike triceratops have, by now, declined from sixteen distinctive varieties, or genera, to only seven. Their decline has run in parallel with a cooling of Earth's oceans (as recorded by isotopes of the element oxygen, in the shells of radiolarians) and a slow withdrawal of shallow seas from the area of the continents (as recorded by sedimentary rocks from central North America to Australia). According to the rat descendants, armored dinosaurs are experiencing a triceratops-like pruning of their family tree during this same time period, declining from nineteen genera to six, while the hadrosaurs (duck-billed dinosaurs) whither from twenty-nine to only nine genera.

The last of the dinosaurs, it seems, are killed by deteriorating climate made worse by the so-called "K-T boundary event." They are victims, apparently, of multiple simultaneous instances of misfortune.

If a 10- or 20-*Thera* event is, as a planet measures explosive events, a serious hiccup, then the terminal Cretaceous event qualifies as a major coronary. About 64.6 million B.C. (give or take two hundred thousand years), an asteroid of stony meteorite composition, measuring roughly the dimensions of Manhattan Island, plunges through the continental shelf east of Mexico's Yucatán Peninsula, at close on 20 miles (32 kilometers) per second. The tidal wave alone, as it washes from end to end over Cuba, plows up mile after mile of bedrock before it reaches the opposite shore. The wave, glutted with boulders and forests, is still more than a mile high when it crosses the center of the island. So much debris is hurled into space that the suborbital splash-streams, as they reenter the atmosphere, blaze forth brightly enough for the sky-shine alone to prove lethal. Across Montana and Ohio, into Louisiana and Florida, entire ecosystems are flash-grilled.

The terminal Cretaceous asteroid is equivalent to 56,000 *Theras,* and it is not alone. In A.D. 2002, petroleum geologists working in the North Sea will confirm the simultaneous arrival of a second object, possibly a smaller, orbiting companion of the Yucatán impactor. On the bottom of the sea, a "fossil impact scar" preserves at least ten concentric rings, resembling ripples in a pond, radiating outward from a central mountainous peak, inside a central pit 1.5 miles (2 kilometers) across. The earth's surface, there, behaves much like water responding to a pebble tossed in a pond, then freezes, fossilizing the shock wave. The North Sea impactor adds up, probably, to another 100 *Theras.*

At this same time, India is a separate continent whose southern tip protrudes into the lower latitudes of the Southern Hemisphere, almost into the antipode of the Yucatán impact, where the shock front from 56,000 *Theras* ripples out from Mexico. As they reach the opposite side of the globe, the ripples, though expanding away from Mexico, are simultaneously compressed into a series of contracting circles—with all of their collective force focused, implosively, on a single point in central India. There, the Yucatán impactor's ripples contract and rebound, like a cymbal clap performed on a geologic stage, at Earth's own planetary scale. Virtually the entire continent loses its rigidity and the mountains themselves swell and roll, snap, leap, and dance like ripples of water. From uncounted new chasms, India bleeds lava fields wide enough to swallow scores of Lake Superiors. Here and there, the continent bleeds so deeply that it coughs up mantle deposits of diamonds—which pick up garnets, sapphires, and rubies along the way. As blistering heat blows toward China and the Pacific, the India eruptions add at least 500 more *Theras* to the terrestrial din.

Though at least a few dinosaurs will deposit bones and eggs in New Mexico's and Colorado's fossil beds during the next 200,000 to 2 million years, the K-T ash layer marks the last chapter of the Mesozoic era: The saurians diminish, and are replaced by mammals and birds.

At the time of the impact, *Ornithomimus* is the newest and brightest creature around—a warm-blooded and rapidly branching lineage of "ostrich dinosaurs." They walk erect, have a high-energy feeding strategy that supports large brains and, just as important, they possess hands.

The origin of the fittest: If, in biology's never-ending arms race, brains, circulatory systems, and digestive systems could be put together to store ever-greater amounts of information outside of DNA—to allow creatures to connect those ever-greater amounts together and to produce anticipation (that is, projection of probability curves, and responses to them)—then an animal will begin to see its own future in reasonable detail, will begin to worry about tomorrow, and will begin to adapt in advance.

Here, at the end of the Cretaceous period, the *Ornithomimus* lineages are analogous to the great diversification of Miocene apes, perhaps even to australopithecine lines of human ancestry. But adaptability and intelligence count for naught, if the most highly adapted brain on Earth ends up in the path of an asteroid, or lava flow, or global dust shroud.

In the time of the last *Ornithomimus,* the ancestors of humans and their cats are insect-eating and root-eating marsupials—ratlike and perpetually underfoot in a world whose chief denizens have scales (and occasionally feathers) and who frequently dine on the "rats." Looking back from futurity, the rat descendants know that if not for 56,000 *Theras,* some distant descendant of the ostrich dinosaurs might have invented street lighting and spread across Earth in multiple billions, then reached outward to the planets and beyond. Or they might have unleashed, against their own kind, the thermonuclear inverse to the Golden Rule, tens of millions of years ago. In either case, the rats might still be underfoot.

The deteriorating climate that preceded the asteroids and the lava seas was merely pruning the saurian family tree, force-feeding change upon them, by increasing environmental stress. In this earthly arena of evolutionary bottlenecks, "the same hammer that breaks glass can also forge steel." Global cooling, all by itself, should not have forced the ostrich dinosaurs into extinction.

Fast-forward to October 1980: As one rat descendant to another, Stephen Jay Gould agreed with me that the 56,000-*Thera* event might only have been a final, contributing factor to the pruning away of the saurian tree. "But," he added, "I do think that the astronomical [and volcanic] disaster may have been more than just a minor coup de grâce. After all, extinctions far less extensive than the Cretaceous event have punctuated the history of life many times during the past 600 million years. Perhaps they never have really great impact unless the general deterioration of conditions that serves as their major cause is greatly amplified in effect by some major extraterrestrial event. Correspondingly, if the extraterrestrial event occurs during 'good' biological times, maybe nothing much happens at all."

So, what *did* kill the dinosaurs?

Bad luck. Simple bad luck. Standing knee-deep in snow, some forgotten, undiscovered branch of *Ornithomimus*, if it thought about that awful time at all, must have wondered how its days could possibly get any worse. And then, looking up: "It's only an asteroid about to strike the earth. (*Should I worry about this?*)" Then India cracks open and bleeds lakes of lava—the whole continent.

That's how the dinosaurs ended, how they cleared the decks for us: one piece of bad luck, piled on top of bad luck, piled on top of bad luck. "*That,* and one other thing," says fellow rat descendant Sir Arthur C. Clarke: "Think upon this, as we hear call after call that our civilization is moving too fast and that we must look away from space as an unwarranted and perhaps even unhealthy distraction. We look away at our own peril. The dinosaurs could not change the asteroid's path, and change their history. They could not even know the asteroid was coming. The dinosaurs are extinct today because they did not have a space program."

134.2 MILLION B.C.

We are deep within the Mesozoic era, in the early part of the Lower Cretaceous. Earth is recovering from a decline in the diversity of ocean plankton, and a similar decline in the diversity of vertebrate animals that marks the Jurassic-Cretaceous boundary. The stegosaurs are now extinct, but most of the other dinosaurs have survived the terminal Jurassic extinctions.

Small birds and protomammals (the cynodonts) have been around for at least 60 million years. But without genetic-mapping equipment (aided by either "mouse hairs in amber" or by the ultimate geologic tool, a time machine), the ancestors of cats and humans cannot be identified, or anticipated, among the egg-laying carnivores. All of them are small and vaguely mouselike. None are particularly common. From these humble beginnings shall arise two major branches: the marsupials and (later) the insectivores; the latter branch pointing the way to such diverse lineages as bats, whales, gophers, and apes.

Dinosaurs have been with us for fully half of our acceleration into the deeps of time, and they will be with us through the Jurassic and Triassic phases of our next leap, utterly dwarfing human existence.

Here, near the Jurassic-Cretaceous boundary, the Moon orbits nearly 4,800 miles (7,872 kilometers) closer to Earth, and each day is shorter by at least one minuté. The central stars of the Big Dipper are nowhere to be seen, for they do not yet exist. Somewhere in the sky, in a dense, stellar nursery of in-falling gas and dust, Mizar, Alcor, and Mergrez are only now about to be born. The general temperature of the universe has risen from 2.80 degrees Kelvin to 2.97 degrees Kelvin, and every cubic meter of space contains at least two atoms of hydrogen, at least two protons.

Temperatures and densities are easy to document, calculate, and recite. But numbers alone are without meaning until we take pause, and think about them, and wonder what is really happening. The whole universe has warmed 0.17 degrees Centigrade since we took our first step backward in time—the whole thing. Its density has increased fivefold, and in our next step backward we will find space and time compressed twice again. It becomes difficult to imagine it ever stopping.

268.4 MILLION B.C.

The Permian extinction, the greatest of all great dyings, approaches. In its wake, the Age of Reptiles will end, the Age of Dinosaurs will begin, and 90 percent of all known genera will vanish from the records kept by stones.

Only 18 million years away, it will become known to the descendants of some obscure reptilian lineage as "the Great Flood." Paleontologists will know it as a flood of fire and molten rock, not of water. Christened the Siberian Traps, the flood lasts for thousands of years (probably many tens of thousands of years), and like Thera in 1628 B.C., and India's post-Yucatán volcanic flood tides, it will be capable of changing the climate of an entire planet. It differs from the later catastrophes only as a matter of degree, only by potency: This flood is more than twice as large as India's, equivalent to more than 1,000 *Theras*— to *thousands* of *Theras*.

The geologists will find hints, in oceanic rocks, that iridium and other heavy metals common in stony meteorites, but rare in rocks of the earth's crust, are injected into the atmosphere about the time of the terminal Permian eruptions, and they will speculate that an asteroid triggered the floods or arrived during the floods and worsened already bad biological times. No one will know for sure. From 268 million through 250 million B.C., most of the continents are huddling together near the South Pole and a whole hemisphere of Earth is open ocean. The positions of the continents will be so extensively reshuffled and so thoroughly reshaped during the next quarter-billion years that any identifying impact crater, if it exists at all, will likely be erased from existence.

In the twenty-first century A.D., Peter D. Ward, a reptile-descendant paleontologist at the University of Washington, will conclude that "it looks like the earth was getting multiple levels of extinction," in which consecutive layers of fossil-bearing shale, when leafed through like the pages of a book, tell of "plant productivity being impacted over and over again, during the period around the Permian-Triassic boundary. Multiple phased cycles of extinction, as evidenced in the fossil record, are compatible with a massive, prolonged flood of molten basalt. We do not see all of the basalt coming out at once, as a steady stream. It was not a single event—like the [hammer fall] of an asteroid striking against the Earth . . . It was really wave, after wave, after wave."

Barely more than 100 million years before the Permian extinction, plants had been drawn out of the sea and onto the land. In rapid succession (as pages of shale and sandstone measure time) they became horsetail weed, shrubs, giant club mosses, and tree ferns—then carpeted Earth in Coal Age forests. The first insects had, by then, taken wing. Beneath them, amphibians, reptiles, and lungfish sniffed the air—portending the hour of a new biological arms race.

In our next step backward through time—a step of a quarter-billion years—all branching lineages, all roads, lead into the sea.

536.9 MILLION B.C.

They would call it the Cambrian explosion.

For more than 2 billion years, and close on 3, simple algal-bacterial reefs, the odd jellyfish-like predecessor, and the organic antecedents of "rusticles" and other complex bacterial Consortia, had been adding their fossil remains to marine sediments. Then, near 570 million B.C., during the first 10 to 20 million years of the Cambrian period, began the seemingly sudden appearance of complex multicellular animals—fully equipped with eyes and gills, circulatory systems, and nervous systems. Immediately below the Cambrian lie the rocks of Australia's Edicaria Province, bearing fossils of sea anemones, fan corals, and a variety of strange and complex worms. Despite the fact that the Australian fossils lie, by only the slimmest of margins, below the base of the Cambrian period, paleontologists of the third millennium A.D., rather than push their time frame for the Cambrian a little bit deeper into the ground to accommodate the Australian fossils, will (to the horror of their students) name an entirely new period: the Edicarian.

Whatever meaning we ascribe to the names of periods and species, an important and endlessly fascinating puzzle lies immediately ahead, and I can describe it in just one word: *equilibrium*. By comparison to the slow parting of European and American eels, the steps we are about to take back through the Precambrian will reduce the whole anguillid divergence to only a chip of time—and yet for 1 billion years, 2 billion years, or more, the essential structure of stromatolites (bacterial reefs) entering the fossil record shall become more changeless, more timeless, than the universe itself.

The oldest known worm fossils (technically of Edicarian age) date from about 600 million B.C. and are embedded in rocks located immediately above an episode of glacial sedimentation in Australia. Once again, an evolutionary bottleneck (or choke point, or natural selection filter) is

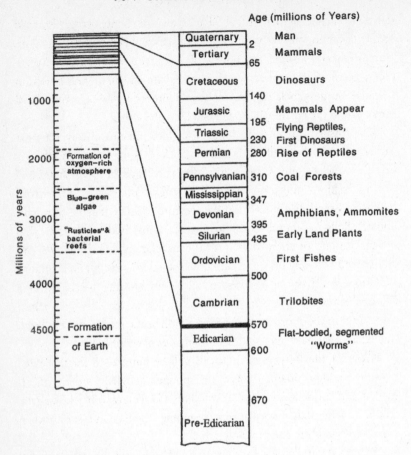

The geological time scale.

associated (coincidentally or not coincidentally) with the spread of ice and/or lava.

Approximately 10 or 20 million years later, there occurred another brief ice age, and by 570 million B.C., megacellular life had diversified into dozens of different phyla. Thirty-three million years after that, about 537 million B.C., in the period that now serves us as "time present," evolution's Rembrandts and Picassos had already formed. Owing to a multimillion-year accident in which periodic avalanches from bacterial reefs carried animals of all shapes and sizes into oxygen-starved waters (whereupon the bacteria of decay crystallized feldspar [calcium aluminosilicate] around the bodies of avalanche victims), a complete record of the Cambrian explosion's immediate aftermath was buried in Canada's Burgess shale region. It was, and forever would be, a miracle of preservation the equal of Pompeii and Herculaneum.

The fossils from the next layer down into the earth, from the next earliest period (Australia's Edicarian rocks), show signs of thorny organic cuticles (built from chitin—the substance of crab shells and "worm bristles") and protective shell casings cemented together from mucus and sand. But none of these creatures display true calcium carbonate shells (as found in the armor of clams, barnacles, and "ship worms"), none of them display true exoskeletons (as in lobsters and crabs). And yet, only one layer higher in the rocks, at Burgess, a burst of evolutionary activity at least the equal of any 10-million-year interval through Silurian, Devonian, Mesozoic, or Cenozoic time has taken place. Within the short span of a few million years, scores of new, hard-shelled lineages have appeared, seemingly out of nowhere.

Many of the Burgess shale fossils will be familiar to their distant, mammalian descendants. There are sponges, jellyfish, worms (both shelled and unshelled varieties), trilobites (which resemble horseshoe crabs), brachiopods (worms that resemble clams), and mollusklike worms (perhaps the ancestors of clams).

Equipped with large eyes, a streamlined body, and prominent dorsal fins—each stiffened by more than a hundred fin rays—*Nectocaris* is an efficient swimmer. It looks like a fish and it swims like a fish, but it is nevertheless a worm. This is, in fact, the Age of Worms.

More than a half-billion years hence, another creature, ordinary by comparison to *Nectocaris* and *Opabinia*, would draw the attention of a worm descendant named Stephen Jay Gould. He would come to know it as *Pikaia*, a swimming animal that looked like a worm but was in fact the beginning of something else. A rod-shaped column of nerve cells, stiffened by cartilage during life (and during death, preserved with Vesuvian precision beneath sheets of microcrystals), is embedded in the animal's back. The beginning of a spine—a *notochord*, the chief axial supporting structure in the bodies of lower chordates ("sea squirts") and in the embryos of higher ones (humans). Gould will place his beloved *Pikaia* in the phylum Chordata. While this fossil is unlikely to be *the* common ancestor of gorillas, hummingbirds, and eels, it does provide a reasonable picture of what some of the ancestral branches of our remotest, wormy lineages looked like.

But the puzzle remains: Why now, at the dawn of the Cambrian, this explosion of such complex and varied life?

The Cambrian explosion will so trouble a worm descendant named Charles Darwin that he shall be driven to concede, in the last edition of his *Origin of Species*, that "the case at present must remain inexplicable; and may be truly urged as a valid argument against the views herein entertained." In frustration, Darwin will posit that either nature is capable of sudden leaps, or the history written in Earth's rocks is imperfectly recorded; that a slow, stately erosion of the planet's surface simply grinds up and eliminates all the earlier stages of life, making it only appear that hordes of exotic invertebrate fossils suddenly exploded onto the Cambrian scene.

"The situation was indeed far worse in Darwin's day," Gould would observe, a hundred years later. "At that time, not a single Precambrian fossil had been found, and the Cambrian explosion of complex invertebrates provided the earliest evidence for any life on Earth. If so many

Stephen Jay Gould's old friend *Pikaia*. Dating back to about 537 million years B.C., this swimming, wormlike animal possessed a rodlike column of cells running the length of its back and stiffened by cartilage. In a biological arms race accelerating mysteriously (and perhaps inevitably) toward the storage and processing of information *outside* of genes and instead within increasingly sophisticated nervous systems, *Pikaia* heralded an Earth that was bound, sooner or later, to spawn intelligent life.

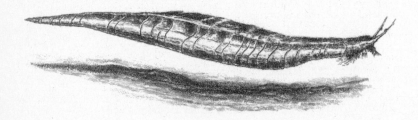

forms of life arose at the same time and with such initial complexity, might one not argue that God had chosen the base of the Cambrian for His moment (or six days) of creation?"

In Gould's time, a record of Precambrian fossils dating back 3.2 billion years to the Canadian Gun-flint Chert, and 3.5 billion years to western Australia's stromatolites, would illuminate (but not eliminate) Darwin's dilemma. Looking backward from the beginning of the Cambrian explosion, even the most complex 1-billion-, 2-billion-, and 3-billion-year-old organisms—displaying internal circulatory systems similar to those seen in sponges, with hints of tissue layers—are built entirely from bacterial cells, just like the bacterial Consortia living near hydrothermal vents and festooning the iron hulls of deep-ocean twentieth-century shipwrecks. In the remotest Precambrian, there is not a trace of a worm, or a snail, or even a true sponge. For most of Earth's history, though multicellularity was there almost from the start, in reef fungi and bacteria, the animal kingdom remained only latent in the seas. If anything, the post-Darwinian collection of a more complete fossil record would only double the size of the original problem by destroying Darwin's theory that crabs and clams and other complex animals had been there all along, before the Cambrian explosion, but that no one would ever find them. Gone was the argument that the "explosion" was more apparent than real. Gone was the argument that God played dice with the geologic record, and sometimes liked to throw the dice where no one could find them.

Something very, very real was at work near the Cambrian's lower boundary. Something extraordinary (and in fact wonderful) had occurred. More than 2 billion years of essentially changeless bacterial fossils said so.

The antecedents of intelligent life on Earth are much more deeply encoded than in mere organs and segments and limbs. Hurtling backward through history, we have witnessed our capacity for the storage, exchange, and use of information in a continual state of contraction: first from storage external of (or supplemental to) the human brain—contracting from a global computer network, to films, to books . . . then to storage in successively smaller brains . . . then to neural nets and notochords with only the most rudimentary capacity for "memory." And now, finally, we are fast approaching a moment in biology when there is no capacity, no ability at all, for storing information outside of DNA. We are on the threshold of a step in which DNA itself becomes the youngest, the brightest thing around, notwithstanding the fact that nucleic acid (this carbon strand of memory) is already ancient even against the standards by which a diamond might measure time.

1 BILLION B.C.

The further back we peer into time, the more numerous and the more violent Earth's geologic upheavals seem to become. At some points in the remote Precambrian, it seems the entire planet is trying to make volcanic basalt and granite, and that life manages to keep a foothold only in the nooks and crannies. Looking back from the early part of the third millennium A.D., some paleontologists will wonder if what the Great Cambrian Diversification really awaited, for close on 3 billion years, was a more quiescent Earth. Looking at an ever-diminishing assemblage of fossils surviving "the dark, backward and abysm of time," they would shake their heads and remark, "Nobody knows for sure." But this is no cause for despair; everyone loves a good mystery.

What do the continents look like in 1 billion B.C.? Where are Italy and Naples, and the piece of continental plate that will spawn Vesuvius, Pompeii, and Herculaneum? No one can even make a good guess. Too few geologic clues survive a billion years of erosion and continental twists, from which we can draw even a crudely accurate, freehand map of the world. Only the Moon looks the same, and only because it is quite dead.

Bacterial reefs still exist. Called "stromatolites," the reefs look much as they will in the Cambrian a half-billion years in the future; they still look much as they will in Australian salt ponds fully a billion years hence; and they still look much as they did 2 billion years in the past.

The newest and brightest things around are the ancestral "rusticles" (though an Australian fossil bed 1.5 billion years older emphasizes, again, that nothing is very new under the Precambrian sun). Rusticles— so named because they often resemble icicles made of rust—are complex Consortia of bacteria, as old as stromatolites and just as long-lived into futurity. What makes them different is that they are complex "cities" of bacteria and fungi (incorporating bacteria-like cells called "Archaea," which typically dwell around undersea volcanic vents). They are arranged into actual tissue layers, built around a functioning (sponge-style) circulatory system. They also possess an immune system based upon chemical defenses against rapidly dividing cells "unwelcome" in the Consortium.

One distant, future line of rusticle descent will be found on the iron hulls of the *Titanic* and other deep-ocean shipwrecks. Another line of descent, the creators of those deep-ocean wrecks, will initially look upon the living fossils as "iron stalactites" or "rust icicles," thinking them to be mineral formations, until they move in closer with microscopes and discover that when they think about their own circulatory systems and immune systems, they must also begin to understand that what they have always believed to be their own cells might actually have originated as collections of bacteria (with the admission of protozoans, or "animal cells," into the club whenever "useful" species became available). And they will begin to see, then, that "their" cells may not truly be "theirs" at all. With such grace shall the ancient concept of "the stranger within" shift from mythology to a dawning reality.

The rusticles, like the termites and sharks that shall come after them, will remain with Earth for a very long time. Even in their most primitive form, they emerge widely adapted to a multitude of environments, moving onward through time with a kind of "neutrality," or invisibility, within their varied and sometimes obscure habitats. "Neutral" organisms need not be eaten by new branching lineages, or competed out of existence by them. Neutral is ignored. Neutral has staying power. Thus might it become possible for rusticle-shaped rusticle descendants and human-shaped rusticle descendants to be living on the same planet, even after the passage of a billion years. Unthinking and forever uncaring, the rusticles have been with us through every backstep—through all the fits and starts of human history, all the fits and starts of human origins.

Fast-forward a billion years: We, the product of volcanic exhalations and regurgitations, live now in a dancing matrix of genomes, constantly testing each other, constantly regulating and adapting. But was it always so? Or did the process of change—as an anguillid eel or a diamond might measure time—once happen much more slowly than in the aftermath of the Cambrian explosion?

Toward the end of his life, Stephen Jay Gould—teacher, paleontologist, fireman—proposed *Contingency* in the descent of rusticles, *Pikaia*, and man. He saw in the beginning of *Pikaia* the question of what would happen if the species had perished under some Cambrian multi-*Thera* event: "We, its descendants, would not exist. The evolutionary outcome is *contingent* on everything that came before. Replay the tape of life and today's biota looks completely different. Contingency is a major factor in macroevolution, not least because the response of organisms to [asteroidal and/or volcanic] catastrophes cannot be predicted. The normal rules of natural selection do not apply. [Darwinian] natural selection is not the only engine of evolution. Major perturbations—catastrophic events—influence the fates of groups. There is no inevitable evolutionary 'progress' to higher forms of life, culminating in man.''

Years earlier, Gould and his friend Niles Eldredge (coframer of the theory that nature might occasionally make biological leaps) came to my defense in New Zealand, after a series of giant fossil crabs in successive layers of volcanic mud began to lend support to their idea. A supervisor had asked, and had demanded an answer of me: "Who are *you* to be questioning Darwin?" My answer that Darwin himself, in a moment of despair over the Cambrian explosion puzzle, had proposed in the sixth edition of his *Origin of Species* that nature might indeed make leaps, fell on deaf ears.[2]

Gould and Eldredge chimed in: "Even suggesting to a young scientist that it is somehow inappropriate to 'question Darwin' is the antithesis of what a young scientist is supposed to learn—to question virtually everything.''

[2] At this same time (the spring of 1982), a lecture I had given about what would eventually become known as the "*Jurassic Park* dinosaur cloning recipe" inflamed a local radio evangelist, and as a result brought much negative attention to my university. Observing what he called "ruffled feathers all around," the vice chancellor commented, "I see that you've managed to alienate both the scientific community and the religious community. How efficient of you. Arrogance and stupidity in one package." Whereupon one of the professors threw a book at my head: Darwin's *Origin of Species*, the original first printing of Darwin's last edition. I carried the book home, repaired the binding, and two decades later carried it to the bottom of the ocean with me, inside the *Mir-1* submersible, into the hydrothermal vent zone called "Lost City"—into a biological wonder world that biology's Einstein had never lived to see.

Question: What if *Pikaia*—the entire species and the entire genus—died in a volcanic or an asteroidal explosion? The first chordate that appears in the fossil record is not telling us that this particular lineage was *the* common ancestor of sharks and hummingbirds. While it is located near the trunk of the chordate tree, the trunk is likely to have developed many branches worldwide even in its birth stages. (We see examples occurring as fossils only after they have become widespread.) *Pikaia* might represent a limb that led, naturally and of its own accord, only to extinction, while its "cousins" lived on to beget sharks and rats, snakes and humanoid lawyer types. Though *Pikaia* provides a reasonably clear picture of what our postrusticle ancestors looked like, we might never learn which chordate branch leads out of the Cambrian to us.

If *Pikaia*, or a *Pikaia*-like cousin that led directly to dinosaurs and humans, died without heir, other chordate branches would have moved onward through time. Even if all branches vanished, they had emerged from an already widespread genetic potential, and would likely emerge again. It would take the extermination of the entire planet, down to the level of bacteria, to prevent this. In the absence of our ancestors, and of dinosaurs, some other vertebrate lineage would stand in the same place as *Ornithomimus*, on the brink of evolution's late-Cretaceous bottleneck.

When, as it turns out, the ostrich dinosaurs find themselves decimated by asteroids and lava flows, the survival advantages of big brains and manipulative limbs (toolmaking hands) are so large as to be unavoidable. Instead of bipedal saurians, it is bipedal humans that spread over the Earth. Electronic civilization is similarly unavoidable. If the Minoan and Byzantine civilizations are cut short by volcano weather, another civilization will simply rise in their place, at some future date.

And Earth will not care one way or the other.

2 BILLION B.C.

In A.D. 2002, the science-fiction writer (and fellow rusticle descendant) Michael Crichton said that if he were God, planning the creation of the universe, he would have set it up in such a manner that simple quarks and gluons could form hydrogen atoms ... which in their own turn, reworked in the cores of stars, could form the basis of an entire spec-trum of newer, heavier elements . . . from which would inevitably emerge long-chain molecules . . . from which systems capable of stor-ing, exchanging, and evolving new sequences of genetic information could arise. "*That* is what I would do, were I a logical God," he said, and added, "And that seems to be exactly how it was done."

While some scientists (myself included) view the origin and evolu-tion of life as an inevitable outcome of carbon chemistry, rather than an improbable coincidence or preordained, godly result, Crichton's obser-vation is worth thinking about, and taking pause, as we step back across 2 billion years of bellowing and burrowing creatures to an encounter with "comparative genomics" before, in just another step, we are only amino acids and volcanic dust.

The science of comparative genomics rests on the premise that if an identical segment of DNA (even a segment of so-called "junk DNA," which codes for no known protein or enzyme) is held in common by worms, salamanders, and humans, then it must be "useful" for some-thing. Replicating it and carrying it along for hundreds of millions of years takes energy and resources from every new generation; and in liv-ing systems, any oxygen- or food-using cog or gear that can be jettisoned in the name of increased efficiency is virtually guaranteed to disappear.

Francis Crick (the codiscoverer of DNA's structure) saw at the root of life a system by which genetic information (or instructions) stored in (or coded in) DNA, flowed from every gene to its multiple RNA repli-cants, then to RNA-constructed proteins. All existence, it seemed, was in the proteins—ranging from the columns of the neocortex to the cellular pump that enables a rusticle to extract iron from a volcanic vent.

And yet, contradictions began to arise once genes from every variety of life could finally be read and assembled into the beginnings of a genetic Rosetta stone. By convention, the "job" of DNA was to orches-trate the construction and support of the proteins that hold our bodies together and keep us moving. Such convention holds that the capacity to blunder slightly, or to drift away from the norm through successive gen-erations, is the real marvel of DNA. An extensive reading of the DNA in yeasts, nematode worms, whales, and apple trees teaches us that the basic formula (DeoxyriboNucleic Acid) is unchanged. No matter how far back we track branching lineages, everything becomes a mere extension and elaboration of the first nucleic acid molecule to make possible a bacterial mat. Convention teaches, therefore, that the engine of growth, replication, and change has itself remained essentially unchanged.

And yet, from the start, the "genetic Rosetta stone" itself has been full of surprises.

When University of Queensland geneticist John Mattick and physicist Michael Gagen saw that only 2 percent of the RNA templates produced by human and insect DNA encode for protein, they exclaimed, "You would have to be blind not to see that non-coding RNAs are a vastly unexplored world."

By comparison, the genome of the bacterium *Escherichia coli* has about four thousand protein-coding genes, and between fifty and two hundred "junk" RNA-coding segments; meaning that, scaled against (the mere 2 percent RNA-coders for) roaches and men, 95 to 99 percent of the bacterium's RNA templates encode for protein. Conversely, up to 98 percent of your genes, and mine, are non-protein-coding "junk DNA."

If we look just a little more closely, you and I, at the secrets of life's origins, you'll begin to see, now, why I believe we must begin to think as kindly about "junk" as we do about volcanic vents.

Segmented worms and houseflies send forth, from their DNA, roughly the same *number* of protein-coding RNAs—which is only about twice the total number of protein-producing genes counted in yeasts and bacteria (bearing in mind, again, that only about 2 percent of the much larger animal genome is encoding for protein, whereas in the bacterial genome the ratio is exactly reversed, with only 2 percent junk RNA being generated). Humans have only twice as many protein-coding genes as worms and flies, and roughly the same number as some fish. Clearly, the number of protein-coding sequences in an organism's genome does not reflect (or explain) its complexity; but the number of noncoding RNAs just might hold the key. Possibly, what at first glance appears to be the excessive accumulation of noncoding "junk," once provided the flexibility (or, rather, the infinitely expanded possibilities) that a rusticle-dominated Earth needed. If so, then the greatest evolutionary advance of all time could have been the proliferation of junk.

Our first tangible (experimentally repeatable) clue to the worth of "junk" arose from a rusticle descendant called *Caenorhabditis elegans*, a species of nematode (or unsegmented worm). In A.D. 2001, nonencoding RNAs were revealed as regulators in the turning on and switching off (and apparently also "volume control") of genes that govern the worm's development from embryo to adult. A year later, a team of geneticists and microbiologists at Massachusetts General Hospital discovered one of the worm's non-protein-coding "junk" sequences faithfully reproduced in the genomes of flies, mollusks, fish, and humans. According to the "Boston theory," this particular gene sequence, though seeming to "dead-end" at RNA, may in fact be a universal regulator in the development of animal embryos.[3]

Shadows of biocomputation . . . As for worms and flies, so also for trees and eagles. There is simply no imagining that the ubiquitous, phylum-crossing worm gene can be alone. I find it far, far easier to imagine that the vast majority of the "junk DNA" segments living in your cells (at least, those not performing such "dormant" functions as preserving blueprints of ancient structures—such as scales and giant claws for birds, in case they are ever needed again) are manufacturing and governing what I have come to call "regulator RNAs." Indeed, it is possible to believe that many of our so-called "junk" sequences may only come into play as "chaperones" during embryonic development, and during the progression from infancy to puberty.

If our bodies are derived from symphonies written in DNA and performed by protein, then regulator RNAs are the conductors in our lives.

---

[3] In 1996, when high-resolution sonograms first came into use, revealing details not previously discernible in developing human embryos, doctors and expectant parents were horrified by what they saw. Nearly a third of all pregnancies appeared to start out abnormally. In one case of first-trimester twins (both of whom lived on to excel in school), brains and spinal cords had ceased development—and then, over the course of two weeks, through what gave the appearance of unnatural acceleration of nerve growth, they caught up to "normal." The developmental program for constructing a human child from the first diploid cell of the yet-to-be-born—written on nucleic acid and etched into protein—does not proceed blindly. An occurrence of accelerated nerve growth, after entire nervous systems had gotten off to a lethally slow start, was without doubt the result of a built-in feedback mechanism contained in the DNA program. There would not have been much need for such a program in Precambrian bacterial slimes. At a guess, this is, as diamonds and DNA measure time, a newly evolved capacity, not much older than the base of the Cambrian explosion.

I suspect that the leap from fewer than 5 percent non-protein-coding sequences in bacterial cells (that is, in Precambrian survivors), to more than 95 percent in goldfish and hyenas, is telling us that "rRNAs" were replicated and preserved only because they imparted a significant survival advantage. Thus, rRNAs did not merely proliferate through higher organisms; they must in fact have triggered the origins of those very same organisms.

Not to be confused in any way with the creationist (religious) concept of "intelligent design," this biocomputation scenario casts such regulator systems (or "junk") as the primary drivers of evolutionary change during and after the Cambrian explosion. Not to be confused, either, with Wolfram's "universal computer," the highly interactive rRNAs are themselves behaving like (or mimicking) a highly evolved computer program by which genes can respond directly to feedback from their surroundings. Such interaction (between DNA and rRNA) does not preclude something very much like the projection (and selection) of probability curves in the "design" of the next generation. In fact, such interaction becomes a mathematical certainty. It is impossible not to imagine, therefore (as when one observes how computer scientists, in designing programs to move entire libraries "from C drive to D drive," have mimicked, serendipitously and unknowingly, the jumping-gene phenomenon), that the designers of computer software are being forced to replicate what nature accomplished more than 600 million years ago.[4]

---

[4] A test of biocomputation theory lies in practical medical applications. When genetic surgeons (or, for that matter, animal breeders) transfer genes from one organism to another, they are not just transferring protein production; there's a whole interactive regulatory program that travels with it. In experiments involving the production of, say, human insulin in milk, the right genes, inserted into early-stage rabbit embryos, were moved unfailingly into just the "right" place in the milk-gland control region, as if by a conveniently "accepting," preexisting program ready to do all the hard work for us. Similarly, once we can identify, in sponges from the *Titanic's* hull, specific genes responsible for what are, potentially, antibiotic-like anticancer drugs, it seems likely that we shall be able to produce new medicines in goat milk or (easier, still) in the egg albumen of cloned chickens. Similarly, the specific genes that allow certain individuals of Italian, Chinese, and African descent to age more than one-third slower than the rest of the human species, once identified, may be literally "bottled." Theoretically, quality of life, not just quantity of life, can be extended hundreds of years (with increased human responsibility extending right along with it). The artificial boosting of human intelligence, in like manner, may lie just a few short steps ahead on the genetic frontier.

At the bottom of all this, the human genome begins to resemble, more and more, a very elaborate CD-ROM or DVD program. From the time of Watson and Crick, geneticists and evolutionary biologists have been thinking of DNA as the hardware, but I'm afraid we've had it backward all along. It's really the software.

Clues to the puzzle of where we came from are scattered through the cells of every living thing. Regulator "junk" emerges not as a mere aberration, not as just the exception that probes the rule but, rather, as the rule. A nematode worm rears its head in Boston as but a twig on a very substantial family tree and reaches backward, perhaps, to the fuse that lit the Cambrian explosion. As such, it becomes the biological equivalent of the unseen "dark matter" that binds the galaxies into gravitational clusters and the elusive "dark energy" that seems to be accelerating the universe's rate of expansion. It is the emergence of a potential to regulate the growth of tissue layers, and to more precisely temper the chaos of growth with feedback from the environment, that probably marks the leap from rusticle or sponge to worm and fish. Anything that can streamline the storage and use of genetic information is bound to be preserved and multiplied by natural selection, and this is exactly what the proliferation of non-protein-coding DNA—in the transition from bacteria to worms—appears to be telling us.

Probing all the way back to 2 billion B.C., rusticles become the most advanced of all living things. In the remote Precambrian (in the time before biocomputation, notochords, and central nervous systems), simple DNA and simple RNA are essentially the only means of information storage, and true Darwinian selection—*slow* Darwinian selection—with random variation producing the raw material of change, and with survival determining the direction of change, holds sway over tomorrow.

In the skies of 2 billion B.C., the Moon and the planets and the galaxy beyond are bathed in a background microwave glow that heats every corner of the universe to a minimum temperature of 7.5 degrees Kelvin. Space is twenty-five times denser than it will be in Minoan and Roman times. The universe is 3.0×10^{-29} times as dense as water, meaning that every cubic meter of space contains at least sixty atoms. Numbers, again. Mere numbers. When, over the course of a 2-billion-year back-step, we watch the universe become denser and hotter, what has really happened?

In another time and another place, a rusticle descendant named Carl Sagan would suggest to me (in a "snail mail" letter to New Zealand, dated May 1981) that the very universe we are now tracking backward toward a state of seemingly infinite density and temperature, a state called the Big Bang, might be "merely the most recent cusp in an infinite series of cosmic expansions and contractions."[5]

If this is true, then the past to which we have just stepped back to, across 2 billion years, may be hidden in time-future, with time-future hidden in an even more remote time-past. As we descend toward the Big Bang, it becomes possible to believe that the way to the past—the way to Pompeii and ancient Rome—is through the past, backward again into the future, and down again from future to past.

Let's step back, then, you and I, and imagine ourselves standing on the shoreline mound of a stromatolite, overlooking an ocean whose days are sped along five hours faster, on account of 2 billion years of tidal friction that lie, still, in futurity. Stand here, in the constricted universe of time-past, and imagine the photons of sunlight and starlight—which exist simultaneously as self-contradictory waves and particles and which are, figuratively and actually, ageless. All the universe is a marvel; it is easy to lose oneself in a single photon of light passing through a grain of Precambrian sand. The same photons released by the Big Bang—which are still present in 2 billion B.C. as the 7.5-degrees-Kelvin cosmic background radiation—have been around for more than 8 billion years, and will be around for billions more. You may think that by producing a mirror and reflecting the starlight back into the heavens—that by sending the

---

[5] Carl Sagan was, in his lifetime, much maligned by some members of the scientific community for popularizing science through such programs as *Cosmos*. "Whoring after the masses" is how some of his detractors put it (although I always thought the name-calling had more to do with Sagan appearing on the cover of *Time* magazine instead of his name-callers). In my own occasional encounters with him, he was always "thinking outside the box." Isaac Asimov, who knew Sagan far better than I, and who was one of the brightest minds I have met anywhere on the planet, once told me that Sagan was one of only three people he had ever known who was smarter than himself. I think that sums up Carl Sagan.

light away from Earth at 186,000 miles per second—you can banish individual photons beyond our galaxy, beyond Andromeda, forever. But if indeed we do live in Sagan's (and Asimov's) oscillating universe, there will come a time, one time in the unending oscillation of times, when the shattering neutrons of your retinal cones shall plunge side by side with your "banished" photons, side by side into the next cosmic singularity, where time itself becomes timeless.

4 BILLION B.C.

The day is as few as ten hours long and the Moon orbits thousands of miles nearer the earth. The smaller member of this double planet system is almost within the Roche limit, which means that Earth's crust— the solid surface of the planet—undergoes tidal variations that shame the Bay of Fundy. In the heavens, the Earth-facing hemisphere of the Moon is erupting entire seas of basaltic lava—which is exactly what protocell descendants, 4 billion years hence, will name the lava fields: *Sea of Tranquillity . . . Sea of Serenity . . . Ocean of Storms*. The lunar eruptions will continue for another 700 million years.

If the Moon is more active than a million Theras very early in its history, Earth is next of kin to chaos. Carbon diverges into two distinct destinies, depending on where it ends up. Four billion years from our present back-step, 300 miles (492 kilometers) underfoot of every protocell descendant's cities, carbon will be able to accumulate in only one form: diamonds. One of the most abundant elements in the world will become one of the most common gemstones on (or, rather, in) the earth. Three hundred miles beneath Naples and Cairo and Manhattan will lie truckloads and shiploads of diamonds—most of them dirty brown or (when "favorably" contaminated with nitrogen) canary yellow, some ranging beyond the diameter of a man's fist, and as clear as water from a mountain spring. The only truly rare diamonds, occasionally enhanced by the steady decay of uranium and thorium, are brilliant green or blue, sapphire pink, or wine red. The protocell descendants will treasure diamonds, in part, because only rarely do the carbon crystals rise to the planetary surface, through only the deepest and narrowest of volcanic wounds. Somewhere underfoot, 300 miles from the nearest sunlight, lies a red diamond more beautiful than any crown jewel ruby, embedded in a diamond cluster bigger than a New York City bus.

High above the diamond beds, where the pressures are, relatively speaking, indistinguishable from the high vacuum of outer space, carbon can bond freely with hydrogen, oxygen, nitrogen, sulfur, and phosphorus. This is the second, even more miraculous carbon destiny. As it turns out, DNA molecules, passing from generation to generation across billions of years, shall prove themselves no less resilient than diamonds.

The Protocell era, from which simple organic compounds shall emerge as living cells with an elaborate genetic machinery, is probably already more than a quarter-billion years old in 4 billion B.C. The first "useful" proteins, those that by sheer chance have appeared on or in preliving bubbles of organic sludge and are able to induce reactions that add to their bulk, invariably prolong the survival of individual protocells. The life span of a protocell is thus directly related to the complexity and effectiveness of its metabolism; and time, the destroyer, sees to it that most protocells and their descendants run down and eventually fall apart, dispersing their contents for future absorption by other protocells. Those bubbles graced with the ability to absorb molecules from their surroundings—and to capture energy and direct it toward the knitting together of absorbed molecules into substances that can promote the survival not only of the bubbles but also of their daughter bubbles— shall be (or have already become) ancestors of the first true life-forms to populate the seas.

What the protocells require, if such compounds as hemoglobin, chlorophyll, and brain proteins are to be evolved, is something akin to a team of carpenters (RNA) and a set of blueprints (DNA), to be passed on to each daughter protocell, guaranteeing that it is able to construct the same enzymes needed for all the reactions important to the parent's survival. What they require is the ultimate parasite: the living gene.

A protocell descendant named Claire Folsome would see, at the cradle of life, an "RNA world," in which the dominant route to the construction of genetic machinery capable of bridging protein and nucleic acids is the emergence of simple "prototype generator RNAs": circular molecules only a dozen base pairs long that are able to specify only four simple classes of amino acids (protein building blocks). Working with a young New Zealand gadfly (in 1980), Folsome would demonstrate, mathematically and chemically, how simple proteins and prototype transfer RNAs could be bond-assembled from a single, randomly generated RNA molecule. From this point forward (so the theory goes), Darwinian selection enters the picture, fashioning the raw material of variation by preserving those systems that work best under prevailing conditions of the day. Adding force to the Darwinian equation, a tendency for Folsome's laboratory microbodies (bubbles and tubes of protein created by a variation on Germany's World War II syn-fuel method) to clump together at the water's surface, and then to separate when shaken, would hint that the inventions of both multicellularity and sex (by protocells) preceded the appearance of true chromosomes. Folsome and the gadfly will guess, from this possibility, that in some cases, their ancestral genetic blueprints must have evolved from back to front, with the strongest, most resilient proteins becoming the actual templates against which the first nucleic acid codes are assembled. Life from non-life . . . Biology . . . The production of order from chaos.

And a day would come, a day in the succession of 40 million centuries of days, when beings that are all but unimaginable and unguessable in Folsome microbodies would look upon their own hands and marvel at the reality of cells coursing through their veins, directing (in their travels) huge molecules to recognize other molecules and to hold on to each other and let go of each other in extraordinarily precise ways—and in this manner to produce structures as diverse as marrow, retinal cones, and eyelashes. And they would discover that the ropes of DNA contained in one of the trees from which this ordinary book is made, if strung end to end, could reach to the Sun and back three hundred times, and yet those very same chromosomes occupy a total volume no bigger than an ice cube. And from this the humans will guess that life could come a long way on a little skeleton of sugars and phosphates studded with nucleic acid bases.

And another of them, a protocell descendant named Francis Crick, will come to suspect that the origin of life requires so many conditions (starting, in Earth's case, with a planet of just the right mass orbiting just the right distance from just the right kind of star) as to be a "miracle" that could happen only once in our whole island of stars. Starting, then, with the premise of DNA as miraculous rarity, and combining this premise with his knowledge that viral contaminants on the *Surveyor* lunar lander were still "alive" when returned to Earth, years later, by *Apollo 12* astronauts, Crick would fashion his "directed panspermia" theory. Looking back to 4 billion B.C., he would ask: What if creatures like ourselves had emerged on other worlds, by this time, and spread outward among the stars, like ripples in a pond, spreading their DNA contaminants as they went and, either by accident or by design, becoming a galactic contagion and seeding life on Earth?

The idea would intrigue a protocell descendant named Stephen Jay Gould (as it would, and has, intrigued me). Gould would shrug and declare, "One dollar will get you five that he's wrong, this time. But it will only get you five, because he's been right about too many other creepy things."

But, in 4 billion B.C., Earth and the Moon and the voids between the galaxies are bathed in a background glow that heats every corner of the universe to a minimum temperature of 10.4 degrees Kelvin. Space is fifty times denser than it will be in Crick's time, and every cubic meter of space contains one hundred atoms. Compared against the composition of the universe in Crick's time, a greater proportion of those atoms are hydrogen and helium, and for a relevant and interesting reason.

Fast-forward to A.D. 1982, when one protocell descendant's theory (directed panspermia) forces another protocell descendant (me) to think a little bit harder about heavy-element accumulation rates as the galaxy ages—as if to drive home the message that the value of any "good" theory is not in how wrong or right it turns out to be, but in the new questions it raises. In order for Crick's theory to be correct, a previous "seeder" civilization would have had to evolve from protocells, through its own Cambrian explosion, by 4 billion B.C.—requiring, most probably (most inescapably), another 4.5 billion years of previous evolution on a planet that formed about 9 billion years ago . . . which brings us close to the estimated age of the universe (13.7 billion years).

That far back, there was precious little material around from which planets could be built, for all elements in the universe heavier than helium and lithium had to be generated during the lives and deaths of stars.

"As near as we can tell, from the deepest peering of our radio telescopes," I said to Crick, "in the beginning there were hydrogen and helium, and almost nothing else, before the first supernovae. From the stars came the substance of our world and our flesh [and it is to the stars, assuming our civilization survives, that we shall one day return]. Looking around, I do not believe (A) that Earth was incapable of generating its own DNA and (B) that there has been enough time since the birth of a hydrogen-dominated universe for civilizations to have developed twice."

Like all truly great thinkers, Francis Crick was not fossilized in his thinking, was not so in love with his own pet theory as to be blinded by it; for he knew that when a favorite theory falls, something even more interesting will often rise in its place.

"You do indeed raise a valid point," Crick wrote. "How long after the Big Bang could planetary systems be formed that were not too dissimilar from the Earth? Obviously, this depends, at least in part, on the composition of interstellar dust [throughout time]. I now realize that this should be looked at more closely. The argument you give rather implies that the density of appropriate elements rose steadily with time and therefore may not have been high enough 9 billion years ago."

Then, in the tradition of the old (orthodox) Epicurean philosophers, he said, "Before we throw out a beautiful theory under the weight of some ugly facts . . . let us first look a little more closely at heavy element accumulation rates . . . and question that . . . and look at this . . . and wonder about that . . . wonder and think about this."

And we began to see that, near 8 or 9 billion B.C., if the galaxy contained "only" 15 percent fewer atoms of silicon, magnesium, carbon, and iron—only 15 percent fewer heavy elements available for the building of planets—there would be, on the "first Earth," 187 fewer miles (300 kilometers) of rock beneath one's feet. A 15 percent decrease in planetary volume adds up to 22.8 billion cubic miles (91 billion cubic kilometers, or the equivalent of 6.6 Moons), and the planet's surface area diminishes by 5 percent (24 million square kilometers, or the equivalent of half the Moon's surface area).

Such a planet would have a substantially lower volume of internal heat than Earth, to radiate through almost the same surface area. The crust would solidify almost twice as fast, and to considerably greater depths. According to the numbers generated by the unbreakable relationships between surface area, volume, and heat loss, continental drift becomes greatly retarded or nonexistent within 2 billion years. Volcanic activity, the process that both sustains and occasionally threatens life on Earth, grinds nearly to a halt. Under as little as 15 percent loss of planetary mass, life-sustaining gases erode away much more easily under the solar wind. Water in the upper atmosphere dissociates into hydrogen and oxygen (just as it does today), the chief difference being that more of the hydrogen, as it reaches the outer atmosphere, is lost to space. The remaining oxygen atoms, left behind by dissociated water, fall to the ground and combine with surface rocks and carbon—lots of carbon.

Carbon dioxide, like oxygen, is soluble in water and, once dissolved, can be chemically bound to form lime ($CaCO_3$) and other minerals. The process of CO_2 absorption is assisted on Earth today by clams and other shell-secreting organisms—also by plants, and by volcanically governed "subduction zones" that are continually cycling carbon, hydrogen, and other substances back into marble and lava.

If a 15-percent-less-massive Earth became volcanically inactive, and began losing hydrogen (read this to mean water), and began building up carbon dioxide, then it would, from the very first, be finished—like the planets Venus and Mars, and for many of the same reasons. The numbers Crick and I produced revealed that if all the carbon dioxide presently on Earth were liberated from limestones and dolomites and oceans, and if all the carbon in living and once-living things (including coal, shale oil, and other "fossil fuels") were bound with oxygen, we would have, overhead, more than one hundred atmospheres of carbon dioxide, and the air would flow liquid, denser than water, hotter than lead emerging silvery white from a crucible.

Without volcanoes—without just the right amount of volcanic activity—there is no water; there is no life.

Looking in the opposite direction, toward a future in which newly formed solar systems will cross a probability threshold that produces planets 15 percent more massive than Earth, we began to see that life becomes just as unlikely. And that is only the meaning of 15 percent. Nine billion years ago, the universal abundance of heavy elements was more likely between 35 percent and 45 percent below present-day values.

(The only biological wild card Crick and I could see in this picture was the emergence of Europa and Ganymede-like ice worlds.)

In this manner, we buried the "directed panspermia" theory, and upon its grave we discovered the theory of "Genesis and Galactic Blight."

Before the Genesis era lies a universe essentially bare of elements from which planets and living things can be made. Genesis begins nearly 5 billion years ago, when enough heavy elements have accumulated to produce a probability threshold at which first a few very rare, Earth-like worlds, and then more and more of them, are likely to form. Billions of years later, as carbon, silicon, and iron continue to be exhaled in the ejecta of supernovae—as hydrogen is used up and as we progress toward an increasingly matter-dominated universe—we reach the era of Galactic Blight: growing populations of black holes, neutron stars, cooling white dwarfs, and worlds of rock and rock ice so gigantic as to be incapable of supporting life. (It is therefore up to civilized life, if such then exists, to "find a way.")

At the root of Genesis and Galactic Blight is the emergence of a specific "instant" during which the universe could begin to produce habitable planets.

In a universe approximately 13.7 billion years old (in accordance with the latest science), Crick and I began to see that no matter what initial heavy-element accumulation rates we projected (faster than present, or the same), Earth seemed to have formed at or even slightly ahead of the "instant" in which all the heavy elements necessary for the building of such worlds had accumulated in quantities that made Earth's appearance likely.

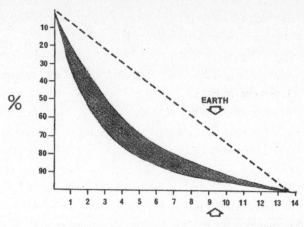

BILLIONS OF YEARS AFTER FORMATION OF THE GALAXY

We live in a universe where studying the fusion of hydrogen atoms, by stars, into the heavier elements from which plants and eyelashes are made, becomes the sincerest form of ancestor worship. Heavy-element accumulation rates, plotted during the 13.7 billion years since the Big Bang, suggest that there was a specific "instant" during which life could begin (on the surfaces of Earth-like planets). The arrows represent the formation of Earth, near 4.5 billion B.C. The dashed line represents constant heavy-element accumulation rates. The shaded curve represents the possibility of a denser, primordial universe producing prompt initial enrichment. According to both curves (based on calculations by Tinsley, Pellegrino, and Crick), Earth formed at the "instant" Earth-like worlds could begin to form (give or take about 300 million years). We were not necessarily the first habitable solar system to arise in the galaxy, but we were certainly present at the starting gate, some 4.5 billion years ago. In a universe where the emergence of intelligent life can be measured as a function of time, the rise and fall of civilizations on this planet take on an added significance, if indeed we are one of the oldest worlds around, one of the newest and brightest creatures around—and alone in the night, or very nearly so.

We were not necessarily the first Earth-like planet to begin the race from protocell, to Cambrian explosion, to civilization building, all those billions of years ago, but we were definitely there at the opening bell. We were at the starting gate. The numbers tell us so.

Crick and I saw then, and still see, one of the two or three most bone-chilling reasons for all the frustrations SETI's astronomers have encountered through more than three decades of searching optical and radio wavelengths for whispers of intelligent life among the stars—"The Great Silence," they call it.

It seems possible—likely, even—that we are among the "First Ones," if not *the* First Ones.

Oh, the responsibilities . . . the wonders . . .

8 BILLION B.C.

Volcanoes.

Of course, there are none.

Not on Earth. Not on the Moon.

Because there is no Earth. No Moon.

What does exist, somewhere in the backward contraction of space-time, somewhere between 8 billion and 13.7 billion B.C., is a point at which the universe is a million times denser than it will be in the days of Pompeii and Manhattan: one atom per cubic centimeter (fifteen atoms per cubic inch). At this point, the universe is "only" 10 million years old, and in an era prior to the fusion of hydrogen into helium nuclei, protons are humanity's remotest ancestors. At 10 million years old, the universal background radiation is warm enough to sustain life: 280 degrees Kelvin (7 degrees Centigrade, 44 degrees Fahrenheit). But nothing breathes. Nothing exists except radiation, forces, space-time expansion, and the lightest of atomic nuclei. All that is, is space, death, and tomorrow.

Stepping backward and backward into the primeval abyss, and watching very carefully, we notice that the third millennium A.D.'s expansion of the space-time between and within the galaxies has been played in reverse. We have been moving toward an explosion that dwarfs a supernova as a supernova core dwarfs the tsunamis of Thera, as Thera dwarfs Vesuvius, as a raindrop is swallowed by the ocean. As the oceans of space-time contract, they carry with them the galaxies. As two proton descendants named Edwin Hubble and Albert Einstein would view the contraction, the back-stepped universe eventually reaches a point of "singularity," or infinitely curved space-time, and infinite density.

One proton descendant would refer to this "point" (with true disdain and true sarcasm) as the "Big Bang." The name, of course, would stick.

Another proton descendant, George Musser, would observe: "Singularities are the toxic waste of cosmology. Theories, let alone children, are advised not to touch anything with infinite density or temperature: the zero time of the Big Bang, say, or the very center of a black hole. At such places, physics dissolves into metaphysics. These mathematical points admit no explanation; they just are."

To see what this can add up to, fast-forward to time-present, and imagine yourself looking out into space for 1 billion light-years in every direction, from any random point in the universe (Earth will serve nicely). Bearing in mind that as you look out into space, you are also looking backward into time, you will have a sphere of vision with a radius of 1 billion light-years.

Now, allow that sphere to expand to 4 billion light-years, to 8 billion light-years . . . hotter and denser, the farther backward and outward you look . . . If four-dimensional space-time is, by analogy, the surface of a sphere, there comes a "moment" when the surface *outside* our expanding sphere is itself a large sphere; the circumference of the large external sphere then contracts toward a point (a *singularity*) and disappears on the far side of the universe.

To understand how this happens, imagine yourself at the North Pole on the spherical surface of Earth. From there, extend your range of vision to latitude 40 degrees north, which runs through Beijing and Philadelphia. Push your range to the equator, and from the equator to 40 degrees south, which runs close to Wellington, New Zealand, and San Antonio Oeste, Argentina. Seventy degrees south carries you into Antarctica, where it becomes apparent that the area outside your expanding range is a large circle with a circumference that has been shrinking ever since you crossed the equator. The shrinkage continues as you advance toward a single point at latitude 90 degrees, on the far side of the globe. This, of course, is a thought experiment, with the four dimensions of space-time compressed into two spatial dimensions on the surface of a globe. In much the same manner as a man walking toward the South Pole, and keeping careful track, sees his circle of latitude contracting toward the center of Antarctica, an object accelerating toward the speed of light sees the universe contracting ahead of it. At 92 percent lightspeed, an object (or a spacecraft) sees the entire universe compressed into its forward field of view, into a "dome" that occupies only one-third of the sky. (Simultaneously, the ship's mass has become three times more resistant to acceleration, and the crew ages at only one-third the rate of the rest of the universe.) Pushing the gas pedal to 95 percent lightspeed halves the diameter of the dome to a circle (with acceleration from 92 to 95 percent lightspeed requiring an additional input of energy at least equal to the amount used to accelerate from zero to 92 percent). At 100 percent, the circle contracts to a single point—to a "singularity." At this point, the universe becomes an all-encompassing black hole (from a crew perspective, this is one of those things that's bad). This is the universe "seen," instantly, by every photon of light—which may, in fact, be the universe's true future.

Every child asks, sooner or later, "Where does the sky end?" If we point out there, in a straight line, where does it all stop? Is there a wall out there? And, if so, what is behind the wall?

In a very real sense, we may be able to answer: "It ends where it begins. Infinity is a snake, biting its tail."

In the three dimensions of space, contracting South Polar circles are ominous reminders that on a larger scale, the four-dimensional space-time of our universe may bend into a finite but unbounded range of spherical space-time. They also remind us that as we look more deeply into space—as we look more deeply into time—we may eventually see ourselves and the whole cosmos squeezed into a single "point"—which can be disquieting enough without creating, in our imaginations, such mathematical aberrations as taking the spherical universe too literally and seeing it as a "ball" contained in some higher-dimensional space (a ball and the room that contains it and—*damnation!*—whatever lies out-side the room). Mathematics—which sometimes only poorly describes the universe—allows this. Mathematics allows us to impart extrinsic sig-nificance to space-time. The universe (probably) does not.

The fact that ships sailing the Atlantic are tracing the curve of the earth is an intrinsic property of our planet's geometry. The fact that we

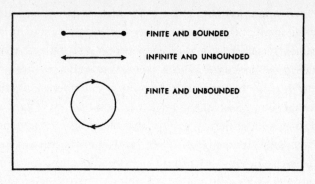

Varieties of the infinite

can step away from Earth and take a grandstand view is an extrinsic geometric feature. But space-time has no extrinsic geometry. Travel in any direction as far as you want and you are still within the universe; travel in any straight line at the speed of light and you may eventually recross your path. If the universe is indeed akin to a finite and unbounded sphere, then its radius is time itself and we cannot step outside and take a grandstand, extrinsic view—which should not trouble us at all, until we approach the primordial singularity: a point at which the mass of the earth (along with all the stars visible to us) squeezes into a space smaller than a gnat, smaller than a virus, smaller than a proton. The universe, at this point, becomes so dense that the speed of light is forced to change, and time itself—the "here" and the "then" and the "now"—loses all meaning.

As Musser has suggested, children (and childishly young civilizations) are well advised not to play with physical infinity. The rules of our universe (the universe of the very large, the universe we know best) apparently break down in the universe of the very small, in the "microverse" within the diameter of a proton. The rules are shattered even more forcefully when the diameter of said proton exists inside the primordial singularity. Many (indeed most) astronomers have opted for divorce, by which "cosmic inflation"—the expansion of the universe that begins with the Big Bang—does not deny the primordial singularity's existence but isolates it from the universe that began with the expansion.

Divorce is never easy. In the case of the universe and the cosmic singularity, it may not even be possible. In A.D. 1981, while debating the significance of organic matter in Jesse Stoff's (and Claus, and Nagy, and Urey's) carbonaceous meteorites, astronomer Carl Sagan and I approached, and began to struggle with, "the toxic waste of cosmology," and to wrestle with the most stubborn of all stubborn questions: What came before the Big Bang?

(Or, as a child might put it, "What existed before the beginning of existence?")

Sagan believed (along with his friend Isaac Asimov) that the Big Bang might be "merely the most recent cusp in an infinite series of cosmic expansions and contractions." And I began to wonder if that infinite series of rebounding universes might in its own turn recurve, so that infinity itself connected somewhere, like a snake, head to tail. What Sagan and I ended up with was the theory of an infinitely oscillating, identically repeating universe: The idea that every grain of dust in every room, every word spoken at every point in history, every letter on every page, repeats uncounted trillions upon trillions of times (indeed, infinitely) without variation (and without memory).

Stephen Jay Gould found such a universe as unbelievable as it was intolerable—"Chaos theory precludes such a dreadful outcome!" he insisted. An identically repeating universe not only removed free will; it also went against Gould's "Theory of Contingency." It implied that there was an inevitable evolutionary progress after all, from simpler to higher forms of life, culminating (on Earth) in man and western civilization. Gould wanted to know if it really was possible for any of us to believe that the history of Earth in the universe really was embedded in time and really could be replayed with the Late Cretaceous asteroid falling upon Mexico's dinosaurs in exactly the same way, on the very same day. If the snake really did bite its tail, was it really at all possible, Gould wanted to know, that the battle of Spartacus at Vesuvius would be repeated not only with the very same outcome but with the firing of every arrow, and with every shout, occurring in precisely the same sequence? He found it difficult to believe that in a replay of Earth's history, even from identical beginnings (an identical Big Bang), there would even *be* a Mount Vesuvius or a human species, much less a Roman Empire or a man named Spartacus.

But . . . Absolute infinity (as when a particle is accelerated to, and views the universe from, 100 percent of the speed of light; or when a particle reaches the center of a singularity [black hole]; or when a singularity oscillates) . . . Absolute infinity, as opposed to numerical or "imaginary" infinity (which becomes slave to a peculiar arithmetic: infinity squared equals the square root of infinity, and the infinite number of points on the length of your eyelash must equal the infinite number of points between here and the end of the visible universe) . . . Absolute infinity may indeed produce a physical universe in which we find ourselves, by the dictates of a very real cosmology, "bounded, or trapped."

No one knows for sure.

The scientist-philosopher Arthur C. Clarke agreed with me and Sagan that any sufficiently advanced future civilization would not accept a universe that played out at random only once (thereafter repeating itself identically and giving only the illusions of randomness and free will).[6]

"They will approach this universe (*we* will approach this universe) with utter contempt," Arthur Clarke predicted. "And even if reintroducing randomness [say, by passing information, or "memories," across the next Big Bang][7] should turn out to be impossible, any sufficiently advanced technology will not resist the urge to tamper."

In A.D. 1989, during the "God, the Universe, and Everything" sessions (conducted largely from Arthur Clarke's home in Sri Lanka), physicist Stephen Hawking added his opinion: "I like Charlie Pellegrino's,

---

[6] Although . . . "random only once" may not be entirely true. In such a universe, infinite and bounded, the truth (and the clue) becomes simply this: You have always been here . . .

[7] It's *Groundhog Day*, again . . . Another paradox of numerical infinity (as opposed to absolute infinity) arises from an old thought experiment in which one is asked to stand facing a wall, and then to imagine successively halving the distance between one's nose and the wall. Mathematical infinity generates an infinite number of halfway points, and in theory (but not in reality) one can never actually reach the wall. Known as Zeno's

Arthur Clarke's, and Father Mervyn Fernando's theory of quantum spirituality—by which all faiths, even lack of faith, may be simultaneously correct, in a universe that sees every photon of light simultaneously as a self-contradictory wave and particle. [But] I hate Pellegrino and Sagan's 'Valhalla theory' [which predicts an infinitely oscillating, identically repeating universe]. The theory is brilliant, evocative, and not without a certain amount of wished-for poetic order. It merely happens to be perfectly wrong."

But in the tradition of Democritus, Epicurus, (doubting) Saint Thomas, Niles Eldredge, and Stephen Jay Gould, we must *question everything . . .*

"Been there, done that," or so said physicists Paul Steinhardt (of Princeton) and Neil Turok (of Cambridge), some twelve years after Hawking. Barely noticed, during the start of humanity's first "shadow war," in the autumn of 2001, they announced that it really might be, in Yogi Berra parlance, "déjà vu all over again." Building upon the work of earlier black-hole and "string" theorists, they began to see, in the then-recent discovery of an unseen force (christened "dark energy"—which appears to be accelerating the rate at which expanding space-time increases the distance between galaxies), hints that space-time can, starting at the scale of the "microverse," act somewhat like a wound-up spring. Masses (or dimensional planes called "branes") push apart when they are close and attempt to snap together when they are far apart, causing the universe to oscillate to and fro. Periodically (and theoreti-

---

Paradox, after the philosopher of the fifth century B.C., this example of numerical infinity gives the illusion that motion is impossible. Absolute infinity tells a different tale. The discovery of so-christened "Dark Energy," through which the expansion of space-time between and within the galaxies appears to have been constantly accelerating for more than 5 billion years, points to a time, after a life of "only" about 35 to 37 billion years, when the rate of expansion, even down to the diameter of a proton, reaches lightspeed, or absolute infinity. At this point, the contracting circle of the universe "seen" by a particle accelerated toward lightspeed, and glimpsed through the peculiar geometry of contracting South Polar circles, comes into play. At infinite expansion, quarks and gluons decouple, photons of light tear apart, and the expansion itself—somewhat like the diminishing circle of latitude seen as an observer expands his range from the North Pole toward the South Pole—becomes indistinguishable from contraction. In a universe inflating toward infinite acceleration, "Then" and "Now," Cosmic Crunch and Big Bang, lose all meaning in singularity.

cally), the "branes" strike, somewhat analogous to cymbals, passing through each other—whereupon one dimension shrinks to zero for an "instant," and the universe (or, as the case may be, two separate universes) will rebound, producing the Big Bang. The running down of energy below lightspeed and its subsequent "freezing" into matter, the cosmic expansion and cooling that leads to the formation of stars and planets, is seen, then, not as a one-of-a-kind event but as part of an endlessly recurring cycle.[8]

How strange (and endlessly fascinating) that such a universe should appear possible. In the second century A.D., the Stoic philosopher–emperor Marcus Aurelius had been schooled in ekpyrotic cosmology. Long before Aurelius was born, Greek science had somehow come to believe in eternal conflagration: a universe caught in a never ending cycle of fiery birth, cooling, and fiery rebirth. Who would have believed, in the days of Thera and Vesuvius, that space telescopes of the future would lead scientists to similar ideas?

"What we're motivated by string theory to believe," said Steinhardt, "is that the Big Bang is not what we've always thought—a beginning of space and time, where temperature and energy diverge. Rather it is a transition between the current expanding phase and a preexisting contracting phase."

One observer commented (for the March 2002 issue of *Scientific American*) that the idea was so impossible as to be simply crazy: "It is like throwing a chair into a black hole and expecting it to rematerialize later."

"When a distinguished but elderly scientist states that something is impossible, or crazy," Arthur C. Clarke had thought of writing . . . but

[8] By some calculations, the acceleration of space-time expansion caused by "dark energy" reaches infinite expansion after about 35 billion years. Again, on whatever remains of Earth at this "moment," the runaway expansion reaches down to the center of every proton and neutron, causing it to fly apart in every direction at the speed of light. The effect is essentially identical to the branes-and-cymbal-clap theory (and may actually describe the same phenomenon). By analogy, much as the outracing ripples from the Yucatán asteroid impact, as they expanded into the antipode of Earth, contracted simultaneously toward a single point in India, infinite expansion becomes infinite contraction. The talon of time becomes a snake, biting its own tail.

he broke the thought off in midsentence, and said, instead, "Hawking did [once] call the idea poetic. If nothing else, we've got to like its poetry. What we all like about the Valhalla theory is that it permits time travel (at least, perhaps, for the most ghostly of subatomic particles) without the grandfather paradox getting into the act [whereby you send something back in time, kill Grandpa, wipe out your own existence]— because you reach the past by going into the future, through the next cosmic Crunch-and-Bang." Sir Arthur evoked something Niels Bohr once said to a friend: "We all know that your theory is crazy; [but] you leave us with a question that refuses to go away: Is it sufficiently crazy to be right?"[9]

The beginning and the end: The greatest single achievement of nature to date was surely the reaction that allowed (and/or will allow) protons and electrons to emerge from a primordial singularity. "Thanks partly to the work of Turok, Steinhardt, and colleagues," says CERN's Gabriele Veneziano, "our community is much more ready to accept that the Big Bang was the outcome of something rather than the cause of everything."

"There is no new thing under the sun," wrote the author of Ecclesiastes 1:9–10 (who is believed by most biblical scholars to have been King Solomon). The text, dating back to at least 950 B.C., resonates poeti-

---

[9] The "Valhalla theory" 's elimination of the grandfather paradox has its own set of consequences; for if it were somehow possible to transfer information, or "memory" (or even yourself) through the next cosmic singularity into the next identical replay of the universe, you could indeed change history at whim without creating a time paradox. You could indeed even kill your grandfather before either of your parents were born, without creating a paradox. You would simply live on, in that universe, as if nothing unusual had occurred (except that you would never see your "twin" born, and you would have to live with any other consequences of getting in history's way). The 1993 Bill Murray classic, *Groundhog Day*, provides basis for a Valhalla thought experiment, if his multiple replays of the same day are viewed as recollections-turned-to-premonitions in an infinite number of identically oscillating universes arranged linearly, like pearls on a string. Viewed in this manner, "Phil" and his entire universe do not merely skip back to the beginning of the same day, with each of his awakenings. Instead, he awakes in each successive universe with vivid premonitions of a single day to come. Not knowing what we know, Phil mistakes himself for an immortal, after a long episode of serial suicide, at the beginning of each recollected February 2. Viewed from a Valhalla perspective, Phil's friends are obliged to live out the rest of their lives, in each previous universe, with the consequences of his actions (so much for the film's seemingly happy ending).

cally—and in the eyes of a few perhaps even prophetically—with the emerging scientific story of Genesis:

> *The thing that hath been, it is that which shall be;*
> *and that which is done is that which shall be done:*
> *and there is no new thing under the sun.*
> *Is there anything whereof it may be said,*
> *"See, this is new?" It hath been already of old time,*
> *which was before us.*

4

THEN LISTEN, JOSEPHUS,
FOR I DIGRESS . . .

In the spirit of "equal time," a creationist alternative theory on the origin of cats: In the beginning was the Dog, and God said unto Adam, "I have created this new animal to be a reflection of my love for you. Regardless of how selfish and unlovable you may be, this new companion will accept you as you are and will love you as I do, in spite of yourself. And because I have created this new animal to be a reflection of my love for you, his name will be a reflection of my name." And it was so. And Dog lived with Adam; and was a companion to Adam; and Dog was a good animal. And God was pleased. And Dog was pleased with Adam, and wagged his tail. And it came to pass that God saw Adam's heart was become hardened with sinful pride, thinking itself worthy of adoration. And the Lord said, "Behold! Dog has taught Adam that he is loved and worshiped as one of us. Now, let us go down and confound the Man, and teach him humility." And God created Cat to be a companion to Adam; and to remind Adam of his true place in the universe; and whence he came, and where he stood. And it was so. And Cat would not obey Adam. And when Adam gazed into Cat's eyes, the Man was reminded that he was—alas, alas—an inferior being. And woe came unto Adam; and Adam learned humility. And it was good. And God was pleased. And Dog was happy, and wagged his tail. And Cat did not care one way or the other.

LUIS T. PILGRIM AND MIMI LEE YOUNG

In a house on the main shopping street of Pompeii, a pair of human skeletons lies. And on the wall beside them, in brightly colored brush strokes, this image is displayed: flowers and songbirds living in a green world on the slopes of a mountain. And by aid of PCR, and electron microprobe, and computer, DNA from the bones teaches us that the skeletons were father and son. In August of A.D. 79, the pair climbed atop a knee-deep drift of volcanic dust that had snowed down from the mount and flowed indoors—flowed from the very same mountain depicted upon the wall. The boy, aged about fourteen years, is lying on his back upon the drift. His jaw hangs open at an angle suggestive of a last conscious moment spent gaping like a fish, and trying to swallow air. His head is turned to one side, as if to fix his gaze forever upon his father's outstretched left hand. They died, apparently, at the same instant, their fingers gently entwined. In the Vesuvian ash, among bones shut out from starlight and from sunlight for close on two thousand years, I have gazed into the eyeless sockets of a skull that never lived to see a pocket-computer-assisted scientist, never lived to see flying machines above the mount or space station *Alpha* speeding beneath the stars. And though the empire of Rome stretches far and away, like a civilization completely alien to us, the bones speak still of our common humanity, speak still, from their last second of life, of love and mutual tenderness.

ACCORDING TO THE FIRST-CENTURY HISTORIAN Flavius Josephus (who lived from A.D. 37 to 100), "the country of Sodom" was a place of brimstone and strange, sudden death. From a Mediterranean perspective, the graves of the cities lay "as far away as Zoar in Arabia."[1] The graves were ancient already, from a Josephean point of view: "It was of old," he wrote, in book 4, chapter 8, of *The Jewish War*, "a most happy land, both for the fruits it bore and the riches of its cities, although it be

[1] While many biblical scholars traditionally place Sodom and Gomorrah in the Jordan Valley or near the Dead Sea, Josephus places the cities much farther east, as part of the Babylonian civilizations of the Persian Gulf and the Tigris and Euphrates Rivers, in present-day Iraq.

now all burned up. It is related how, for the impiety of its inhabitants, it was burned by lightning; in consequence of which there are still reminders of that divine fire."

Josephus claimed that easily destroyed or dissolved objects, including the table settings and meals of the dead city, were, in his time, "still there to be seen": And the "shadows of the fruits," in shape and apparent texture, gave the illusion of still being fresh, perhaps even fit to be eaten—"but if you pluck them with your hands, they dissolve into smoke and ashes—and thus what is related of this land of Sodom has these marks of credibility which our very sight affords us."

Josephus published his history of the Jewish War about A.D. 78 or 79, following reading and approval by Agrippa II. His mention of the extraordinary preservation of food and other organic furnishings within buried buildings, seems curiously prophetic of breads and vegetables (and pizza before the invention of tomato sauce) now variously carbonized and fossilized in the ruins of Pompeii and Herculaneum. On close reading, one is tempted to suppose that Josephus wrote (or amended) his history at some point after the eruption of Vesuvius—not, as convention holds, before the August A.D. 79 eruption. Surviving records of senatorian hearings reveal that an excavation was begun at Pompeii, aimed at recovering vaults and other property, as an additional financial support for history's first recorded disaster-relief program. Given these records, it becomes easy to imagine sappers tunneling into the still-smoldering ash of Vesuvius, seeking gold and other entombed treasures and discovering preserved food items en route. It becomes easy to imagine that Josephus heard about these finds and subsequently embellished his account of biblical Sodom with an eerie but genuine detail of volcanic preservation.

Later, while penning his annotated edition of the Hebrew Bible, Josephus described distinctly volcanic phenomena in association with the Exodus plagues of Egypt (in *Jewish Antiquities*, book 2, chapters 15 and 16). In the Josephus bible, the oldest complete edition known to have survived (exceeded in age, just barely, by biblical chapters found among the Dead Sea Scrolls), Josephus quotes Moses as saying, "For even these mountains, if God so please, may be made plain ground for you, and the sea become dry land." The line seems to echo Pliny the Younger's eye-witness account of Mount Vesuvius turning the Bay of Naples into dry land: "We saw the sea sucked away and apparently forced back by the earthquake," wrote Pliny. "At any rate it receded from the shore so that quantities of sea creatures were left stranded on dry sand. On the land-ward side a fearful black cloud was rent by forked and quivering bursts of flame, and parted to reveal great tongues of fire, like flashes of lightning magnified in size . . . a dense black cloud was coming up behind us, spreading over the earth like a flood . . . Darkness fell—as if the lamp had been put out in a closed room. Many besought the aid of the gods, but still more imagined that there were no gods left, and that the universe was plunged into eternal darkness forevermore."

And the mountains would "open themselves," if the prophet com-manded them, God told Moses, in a message unique to the Josephus account—which links a mountain to Moses' parting of the waters: "These mountains will open themselves if you command them, and the sea also, if you command it, will become dry land." The parting of the sea in Josephus's Exodus is associated with the idea that a mountain would open itself (whereas the Hebrew Bible specifies a sea forced back by "a strong east wind all that night"); and, though the Testament (as in Exodus 13:21 and 14:19) associates pillars of fire and black cloud with the "miracle of the waters" (mere hints of an ancient volcano), Josephus has left us with an Exodus story more reminiscent, still, of Pliny at Vesu-vius. Book 2, chapter 16, of *Jewish Antiquities* begins: "[Moses] struck the sea with his rod, which parted asunder at the stroke, and receiving those waters into itself, left the ground dry . . . Now [Moses] went first of all into it, and directed the Hebrews to follow him along that divine road" while behind him the Egyptians were consumed by "a torrent raised by storms of wind," and by "dreadful thunders and lightning, with flashes of fire [which also "came down from the sky"]. Thunderbolts were darted upon them. Nor was there anything which used to be sent by God upon men, as indications of His wrath, which did not happen at this time, for a dark and dismal night oppressed them."

A Josephean embellishment, based upon survivors' accounts from Pompeii? To one degree or another, perhaps so. But Josephus was, by his own account, a religious Jewish scholar. Why then would he infuse volcanic phenomena into the Exodus story more than 1,500 years after it had become sacred?

So complex an issue as divining a writer's motivations resists simple resolution (especially as we are attempting to parse a dead historian in his own parlor, two millennia in the past); but I feel confident enough to venture one guess: Josephus associated "modern" volcanic phenomena with the Exodus because the (volcanic) association was already present, from antiquity. In book 2, chapter 16, of *Jewish Antiquities,* Josephus wrote, "As for myself, I have delivered every part of this history as I found it in the sacred books; nor let anyone wonder at the strangeness of the narration . . . whether it happened by the will of God or whether it happened of its own accord . . . But as to these events, let everyone determine as he pleases."

The old records, the "sacred books," have left only fragments surviving into the present (as in the case of Egypt's Ipuwer, or "lamentation," papyri), but these must have existed as multiple fully intact copies in the time of Josephus. Such records appear to have been accessible (and quotable) at least as far back as the time of David, for although King David's Psalm 77 fails to mention the mountains opening themselves for Moses; for although it fails to describe flames descending from a dark and terrible cloud on the day water gave way to dry land, the psalm specifies, in parallel with Josephus, earthquake and lightning: "I remembered God, and was troubled: I complained and my spirit was overwhelmed. Selah . . . The waters saw thee, O God, the waters saw thee; they were afraid: the depths also were troubled. The clouds poured out water; the skies sent out a sound: thine arrows went abroad. The voice of thy thunder was in the heaven: the lightnings lightened the world: the earth trembled and shook. Thy way is in the sea, and thy path is in the great waters, and thy footsteps are not known. Thou leddest thy people like a flock by the hand of Moses and Aaron."

Twenty-first-century theologians place the time of these legendary events near 1200 B.C., about 250 years before King David's time, during the reign of the Egyptian pharaoh Ramses II. The dating is entirely dependent upon the Bible's mention, in the time of Exodus, of an old Minoan outpost in Egypt, named Avaris. During the reign of Ramses II, the city's name was changed to Ramses, and the Bible later referred to it by this more well-known name—which provides no clue whatsoever to dating events there. (By analogy, the fact that even old New York was once New Amsterdam allows neither theologians nor historians to place two hundred years of pre–Revolutionary War colonization, and six thousand years of tribal history, *after* the name change.)

Josephus, having access to documents long since bonfired by Christians and Muslims or turned to dust by neglect, placed the legend of the Egyptian catastrophe ahead of the name change, some five centuries before David's son, Solomon, began construction of the Temple in Jerusalem (during the fourth year of Solomon's reign, a thousand years before Josephus, in 961 B.C.). Josephus's accounting puts the event back at least as far as 1461 B.C., during the rise of the Philistines (known to the Egyptians as "the Sea People," to the biblical prophet Amos as a remnant of Crete, and to those of us who explore the Bronze Age, as remnants of Minoan Crete). Stepping back at least this far, we see Egypt reeling from the "heretic pharaoh" Akhenaton's attempt (about 1510 B.C.) to impose upon his people a belief in one all-powerful, all-knowing god. Josephus's best guess brings the Exodus phenomenon into the time frame of Jericho "City Four's" destruction by fire (1450–1540 B.C.). Archaeology teaches us that this is also the time frame of the Joshua story (whether or not Joshua himself ever existed).

The time of Exodus, therefore, can be pushed down a little deeper than the (post-Exodus) Joshua story . . . beyond Jericho IV and the Philistines and nearer Egypt's Eighteenth Dynasty. This was, by any measure, a chaotic period in Egyptian history (as told by records that still survive). The Eighteenth Dynasty was marked by such royal intrigues as patricide, fratricide, and incest—out of which emerged a series of coregencies that sometimes made it impossible to tell who was in charge at any given moment, especially as at least two of these rulers—Tuthmosis II and Hatshepsut—reigned as history's most fascinating pair of cross-dressers. Tuthmosis II, known from Egyptian graffiti as "He with the dainty fingers," preferred to stay at home and have his nails manicured while his half-sister bride Hatshepsut (who was, by every written and sculptural account, strikingly beautiful) dressed as a man and led her husband's troops into battle, where she proved herself a most brilliant (and unusually merciful) general. In time, the priests declared her divinity as a man, and she was thereafter required, under Egyptian law, to wear a false beard made of gold and lapis.

Amid such rapid-fire chaos, if we push the Exodus or any other event back to this time, we find ourselves hard-pressed to name a specific pharaoh in any given decade. While the Bible names pre-Exodus leaders all the way back to Nimrod (about 2500 B.C.), the pharaoh (or pharaohs) of the Exodus period (nearly one thousand years after Nimrod) remain distinctly nameless.

The Eighteenth Dynasty is known for one other chaotic event: the explosion of the volcanic isle of Thera in the autumn of 1628 B.C., with a force equivalent to 1,000 *Pompeiis*. The dust cloud of Thera reached deep into Egypt, depositing a layer of ash that can, to this day, be easily read in Nile River mud. The writings of the wise man Ipuwer—which can also be read to this day—appear to describe the environmental effects of a volcanic death cloud. Ipuwer's rage at a sun god who abandoned his people, a rage contemporary with the Eighteenth Dynasty eruption, reads as if the author believed civilization itself had come to an end:

"The land—to its whole extent confusion and terrible noise," Ipuwer laments (in the Museum of Leiden and St. Petersburg's Hermitage Papyri). "No one really sails north to Byblos [Lebanon] today. What shall we do for cedar for our mummies? . . . Men of Keftiu [Minoans from Crete and Thera] come no longer. Gold is lacking . . . For nine days there was no exit from the palace and no one could see the face of his fellow . . . Plague is throughout the land. Blood everywhere. The river is blood. Men shrink from tasting, and thirst after water. All is ruin! Forsooth gates, columns and walls are consumed by fire. The towns are destroyed. Oh, that the Earth would cease from noise, and tumult be no more. Trees are destroyed. No fruits or herbs are found . . . The land is without light . . . The sun is covered and does not shine to the sight of men . . . Ra has turned his face from mankind."

The similarities between Ipuwer's lament and the story of Exodus (as told by Josephus and by ancient Hebrew scribes) are nothing short of striking. For the Minoans of Ipuwer's time, and to a considerably lesser degree for Ipuwer's Egypt (located some 490 miles, or 800 kilometers, southeast of the Thera explosion), this was the beginning of a Bronze Age dark age.

IN JOSEPHUS'S VIEW, when in a just universe the mountain exploded or the sea rose up against a city or a civilization, the victims were villains, because they had become victims. Josephus, recording his people's history and legends some four centuries after Plato, writes much like him. Plato's Atlantis (which either did not exist at all or was based on the fall of the Minoan Empire in the time of Eighteenth Dynasty Egypt and Thera) was a once-noble civilization that descended into pride, decadence, and corruption. In a cautionary tale dating from 347 B.C., Plato wrote that the people, having fallen from grace, drew upon themselves the wrath of Zeus, "who rules according to law, and is able to see into such things, perceiving that an honorable race was in a woeful plight." Zeus then decides to inflict punishment by sinking their land beneath the waves, "that they [or, rather, a handful of surviving forefathers of Greek civilization] might be chastened and improved."

In chapter 3 of *Jewish Antiquities*, Josephus writes similarly about a kingdom descended from Seth—which became "perverted and forsook the practices of [its] forefathers; and did neither pay those honors to God which were appointed them, nor had they any concern to do justice towards men. But for what degree of zeal they had formerly shown for virtue, they now showed by their actions a double degree of wickedness, whereby they made God to be their enemy." God then decides to inflict punishment by "turning dry land into sea," that he might "make another race that should be pure from wickedness," from a handful of survivors sent forth by a Seth descendant, whom Josephus calls Noah.

The "Noah" story is a Babylonian legend dating more than a thousand years before Eighteenth Dynasty Egypt, and it is far removed by geography, as well as by time. What the apocalyptic legends of Josephus's era have in common, from Babylon to Egypt, from Thera to Vesuvius, are the monstrous engineers of godly vengeance: monsters from the earth.

Plato speaks of half-man, half-god Titans under the Mount of

"Atlantis." Josephus names agents of devastation sent against Seth's descendants. They are the same agents that Dio Cassius claimed (about A.D. 230) to have been moving busily to and fro over the slopes of Vesuvius and flitting through the air before the end came in A.D. 79.

Dio called them "giants."

Josephus elaborated: "For many angels of God coupled with women, and begat sons that proved unjust, and despisers of all that was good, on account of the confidence that they had in their own strength; for the tradition is, that these men did what resembled the acts of those whom the Grecians call giants."

The concept that fallen angels, or lesser gods, occasionally fathered misshapen, wicked, or otherwise powerful and even superior human beings, had already ripened by the time a Jewish reformist movement known as Christianity came to Pompeii, Herculaneum, and Rome. Josephus tells us so. His works came to be favored by the new faith, after it came to dominate Vatican Hill and by fits and starts evolved into the Holy Roman Catholic Church and the Byzantine Empire. Favored, his works were preserved and copied by monks after the fall of the Eastern Empire and the onset of the Dark Ages. This is why we are able to read Josephus today. With but a handful of prominent exceptions, all other historians, philosophers, and scientists who lived a millennium before and a millennium after his time survive (at best) only as fragmentary works. They provide only whispers and glimpses of everyday life in worlds lost so utterly that their very light has crossed the Pleiades and burns now beyond Ursa Major and the shoulder of Orion. Only whispers and glimpses for archaeologists—but they are the most precious sights and sounds we have.

We know from Greek texts preserved by Roman scholars (among them an entire library of scrolls lying under the ash of Vesuvius, in Herculaneum's Villa of the Papyri) that the Epicurean philosophers who had been following Democritus's theories about atoms, planets, and stars for nearly four hundred years understood, in A.D. 79, that the wandering red star Mars was really a planet (believed then to be more or less like Earth). By careful observation of Earth's shadow during lunar eclipses, and from measurements of shadows cast down wells at noon, at far ends of the empire, Greek and Egyptian philosophers and astronomers had also concluded that Earth was a sphere with a diameter of approximately 8,000 miles (13,120 kilometers). They knew that day and night arose from the rotation of the earth . . . knew that the Moon orbited Earth . . . that Earth and Mars orbited the Sun . . . that the stars were suns other than ours, seen at immense distances. Some of this knowledge—the orbits of planets and the sources of eclipses—became preserved in the hand-cranked analog computers known as "Antikithera."

To the best of our knowledge, theories about natural selection as a mechanism of evolutionary change did not exist at the dawn of the first millennium A.D., but history teaches us that the theory of evolution itself did not begin with Darwin and was a common "heresy" long antedating him. The idea that life had undergone changes throughout time and that even humans might be the descendants of more primitive creatures goes back at least to Democritus, about 400 B.C. The idea that dinosaurs had once ruled the land and the seas, and that extinction events might be viewed as measuring points through Earth history, was already of long standing by the time of Emperors Augustus, Claudius, and Titus. The Roman historian Gaius Suetonius (who was ten years old when Titus ruled and Vesuvius erupted) noted in his biography of *The Twelve Caesars* that Augustus (who ruled from 31 B.C. to A.D. 14) had collected and reconstructed at his estate on the isle of Caprae "the huge skeletons of extinct sea and land monsters"; his estate was "less remarkable . . . for its exquisite statuary and frescoes, than for these rarities on display."

Later generations would come to insist that Augustus's dinosaurs were fallen angels, related in some way to the monsters believed to have heralded hell itself, breaking out from Pluto's underworld to punish Pompeii and Herculaneum and the isle of Caprae for the sin of pride. But a century before the Vesuvian catastrophe, the architect and military engineer Marcus Vitruvius understood the geologic origins of lava and volcanic ash. "It must be remembered," he wrote in *On Architecture*, "that in ancient times fires had been generated below Mount Vesuvius, and, from it, flames had burst forth upon all the country round about. Because of this, the material we call 'sponge stone,' or the pumice of Pompeii, may actually have been brought into this state of being out of another type of [liquid] stone through the process of heat."

In what they saw as a coming age of "Enlightenment," an age of potentially never-ending scientific advancement, men like Vitruvius frowned upon their ancestors because they had lived in a dark age of political excesses force-fed by superstition and religious extremism (for how else could one explain the death of Socrates?). They looked to the past and frowned upon it, because their forebears seemed all but scandalously ignorant about nature. And while Vitruvius expected that continued advancement would lead his children's children's children to frown upon him for similar reasons (for this, according to Vitruvius, was the way the future was supposed to be), futurity would prove to be stranger than any Roman architect or engineer, naturalist or philosopher could have anticipated.

Knowledge of geology was eventually replaced by hollow-Earth theories, and by a widespread belief in subterranean demons. In the time of Vitruvius and Pompeii, the power and potential of the steam engine was already known, and the first printing presses (evolved from winepresses) were being used to reproduce decorative patterns on Rome's finest silks—one such device still survives in the ruins of Herculaneum.

But something—many things, evidently—went awry. Great potentials were moving through civilization, unrealized. Out of the southeast, a new astronomy was on the verge of taking hold. When Alexander the Great conquered Egypt, he took with him his close friends the Ptolemies. He named Alexandria after himself in 304 B.C. and left King Ptolemy I in charge. In 30 B.C., some 109 years before the Vesuvius eruption, Queen Cleopatra VII ruled. Neither a brunette nor a stereotypical Egyptian, Cleopatra was in fact a Greek descendant of Ptolemy I, most widely known for her astonishing beauty and a fiery temper that matched her fiery red hair. Best described as Hatshepsut with an inferiority complex, Cleopatra brought the Ptolemy dynasty to an end through disastrous romantic entanglements with rivals Julius Caesar and Mark Antony. The dynasty disappeared but, tragically, not the Ptolemies.

A century after Vesuvius, Ptolemaic astronomy began to take hold and to do away with distant suns and other worlds. The new astronomy placed Earth, by the divine decree of Zeus and his master architects, in the center of the solar system—which was the center of a much smaller universe than that revealed by Democritus. The Moon, the Sun, and the planets were presumed to be revolving around a *stationary* Earth—glued, as they were (all these worlds), to a series of concentric spheres made out of crystal.

This new reality, Ptolemy's universe, eventually became the mainstream in astronomical (or, more correctly, astrological) thought. After Constantinople and the entire Eastern Roman Empire fell in the mid-sixth century, the Earth-centric view of the cosmos, because it elevated the relative importance of humankind and appeared to emphasize the idea of "special creation," was adopted by the Holy Roman Catholic Church. For more than a thousand years (throughout the Dark Age and into the Renaissance) Ptolemaic astronomy survived as Christian doctrine—which, for most of the western world, rendered as law an unfailing belief that the Moon and Mars and Jupiter were embedded in spheres of solid glass.

To anyone who did not look a little deeper into the mystery, the Earth-centric glass was real. In the worst of times, perception became more important than reality. Worse still, it sometimes created reality.

Between A.D. 1530 and 1540, a Polish astronomer named Nicolaus Copernicus resurrected the old, pre-Ptolemy model of the solar system: Earth rotates, he said (and that is why the Sun appears to circle the sky, producing day and night); Mars and all the other planets, of which Earth is only one relatively small member, orbit the Sun; and the Moon orbits Earth.

In 1548, five years after Copernicus died, the Italian astronomer-philosopher Giordano Bruno was born. He grew up to support and refine (with a more precise charting of Mars, Jupiter, and Saturn moving against the background of stars) Copernicus's heliocentric view of the solar system. By 1600 he was writing about an infinite universe of numerous solar systems moving in space, adding mathematical reasoning and observational credibility to Democritus's ancient idea that the stars were distant suns. Bruno had rediscovered and refined the right ideas, but his timing could not have been more wrong. For denying that Earth and its inhabitants were the center of all things and that the Moon and Jupiter were embedded in glass, Giordano Bruno was tried by the Inquisition in 1600, convicted of "heresy," and burned at the stake.

Some three decades after Bruno's death, Galileo Galilei was allowed by the church to keep the telescope he had perfected, in part because he was able to observe ships on the horizon from the Tower of Saint Mark's and to know long before anyone else precisely when new cargo was coming in. So long as Galileo and a few wealthy church-donor merchants continued to profit from history's first-known price-fixing and insider-trading scheme, the church fathers did not care that he was aiming a telescope where no one else had thought to aim it, or that he was seeing what no one else had seen. And no one really took notice, until he began publishing his drawings of moons orbiting Jupiter, and concluding from this that neither Jupiter nor any of the other celestial bodies could possibly be embedded, like bubbles, in glass. Galileo spent the remainder of his life sentenced to house arrest by the Vatican. As it turned out, he was much luckier than Giordano Bruno, and more than a little luckier than many who were then fleeing the religious oppressions of western Europe, so that they could go to America to start new lives, and occasionally become religious oppressors themselves. The Salem witch trials of 1692 were only fifty years away, when Galileo died in exile in 1642.[2]

Two decades after *Apollo 13* astronaut Fred Haise (in April 1970) photographed and named the crater Giordano Bruno from a lunar flyby, one decade after the *Voyager* space probes sailed under the Galilean moons of Jupiter, and on the eve of a robotic spacecraft named *Galileo* settling into

---

[2] In the autumn of 2002, the governor of Massachusetts released a final legal judgment that those poor souls who were imprisoned, tortured, crushed to death under stone weights, and hanged 310 years earlier were beyond all reasonable doubt not guilty of flying over the Moon at night—or of any similar acts of witchery—and should henceforth have their names legally cleared. After reading the trial records, the historian Ed Bishop wondered: "If the accusers ever did really believe that their neighbors could fly, strike people dead with a mere glance, summon fire and demons out of the air, cause crops to fail—if they really did believe it, don't you think they would have thought that perhaps these 'witches' were the last people on Earth anyone wanted to be angering?" As if to drive home the message that human civilization was still haunted by superstitious extremism, several months after the governor of Massachusetts pardoned the Salem witch trial victims, four teachers in Africa's Congo Republic were accused of witchcraft (among them two science teachers charged with casting spells that had caused an outbreak of Ebola fever). Despite appeals for help from the United Nations and the World Health Organization, all four were convicted of witchery and stoned to death.

Jovian orbit, the Vatican's Pontifical Academy of Sciences offered its official apology to Galileo Galilei.

In the empire of Rome, during the days when Pompeii and Herculaneum still gleamed and thrived under the sun, the hour of spacefaring ambition still lay on the horizon—perhaps only a short distance on the horizon—yet with no guarantee that it would ever come, or endure. In this universe, in a far-flung corner of it, electronic civilization was struggling to be born.

THE PERIOD IN WHICH Vesuvius erupted, the same period in which Jerusalem was destroyed and Josephus wrote his histories, was haunted by superstition, and by the fragmentation of old religions into so many new ones that it became difficult for the Romans to keep track. Contemporary letters sometimes complain about the fragmentation. The increasing efficiency of Roman roads seemed to be force-feeding the process. East of Vesuvius, along the river Jordan, Buddhists from India had (some one hundred years before the eruption) introduced the concept of reincarnation—which was embraced by at least three Jewish factions. Accordingly, some of the devout came to believe that one returned after death as an animal or even a plant; and in a final incarnation the soul might inhabit food, communing with the living through water, bread, and wine.

Somewhere within the long habit of conquest and imperial expansion, Roman priests and knights had become fearful of offending any gods—even the gods of conquered lands—so they hid their fear in the smoke of new doctrine. By the time of Josephus, they had added to their habits the invitation, over to Rome's side, of gods from every country the empire assimilated. The wrath of gods other than Rome's was to be limited wherever possible (or at least where politically expedient)—which explains, perhaps, how Josephus came to be regarded by pagan Rome as "a Jewish Prophet," and how he survived to write his histories.

According to Josephus's autobiographical accounts in *Life* and *The Jewish War* (which are equally self-glorifying and self-defensive in tone), he was a prodigal child to whom the priests of Jerusalem came for interpretation of holy law. Interestingly, he assigned to himself the very same fourteen-year-old-prodigy-amazing-his-teachers motif used by Luke (2:41) to describe Jesus, who was, according to Scripture and according to Josephus, crucified in A.D. 33, four years before Josephus was born. (Much as the story of an infant prophet being set adrift and spared miraculously from slaughter has counterparts to Moses [Sargon the Great, about 2450 B.C., the pharaoh Akhenaton, about 1550 B.C.], Josephus and Jesus have student-lecturing-teacher antecedents in Alexander the Great [342 B.C.] and Emperor Augustus [49 B.C.].)

In A.D. 66, Josephus was a commander of Jewish forces in Galilee during the Jewish War against Vespasian. This was the time of the Essene sect, the burial of the Dead Sea Scrolls, and a legendary mass suicide at Masada. As the Roman legions advanced, more than half of Josephus's Galilean soldiers decided that desertion was the better part of valor, and ran away. Josephus recounts that he then reorganized his forces and retreated with them into the fortified city of Jotapata—which Vespasian promptly surrounded. After forty-seven days of catapulting fire bombs at Vespasian's siege works and encampments, the Romans (many hundreds of them, backed by thousands more in nearby fortifications) broke through and put most of Josephus's rebels immediately to the sword.

With forty surviving zealots, Josephus retreated through hidden fortress passageways into a cave. There, knowing that the Romans were searching for them and that they would leave "no wall unbroken, nor any stone unturned" till they found their prey, Josephus's compatriots made a pact to die rather than be captured by pagan, polytheist Gentiles.

Josephus tried to convince them that this did not sound like a good plan; but an assurance, with swords leveled at his throat, that he would die first if he did not hold his tongue, convinced him to (at least on the surface) go along with the pact. After Josephus pointed out that Jewish law specifically forbade the Roman ritual of simply falling upon one's own sword, the soldiers decided that half of them would run the other half through, then half of the remaining half would kill the other half, and so on, and so on—until only two remained. Then, one would kill the other, and the last would be obliged to fall upon his own sword, damning himself for all time. It was decided, also, that the last two to remain would be determined by drawing lots, and Josephus, in his writings, has left archaeologists and historians to guess forever who held the straws (which is not to say that, as a suicide squad member who lived to write his memoirs, he leaves us no substance for guessing).

As it turned out—"by the fortune or the providence of God," according to Josephus—only Josephus and one other remained standing. The sole survivors then contrived a new pact, "a pact of life." They climbed back into daylight and surrendered to the Romans. Brought before Commander Vespasian, they were made to kneel. Minutes later, the head of Josephus's companion lay neckless and bleeding upon the floor, and Vespasian's advisers recommended an equally quick dispatch for Jotapata's last rebel.

Josephus merely (and, according to Josephus, "fearlessly") spoke, in Latin tongue, his God-given vision that the Emperor Nero would soon die young and hated by his own people, and that Vespasian and his son Titus would become emperors in Nero's place.

The prophecy struck a chord with Vespasian—whether by religious belief in prophets or by the ego of the emperor-to-be—and so, declaring Josephus a "prophet," Vespasian sentenced him to imprisonment rather than death.

Months later, at the age of thirty-one (as Gaius Suetonius told it), Nero gasped his last: "Dead! And so great an artist!"

A brief civil war ensued, with four successor caesars: Emperor Galba died in A.D. 69. Emperor Otho died in A.D. 69. Emperor Vitellius died in A.D. 69. And Vespasian's legions proclaimed him emperor in A.D. 69, whereupon he ordered Josephus freed from his shackles and confirmed him as "a *true* prophet."

Awarded privileged and exalted status, Josephus accompanied the emperor to Alexandria, then returned to the Jordan Valley with Vespasian's son, Titus. There, during the year of imperial confusion in which four caesars died, the Judeans had united in all-out warfare against Rome. Josephus, one of history's true survivor types, acted as intermediary and interpreter between Roman and Jewish forces. In this role, he begged his countrymen to accept Roman rule and to thereby avoid the burning of Jerusalem and the leveling of its sacred Temple. All things considered, the Judeans were well advised by Josephus; but they cursed him as a traitor, and in A.D. 70 Jerusalem, the Temple, and the population of the city were burned to a cinder. For the authors of Christianity's earliest books, this produced a vision of apocalypse on Earth as legendary as the Vesuvius eruption. Indeed, as legends measure time, the two destructions were exact contemporaries.

The Roman prophet Josephus returned to the capital with victorious Titus, where he was rewarded with an apartment in Vespasian's mansion, a library of his own, and official adoption into the family of what was to become the Flavian dynasty. Thereafter, he changed his name (from Joseph ben Matthias) to Flavius Josephus.

From fragmentary writings (including the surviving works of Josephus himself), from shrines, household artifacts, and frescoes under Vesuvius, we know that this was the era of an ever-growing pantheon of Roman gods and lesser gods (sometimes called "spirits," other times called "angels"). When the empire subdued Egypt and the Jordan Valley, the generals, even as they occasionally killed rebellious priests and demolished their temples, continued the long habit of inviting over to their side, to be worshiped, the foreign gods of the vanquished. It is easy to guess that at Jotapata, Josephus was already aware of this trend and used a Roman Achilles' heel (Roman superstition) to his best advantage, so that his capture and promotion to "prophet" was not so much an act of divine providence as it was shrewd observation combined with excellent survival instincts. It is just as easy to guess, from this preexisting tendency to assimilate foreign gods, how Jewish reformist movements of the first century A.D., including Christianity, could (despite occasional purges) spread through the Roman Empire. Such spread could occur with astonishing ease if something extraordinary (or inexplicable, or miraculous) had happened to, or around, a founding prophet.

By A.D. 79, the pantheon of gods had become so diverse, and so cumbersome, that a specific god might have acquired ten different foreign names, none of which could be offended. One Roman prayer—which was later rewritten into Christianity's "Our Father"—addressed this problem by adding to the usual formula of "Hallowed be thy name," the all-inclusive remedies: "whatever name it is that you prefer," and "whomever or whatever you may call yourself today."

This pantheon had grown so weighty that there were individual "numina," or angels, assigned to one's own garden. Spiniensis presided over the digging out of thornbushes, Sarritor over hoeing. Sterculinus was the god of manure's breakdown into fertilizer, while Subruncinator was the deity assigned to assist with the weeding out of thorny plants. (And this was but a fraction of the deities to which one owed prayers simply to tend a garden.)

Terminus was the god of boundary stones.

Verminus was the deity who protected cattle from worms.

Vulcan had fathered the fire-breathing monster Cacus, whom Hercules slew.

Sol Invictus was the source of an empire-wide solar birthday celebration—a time of feasts and gift giving marked by the midwinter solstice on the Julian calendar: December 25, "the birthday of the sun." Every April, Jupiter was honored by the sacrifice of the white heifer—which was then eaten in a communal meal. Later in the month, the resurrection of Ceres would be celebrated by letting foxes loose with burning brands tied to their tails. Surviving records fail to say why.

During the decades leading up to Vespasian and Josephus, and especially during the reign of Nero, a cult celebrating the resurrection of a minor god named Attis became strangely popular. The April festival of Attis's rebirth was celebrated with self-flagellation and piercing. Priests were initiated by standing beneath wooden slats while a sacred bull was sacrificed on a platform, or "altar," overhead. As bull's blood streamed down between the slats, the devout publicly firmed their vow of celibacy by self-castration. The crowd cheered, and then burned the bull.

About this time, Rome became ripe for the spread of a simpler, one-god faith. Polytheism was beginning to lose its charm.

The time was also ripe for the resurging popularity of Prometheus, Osiris, Dionysus, and other "suffering servants" of humanity. The Derveni papyrus describes the death and resurrection of Dionysus, a son of Zeus (and a deity of wine) who lived and died in human form. Humans were regarded as somehow bearing the sins for which Dionysus died—and it was through the suffering of Dionysus (called "the Passion of Dionysus") that humans would pay their debt after death, be spared punishment in the afterlife, and rise to a higher existence in heaven. The Derveni papyrus predates the eruption of Vesuvius, the writings of Josephus, and the first books of the New Testament by more than two hundred years.

There was another suffering servant, known to Josephus and Suetonius, who had risen in defiance, above such Roman humiliations as gladiatorial sacrifice and crucifixion, to become both cursed and revered by his own people. Toward the end of his life, he brought forth, from the throat of Vesuvius, a conquering army of the formerly downtrodden; he was henceforth known as the "deliverer from evil"—to a few, even, as "Messiah." To others, he was simply "the devil," or "the lowly one," or "the Greek."

Josephus and Suetonius called him Spartacus.

5

SWORDS AND SANDALS: SPARTACUS AT VESUVIUS

*Everywhere, you see things that make you wonder how old these [buried]
houses were before the night of destruction came—things, too, which bring
back those long dead inhabitants and place them living before your eyes. For
instance: The [stone] steps that lead out of the school . . . For ages the boys
hurried out of that school . . . [the steps] are almost worn through! And the
nervous feet that have been dust and ashes for eighteen centuries have left
their record for us to read today . . . In the bake-shop—the exhumers of
Pompeii have found nice, well baked loaves which the baker had not found
time to remove from the ovens the last time he left the shop, because the circumstances compelled him to leave in such a hurry . . . [I] went dreaming
among the trees . . . of this city which perished . . . when the Disciples
were preaching the new religion, which is as old as the hills to us now—till
a shrill whistle and the cry of "All aboard—last train to Naples!"
reminded me that I belonged to the 19th century, and [that I] was not a
dusty mummy, caked with cinders and ashes, 1800 years old. The transition
was startling. The idea of a railroad train actually running to old dead
Pompeii [on a modern, coal-fired steam engine], and whistling irreverently,
and calling for passengers in the most bustling and business-like way, was
as strange a thing as one could imagine, and as unpoetical and disagreeable
as it was strange.*

MARK TWAIN, 1875

They say that every time he failed in his aims or desires, Socrates judged that his failure should be turned into a learning experience. Or so the wealthy slave owner Symmachus believed, when he tried to explain, in an A.D. 393 letter to his brother, the mass suicide of twenty-nine of his best slaves, handpicked for a gladiatorial contest he had in mind.[1]

"I am," Symmachus wrote, "following the example of this wise man and count the following episode as a good thing for me. Death has subtracted a number of the Saxons from the total number of men that I had decreed to be displayed for the pleasure of the people—a modest number, I must emphasize, so that our exhibition of gladiators would [not] appear to be extravagant. How, indeed, could the best private security have stopped the impious hands of such a desperate group of men? The first day of the gladiatorial games had barely begun when these twenty-nine Saxons managed to strangle themselves without even having the rope to accomplish the task. I will, therefore, not trouble myself with this gang of slaves, worse than Spartacus himself."

The Symmachus document, beyond what it reveals about the letter writer as human being (or his failures as such), is remarkable for two reasons. First: It was written at the beginning of the Theodosian Dynasty, only seven decades after Emperor Constantine made Christianity (the Holy Roman Catholic Church) the religion of the empire. Excommunicated by the Bishop of Milan after his punitive expedition of A.D. 390 (in which the citizens of an entire town were massacred in retaliation for the murder of an army commander), Flavius Theodosius had only recently been permitted to rejoin the Church of Rome, having done "adequate" penance and banned, by law and by penalty of death, all pagan worship, whether public or private. Despite the closing or conver-

---

[1] The A.D. 393 slave-gladiator incident occurred well into the Christian era, some sixty-eight years after Emperor Constantine and the Council of Nicaea in A.D. 325. This was a particularly chaotic period in which the Eastern and Western Roman Empires frequently came to blows against each other; in which four-year-old Valentinian II was appointed emperor in the west, and eighteen-year-old Arcadius in the east (he would be succeeded by his seven-year-old son). Fractionation of the empire at this time was being accelerated by Visigoth and Goth invaders who, through a combination of siege and treaty, were literally forming a wedge between Constantinople and Rome by occupying Greece. It was not the invaders who were putting the empire upon the wane. The invaders were merely an opportunistic infection, moving in and taking advantage of the empire's own internal weaknesses.

sion of all pagan temples to "the Cross," gladiatorial combat—a pagan variation on the themes of human sacrifice and public execution as entertainment—was allowed, interestingly, to persist in the Christian era. One other fact renders the Symmachus letter a document of rare design: More than four and a half centuries after the Spartacus Slave War, the name of Spartacus is both unforgettable and disturbing to a powerful Roman citizen.

From Sallust in the first century B.C. to Orosius in the fifth century A.D., surviving historical accounts of the slave warrior are quite consistent. They also provide us with clear views of Mount Vesuvius and its surrounding countryside some 150 years before the A.D. 79 eruption.

Plutarch, writing about A.D. 100, mentioned that the land was once covered by dense forest, famous for its wild boar. But by the time of Spartacus and the rebellion of 73 B.C., farms and vineyards had spread up the slopes of the volcano; forests had given way to pastures and towns. According to Plutarch, Spartacus seized Vesuvius and made it his stronghold: "Many of the herdsmen and shepherds from the surrounding regions—hard-bodied and swift-footed men—came to join the slaves."

"Spartacus and his troops had shields made from wild vines, which were then covered with hides," according to Frontinus. Writing as a contemporary of the Vesuvius eruption, he described a mountain summit very different from the lifeless moonscape that has existed ever since: steeply cliffed, green with vegetation, and habitable.

"When he was besieged on Mount Vesuvius," Frontinus wrote, "this same Spartacus had chainlike ladders made from wild vines on that side where the mountain is most rugged and therefore was unguarded. Letting himself down by these, he not only escaped the siege but also terrorized [General Claudius Glaber] from a different and unexpected direction, with the result that a number of cohorts of Roman soldiers retreated before seventy-four gladiators."

Florus, in the second century A.D., described the breakout from Vesuvius: "I do not know what to call the war that was incited under the leadership of Spartacus. For when slaves served as soldiers, and [when] gladiators were their army commanders—the [soldiers], the lowest sort of men and the [gladiators] the worst—they simply added mockery to the disaster itself . . . Not satisfied with having made their escape, they also wished to avenge themselves. The first place that attracted them . . . was Mount Vesuvius. When they were placed under siege by [Claudius] Glaber, the slaves let themselves down through a crevice in the mountain by means of ropes woven from wild tendrils and made their way to [the crevice's] very foot. Then, by way of a hidden egress, they launched a surprise attack on the unsuspecting Roman general and captured his camp. Next, they captured other Roman army camps . . . [Spartacus at Pompeii] celebrated the deaths of his own generals who had died in battle with funerary rituals usually reserved for regular army commanders. [In the amphitheater] he ordered prisoners of war that his armies had captured to fight one another around the funeral pyres, hoping to demonstrate, I suppose, that he could expiate his past shame by transforming himself into an exhibitor of gladiatorial contests."

Varro, writing in the time of Spartacus, in the first century B.C., placed the seed of Spartacus's stand at Vesuvius in an accusation: "For although he was an innocent man, Spartacus was condemned to the professional life of a gladiator."

Lucius Seneca, a tutor to Nero who lived in Pompeii before the great eruption, provided (in *Moral Letter* 70:22) a glimpse of just how hopeless the professional life of a gladiator could be: "The following incident happened recently in a school that trains beast fighters. While one of the Germans was engaged in a training session for the morning spectacles, he went off to relieve himself. No other opportunity was ever allowed to him to have an unguarded moment of privacy. In the latrine, he picked up a stick tipped with a sponge [the Roman equivalent of toilet paper]—which was provided for the purpose of cleaning one's obscene parts. Then, jamming the whole thing down his throat, he blocked his windpipe and suffocated himself to death. What a joke to play on death! That it was, indeed. Not very genteel and not very decent. But what can be more stupid than to be overly choosy about our manner of death? What a brave man, worthy of his chosen fate. How bravely he would have used a sword . . . Do you see that even the lowest of the slaves, when pain provides the incitements for them, rise to the occasion?"

As the fifth-century historian Orosius told it: "In [73 B.C. in] the 679th year from the founding of the city of Rome, sixty-four slaves escaped from Gnaeus Lentulis' school for gladiators at Capua [a city 25 miles north of Pompeii]. The fugitives moved immediately to occupy Mount Vesuvius [and] soon attracted a large armed following . . . Wherever they went, the slaves indiscriminately mixed slaughter, arson, theft, and rape . . . [T]hey staged gladiatorial games, using four hundred prisoners they had taken. Those who had once been the spectacle were now to be the spectators."

Writing from a time nearer to the events, the first-century-B.C. Roman historian Sallust is consistent with (and evidently a source for) later accounts: Spartacus, "a leader of the gladiators," escaped Capua with threescore from the gladiatorial school and, from the volcano, "waged a major war against the Roman people." The men who came to Spartacus at Vesuvius "were very knowledgeable about the region," but though the region was rich in cattle and produce, this did not protect the rebels from being surrounded and starved off by the arrival of increasing numbers of soldiers sent from Rome: "Varinius established his camp—which was well-defended with a wall, trench, and large scale fortification—close to the camp of the rebellious slaves. Since they had used up their own food supplies, all the fugitive slaves silently departed from their camp about the second hour of the night watch. To avoid a surprise attack from the Romans while they were away raiding the countryside, the rebels, according to regular army practice, usually appointed night watchmen and guards. [One time, to make an escape from the camp], they left behind only a signaler in the camp. Then they propped up fresh corpses on stakes at the gates of the camp, so that those who saw them from afar would be led to believe that night guards had been stationed. They lit many fires in the camp so that by [the manuscript is disintegrated here] . . . Nothing was either too sacred or too wicked to be spared the rage of these barbarians and their servile characters. Spartacus himself was powerless to stop them, even though he repeatedly entreated them to stop and even attempted by sending on ahead swift . . . messenger [the manuscript is disintegrated here] . . . Spartacus was finally killed, not easily nor unavenged."

Plutarch, in his *Life of Crassus*, provided additional details: Spartacus's wife was a priestess in what was loosely known as the Orpheus-

Dionysus cult, or "Orphism." According to legend, Orpheus was a Greek poet who, before Homer lived, descended into the underworld to rescue (or resurrect) his true love, Eurydice, by leading her out with a sacred thread. But in the end he disobeyed the instruction of his would-be savior not to look back—the instruction to trust that Eurydice was following safely behind him—and he lost her; he suffered a fate worse than that of Lot's wife. Dionysus, too, descended into the underworld. He suffered, died, and was resurrected. According to Orphic-Dionysiac doctrine, after three reincarnations—after three lifetimes striving for high ethics and enlightenment—the truly virtuous ascended into something very much like heaven.

Spartacus, according to Plutarch, "not only possessed great spirit and bodily strength, but he was more intelligent and nobler than his fate, and he was more Greek than his [rural] background might indicate. People tell the following story about him when he was brought to Rome and sold as a slave: While he was sleeping, a snake coiled up around his head. Spartacus' wife, a woman who came from the same tribe as Spartacus, was a prophetess who was possessed by ecstatic frenzies that were part of the worship of the god Dionysus. She declared that this was the sign of a tremendous and fearsome power."

Plutarch states that the prophetess was living with Spartacus at the time of his enslavement in Rome, and that she managed to run with him when he escaped from the city of Capua, 125 miles (205 kilometers) south of Rome. Then, "Glaber was sent from Rome with 3000 soldiers. He laid siege to the gladiators on the mountain they now occupied [and] placed a guard post on the one narrow and difficult access road that led up the mountain."

Again, describing a terrain very different from the lifeless, relatively gently sloping volcanic cone of time-present, Plutarch recorded: "All the other parts of the mountain [except the occupied road] were formed of smooth and steep precipices—nothing but sheer cliffs. The top of the mountain was heavily overgrown with wild vines." Seeming to corroborate other accounts of the Vesuvius battle, Plutarch wrote, "The slaves cut off the useful parts of these climbing plants and wove ladders out of them. These were strong, and long enough so that when they were fastened at the top of the cliffs, they reached down as far as the level plain at the foot of the mountain. All the men, except one of them, descended safely by these devices. This one man stayed behind with the weapons. When the others had reached the bottom, he [lowered] the [weapons] down. Only when all of the weapons had been [sent] down did he [descend] himself, last of all. The Romans knew nothing of these developments and consequently were the slaves able to surround them and to shock the Romans with a surprise attack."

After a series of empire-humiliating victories against entire legions of Roman soldiers, Spartacus led his ever-growing army of rebels into the safety of the Alps, declared them a free people, and urged them to disperse to distant lands. "But his men," Plutarch seemed to lament, "who now had confidence in their great number and had grander ideas in their heads, did not obey him. Rather, they began to pillage Italy far and wide."

Of Spartacus's refuge on Mount Vesuvius, the second-century-A.D. Greek historian Appian wrote: "Many fugitive slaves and even some free men from the surrounding countryside came to [the Mount] to join Spartacus. They began to stage bandit raids on nearby settlements . . . Since Spartacus divided the profits of his raiding into equal shares, he soon attracted a very large number of followers . . . Many deserters from the Roman army came to him, but he accepted none of [these]."

The war drew on for three years—a war that, as Appian told it, "had become particularly fearful for the Romans, although at the beginning they had treated it as a laughing matter and a contemptible thing, since it involved only gladiators, only slaves."

Two generations later, when another "liberator," another "suffering servant" began speaking of freedom and apocalypse, the Romans would not find Jerusalem's "Teacher of Righteousness" nearly so funny as they had found Spartacus at the beginning of his revolution. The Romans would see to it that anyone who sounded even remotely like Spartacus (especially if sermons on mountaintops became a motif of choice) must, like Spartacus, die badly.

In 71 B.C., the military commander Crassus became so desperate, according to Appian, that before engaging the enemy he crucified one of his own men as an example of what he would do to every tenth man should his legions fail to win. "Since so many tens of thousands of desperate men were involved," wrote Appian, "the result was a protracted battle of epic proportions. Spartacus took a spear wound in his thigh. Collapsing on one knee, he held his shield up in front of him and fought off those who were attacking him, until he and the large number of men around him were finally surrounded and cut down. The rest of his army was thrown into disarray and confusion and was slaughtered in huge numbers. The killing was on such a scale that it was not possible to count the dead. The Romans lost about a thousand men. The body of Spartacus was never found. When the survivors among Spartacus' men, who were still a large number, fled from the battle, they went up into the mountains [near Capua and Vesuvius], where they were pursued by Crassus' forces. Splitting themselves into four groups, they continued to fight until all of them had perished—all, that is, except 6000 of them, who were taken prisoner and crucified along the whole length of the highway that ran from Capua to Rome."

The distance between Capua and Rome is 125 miles (205 kilometers). If Appian's figure of six thousand crucified slaves is accurate, then the road to Rome was marked, at one point in time, by men raised on crosses every 35 to 40 yards (or meters) along the entire distance of 125 miles.

ITEM: Inscription Number 1189, advertising a forthcoming event in the Amphitheater of Pompeii; red paint on white plaster; five generations after the Spartacus revolt:
THE COMPANY OF GLADIATORS OWNED BY AULUS SUETTIUS CERTUS, THE AEDILE, WILL FIGHT AT POMPEII ON MAY 31. THERE WILL ALSO BE A WILD BEAST FIGHT. AWNINGS [shades from the sun strung over viewing stands] WILL BE PROVIDED.

ITEM: Inscription Number 7991; red paint on white plaster:
GNAEUS ALLEIUS NIGIDIUS THE ELDER, QUINQUENNALIS, PRESENTS TWENTY PAIRS OF GLADIATORS AND, IF NECESSARY, THEIR REPLACEMENTS, TO FIGHT AT POMPEII, AT NO EXPENSE TO THE PUBLIC PURSE.

GLADIATORS, SLAVES, AND CRIMINALS were synonymous and often interchangeable, in writings contemporary with Vesuvius.

"For although slaves are persons who have been made subject to punishment in every possible way by some stroke of misfortune," wrote Florus, in reference to the Spartacus revolution, "they are still a type of human being, albeit an inferior type, and they are capable of being initiated into the benefits of freedom which we enjoy."

How astonishing, when we take pause in the shade of the twenty-thousand-seat amphitheater at Pompeii. How astonishing, to think that those twenty thousand seats accommodated not only the populace of Pompeii but also the people of its sister city whose god was Hercules. And strangest of all, to think again, how the wealthiest of Herculaneum's merchants counted among themselves freed slaves and freed gladiators—turned, then (some of them just prior to that last Vesuvian dawn), into owners of slaves and presenters of gladiatorial spectacles.

And woe to the slave who showed too much strength, too much intelligence, too little docility. The earliest hint of rebellious nature, or of independent thought, more often than not brought him straightway to the games, or to the cross.

From the first century A.D., the agricultural handbook of Columella shines a light into the minds of the slave owners, and into the lives of the owners' chief economic assets: "I have never had cause to regret that I have maintained [either slaves, or these rules] myself." First, Columella recommends jesting with slaves and making them think he cares, but when counting the animals, slaves, and all the farm equipment and household furnishings, he regards slaves and cattle and furniture equally. The Columella pamphlet recommends arranging to talk with slaves about any new work, "engaging in the pretense" that the master is listening, that he regards the slaves as experienced, and that the master cares—for Columella had observed "that the slaves undertake their work more willingly when they believe they have been consulted about it and that their advice has been accepted."

Columella warned that careful (post-Spartacus) masters "must inspect the slave barracks nightly—making certain that [the slaves] have been securely *chained* and that the places of housing them are secure and well-guarded . . . On occasion, I myself uphold the complaints of those slaves who have suffered genuine wrongs, just as I punish [by sending to the games] those who incite my slaves to rebellious behavior or who make false accusations against their overseers. On the other hand, I reward those slaves who work strenuously and assiduously at their tasks. To the more fertile female slaves, who ought to be rewarded for producing a specific number of offspring [all of them, by birthright, destined themselves to become slaves, to the increased value of the farm], I have allowed [for these women] some respite from work. To a few of them, I have even granted freedom when they have raised an especially large number of [enslaved] children. When a female slave has produced three children, she is granted leave from work. When she produces more, she even receives her freedom."

Another view of slaves and gladiators was penned by Diodorus Siculus, within a generation of the Spartacus breakout from Vesuvius. Other glimpses survive as lines of graffiti on the walls of a Pompeiian tavern where brick-oven cheese bread and heated wines were served. The written words come down to us, across time, like scraps of attitude and neighborhood gossip passed over a backyard fence: "Spartacus, the barbarian," wrote Diodorus Siculus, "having been done a favor by someone, showed himself to be grateful to the man. For even among barbarians, human nature is self-taught to return an equal favor to those who bestow benefits on us . . . SUCCESSUS THE CLOTH-WEAVER LOVES IRIS, THE INN-KEEPER'S SLAVE GIRL . . . CRESCENS, THE NET FIGHTER [a powerful gladiator] HOLDS THE HEARTS OF ALL THE GIRLS . . . CALADUS, THE THRACIAN [gladiator], MAKES ALL THE GIRLS LAUGH."

Elsewhere in the city, an inscription preserves the names of the Roman officials responsible for building Pompeii's amphitheater—Valgus and Porcius—in the second year of Dictator Sulla's reign, a decade before Spartacus was brought in chains to the theater's gladiatorial school (and chief supplier of "entertainment") at Capua. A century and a half later, surges of air, weighted down with volcanic dust, emerged from a volcanic downblast and followed streambeds toward the Bay of Naples. The dust-laden air—in places hotter than live steam, hotter than an iron blade emerging white from a furnace—behaved more like a fluid than a gas. Trees on either side of one streambed were tossed right and left of the bed—parted to either side and flattened, as one might part hair with a comb. The surge cloud moved like a tidal wave over the land, faster than any man on horseback could flee, faster than any steam-driven device (still all but latent in copies of Gaius Orata's notebooks) could possibly propel itself. Here and there within the surge, entire houses exploded to pieces, as if a tornado had touched down upon them. They came apart and were carried away. In Herculaneum, massive stone columns were thrown down, all in the same direction. Their plaster cladding baked as they fell, while men standing nearby were converted to gas and charcoal before their bodies struck the ground. Yet only a sprint from their carbonized tongues and exploded teeth, a home stood with its tables still set for the next meal, with oil lamps still hanging from their bronze brackets, undisturbed. Surge clouds, like tornadoes, can be capricious. In one Herculaneum room, where the cloud touched wooden beams at 1,200 degrees Fahrenheit (and vaporized their outer surfaces instantly), a drawer somehow managed to preserve legal documents with their wax seals unmelted. No one has explained how the most delicate objects tend to be cocooned, or protected, in the epicenters of almost inconceivable destruction, but the phenomenon is seen in all explosive events, without exception. Tornadoes, tsunamis, nuclear explosions, and volcanic surge clouds: They are alive with contradictions.

After each of the Vesuvian surge clouds passed, the air that flowed behind it, though slower and often less dense than the leading edge, continued to behave like a fluidized hybrid of atmosphere and cracked rock. The last two surge clouds (the largest and most violent horrors of all) reached the amphitheater of Pompeii between 7:30 and 7:45 on the morning of August 25, A.D. 79. Piling up behind and on top of the surge deposits, the "pyroclastic flows" (so named from the Greek words *pyros*, for "fire," and *klastos*, "cracked," meaning "cracked fire"), despite being cooler than the preceding surges (or precursor waves), and despite their more leisurely pace (or rather, because of this), filled the arena to a substantially greater depth. Falling in behind the surges, these secondary death clouds overflowed the high arches of the outer walls, spilled indoors, and sank the amphitheater as if it were a ship tossed upon seas of high-viscosity mist.

Several blocks east of the amphitheater, near the Temple of Isis, the gladiatorial compound (or barracks, or prison, as the case may be) disappeared beneath the same clouds. There, in the barracks, excavators have found the securing foot chains and locks mentioned in Columella's pamphlet on the care and management of slaves. Although merchants throughout Pompeii and Herculaneum sold oil lamps displaying portraits and descriptions of famous gladiators ("SEVERUS—CHAMPION OF 56 BOUTS!"), and though fighters such as Auctus enjoyed what the twenty-first century would call heavyweight world-champion status, the fossils of Pompeii are telling us that this was far, far from the norm. The career (that is, the life expectancy) of a young gladiator must have been measured, not in years, but in weeks. In one corner of Pompeii's gladiatorial compound, four skeletons were preserved in a locked room labeled "DETENTION." Two others are still chained to a wall. All told, more than a dozen gladiators were unable to escape the compound, while the lions' den and all the other animal compounds went into the earth utterly free of bones. One wonders if the sponsors of the games valued exotic beasts as being more difficult to replace than trained gladiators—and one wonders if the overseers, judging animal life more important than human life, found time enough to cart away the lions and the bears, but not the men.

Directly behind the gladiators' compound-turned-gladiator-tomb, the Temple of Isis, as its pillars toppled under the heat and horizontal velocities of downblast and surge cloud, preserved a beautiful fresco depicting holy water from the Nile being blessed beneath pillars of rising smoke. The surge preserved images of baptism and rebirth, and it preserved priestly cymbals of the kind typically imported from India. Down the road, in the "House of Four Architectural Styles," it preserved an ivory statue of the Hindu fertility goddess Lak shmi, testifying that Roman roads, in the days of the apostles and Vesuvius, were importing—along with bronze, frankincense, and ivory—Hinduism, Buddhism, and other reincarnation or rebirth-centered faiths.

Among the distant eastern philosophies circulating around the foothills of Vesuvius was the admonition "Do not do unto another what

Found in Pompeii, an ivory carving of the Hindu fertility goddess, Lak shmi, testifies to the influx of eastern religions—which might explain how first-century Gnostic Christians adopted Buddhist-like beliefs in reincarnation, the Golden Rule, and meditations about multiple planes of existence. A knowledge of Chinese antibiotics also appears to have been imported about the time of the Hindu "Venus." Appropriately, the ancient volcanic soils made Vesuvius one of the most fertile wine-growing regions in the Empire. Vineyards ascended almost to the tops of the mountain's slopes. Lak shmi is shown against the backdrop of a painting from the home of a Pompeiian wine merchant. Trees reach almost to the summit, where the Spartacan cliffs overlook a landscape that would never be the same again. In the original painting, clouds and a pattern of leaves reaching up toward a garland are vaguely suggestive of smoke rising from the volcano: the shape of things to come.

you would not want done unto you"—dating back more than five hundred years, in A.D. 79, to an Indian prince-turned-prophet, named Buddha. Evidently, the Empire, in the time of Vesuvius, was becoming a melting pot of newly received ideas, some of them popular and readily embraced by merchants, senators, and knights—others embraced just as easily (and perhaps more easily) by slaves and abolitionists, and therefore judged to be "dangerous."

In A.D. 79, a variation on the Golden Rule (Do unto others as you would have them do unto you) was spreading quickly through preachings and writings attributed to prophets and apostles of what was still, in those days, known as the Jewish reformist movements of Gnostism and Christianity. Both movements, still highly Egyptianized, preached resurrection and rebirth. The Gnostic Christians (doomed to eventual extermination under Roman Christianity) worshiped, as a kind of trinity, Jesus, Isis, and Osiris. The Isis cults portrayed the fallen angel, Seth—who deceived and dismembered Osiris (thus requiring Osiris' resurrection)—as the embodiment of evil, the god of darkness. Isis was often represented, in statues, as holding her baby son Horus in a manner paralleling the medieval image of Madonna and Child. The cults of Isis and the Gnostics practiced baptism and prophesied salvation through "the resurrection"—with Jesus and/or Osiris (both previously resurrected, according to scripture, after temporarily inhabiting, and suffering in, human bodies) forming spiritual bridges between humanity and God (or, as the case may be, gods).

The Isis-Osiris cults, the Orphic cults, and the earliest Christian sects of A.D. 79 all shared a belief in attaining grace and even resurrection through suffering and bloodletting. The priests and "parishioners" in Pompeii's Temple of Isis stayed with their goddess as long as they could, into the second and final day of the eruption. Some clutched ceremonial objects as the end drew near—conceivably they had been offering prayers at their communal breakfast, begging salvation from the volcano. The meal of eggs and fish is still there, in the fallen temple. The priests, too, are still there, in the shapes of fossil casts, still clutching their ritual vessels. The Egyptian communion, though briefly interrupted, has been going on for a very long time.

In the gladiatorial school next door, the concept of grace through suffering carried on a religious tradition dating back to the people whom Roman writers called Etruscans, who had dominated central Italy before the rise and spread of the Roman Empire. The Etruscans believed that the offering of fresh blood in staged combat supplied a recently deceased general or national leader with grace or energy in the afterlife. By A.D. 79, the Romans had turned staged, gladiatorial combat into performance art, if not semireligious theater. Gaius Suetonius described gladiatorial games presented by Emperor Claudius in which the combatants were called "actors," in which mythical and historical dramas were re-created to the accompaniment of music and "massacre." At one event, about A.D. 50, near (or in) Pompeii's "Great Circus [Amphitheater—which was] built of volcanic tufa and wood," Claudius created an artificial lake in which twelve Rhodian warships "then engaged twelve Sicilian ones; the signal for the fight being given by a mechanical silver Triton [statue], which [steam-operated] emerged from the lake bottom and blew a conch." In another gladiatorial ritual, or "game," the drama of Orpheus descending into Hades to resurrect Eurydice was played out with an unexpected plot twist. As the human figure wearing the mask of Greek tragedy approached the world of the living, he was surprised by a bear and torn to pieces. This departure from the known legend "pleased the crowd mightily."

According to Plutarch, Spartacus's wife was a priestess in the Orpheus-Dionysus cult, and Spartacus himself had risen high in Orphic legend by the time Vesuvius buried the Pompeiian amphitheater. If Spartacus was indeed an Orphic cult figure at Vesuvius, he was not alone. He had Isis, Osiris, and Jesus for company.

AT FIRST, when archaeologists of the late twentieth century A.D. discovered the perfectly preserved body of a young girl (she was about eight years old and heartbreakingly frail), they thought the small wooden object she had been clutching close to her chest was simply a carved head broken from a sacred statue, as if to bring the household gods along for company when, finally, the girl's family began a desperate last-minute dash toward the city gates. Archaeologists have a habit of jumping to conclusions that every object treated as precious, and clutched close to the heart, was so treated because it bore religious-icon significance. In the eyes of some, the little wooden head of an infant child became Horus, the child of Isis . . . or the child of the first Christians . . . until closer inspection revealed that the head had once been attached to a now-all-but-vanished mass of cloth and padding. Fleeing a Vesuvian death cloud, the young girl whose name history cannot remember—seemingly alone and separated from her parents in the

At first, the miniature human head from the city of Hercules was believed to be a religious icon rescued hastily from a home. However, the charred remnants of soft stuffing revealed that the head had been attached to a body made of cloth—a *doll*, clutched close to the heart of a little girl turned to ashes and bones. The wooden head and the cloth remnants were removed to the Naples Museum, and the little girl's bones were left where she had fallen, inside the city gates. Then, in 2001, forensic archaeologists working at Ground Zero in New York City discovered a new understanding of hallowed ground. When they returned to Vesuvius, some of them began to leave roses with the dead, just as they had done at "Zero." One of them returned with a new doll, and placed it in the earth with a hand-written note: "From the children of New York to the children of Vesuvius."

stampede—fell to the ground and hugged the only familiar and comforting shape still left to her. All alone in the dark, she clutched her little toy doll.

DURING THE DAYS and weeks that followed, grieving friends and relatives of the lost (joined by treasure-hunting salvage operators) returned to the dune fields where the cities had stood. The salvors began sinking wood-braced shafts down along the walls of houses whose tops still jutted above Pompeii's new ground surface. Around the time the digging began, the Roman poet Satius, then thirty-four years old, visited the site and wrote: "Will future centuries, when new seed will have covered over the waste[land], believe that entire cities and their inhabitants lie under their feet?"

After digging straight down, some two stories into Pompeii, the salvors tunneled sideways, receiving fresh air through tubes and hand-pumped bellows as they propped up ceilings with mine-shaft beams. Burrowing from room to room, they broke through walls and sliding oak door panels mounted on bronze tracks. Statues were removed from pedestals, marble veneer from walls and floors—along, undoubtedly, with gold from ransacked drawers. One team had worked its way, prob-ingly, around the entire perimeter of a courtyard garden, radiating tun-nels outward from the perimeter, into the mansion itself. The ground floor was evidently cleared of all valuables, and a new tunnel was being extended, feeler-like, toward the house next door—which concealed a complete silver table service and a cache of gold jewelry, when some-thing interrupted the salvage operation.

The tunnels were still there when treasure hunters of the nineteenth century excavated the entire street. Some of the Roman tunnel builders were there, too, exactly where a posteruption earthquake had caught them, with their bellows tubes and their digging tools. Without any warning or fuss, the mountain had added their numbers to the perma-nent residents of Pompeii.

All further salvage appears to have ceased abruptly, about the time of the cave-ins, somewhere near A.D. 79. Along the tunnel paths, the recovery workers had passed through carbonized flower gardens, black walnut drawers filled with ghostly black cloth—and pewter vessels filled with eggs, nuts, and spiced bird tongues turned to charcoal. These first excavations were under way, and such discoveries were being made (dis-coveries of once-living things converted to traces, or *"shadows of the cities,"* as a Josephean phrase so aptly describes it), during the very year in which Josephus was putting the finishing touches on his history *The Jewish War.* To this book, Josephus added his famous description of Sodom's shadowy ruins, uniquely Pompeiian. And to this day, in Hercu-laneum's "House of the Wooden Partitions," a piece of bread still lies where someone broke it from a loaf, its carbonized remains fused to a tablecloth that was likewise converted to carbon.

According to Josephus, there were, within the earth, shadows of lost cities, in which living things had been transformed into strange fossils. Two millennia later, the original woodwork, with lamps and table settings still in place, and with charred fava beans and chickpeas still in storage, have been unearthed in a shock-cocooned corner of Herculaneum's "House of Neptune."

Slavers and bakers, merchants and priests—children with their dolls—all flash-frozen into futurity. They could not sanitize and tidy up. They could not hide from us, behind Josephean and self-glorifying writings, who they were, what they believed, how they lived.

Rarely does the earth preserve with such haunting fidelity. I know of a Portuguese carrack that sank into the protection of the coldest, most isolated, most oxygen-starved reaches of an undersea mountain range. A sample of wooden railing has aged only about four weeks in four hundred years.

Two and a half miles (4 kilometers) beneath the Atlantic, I have intruded upon the Royal Mail Steamer *Titanic* and peered through robotic eyes into Stateroom A-11. Almost everywhere else on the ship

No one knows for certain how shock cocoons occur. In a neighborhood where houses were blasted out to sea in pieces, no one in Herculaneum would have believed, in the predawn hours of August 25, A.D. 79, that a container of walnuts would be so perfectly cocooned that the nut meats (albeit just barely) would still be edible more than 1,900 years later.

was total destruction, most of it dating back to that cold April night in 1912. The *Titanic* had stood on end and broken in half, and the bow section had impacted the bottom at approximately 35 miles (57 kilometers) per hour. In the space of two seconds, perhaps three, compression and downblast had pancaked deck upon deck and stamped many of the rooms perfectly flat; yet in A-11 the mattress was still upon the bed, the dresser drawers were unbroken and, though the mirror had cracked, a drinking glass still stood upright in its wooden cup holder, beside the silvered pane. The room had belonged to a fashion reporter named Edith, who survived to record in her diaries the syndrome that now bears her name—the Edith Russell response: the tendency, in time of crisis, to forestall panic by focusing on an absurd detail, such as returning to room A-11 and tidying up, making sure all the clothes were packed neatly into drawers and that the cup was placed properly in its cup holder, before seeking out lifeboats on the sinking *Titanic*. The historian Walter Lord, one of Edith's closest friends, had no doubt that the cup had held "a few stiff shots of whisky" before she set off for the boats. In the rooms beyond, similarly shock-cocooned—entire walls of stained glass stand perfectly intact . . . and in the corners: The stems of palm trees are still in their pots . . . and the ceiling fans are still in place . . . and a jar of olives appears still edible. And over there lies a crate broken open with books spilling out . . . and the telegraph equipment, with the last actions of Jack Phillips and Harold Bride still readable on the dials . . . and decorative carved oak . . . and a new species of winged squid peering down at our robot from high in the eaves. And paper, in this place, is every bit as readable as the telegraph dials, and the clock in the poolroom.

Save for a ship fallen into the frozen depths nearly 3 miles below the ocean surface, nothing in the realm of archaeology can compare to cities lost beneath volcanic death clouds. The only fossilization events that come close are Pleistocene mammals embedded in ice, or Cretaceous flies trapped in amber. Pompeii and Herculaneum are preserved almost as well as Cretaceous flies. They are, in effect, entire cities in amber.

PART II

GHOSTS OF FUTURE-PAST

6

CITIES IN AMBER

Stand at the bottom of the great market-place of Pompeii, and look up the silent streets, through the ruined temples of Jupiter and Isis . . . away to Mount Vesuvius—and lose all count of time . . . in the strange and melancholy sensation of seeing the Destroyed and the Destroyer making this quiet picture in the sun . . . [Then, feel] the solitude and deadly lonesomeness of this place, ten thousand times more solemn, than if the volcano, in its fury, had swept the city from the earth, and sunk it in the bottom of the sea.

CHARLES DICKENS, 1845

Life in Darwin's universe—a universe in which volcanoes reveal themselves to be severe and paradoxical parents, holding sway over the beginning and the end.

Somewhere under the volcanically stressed ice of Jupiter's Europa and Ganymede, or Saturn's Enceladus and Titan, or under some remote iceworld between Centaurus and Ursa Major, the universe has probably succeeded in making life, and is trying to make (or has already made) intellects who will one day look down upon Earth and judge us either fit or unfit for exploration. A quick look around our own solar system teaches us that worlds like Ganymede, Europa, Enceladus, and Titan— lying in "just the right zone" of gravitational flexing, orbiting somewhere between, say, Jupiter's volcanically hyperactive Io and the geologically quiescent Callisto—outnumber worlds like Earth by at least four to one. In order for Earth's volcanic vents to send forth life and to infest the entire planet, we needed to accumulate just the right amount of mass to hold just the right kind of atmosphere, set just the right distance from an unusually stable star of just the right magnitude and temperature. In a far-flung iceworld, a volcanic vent need only be warm and wet for a very long time. Worlds like Titan and Europa do not even need the right kind of star.

So goes the so-called "Europa theory," first put forth by a couple of "geek-and-proud-of-it" teenagers sitting on a fence at a Long Island 4-H camp, way back in the 1970s ("way back," I say, though such a span is but a gnat's breath in Pompeii years).

The author of *Stand by Me,* Stephen King, once lamented that he never had friends again like the ones he had when he was twelve years old. "Who does?" he asked. Well, I still have the same friends I had when I was twelve. I also have a cat named Europa. And I understand, now, that we live in a universe whose life-bearing seas will more commonly be found under volcanically warmed ice—under Europa conditions—than on the surfaces of Earth-like worlds. A planet like ours, with its water and its habitable zones on the "outside," becomes a galactic minority, if not downright freakish.

Under the iceworlds theory, every star in the heavens becomes a potential site for hydrothermal seas locked inside giant orbiting "snowballs" (actually, they are ice-covered volcanic globes of rock). Every star in the sky, including each of the miniature "gas giants" in our own solar system, is a candidate neighborhood for hidden seas trying to make life.

It was Europa (the theory, not the cat) that brought about my first meeting with volcanologist Haraldur Sigurdsson, late in the autumn of 1985. Expedition Argo-RISE was a voyage to the edge of creation, a voyage to the Galápagos Rift and the East Pacific Rise, with explorer Robert Ballard in command. Using the robot Argo, we were able to zero in on a small corner of the system of hydrothermal vents and undersea oases that ran along some 40,000 miles (66,000 kilometers) of ocean floor and literally girdled the planet. For me, the gallery of robotic views was a window on Europa and Titan—a glimpse of undersea geysers throughout the universe.

Only a few weeks earlier, Argo, our deep-ocean robot, had conducted history's first photographic reconnaissance of the *Titanic,* whose wooden and glass fixtures, manuscripts, and even items of food would eventually be found almost as impossibly well preserved as manuscripts and loaves of bread in the "ghost houses" of Herculaneum.

On most oceanographic expeditions, in those days (cut off, as we were, from contact with the outside world), reading medical books in the ship's library was what often passed for entertainment in off-hours. The research vessel *Melville* was different. Apart from the oases 1.5 miles (2.5 kilometers) underfoot, there were pictures of the *Titanic* with its aft section missing and its fore section looking as if something like a volcanic surge cloud had downblasted upon it, blowing the center of the Boat Deck apart.

"Why is the stern more than a half-kilometer away?" I asked in amazement. "Why are the officers' quarters stamped flat and bulldozed outward, from the center of the ship?"

"You're the bone-peddler," Ballard said. "You figured out how the *T. rex* got all broken up. And you put its toes back together again. Go figure out the *Titanic*'s breakup."

And thus did the *Titanic* become, for a paleontologist-turned-astrobiologist, a baptism in archaeology. Haraldur Sigurdsson and the other Argo-RISE volcanologists said, "If you think the *Titanic* is an archaeological puzzle, you haven't seen anything yet." They then pointed me toward the volcanic isle of Thera, and to the civilization buried underneath. And from there it was only a matter of time before our paths recrossed, only a matter of time before I turned up at one of Haraldur's favorite haunts: the cities buried under Vesuvius. And so it has been, ever since the winter of 1985–1986: we disembarked *Melville* and dispersed, but we became something like a family whose members can never really get away from one another. We know this to be true, we of the *Melville.*

As way leads onto way (from the *Titanic* to Thera, to Iraq and Egypt—and back again to *Titanic*), Haraldur and I found ourselves drawn to the puzzle of downblast and surge-cloud effects produced by New York's Twin Tower collapse columns. We were drawn to it, not by mere curiosity but by the realization that the knowledge gained from solving the puzzle might save lives during a future volcanic collapse and surge. Like volcanic collapse columns, the power of the World Trade Center columns was in their mass; like volcanic collapse columns, they were 90 to 95 percent air. The behavior of dust-heavy air in Manhattan was governed by the very same physics that sent volcanic death clouds crashing upon the Minoans and the Egyptians about 1628 B.C., and upon the cities of Vesuvius in A.D. 79. Inside Ladder 10/Engine 10 House, on Liberty Street, the dust-laden air—*the cloud itself*—burst every one of the steel pole doors outward from the center of the truck bay. Southward along West Street, cars were flipped upside down, on top of fire trucks; and firefighters were tossed nearly a full city block, past cars that were telescoped under each other near Albany Street. Six blocks farther south, the cloud lifted a man toward a pillar—which was clad in granite plate a quarter-inch thick—and the cloud killed him there, with granite-cracking force. His bones suffered the same magnitude of breakage inflicted upon a Roman soldier at the Herculaneum marina—inflicted instantly by a Vesuvian death cloud, nearly two thousand years earlier.

Together, the 110-story buildings—crashing into the earth at a terminal velocity of 120 miles (197 kilometers) per hour—were a force equivalent to 1.6 kilotons. They produced a crater a third of a mile in diameter. New York took between 10 and 15 percent of a *Hiroshima* that day—about one ten-thousandth of a *Pompeii*, one ten-thousandth of the next Vesuvius or Mount Rainier eruption.

Volcanic surge clouds rarely produce survivors' accounts, but the fires of September had unleashed what were, in most essentials, "room temperature pyroclastic surges." And because, by volcanic standards, the New York City surge clouds were small and reasonably cold, they had produced something volcanoes never leave behind: more than three hundred survivors at close range, three hundred clarities born of atrocity. And within these clarities, if we were wise and if we paid attention, Haraldur and I believed we could learn enough about surge clouds to convince people of the need to evacuate, say, Naples or Seattle, when the volcanologists say a major eruption seems likely. It became possible to believe that, in volcanic zones far removed from Ground Zero, the Twin Towers might ultimately save more lives than the invaders took.

"Trying to create goodness from an evil deed?" asked a rabbi in Saint Paul's (the chapel on the edge of Ground Zero). He laughed, and said, "They'll make a Buddhist of you yet."

"That'd be a new one," I replied. But the crater in lower Manhattan, the crater where skyscrapers once stood, was if anything a place for firsts. Where else had a forty-seven-story building called "Tower 7" imploded and surge-clouded almost entirely without mention? At Saint Paul's they called Tower 7 "the Rodney Dangerfield Building" (after a comedian whose catchphrase had been, "I don't get no respect").

And strangest of all, in this limbo of strange firsts, to understand that the fury unleashed by those remarkable pigs at the helms of American Flight 11 and United Flight 175—*1.6 kilotons*—was, by comparison to nature's fury, the work of rank amateurs.

Even Hiroshima was a thousand times weaker than Vesuvius in A.D. 79, and Vesuvius, in its own turn, was a thousand times weaker than Thera in the seventeenth century B.C. Up to the first year of the third millennium A.D. (just a few short steps ahead of the immunogenetic revolution and the fantastic robot technology still latent in the brains of ants and flies), humanity had been, and still was, of but trifling magnitude. You could read it any day in the dust pit west of Saint Paul's—and *in* Saint Paul's (even with eyes widened by science and forensic analysis), you could read it, and never tire of reading it, in an almost identical message from the author of Psalm 90: "To you, a thousand years are but a single day. Before the mountains were born, before the earth and the world came to birth, you were God. You can turn a man back to dust by saying, 'Back to what you were!' "

Dust to dust. Twenty-four megatons, or even 1.6 kilotons, have a way of turning things back to what they were. Near the cores of the twin collapse columns, pressures soared upward of 3 tons per square inch, and some of the people—the people themselves—vanished so quickly, and so utterly, that it appeared they had merely been spirited away.

I saw necklaces and rings made of the softest 22-karat Chinatown gold—perfectly intact with the inscriptions still readable. I could not explain this: It was as if many of the people had simply disappeared into the dust, leaving their jewelry and their other worldly possessions behind, inexplicably intact.

And I remember Tommy Foley of Rescue 3, who had returned to duty against regulations, with a not yet fully healed knee replacement. Foley was a cowboy displaced from riding bulls in rodeos to fighting the "red demon" in New York high-rises. In the last year of his life, at age thirty-two, he was noticed by a filmmaker, and he had made guest appearances on shows called *Third Watch* and *The Sopranos*. "But his knees were pretty banged up," recalls Battalion Chief John Salka. "I don't know if the Fire Department knew, but he had all sorts of nuts and bolts and hardware holding him together. And his brother recognized a piece of metal at the site—an artificial joint—in the remains of the [South] Tower. And it turned out that it was in fact Tommy Foley."

Scraps of Foley's rescue gear were found nearby—and a woman's credit cards, undamaged; but nothing else remained.

One night, in the chapel, I met a security guard who had missed work on that last day—who, because of a flu virus, had lived to recall the last day of the old world. In the North Tower, more than thirty security guards had received, and acknowledged, an order to get out of the building, but every one of them had refused to leave so long as anyone remained trapped and potentially "retrievable" below the fires. Not one of the woman's coworkers ever returned to the streets. Not one of them, ever again. But two wristwatches had survived, one of them still keeping time. I told the security guard—Mary was her name—that the intact items (though I would never believe this) reminded me of something the Christians used to say about a so-called "rapture," about something in the Book of Revelation . . . something about people disappearing one day while everything they no longer needed—their laminated driver's licenses, their papers, their jewelry—was left behind. "Something like that," I said. "Something like the vanished airline passengers in Stephen King's *Langoliers*. Something strange."

"You'll never know how much comfort a statement like that brings to people [of faith]," Mary explained. "Coming, as it does, from an agnostic."

ALL FROM A FEW BOX CUTTERS: roughly one-tenth of a *Hiroshima* . . . one ten-thousandth of a *Pompeii* . . . one ten-millionth of a *Thera* . . .

Scientists and theologians may use different words—and sometimes even different numbers—to describe what they see; but the lessons from the rocks, and from ancient religious texts, are the same: We are small, we human creatures struggling down here on Earth. And . . . whatever we're coming to . . . we're almost there.

On September 10, 2001—on the last day of the old world—I went to *Titanic* again. From the abyss, I went to New York: I emerged from the forensic archaeology of a relic not quite old enough to qualify as "archaeology" proper, into the archaeology of my own time. Ever since *Titanic* and the Towers, it has been impossible for me to sift through dust and broken glass without renewed sorrow for the Minoans; for as the Mount of Thera rumbled to life more than 3,600 years ago, the people had no idea that they were the beginning of an Atlantis legend . . . No idea, even as it happened before their eyes, what was happening to their civilization. And from this revelation, the question that begs asking: Is it possible that my poor Minoans, if gifted and cursed with an omnipresent view, would have pitied us for the same reason?

Well, and why not?

The difference between their time and ours is that civilization today creates its own volcanoes. The past never lets us forget this, as we sweep our gaze from the Thera surge cloud to the collapse columns, downblasts, and surge clouds of Pompeii and Herculaneum, as we look from Herculaneum to the twin surge columns and downblasts that followed the *Titanic* to the floor of the Atlantic. Nature reminds us, as we climb from Bronze Age Thera into the footprints of downblast and ground surge left in the wake of two World Trade Center collapse columns—as we sense in those footprints an eerie familiarity—and as we realize that whenever it wants, when you least expect it, the past can sneak up from below and take hold of you. And you never know where it will bring you, warns an old scholar and horror writer who finds, in the lost worlds of the Minoans, a favorite haunt. "No," warns King. "You just never know where the past is going to take you. All you can do is hope it's somewhere you want to go."

AT THE BEGINNING of the Manhattan surge-cloud investigations, I met Haraldur Sigurdsson again. I was not the only *Melville* "escapee" whose journeys into the past had carried him far and wide, along unexpected and often untraveled roads. On an island just offshore of Tambora, Haraldur had discovered a crater lake filled with huge bacterial colonies called stromatolites. In a volcanic pool hostile to most earthly life, he found living fossils from the remotest Precambrian. "The only time I've seen live stromatolites," he recalled for me. "It was an amazing place—because the rim of the crater was a thick carpet of trees, and during the day, when I went in, I noticed that the forest was black. Then I realized that the black crowns of the trees were fruit bats—huge bats in all the trees. And because nobody ever goes in there and the presence of humans was new to them, the animals started to get restless, and to take flight—these *monstrous* things, with six-foot wingspans and the heads of dogs. The people [the guides] called them flying dogs—each, with its wings spread out, as large as a man."

Most people would shrink away from an encounter such as this, with the living Precambrian underfoot and a living mammalian cloud overhead—a cloud so strong with life's surge that it cast a false twilight over the island and the sea, a twilight such as one knows during a total eclipse of the Sun. People taking in air and in their right minds shrink back from the moment. Seekers live for it. Haraldur lived by the explorer's creed—which could never be too often recited and which defined the moment of turning back forever (or premature retirement, as the case may be): "If you cannot bear the darkness, if pushing half-blind into new frontiers becomes not a longing for the mysterious so much as a dislike of shadows leering from odd corners, then you should go back to the sunshine and never make exploring your profession. The frontiers of the night were never meant to be inhabited by the meek."

Haraldur's longing for the mysterious, and his love of things volcanic, had carried him from Iceland onto and under the high seas, onto the Greenland ice sheet and deep under it.

In that last bright year of the old world, the ice sheet began yielding up secrets from the last days of the Minoans. Layers of Greenland ice can be added up and dated somewhat like the rings of a tree. A number of clues, beginning with accounts of winter during summer in China's Bamboo Annals (dated by records of eclipses in the margins) and ranging through summer frost scars in the rings of California's oldest trees, had allowed us to narrow the brackets on Thera's "year of the damned" and led me to favor a 1628 B.C. date (autumn, to judge from the direction in which prevailing winds blew the volcanic dust).

Haraldur was glad to tell me that a vein of microscopic glass particles dated close to the 1628 B.C. time frame, when approached by counting downward and backward into successively older layers of ice. Most important: The glass in the ice could be fingerprinted, chemically, to ash from the Thera eruption. The ratios of silicon to iron, calcium, aluminum, and magnesium were identical, providing us with not merely a smoking gun from Thera but a gun with fingerprints and a time card attached.

But Haraldur's ice date was about a dozen years away from the tree rings, very close to 1644 B.C. "I think the ice is accurate within five years, plus or minus," he said. "Possibly a little more." We both knew that two layers of ice could, on rare occasions, be compressed indistinguishably. Or, every few centuries, a tree might under some unusual condition skip a year of ring growth, or add one. We did not need many rare events, over a span of nearly four millennia, to throw the clock off by a half-decade or more.

Perhaps on account of my personal bias toward all things living or paleontological, I placed more credibility on the tree-ring calendar. Haraldur, perhaps because of his bias in favor of all things geologic, placed more credibility on the ice-layer date. Neither of us can know for sure, until or unless a near-immortal tree is found with Theran glass embedded in its rings.

Pompeii and Herculaneum can be dated with far, far greater certainty, not only because we can examine ash flows, skeletons, household furnishings, and tree rings in situ but also because written records have survived. Descending into ash layers with spade, paintbrush, and even on occasion with toothbrush, descending sometimes by mere fingernail lengths in a day—and by comparing the ashes and fossils, inch by sequential inch, with the experiences of firsthand eyewitness participants—we can bracket the events of A.D. 79 not merely to a specific month, or to specific days within a month, but to specific hours within specific days.

WORKING WITH ITALIAN, British, and American colleagues (among them volcanologists Steve Carey and Steve Sparks), Haraldur Sigurdsson identified, at the very bottom of the Vesuvian eruption layers, a paper-thin dusting by very fine ash, extending barely more than 2 miles (3.3 kilometers) from the old Spartacan cliffs. This fingerprint of a small precursor explosion (essentially an impressive but short-lived puff of smoke) was probably produced during the late-night and early-morning hours of August 23–24, A.D. 79. Haraldur's measurement of the initial ash layer's depth and extent convinced him that the first airburst was probably not loud enough to alarm the populations of the cities below the Vesuvian foothills. The burst was a warning, but most of the people, if roused at all, must have gone back to sleep or resumed their morning chores. The roads leading away from Pompeii are so thickly littered with human bones that when finally the inhabitants did begin to stir and to leave, it becomes possible for us to believe that it was already too late for any of them to escape.

The city of Pompeii was located 7 miles (11 kilometers) southeast of Vesuvius's peak and the now-disintegrated Spartacus stronghold. Herculaneum was 4 miles (7 kilometers) west, and a city called Misenum (home to the Plinys) lay 20 miles (33 kilometers) west across the Bay of Naples.

According to the story coded in rocks and translated by Haraldur Sigurdsson and Steve Carey, the first major release of energy missed Herculaneum altogether. The rate and extent to which deep-Earth magma frothed and cooled, as it jetted into the atmosphere and became

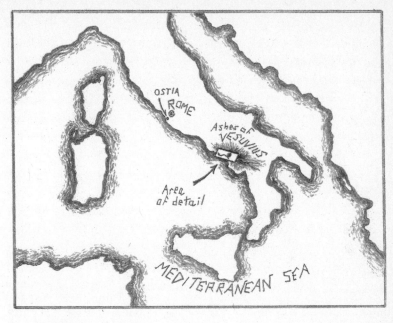

128 mi.

0   100 km.   200 km.

"sponge stone," reveals that the first pumice burst exited Vesuvius at approximately 2,000 feet (0.66 kilometer) per second, or twice the speed of sound. Any portions of the Spartacan cliffs avalanching into the jet would have converted immediately from boulders to dust. The jet did not weaken but, rather, strengthened, like a mighty engine aimed at the heavens. Supersonic pumice froze in the stratosphere, reaching a minimum altitude of 12 miles (20 kilometers), before powerful stratospheric winds, blowing two times higher than twenty-first-century jet routes, pulled the smoke apart and nudged it eastward in the direction of Pompeii. There, dust and pumice began to fall as a kind of volcanic snow, along a path 2 miles wide and more than 65 miles (100 kilometers) long.

"Pompeii was dead-on the axis of the main dispersal of fallout," according to Steve Carey. During this initial fallout phase, the city was

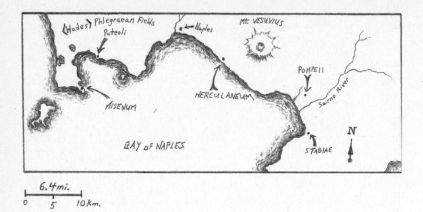

essentially experiencing a gentle "snowing under" by dust and spongy white pumice stone.

For more than a century, textbook dogma had dictated that the Pompeiians had suffocated under the fallout, but Sigurdsson and Carey did not see eye to eye with the textbooks, partly because very few bodies had ever been found *under* the fallout. Most of the casualties were located on top of the pumice—which did not surprise Haraldur, for he never did understand how chilled pumice was supposed to have been lethal in the first place. The largest particles of "sponge stone," at the onset of the Pompeiian catastrophe, were barely wider than acorns— and they were made mostly of air. Alongside the pumice stones, starting at the bottommost Pompeiian ash layers, fell equally small fragments of pulverized black rock (called lithics). These comprise between 2 and 10 percent of the deposit, and they teach us that the "nozzle," through which ash was being ejected, was eroding wider and wider with each passing hour.

Some of the fossilized citizens of Pompeii were holding pillows over their heads. While low-density nuggets of sponge stone could scarcely sting, the lithics had terminal velocities upward of 120 miles (197 kilometers) per hour. They fell from the sky like random volleys of slingshot ammunition, breaking roof tiles and threatening to shatter skulls. As the people went into the streets or evacuated through the city gates, they protected their heads as best they could with leather helmets or pillows and blankets. Their fossilized remains give testimony of this. So, too, do the letters of Pliny the Younger.

"Thank you for asking me to send you a description of my uncle's death," began a letter written between A.D. 103 and 107 to the historian Cornelius Tacitus by Pliny the Younger. "It is true that he [Pliny the Elder] perished in a catastrophe which destroyed the loveliest regions of the earth." Pliny recounts that his uncle was in command of the Roman fleet at Misenum, 20 miles (33 kilometers) west of Vesuvius. From his vantage point at Misenum, the younger Pliny, then seventeen years old, witnessed and documented the eruption. Pliny gives us the date and time at which the fallout phase began, a phase commonly called the "Plinean phase" by volcanologists, in honor of the Plinys.

According to Pliny, near midday on August 24, shortly after lunch, his mother drew attention to a cloud of unusual size and appearance rising from Vesuvius, some 20 miles away in the east. Its appearance was described by Pliny the Younger "as being like an umbrella pine, for it rose to a great height on a sort of trunk and then split off into branches." Corroborating the pumice record, he appears to describe stratospheric winds cutting through the top of the cloud, pulling it apart into long streamers of fallout, eastbound, where "borne down by its own weight, [the fallout] spread out and gradually dispersed. Sometimes it looked white, sometimes blotched and dirty."

Present-day observers might more closely associate the eruption column with an ascending mushroom cloud than with the shape of an umbrella pine. But the image of a stem and a spreading crown is the same in either case, and the image speaks to the precision of the Pliny report.

Under the distant fallout plume, from Stabiae and other towns downwind of Pompeii, Pliny records secondary eyewitness testimony that even though falling pumice stones "were light and porous," there was danger from them. The survivors were probably referring to falling "lithics" mixed in with the pumice hail. Two lines further into his report, agreeing independently with the story told by stones, fossils, and artifacts, Pliny tells us, "As a protection against falling objects, they put pillows on their heads tied down with cloth."

Of his uncle's habits—which foreshadow his march toward an

erupting volcano—Pliny says (in a separate report to Baebius Macer) that the admiral had produced eight volumes titled *Problems in Grammar:* "This he wrote during Nero's last years [A.D. 54–68] when the slavery of the times made it dangerous to write anything at all independent or inspired." After Nero, the elder Pliny, during the last decade of his life, wrote *A Natural History* in thirty-seven volumes—which the younger Pliny refers to as a learned and comprehensive work as full of variety as nature itself.

"You may wonder," Pliny the Younger records, "how such a busy man was able to complete so many volumes, many of them involving detailed study; and wonder still more when you learn that up to a certain age he practiced at the bar [within the court system], that he died at the age of fifty-five, and throughout the intervening years his time was much taken up with the important offices he held and his friendships with the emperors. But he combined a penetrating intellect with amazing powers of concentration and the capacity to manage with the minimum of sleep."

We have it from the younger Pliny that his uncle, when in Rome, had usually visited the emperor Vespasian—"who also made use of his nights"—before daybreak, and that upon returning home from his official duties, he devoted every spare moment to his work. Indeed, the only time he took from his work was for a bath, during which he dictated notes: "He kept a secretary at his side with book and notebook, and in winter [he] saw that his hands were protected by long sleeves, so that even bitter weather should not rob him of a working hour.

"It was this application," his nephew tells us, "that enabled him to finish all those volumes, and to leave me one hundred sixty notebooks of selected passages, written in a minute hand on both sides of the page, so that the number is really doubled."

None of these notebooks has survived.

According to Haraldur Sigurdsson, "What Saint Augustine said of the Roman scholar Varro can apply equally well to Pliny the Elder: That he read so much, it was a marvel he ever had time to write anything; and he wrote so much that it was difficult to see how he found time to read."

For *A Natural History* he had, by his own account, consulted no fewer than two thousand volumes. "He was possessed," Haraldur observes, "with a mania for acquiring (and digesting) information; and he searched the great libraries of [his] time for books on science, most of which (like Pliny the Elder's notebooks) have been lost to us, either burned in the great fire of Alexandria in Egypt or destroyed when the Roman Empire fell. But in the end, his mania for seeking out fresh avenues of knowledge led to his death at Stabiae, 4 miles (7 kilometers) south of Pompeii."

Pliny the Elder, according to his nephew, saw at once that the towering cloud seen from Port Misenum was a natural phenomenon worth closer inspection. As an admiral, it was easy for him to order a boat made immediately ready for an expedition to Vesuvius—which we are told, in fact, he did. As he prepared to leave, he told Pliny the Younger that he could come aboard if he wished, but his nephew declined, writing later, "I replied that I preferred to go on with my studies, and as it happened he had himself given me some writing to do."

Pliny tells us that the cloud appeared after lunch, and that his uncle ordered a boat crewed for the 20-mile trip, bringing his secretary along to take dictation of his observations. The preparations could not have required more than an hour, meaning that it was (depending on what time the Plinys took lunch) approximately 2:00 P.M. when, "as he was leaving the house, he was handed a message from Rectina, wife of Tascius whose house was at the foot of the mountain, so that escape was impossible except by boat. She was terrified by the danger threatening her and she implored him to rescue her from her fate."

The port at Misenum was 20 miles from the mountain—20 miles (33 kilometers) along winding roads. Somehow, Rectina sent Admiral Pliny a message faster than men on horses could travel by relay. A rider would have traveled the better part of a day to hand-deliver a message that a large eruption was cutting off all landward escape. A ship traveling west would have taken even longer, for the distribution of dust teaches us that (at sea level as well as in the stratosphere) the wind was blowing eastward. Traveling by sail from Pompeii or Herculaneum to Misenum would have required a tedious path, tacking against the wind, in a north-south zigzag.

Haraldur Sigurdsson found a likely solution to the mystery of Rectina's rapid communication in Roman references to "flag signals" used by the military, and it occurred to him that by putting keen-eyed soldiers in towers spaced a half-mile apart, a preelectronic era "Morse code by flags" could be transmitted swiftly along strategic roads. The theory of a signal relay rests on the likelihood that the Romans appreciated the strategic significance of the region and would have invested resources in flag towers. The probability is high, for the Bay of Naples was a natural harbor and crossroads to the Tyrrhenian Sea; it was headquarters to the Mediterranean fleet, for the same reasons that it became, 1,900 years later, headquarters of NATO's Mediterranean naval fleet.

As the eruption strengthened, the connection to Misenum, at the far end of the relay, would have been cut from the moment that sheets of ash began to obscure the easternmost flag stations. According to Pliny the Younger, as related to him by survivors of the admiral's expedition (and by the admiral's notes), they encountered thick curtains of sponge stone and ash within a few hours of their eastward sailing. Therefore the flag towers (if such existed) were, by late afternoon, ceasing to transmit any news from the east except, perhaps, "Loss of signal."

After Rectina's message was received, the admiral changed his plans. According to Pliny the Younger's letters, "What he had begun in a spirit of inquiry he completed as a hero. He gave orders for the warships to be launched and went on board himself with the intention of bringing help to many more people besides Rectina, for this lovely stretch of coast was thickly populated. He hurried to the place which everyone else was hastily leaving, steering his course straight for the danger zone. He was entirely fearless, describing each new movement and phase of the portent to be noted down exactly as he observed them. Ashes were already falling, hotter and thicker as the ships drew near, followed by bits of pumice and blackened stones—[lithics], charred and cracked by the flames: Then suddenly they were in shallow water, and the shore was blocked by the debris from the mountain [blocked by impenetrable rafts of floating pumice]. For a moment my uncle wondered whether to turn back, but when the helmsman advised this he refused, telling him, 'Fortune favors the brave,' and [that] they must make [south] for Pomponianus at Stabiae. He was cut off there by the breadth of the bay (for the shore gradually curves round a basin filled by the sea) so that he was not yet in danger, though it was clear that this would come nearer as [the eruption strengthened and] spread."

The skeletons of the Pompeiians are always found in hollow cavities, their softer parts (even the fossilized folds in their clothing) having

As if merely asleep within the earth, those Pompeiians who were packed tight inside a bedding plane of fine-grained pyroclastics (which followed the 7:30 A.M. surge cloud) were flash-fossilized for all time. After centuries, their flesh, their hair, and their clothing had disintegrated, leaving behind hollow spaces in the shapes of people. No matter how disquietingly perfect a face may appear after a "hollow" is filled with shape-fitting plaster or resin, each of the casts becomes, in essence, a statue filled with bones. On occasion, an earthquake or other disturbance had collapsed part of a hollow space, permitting an excavator's resin intrusions to replicate only half of a man's face.

long since been removed by a combination of bacteria and water seeps, the end result being bone-filled caves in the shapes of people.

In A.D. 2000, a road-widening operation exposed five human skeletons huddled together just outside Pompeii's city gates. Haraldur Sigurdsson saw in their deceptively peaceful poses, signs that something very hot and instantly lethal had reached them. The awkward attitudes of sudden and severe contractions in the musculature surrounding the bones of the feet belied quiet death. When University of Naples radiologist Francesco Sasso examined the skulls, he found the sinuses to be plugged with dust. Closer inspection revealed faint but clearly successive layers of inhaled volcanic microglass. The plugs had grown like the successive layers of pearls, over many hours before death caught up with this one small group of fleeing Pompeiians.

Pliny the Younger places the emergence of the cloud and start of the ashfall just after lunchtime, on August 24, A.D. 79.

Initially, and for many hours thereafter, there is no ashfall on Pompeii's sister city, Herculaneum. "Absolutely none," Haraldur emphasizes. "We've looked hard, everywhere, and there's no sign of fallout, underneath what we've come to call 'the midnight surge layer, the midnight surge glass.'

"And meanwhile, Pompeii is in total darkness, and getting buried. So, the Pompeiians are having a very different experience of the eruption, by comparison to the inhabitants of its westward sister city." Pompeii experiences midnight in midafternoon, while Herculaneum is still in sunlight. Rectina's distress call to Pliny the Elder, if relayed by flag tower from (or through) a city, has gone to the port of Misenum from a city outside the Plinean shadow—westward of it, like Herculaneum.

By 4:00 P.M., as Admiral Pliny's ships are sailing toward floating pumice fields and a blackened southeast horizon, the Pompeiians are already climbing atop a deepening snowfall of crystallized pumice and powdered glass. A few little knots of people, huddling together indoors, become the first to enter the fossil record, as rooftop after rooftop begins to fail. Herculaneum enjoys nearly twelve hours' respite, its people no doubt frightened by the towering column, but nonetheless thinking themselves lucky, as they watch the crown of Pliny's "umbrella pine" cloud spreading eastward and dropping pumice on distant Pompeii. Fright there is, in great abundance; but also there must exist, among the Herculaneans, an inescapable feeling of "better you than me."

To judge from excavations and road cuts revealing, somewhat like geographic X rays, the approximate land surface area covered in fallout, and to what depth the pumice accumulated between specific eruption phases, Haraldur estimates that, initially, magma is jetted out of Vesuvius at the rate of 1,000 tons per second (the approximate mass of one thousand automobiles per second).

All of the terrifying phenomena associated with those sixty thousand Toyota masses per minute are governed by a disarmingly simple physics: Relatively low-density magma and compressed gases are "seeking" the surface of the earth, finding their way blocked (or corked) by a mountain. The volcano, for its part, is always sinking under its own weight, always "wanting" to fall into the earth. Once its cone is breached, the sheer mass of overlying rock force-feeds the eruption, somewhat as an inflated tire with a pinprick in one side will respond to the weight of the truck it has been forced to support. (For a clearer picture, simply multiply the truck analogy by the mass of Vesuvius or Everest.) In the end, the eruption is reducible to physics—and the physics, in turn, is reducible to mathematics. Such is the fate of the Pompeiians and the Herculaneans: The mountain transforms and reduces them into victims of mathematics.

During some of the post–Roman era "cone-building" eruptions, whenever the Vesuvian magmas lacked great quantities of compressed gas, they simply bled lava, nonexplosively onto the earth's surface—whole lakes and streams of molten rock. The 1944 lava flows are an example of this. By comparison, a gas-filled eruption dating from April 1906 had dusted nearby towns (including the one then sprouting high above the streets of Herculaneum) in knee-deep drifts of volcanic dust. The A.D. 79 eruption was larger, of course, and roiling with compressed gas.

In its present incarnation, the Vesuvius magma pool is capped by 2 miles (3.3 kilometers) of down-pressing rock. Two miles below Earth's

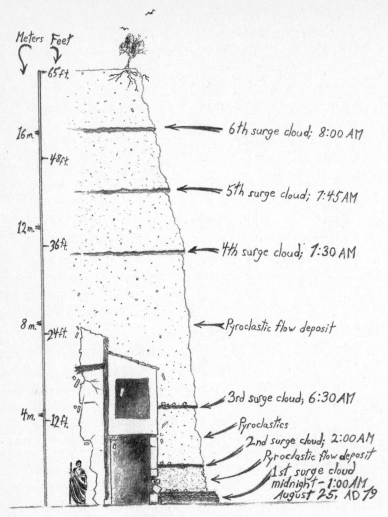

Meters Feet

65 ft.

16 m. ← 6th surge cloud; 8:00 AM

48 ft.

← 5th surge cloud; 7:45 AM

12 m. ← 4th surge cloud; 7:30 AM

36 ft.

8 m. ← Pyroclastic flow deposit

24 ft.

← 3rd surge cloud; 6:30 AM

Pyroclastics
2nd surge cloud; 2:00 AM
Pyroclastic flow deposit
1st surge cloud
midnight – 1:00 AM
August 25, AD 79

4 m. 12 ft.

HERCULANEUM

surface, water cannot boil, no matter how hot it gets. Even hydrogen gas is compressed down to a liquid and behaves like a thick oil. Compressed into thick magma, the gases, at depth, are indistinguishable from molten rock.

But as cracks develop in the pool's roof, and the Vesuvian cone (or clot, or cork) gives way to a magma channel, any compressed gases dis-

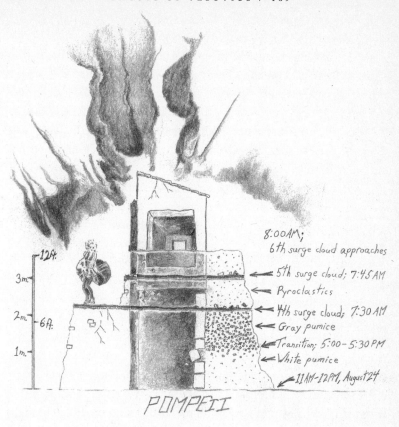

8:00 AM;
6th surge cloud approaches

5th surge cloud; 7:45 AM

Pyroclastics

4th surge clouds; 7:30 AM

Gray pumice

Transition; 5:00 - 5:30 PM

White pumice

11 AM - 12 PM, August 24

POMPEII

solved in the magma will expand as they move toward the surface and into decreasing pressure. To these gases, sea-level air is like a vacuum. Bubbles form as the lava ascends, becoming larger and more numerous with each passing league, effervescing. By the time it reaches an altitude equivalent to the volcano's foothills, gaseous lava is already fizzing, boiling, and exploding—obeying the same laws guiding hot gases from a flash of black powder through the barrel of a gun. The lava shoots out as foam, its air pockets (or bubbles) filled mostly with steam. The foam, as it ejects, is sometimes blasted to bits of siliceous or granitic dust, and other times manages to hold together as rice-sized, acorn-sized, or hen's egg–sized grains. The larger particles, as they jet into the stratosphere, solidify into pumice (or foamy volcanic glass). What begins journeying toward the surface as highly compressed material explodes into the upper atmosphere as a very lightweight, low-density substance—pumice stone—the only rock in the world known to float on water.

By comparing the square mileage (or surface area) of pumice falls against the starting and ending times given by Pliny (for an eruption lasting nearly twenty-four hours), Haraldur Sigurdsson has clocked the accumulation rate in Pompeii at—*initially*—approximately 8 inches (20 centimeters) per hour. During the first two or three hours, most of the buildings had sufficient load-bearing strength to resist the accumulation, for not only did the hail of air-filled rocks resemble a gentle snowfall, the pumice was in fact no heavier than snow. "But the rate of accumulation was not steady," according to Haraldur's inch-by-inch analysis of the pumice, from the original Roman ground surface upward. The rate increased during the first few hours, and the false hope that the eruption would not increase its fury, or would soon subside, must have trapped many.

Pliny the Younger has recorded, for all time, his own hesitation to believe what his own eyes were showing him and to leave the danger zone: "After my uncle's departure, I spent the rest of the day with my books, as this was the reason for staying behind." Intent on finishing the work assigned by the admiral, Pliny stayed home and read Livy's history of Rome, while all around him the danger became increasingly apparent. Even after a friend from Spain arrived at the house to tell him that he must be insane to be staying home at this kind of time, common sense was slow to take root, and a nesting urge (or Edith Russell response, call it what you will) continued to hold sway.

During the hours after his uncle departed eastward with the fleet, Pliny the Younger tells us: "I took a bath, dined, and then dozed fitfully for a while. For several days [previous to August 24] there had been earth tremors which were not particularly alarming because they were frequent in Campania: but that night [20 miles west of Vesuvius] the shocks were so violent that everything felt as if it were not only shaken but overturned. My mother hurried into my room and found me already getting up to wake her if she were still asleep. We sat down on the forecourt of the house, between the buildings and the sea close by. I don't know if I should call this courage or folly on my part (I was only seventeen at the time) but I called for a volume of Livy and went on reading as if I had nothing else to do. I even went on with the extracts I had been making. Up came a friend of my uncle's who had just come from Spain to join him. When he saw us sitting there and me actually reading, he scolded us both—me for my foolhardiness and my mother for allowing it. Nevertheless, I remained absorbed in my book."

Meanwhile, the quaking worsened, and the volcano began to send out tsunamis. And all the while, on the opposite side of the bay, "a fearful black cloud" roiled in the east, "rent by forked and quivering bursts of flame." Of his uncle's passage toward the cloud, Pliny the Younger records that by late afternoon the ships were being pummeled by hot ash, pumice, and blackened (lithic) stones. Pliny emphasizes that their path toward the endangered eastern cities was blocked "by the debris from the mountain," by vast floes of floating pumice so thick that the admiral seemed suddenly to have mired his ships in shallow mudflats, through which it was evidently impossible to forge a new path. They were forced south by the growing barrier, south toward the harbor of Stabiae.

Probably, the turn southward occurred after 4:00 P.M. At this time, the streets of Herculaneum remained ash-free, and sunny, and they must have been safe-appearing still.

On the other side of the volcano, 10 miles (16 kilometers) east of Herculaneum, pumice has, at this time, been falling since noon, since about the time Pliny the Elder finished his lunch. Initially, in accordance with the story written by volcanic debris lying immediately on top of Pompeii's original road surface, the pumice grains started arriving as rice-sized pebbles. Then, after about 2.25 inches (or 6 centimeters) of accumulation, some of the grains have enlarged to the diameters of quail eggs. At a depth of 8 inches (or 20 centimeters), probably not much more than an hour into the eruption, with Admiral Pliny's ships still more than two or three hours from their encounter with a floating pumice barrier—a mere 8 inches above ground level, 8 inches into the eruption sequence—*all* of the deposited pumice stones have become quail egg–sized or larger.

"It's getting coarser," Haraldur emphasizes. There is a sense of urgency in his voice, as if, spade in hand, he can look down the streets of the dead city and still see the Pompeiians coming out of their homes, each of them hoping that the Vesuvian snowfall will soon diminish and die. The rocks tell us otherwise. Haraldur sees what is going to happen to these people. They don't. "The coarsening of the pumice fall is due to the increased intensity of the eruption. The eruption is getting more violent. There's more energy; a higher rate of magma ejection."

Initially—and only initially—as dictated by Sigurdsson and Carey's estimates of total depth and surface area, the magma was being ejected at a rate of approximately 1,000 tons per second. But by the end of the first hour, when the "quail egg stones" begin to fall, the ejection rate has increased tenfold, to 10,000 tons (or the mass of ten thousand automobiles) per second. By this time, the downwind fall of large pumice stones and lithics (almost as far away as Stabiae) has increased by a factor of three, suggesting that the stem of the Plinean cloud (the eruption column) is now rising 18 miles (30 kilometers) into the atmosphere, halfway to the edge of space.

With Pliny the Younger supplying the start time, Haraldur Sigurdsson's estimates of magma ejection rates suggest that the fallout in Pompeii reaches the height of a man's waist (40 inches, or the 1-meter mark) about four o'clock on the afternoon of August 24.

By this hour, on this day, wooden roof beams are beginning to creak and groan under the weight of pumice and ash. By A.D. 2001, archaeological maps would record 1,044 bodies discovered within Pompeii, suggesting that the remainder of the city's approximately twenty thousand inhabitants eventually fled outside the gates. Every new twenty-first-century road cut finds Pompeiians—more and more of them—miles from the city gates. Condemned to being felled as they flee, something far, far deadlier than pumice is waiting for the people; and even as it dwells, at 4:00 P.M., under the throat of the mountain, it is gaining on them.

By Haraldur's estimate, even those who took heed of nature's warning signs and fled at the first trump—the alert ones who never took pause to gather their valuables in a sack, or to look back—even they might have fled too late.

Two miles outside the city gates, someone sheltering at or fleeing through the Villa Pisanella tossed a sack of silverware into a wine vat. Beside the vat, the skeleton of a woman entered the fossil record. Inside the vat, a silver-garlanded cup preserves first-century Rome's sense of dark humor, and perhaps (if one looks closely enough) the irony of random chance as well. The cup's entire outer surface is decorated with silver skeletons holding silver sacks, each corpse a laughing figure inscribed with the name of a dead philosopher. The skeleton identified as Epicurus stands at a table, with a dog at his feet. He grabs a large handful of cake from the table, while the dog appears to bark disapprovingly. Beneath the dog, these words appear: "Enjoy life while you have it, for tomorrow is uncertain."

THE BEGINNING OF THE END is marked by a transition from white pumice to gray pumice, deposited about waist-high from the original ground surface. At a depth of just over 4 feet (125 centimeters), the nature of the eruption begins to change—subtly, at first. According to Haraldur's accumulation rates, this depth corresponds to between 5:00 and 5:30 P.M., and possibly as late as 6:00 P.M. Admiral Pliny's ships had probably turned southward toward Stabiae by this time. If not, the arrival of gray pumice on his decks, accompanied by a corresponding increase in the destructive power of dense, lithic stonefalls (spreading from the diameter of quail eggs to hen's eggs, from 3 centimeters to 7 centimeters), was soon guaranteed to force a retreat.

Near the transition between afternoon and evening, the gray pumice, snowing down upon the white, marks a compositional change. Two miles beneath the mountain, the magma reservoir was stratified compositionally, somewhat in the manner that a froth of fresh cream will float in a cup of cappuccino. The cup's contents simply separate, or stratify, into layers of thick cream and less buoyant coffee. Up to this point in the eruption, the white pumice, covering the streets, rooftops, and gardens of Pompeii, has been emerging from the "cream," floating on top of the magma reservoir. The eruption, as it progresses, is tapping different levels, emptying first from the top, then excavating deeper and deeper into the constantly rising pool. As evening approaches, the volcano, in a manner of speaking, is reaching for coffee.

One interesting result of this sequence puts the material at the top of the magma chamber (the cream) at the bottom of Pompeii's pumice record, while the material nearer the bottom of Vesuvius (the dark coffee) ends up settling on top. Like a Vesuvian upside-down cake, the strata (or succession of layers) occurring within the earth are found inverted upon the earth.

The white magma, from the top of the reservoir, emerged cooler than the gray, and its bubbles of frozen glass had trapped more water. The gray magma that erupts behind it is, by comparison, drier than an old bone; yet in water's place are liquid carbon dioxide and other compressed, deep-Earth gases. Thus, as the sun sets upon the still ash-free streets of Herculaneum, and evening progresses into night, the dark magma erupts more ferociously than the white.

According to Pliny the Younger, in the direction of the mountain, broad sheets of fire appear at several points—leaping out there—and the coming of night amplifies their brilliance and terrifies those who watch from afar, either from land or aboard the admiral's ships.

"My uncle tried to allay the fears of his companions," Pliny the Younger reports. By 9:00 or 10:00 P.M., Pliny the Elder reaches Stabiae and will soon find himself trapped in a house, under a deepening tomb of gray pumice. As it turns out, most of the elder Pliny's companions (but not the admiral himself) will live to tell the tale of Stabiae. While it is possible for the admiral to still walk freely about the town, dictating notes, almost 6 miles (10 kilometers) north of him, in Pompeii, the fallout is rising toward 7 feet (2 meters), and it will soon be a story deep. Throughout the northern city, by 10:00 P.M., some of the homes have undoubtedly collapsed. But very few of the people who remain behind have actually died in the collapse of Pompeii's buildings. Most survive by continuing to walk on top of the deepening layers of sponge stone and ash, as one walks upon deepening snow. Most of Pompeii's stragglers will still be alive when the sun rises.

Pliny the Younger tells us that his uncle was always able to manage with a minimum of sleep; but after reaching Stabiae and trying to allay people's fears, "[h]e then went to rest and certainly slept, for as he was a stout man his breathing was rather hard and heavy and could be heard by people coming and going outside his door."[1]

---

[1] There is no mention that Pliny the Elder either married or stayed married for very long. Given his nephew's mention that the admiral-explorer was able to snore louder than erupting Vesuvius, it becomes easy to understand why Pliny the Elder also came to be known as Pliny the Lonely.

The younger Pliny notes that, while the admiral sleeps, the court-yard outside his room fills with pumice stone and powdery ash, making it difficult, by the time the fallout is ankle-deep, to pull doors open from the outside and gain access to the room. Pliny does not give us the time his uncle went into the room and pulled the door shut behind him. Exhausted from the voyage, it appears likely that he retired before midnight, earlier than usual, while Pompeii lay under a shroud blacker than the deepest mine shaft and while Herculaneum still lay in starlight.

No one knows, for sure, how long the admiral remained awake at Stabiae. But around midnight, while Pliny the Elder sleeps, or while he prepares for sleep, every living creature in Herculaneum dies within a span of split seconds. Every plant dies. Even the bacteria die.

"STRONGER," Haraldur Sigurdsson says. "The eruption column (the stalk of the mushroom cloud) is getting stronger—which means it is, at the very same time, developing weaknesses. Sooner or later, it's bound to happen. Sooner or later, gravity wins and takes over, with increasingly powerful downblast effects."

Born of a balancing act between a mountain that "wants" to sink toward the center of the earth, and a chamber of magma ballooning toward the surface, the eruption column is, in its own right, a balancing act—one of nature's most precarious and spectacular.

At Vesuvius, the inevitability of imbalance, and eruption-column collapse, is dictated by a simple (and deadly) mathematics: As objects of the same shape increase in size, volumes increase faster than surface areas. As the eruption column increases in width, it suffers a continual decrease in surface area relative to volume.

The throat of the volcano, or nozzle, is like a gravel-filled rocket engine aimed at the stars. For the first mile or two, bits of glowing dust and pumice are dominated by the forces rocketing them out of the earth. Emerging at twice the speed of sound, the magma debris reaches an altitude of 2 miles (3.3 kilometers) in just over five seconds. During this interval, the particles have transferred much of their heat to air scooped up through the sides of the ascending exhaust plume; and the buoyancy of superheated air (which enters the plume, or column, through its surface area) becomes, during the next few miles and seconds, more dominant than the force of ejection. If the eruption debris is to continue ascending, the column must be able to take in tremendous volumes of air through its sides; the column must be able to breathe. Should the diameter of the mountaintop's puncture, or "nozzle," be increased, the unbreakable relationship between surface area and volume will begin to choke the eruption column. Portions of it may even stall and collapse. When this happens, one's only hope for survival is to be very, very far away.

"Now, the diameter of the nozzle inevitably increases during the eruption," says Haraldur. "Pushing all this material through, at high temperature and pressure, erodes the walls of the nozzle. And in Pompeii, during those first twelve hours, we see the signal of erosion and widening embedded in the white and gray pumice, in the fragmented rocks we call lithics."

As the eruption column dilates toward instability, boulders avalanching from the nozzle wall, into the nozzle itself, may be all that is required to break the balance between the forces trying to keep the column jetting skyward and the forces trying to drag it earthward and pull it apart.

Sections of the column, and finally the column itself, are forced into collapse six times during the second day of the eruption. The shock wave from the third collapse dissipates just short of Pompeii's northern gate, between 6:00 and 6:30 on the morning of August 25. Tracking backward through accumulations of gray pumice, Haraldur Sigurdsson is able to map an earlier, second surge of fused glass, residing 8 feet (2 meters) below the third collapse. This second, ankle-deep sheet of glass extends halfway between Herculaneum and Pompeii. The intervening 8 feet of pumice, between the third glass surge and the second (given an approximate pumice accumulation rate, at this point in the eruption, of 35 to 45 centimeters per hour), places the second collapse between 1:00 and 2:00 A.M. In Herculaneum, a knee-to-waist-deep accumulation of gray pumice separates the second collapse layer from the streets and the first collapse, suggesting that the first of six volcanic death clouds reaches the city about midnight, or shortly thereafter.

When the delicate balance between gravity and the forces trying to hoist the eruption column through the stratosphere is finally undone, gravity cannot fail to take over.

The early-morning collapse—the first downblast, the first surge cloud—must have resembled an atomic mushroom cloud turned on its head, descending from its stem instead of rising upon it. Within the cloud, every volcanic grain, as it falls to Earth (whether it is as large as a basketball or smaller than a grain of sand), trails a tiny slipstream of air. Every slipstream, the uncounted trillions of them, adds its own mass to the collective, descending whole.

The resulting downblast is not controlled by ejection rates, or by the tendency of heat to rise, or by the force of the southeasterly wind pushing away from Herculaneum and toward Pompeii. Crashing to Earth, it takes no notice of anything except gravitation.

Finding its path blocked by the earth itself, it explodes outward—"its path controlled, now, by the geometry of the ground it is collapsing into," Steve Carey explains, "and by the geography of the land over which it is flowing." It plows along streambeds, tossing the trees to either side, away from the stream center. "Once it starts to flow," says Carey, "it's a gravity curve, basically. A gravity bomb."

Haraldur Sigurdsson, Steve Carey, and the other tunnelers into Herculaneum have a very clear picture of what happens to the city as the surge cloud passes through. The pool in Herculaneum's sports complex is filled with seething volcanic dust particles left behind in the wake of the surge, whereupon they fuse together and harden, instantly, into dark granular glass. The hardened glass, like the organic gemstone amber, is a natural preservative of everything dislodged, and stirred into, and carried by the surge. Bits of carbonized paper and wood, uprooted stone columns, shattered roof tiles, parts of someone's mosaic floor, chunks of brick, a shred from a priest's robes, another shred from a slave's rags—all are stirred impartially by the storm, then baked and hidden in the earth, with an efficiency exceeding an entire army of Pharaoh's embalmers.

Nearly two millennia before Vesuvius, the Egyptians and Minoans had discovered that blending tin and copper produced a newer, stronger composite material possessing the properties of both metals, and yet at the same time like neither of them. In similar fashion, air mixed with pulverized rock is a composite of rock and atmosphere that behaves like neither. The air flows liquid, superheated, with the power of a tsunami. And this composite surge is capricious, with complex eddies and flows of varying density and temperature. Here, at the Herculaneum pool and sports complex, bronze statues have been pulled apart by the first surge cloud and strewn over an entire city block. Some of the nearer buildings are swept away and massive columns are overthrown, then telescoped one under another. And yet, only a few steps across the street, a table (at once undisturbed and disturbing) is still set for lunch when the first archaeologists arrive more than 1,900 years later. The room teaches us that the owners of a summer villa evacuated at the first sign of trouble, some twelve hours before the first Herculaneum surge. Oil lamps still hang from their brackets. Eggs, pistachio nuts, and a bowl of honey-sweetened cookies baked with a flower pattern are still intact—moderately overcooked by hot volcanic dust and clearly off the menu long before da Vinci was born, but intact nonetheless. A portion of a napkin, still upon the table when the dust was rafted (ever so gently) into this room, hints that the family maintained its poise at the moment of departure . . . around lunchtime, according to Pliny the Younger. His letters tell us that the umbrella pine cloud went up from the mountain around lunchtime, and shortly thereafter came the distress call from Lady Rectina, possibly from Herculaneum itself. But in the villa of the interrupted lunch, there is no impression of panic. A napkin and spoons are simply laid aside, and in orderly, polite fashion, a family slips away into history . . . And southward, down the street, part of a wooden partition in the Suburban Baths carbonizes to the core while, oddly, other pieces of wood on the same partition, as near as an arm's length away, are merely singed. The wood, as it enters the fossil record, preserves some of Herculaneum's smallest victims: termites . . . And in another home—archaeologists call it the "House of the Christians"—the wave from the east makes wood flash into charcoal; yet in an adjoining room of the same house, the dust has cocooned and preserved an entire drawer full of legal documents. The court battle is inscribed by stylus onto wax pages. The wax is unmelted.

In A.D. 79, on August 24, about lunchtime, some four thousand people are living in Herculaneum. Twelve hours later, when the first Vesuvian surge cloud reaches the sports complex and the House of the Christians, it finds scarcely more than a dozen people within the town itself.

"It must have been a very frightening sight, from the very first—this towering column," says Steve Carey. "Even today, standing in Herculaneum, Vesuvius looms so. It's easy to envision an eruption column towering 20 or

A city that died—to live on the edge of forever. The roots of trees, in the background, mark Herculaneum's posteruption ground surface. Sunrooms, palm verandas, and garden dining saloons took advantage of the Bay of Naples' natural beauty. In A.D. 2000, forensic archaeologists turned their attention to the strange physics that overtook three hundred people crowding the beach and sheltering under the arches of the Herculaneum marina. The first surge cloud had shattered their teeth and, before their nerves could respond, vaporized the people to the bone—all three hundred of them, all within two-tenths of a second.

30 kilometers overhead. Add lightning and seismic activity, and from the moment of the interrupted lunch, it had to be absolutely terrifying. You hear an explosion outside and you step into the street and you see this, and you know: 'This is not a place I want to be today.' So, the direction to go is away from it—west of Vesuvius—and that's basically out to sea.

"And it's not until this area near the beach is excavated that we begin to find the people—scores and scores of people, entire bedding planes of carbon and bone. It had been somewhat of a mystery, up to this point: Where did all the people go, in Herculaneum? Now, as the beach, and the boats, and the boathouses are excavated, we realize: They had left the town and gone down toward the coast."

There, in the boathouses, lie the Herculaneans. When you read your Pliny, you know that this is just as the witness had said it should be: According to the lunch-hour distress call received by the admiral, who was west of Herculaneum, across the Bay of Naples, Rectina's home was (just like Herculaneum) at the foot of the mountain, and (just like Herculaneum) was near water. With the local signaling towers apparently unobscured by the southeastward veils of Plinean phase ash (just as Herculaneum's towers would have been), Rectina implored the elder Pliny to rescue her by sea. Rectina reported that she was terrified, and that escape was impossible for her except by boat (again, just as in Herculaneum).

As the eruption column collapses and sends forth the first surge, the dust is five times hotter than seawater flashing to steam. It glows brighter than iron emerging yellow-white from a metalsmith's furnace, and, as near as forensic archaeologists can guess, it covers the 4 miles (or 7 kilometers) between the nozzle and Herculaneum in three to four minutes, probably in as few as two. But even two minutes in such situations can become elastic in the human mind, and time can be stretched to its outermost limits.

Glowing and roiling, and shedding lightning as it approaches, the midnight surge cloud doubtless gives people on the beach and near the boathouses a very clear portent of what is about to happen to them. The skeletons, as we see them today, have had time to see and to understand—and as the final approach vibrates through (and is amplified by) the ground itself—they have time for the beginning of a response; for to them, as their brains snatch up every detail, trying to find a way out, their world becomes high-definition video played out in slow motion, and seconds become lifetimes.

It can be a strangely quiet and peaceful end, once the brain shifts into maximum overdrive and the time-dilation effect kicks in. For some of the Herculaneans, in that final split second, there is a surprising and overwhelming sense that they are somehow watching their deaths through the eyes of someone else. And on the heels of this, fascination predominates, mingled with a strange regret: "No one I love who survives this, out there, beyond the fires, beyond the danger, will know that this is really not so bad as their imaginations will make it seem to them . . . This isn't so bad . . . It's more astonishing than bad. And my only regret is that I'll never live to tell—"

I know this to be true, for I have walked my mile in the Herculaneans' sandals. In 1975, the truck I was driving was pierced by engine parts from a crashing 727 jetliner. One hundred twenty people died around me; yet I regained consciousness in an apparent shock cocoon, with the truck somehow still able to be driven away under its own power. I survived the afternoon with only a bump on my head, and an inexplicable craving for chocolate. Sir Arthur C. Clarke has theorized that I also survived with a craving for "maximum overdrive" and "time dilation." It's only a theory, and I don't entirely agree. Nevertheless, I've since been taken to the brink of death (and back from it) by a disease most physicians had never seen before, I've been plane-crashed again, then submarine-crashed (but no one was hurt). I've been rock-slided, tornadoed, shot at, slashed, stabbed, hand-grenaded, and almost blown up with the Dead Sea Scrolls (the grenade landed near me and fizzled, and no one was hurt).[2] And always, as time begins to distort, as the world becomes at once more real and more unreal, a sense of fascination takes hold, and there comes with it a

[2] This was in Jerusalem, during a 1991 incident at the Rockefeller Museum. In the aftermath of a failed attack in which the grenade turned out to be a dud, an archaeologist told me that "someone above must have really been watching out" for me, on account of the fact that while everyone else in the room had ducked for cover, I had remained standing, looking stupidly at the grenade, trying to decide whether or not it really was a grenade or just something that "really did look like" a grenade. "Don't let Pellegrino's head inflate with self-importance," said a rabbi. "God wasn't watching out for Pellegrino. Pellegrino just happened to be standing near the scrolls, and God did not want the scrolls to be harmed." Well, that just about sums up my place in the universe, doesn't it?

momentary but profound sadness born of the knowledge that no one outside the event will understand how it is rarely, if ever, so bad as they imagine it to be for those of us actually experiencing the event from the inside.

So it must have been for the Herculaneans.

(And so I know it must have been, 1,922 years later, for Captain Patrick Brown, up there with the burn victims he had found on the forty-fourth floor of Tower One. So it had to be—and I draw some small comfort from knowing this—so it *had to be* for him, and for Rescue 1's Terry Hatton and for John Sherry. So it had to be for my cousin Donna on the ninety-eighth floor, west side of Tower One, and for her coworkers Wayne Russo and Kristen Fiedel.)

So it must have been, even under Vesuvius, even in A.D. 79.

"And so, the first surge cloud starts out about midnight, or shortly after," says Haraldur. "It goes out radially from the volcano, with great speed and intensity. And nobody in Herculaneum lives to tell the tale."

As the hours pass, subsequent Vesuvian collapse columns (preserved in rock-forming strata of their own creation) produce the same radial surges, except that they are successively larger: first washing again over Herculaneum, solidifying over a dead city filled with dead people; then reaching the northernmost outskirts of Pompeii; then bursting through Pompeii itself; and finally reaching Pliny the Elder at Stabiae, and Pliny the Younger at Misenum. One Pliny is spared, the other taken.

Haraldur has supposed that some of those who ran to the Herculaneum boathouses might have witnessed the actual collapse of the column—20 miles high, glowing and collapsing, as if from directly overhead. It strikes the ground, less than 4 miles away, and as it splashes toward them, it is all downblast and fire and expanding dimensions.

On the beach, a Roman soldier is slammed facedown into the black sand with a force sufficient to crack every bone in his body, except those of the inner ear. Whatever the people see or hear, whether they are aware of it or not, they are trapped between the sea and the surge.

Haraldur has studied the skeletons of two horses in the Herculaneum marina's boathouses. There are forensic archaeologists who can describe year by year, from an analysis of teeth, how well a Roman workhorse, slave, or knight was fed throughout life. They can tell us, from an analysis of carbon isotopes, the ratio of meat to vegetables in an aristocrat's diet; but Haraldur Sigurdsson is much more interested in the positions of the skeletons: "Excavating very carefully, we can actually reveal footprints in the sand, leading under the arched brick-and-stone roofs of the boat shelters—and never coming out again. The horses are just in the bone pile, with the people, not very far from an overturned boat."

It is easy for us to imagine the riders; they almost definitely saw the incandescent tidal wave spreading over the earth, full of light, full of sparks. Most of the others must have seen it, too—which is why we find them under the arched roofs, with the horses. If the first instinct of the Herculaneans, from the start of the eruption, has been to move away from the volcano, then those who do not flee along the roads will attempt to evacuate by boat. When the surge cloud starts toward them, they have a minute—perhaps two—in which to seek shelter. (As a thought experiment, count off sixty seconds and you'll soon discover that a minute can be a very long time, infinitely longer when dilated by astonishment and fright.) Even those Herculaneans who are not on the beach—who happen only to be located nearby, on the terraces and foot-paths overlooking the marina—are driven instinctively away from the approaching cloud. "And that would take them right down to the beach," says Haraldur. "And then, when they reach the shore, there's nowhere to go. They have only two directions from which to choose: into the sea or under the arches (under the dry-dock garages).

"They are dead, either way.

"Their bones are still there, whispering of what actually happened to them. So many human skeletons lie next to the horses that still I can-not discern which of them were the riders. There are many questions still to be explored. I knew a woman who could tell from the pattern of muscle scars on a bone just how strong a cavalryman's shoulders were, and how hard he had worked during the last year of his life. The foren-sics people can tell you exactly how much lead had been consumed by any particular boathouse victim, putting to rest, as the archaeological equivalent of urban legend, the old theory that lead pipes were spreading an Empire-wide variant of 'Mad Hatter's disease,' and that heavy-metal poisoning would soon herald the fall of Rome. Pompeii and Herculaneum are honeycombed with lead pipes, and the lead content of the bones is, in general, barely detectable—as we might have anticipated from what had long been known about the pipes themselves. They are heavily encrusted, on the inside, with a Roman plumber's darkest cloud: thick layers of calcium (but this cloud does have a silver lining; it forms a natural barrier between lead and the water supply).

"The forensics people, working from boathouse skulls, can even [by precisely reconstructing the original muscle structures that once covered the bones] answer the question of what these people looked like. The Roman soldier, for example (the soldier with the shattered bones), looked strong and brutish even without the battle scar that crossed his mouth. A slave girl of about sixteen, holding close to her the master's child, turned out to be remarkably beautiful—which could only have complicated her life."

But Haraldur, coming to the boathouse from the field of volcanology (and bringing with him, therefore, new questions about the physics of eruption), is much more interested, when thinking about bones and ash, in asking, "How many people are facing the rear wall, or glancing back toward the boat shelter entrance? How many people are lying on their faces? How many are on their backs?"

Haraldur notes that most of the people died facing the rear wall: "Facing *into* the boat chambers, virtually all of them. Their heads are pointing aft, and most of them are lying facedown, or with their arms sheltering them from something that is approaching the front door. They do not want to see what is coming."

The cloud shoots seaward, over the beachfront villas and terraces, three stories above the boathouses. For a second or two it surges westward over the water; but the beach and the boathouses, now located below and aft of the overburst, draw the lower surface of the cloud down, and whip it eastward and landward, as if into vacuum.

"The people, at this instant," Haraldur observes, "are crowded into the far ends of the chambers, as far away as they can get from the openings. Some, including a mother and daughter, are stacked on top of each other. A few—very rarely—are lying on their backs. I'm not sure what's going on with *them.* Perhaps they were picked up and flipped over, or rolled by the force of the surge. That's quite likely. Or maybe a small minority of them, in the very end, wanted to stare, dead-on, at whatever was about to catch up with them, at what was about to come through that door."

Outside the door, an overturned boat lay in 20 inches (0.5 meter) of water. As the lower surface of the cloud whiplashes, reverses direction, and advances on the boat shelters, it converts the upturned wooden keel to charcoal, then continues, unimpeded, to the men hiding in an air pocket beneath the boat. Probably these men—almost certainly would-be rescuers—used the final minute separating them from the surge to tip the 26-foot (8-meter) boat over and scrabble underneath, hoping to use it as a shield. It is the most logical move available to them at this kind of time. The maneuver actually buys them a little more life. By the time the cloud reaches through the wood, and converts the men to gas, they have outlived the soldier on the beach and the people in the boathouses by almost three seconds.

The boat chambers are a grave for more than three hundred people. The ash, when it reaches them, is hot enough to immediately vaporize all soft tissues, leaving only bones, traces of tendon, and, oddly, singed clothing. To bring such rapid devastation, the cloud, as it enters the chambers, must be burning at five times the boiling point of water (about 1,060 degrees Fahrenheit, or 500 degrees Centigrade), a temperature exceeding the thermal shock that, 1,000 feet (or 0.3 kilometer) from the Hiroshima bomb, created "shadow people."

Within the chambers, the cloud shatters teeth. The inner surfaces of skulls are blackened by the sudden expansion and disintegration of brain tissue, and by the instantaneous boiling of blood. The flesh simply disappears, leaving only glowing bones, rafting slightly on the settling ash, as ripples in a pond might raft sticks of wood. In one corner, the bones of an unborn child lie caged beneath his mother's ribs.

Except for the soldier, whose fingers are either grasping at air as he is thrown down, or curling involuntarily as they disintegrate, none of the skeletons are in positions suggestive of agony. Indeed, their eyes and tongues and brains have ceased to be, by the time the nerves in their fingertips can even begin to register and transmit pain. Once it touches them, the cloud leaves no time for grimacing, no time even to flinch. The time frame in which the activity of nerves and muscles stops is shorter than conscious reaction time; the velocity of volcanic dissolution exceeds the speed of astonished thought. The muscles themselves, with some of their localized nerve bundles intact, last several hundredths of a second after death—just long enough for a single involuntary contraction to occur before ash surrounds the bones and solidifies instantly in the spaces left by disappearing muscle and tendon. (Invariably, the feet are flexed away from the calves and thighs, as if to strike a swimming pose; but the toes are flexed in the wrong direction for a swimmer—they "curl" upward, toward the shins.)

Within two-tenths of a second, it is all over. What happens next requires five additional full seconds. By comparison to death itself, the condensation and crystallization of the ash, as recorded in the first boat chamber surge layer, unfolds in slow motion.

A human body is more than 70 percent water. The same cloud that disintegrates three hundred human beings (and two horses) releases into the air of those chambers a volume of steam that at first contact (at the instant before disintegration and release) is seventeen times cooler than the surge cloud itself. The boathouse becomes, in effect, a large and very efficient heat exchanger. As the surge cloud converts blood and fat into incandescent gas and black steam, the cloud's heat is simultaneously absorbed by its victims. As blood boils, the cloud cools.

Two seconds after the cloud enters the chambers, its temperature has plunged nearly 80 percent (down to nearly 212 degrees Fahrenheit, or 100 degrees Centigrade, while the world outside still roils at approximately 500 degrees Centigrade). Still hotter than live steam but several times cooler than eruption column ash, the boat chamber cloud (after an initial split second of steam-driven expansion) begins to condense implosively. For an instant there is a geologic fog in the air, then a snowstorm indoors, its flakes made of crystalline granite and basalt. The "cold" condensate deflates toward the floor, naturally. During the next few tenths of a second, deflation is amplified by fresh surge-cloud air and dust—which falls in immediately behind the implosion and presses the condensate more forcefully into the spaces between the bones. The newly arriving material is, in its own turn, cooled upon contact with the deflationary layer, and rapidly hardens in place.

Throughout the city, wood proves to be more resilient than flesh. On an avenue where the newest, cheapest apartment houses are built in a style anticipating English Tudors, the cross-beams and the supporting structures of balconies develop black "alligator skin" blisters more than an inch deep. And then, for two reasons, the burning stops. First, as fire-walkers prove every day, carbonized wood is a very effective insulator. Second, as the surge-cloud dust coats and ignites every object in its path, it acts very much like sand thrown onto a campfire: The dust, though hot, smothers the very fires it starts, before the buildings can actually burn.

In most instances, the depth to which wood converts to charcoal is determined entirely by the temperature of a localized eddy within the cloud. Above the boat shelters, outside the Suburban Baths, major support beams, wider than a human skull, are carbonized to the core. Inside the entrance to the baths, a beam thicker than a man's fist also carbonizes to the core; and yet within arm's reach, the vagaries of the cloud are demonstrated by finger-thick planks that are merely baked brown inside, beneath paper-thin surface singeing. The undamaged planks are then smothered and encased—instantly—in a relatively cool and crumbly sheath of fossil-impression-forming ash. If the surge cloud sheath were to prove itself imperfect and if the uncarbonized wood were to vanish utterly (as in the case of Pompeiian wood), a plank's individual growth bands would still be visible in the hot-ash impression, nineteen centuries later.

Hot pumice and ash, trailing behind the surge cloud, continue to spill from the eruption column—slower and in some places cooler than the surge, but in most places above 300 degrees Centigrade (Fahrenheit 636), a heat sufficiently fierce to make glass glow and drip, and to fuse individual ash particles together. Streets and balconies, gardens and rooftops, are encased in a city-spanning bedding plane of solid rock, hard enough to resist the archaeologist's chisel. Flowing seaward, like a semiliquid mist, the bedding plane is waist-deep within an hour or two of the first surge.

Sometime after 1:00 A.M., the second surge cloud sweeps over

Herculaneum. As yet, no one in Pompeii, Stabiae, or Misenum knows that the city is quite dead. During the next four or five hours, as the eruption intensifies, Herculaneum is buried fully a story deep in a variously glass-hard and siltstone-hard bedding plane of solidified fallout.

Then, about 6:30 A.M., the third surge cloud sweeps over the city and fells every refugee still on the road between Herculaneum and Pompeii. When finally its southward edge stalls, the cloud deposits the southernmost samples of its distinctive glass just outside Pompeii's north gate.

An hour later, Vesuvius has buried Herculaneum's third surge deposit under two additional stories of pyroclastic fallout—which now cocoons the buildings and cushions their walls against increasingly violent tremors. It is almost 7:30 A.M. when the fourth Vesuvian downblast surges forth.

"In Pompeii, the pumice and ash are relatively loosely settled and relatively cold," says Haraldur. "But it is still fully one story deep.

"We find fewer than two thousand bodies in Pompeii itself, meaning that about 90 percent of the population has been able to get away from the city, by the time the fourth surge cloud crashes through. This fourth cloud—the 7:30 surge—has shed much of its heat along the way and is not quite so hot as the Herculaneum clouds: 'only' about twice the boiling point of water (Fahrenheit 424), just below the flash point of paper. But this is enough.

"Clearly, the evacuees have been moving southward throughout the night, away from the volcano and toward Stabiae. Probably they were walking in total darkness, under heavy ashfall, from the moment of their departure, between the afternoon of August 24 and the early morning of the twenty-fifth. They have managed to get away from Pompeii by the time the fourth surge cloud arrives in the city, but I suspect they are then overtaken by the fifth surge, and certainly by the sixth, because the last two surges extend all the way to Admiral Pliny in Stabiae, more than 4 miles (7 kilometers) south of Pompeii."

Haraldur does not believe that most of the people on the south road have abandoned Pompeii prior to the early-morning, post-Herculaneum earthquakes or before the third surge cloud almost reaches the north wall of Pompeii, near 6:30 A.M.: "The third surge cloud stirs many of Pompeii's stragglers to action and shepherds them south. Then, about

The skulls of the Pompeiians are usually found inside hollow fossil impressions of their bodies. Even folds and wrinkles in clothing have been preserved by the surge cloud, during the last seconds of life, as the cloud overtook the people. When explorers encounter the Pompeiians, their bones are lifted out of the earth within coffins of cement pumped into the hollow spaces. The resulting casts memorialize Vesuvius's mysterious Medusa effect, in which the people of Pompeii appear to have been converted instantly to stone, as if they had looked upon the face of the Gorgon.

7:30 A.M., seven or eight hours after Herculaneum dies, the fourth surge totally decimates Pompeii. As in Herculaneum, the bodies of the Pompeiians are not found in the pumice layers. They are not found (as archaeological legend would have it) suffocating quietly on the original ground surface and then being buried by the fallout. Instead, they are, in the end, walking on top of the pumice layers—one story deep—when the sun rises on the eruption column during the morning of August 25, 79."

Within Pompeii itself, the last stragglers are located atop drifts of pumice, at the surge-four level, about 7:30 in the morning. No one has explained what they were seeking, or why they continued to wander vacant streets in which fields of ash reached to second-floor balconies, and entire houses were continually imploding under the press of pumice, threatening to suck passersby into the earth, much as ants are drawn into the tiger beetle's den.

Half buried—
—under the
Gorgon's gaze.

I have recalled, for Haraldur, the example of stragglers aboard the sinking *Titanic*. Passenger Edith Russell's letters to Walter Lord memorialize how she returned to her stateroom to tidy up drawers and closets, before seeking the safety of a lifeboat. Helen Candee's diary recorded how her friend Colley had simply announced, early in the sinking while Officer Murdoch was allowing men to enter the boats, that he was going to his bed in a cabin located several decks below, and that he intended to stay there. He was never seen again.

Haraldur noted how Pliny the Elder—after reaching the imagined safety of Stabiae—had gone to bed during the eruption, and how Pliny the Younger had decided to stay home and read a book, as if, in a time of obvious danger, an Edith Russell–esque nesting instinct had taken hold of them.

"It's always interesting to study how we human beings behave in extraordinary situations," says Haraldur. The Pliny letters make clear how even people who should know better, when they are endangered, may deny that any danger exists at all, and will often latch onto the imagined safety of the familiar, the comfortable, the commonplace.

"Thus," observes Haraldur, "Colley's attitude, or Pliny's: 'There's nothing to worry about! I'm going to bed! Leave me alone!' That's a natural reaction."

And then something rumbles down from the sky, and it is easy to imagine Pliny the Elder awakened by hurrying feet in the hallways, and by people knocking on his bedroom door—

And at 7:30 A.M. Pompeii, like Herculaneum before her, becomes a dead city filled with dead people. And the eruption continues to intensify. Fifteen minutes after it forms, Herculaneum's fourth surge layer is buried under 7 feet of fused ash, and Pompeii's first surge layer (this same 7:30 surge) lies under more than 2 feet (0.6 meter) of glowing dust. In the second dead city, this fourth Vesuvian surge cloud, and the ash that flows in behind it, is instantly lethal, despite being an iced-over lake by comparison to the Herculaneum fossil beds. The Pompeiian ash consolidates around clothing, hair, and soft tissues. It does not, like Herculaneum ash, vaporize flesh and close in on the bones; in time, bacteria-laden rainwater seeping down from above will remove all but bones, leather garments, and items of jewelry—which will collapse into piles at the bottoms of fossil impressions turned to voids in the ground.

When archaeologists of the future pump the voids with quickhardening plastic and scrape the ash away, they will find a vanished child clothed in vanished silk, his final, deceptively sleepish movements visible in the folds of silk, the tilt of the head, the expression of his fingers, as if he were a life-size Michelangelo sculpture rendered in marble and not a fossil cast filled with the bones of a child.

Pompeii's second surge layer (Herculaneum's fifth) arrives about 7:45 A.M., sweeping through town at about 120 miles (200 kilometers) per hour. Despite the cocooning effect of the previous night's fallout, the ash-heavy air has a power comparable to a tsunami rushing through midtown, or to a column of advancing tornadoes. The fist of rock-laden air passes through the upper stories of houses, protruding through the sea of pumice, as if their walls do not exist. With few exceptions, they are imploded and instantly buried, or their contents are scooped up and flung southward; sometimes both fates are suffered simultaneously by the same building.

Fifteen minutes later, Herculaneum's fifth surge layer lies under another full story of glowing debris. Then, about 8:00 A.M., the sixth and final surge cloud—the largest and deadliest of them all—spreads radially over Herculaneum and Pompeii, surges outward to all points of the compass, south toward Stabiae and Admiral Pliny's fleet, west toward Misenum and Pliny the Younger.

By 9:00 A.M. the eruption is abating. The sixth Herculaneum surge layer has gained an additional story of postsurge fallout, and the entire city now lies beneath a fusion crust more than six stories deep. Pompeii, in sharp contrast, is buried under cooler, looser material and lies barely more than one story ("only" 12 feet, or 3.6 meters) underground.

"The lethal agent in Pompeii was the fourth surge," Haraldur emphasizes. "The fifth and the sixth—following in quick succession over the course of an hour—simply helped to fossilize everything (and everyone) underneath. In addition to bodies, the surge layers contain all of the building material that was carried along by the cloud. The surge layers (though rarely more than 3 inches, or 7 centimeters, thick) contain all the carbonized wood, shattered roof tiles, melted glass, and pieces of brick. The fallout deposits—even the pyroclastics trailing in the slipstream of downblast and ground surge—contain none of this material. So we have two very different behaviors in these killing winds. The pumice and ash layers are formed mostly by vertical deposition, as during a gentle snowfall on a windless night or, at worst, under moderately blizzard-like conditions. In between these [lightly packed] layers we have the thinner, darker surge-cloud events," and these are nothing except lethal, horizontal velocities.

In Pompeii's first surge-cloud layer (the 7:30 A.M. layer), all the clothing surrounding the victims, and all the bacteria lining the insides of their mouths, their throats, and their lungs, had been sterilized. The bacteria died with the same amazing rapidity as their hosts. Only deep inside their bone marrow and in the roots of tooth abscesses do forensic archaeologists find evidence that bacteria survived the Pompeiian surge and burial. This means that, at 7:30 A.M., the immediate environmental surroundings where the Pompeiians fall are hot enough to boil and sterilize skin, clothing, and throats—to autoclave people, hundreds of people, while still alive.

By 9:00 A.M., the three Pompeiian surge clouds have come and gone, and the eruption is ending. The Pompeiians lie bleeding under the earth, but deep in their abscesses and their marrow, methane- and iron-metabolizing bacteria will live on and multiply, until the food runs out, about two hundred years later. Then they will form protective clots, or "cysts," and in this manner, in suspended animation, they will still be alive when biologists of the twenty-first century find them.

It is 9:00 A.M. in Pompeii. And several miles to the south, in the town of Stabiae, Admiral Pliny has breathed his last.

Some nine hours earlier, the admiral was likely asleep when Herculaneum died; but none of those who lived through the night said so definitively, in any record that survives. Pliny the Younger, in his letters to Tacitus, makes reference to his uncle trying to convince the people with him in Stabiae that the "broad sheets of fire" moving ominously in the north, over the ground, "their bright glare emphasized by the night," were in fact nothing to worry about, and that the better part of valor, that night, was to go to bed and try to get some sleep. If the admiral went to sleep after midnight, after the death of Herculaneum, it is possible that the broad sheets of ground-hugging glare, about which the admiral tried to allay fears, were in fact the last moments of Herculaneum, seen from 12 miles (20 kilometers) away.

Pliny the Younger tells us that sometime during the night, after watching the distant and widespread glare, his uncle "went to rest and certainly slept." While he slept, the eruption intensified, the column climbed 20 miles (33 kilometers) into the sky, and its fallout began descending upon Stabiae. The courtyard giving access to the admiral's room filled with a constantly rising layer of "ashes mixed with pumice stones," and, as Pliny the Younger tells it, "If he had stayed in the room any longer, he would never have got out."

Evidently, the admiral's door opened onto the courtyard from the inside of the house. To make egress so difficult as to preclude escape, the fallout must have, by this time, accumulated knee-deep at Stabiae, and perhaps deeper. At this depth, collapsing roofs have become a legitimate worry. Probably, the pumice level has required several hours to rise knee-deep, suggesting that Admiral Pliny slept at least as long: up to, or about, sunrise.

Pliny the Younger records, from the accounts of those who survived his uncle's voyage, that "the buildings were now shaking with violent shocks, and seemed to be swaying to and fro as if they were torn from their foundations. Outside, on the other hand, there was the danger of falling pumice-stones, even though these were light and porous; however, after comparing the risks [of staying indoors and awaiting collapse or going outdoors and facing a pelting], they chose the latter. In my uncle's case one reason outweighed the other, but for the others it was a choice of fears. As a protection against falling objects they put pillows on their heads tied down with cloth.''

The increasing ferocity of the eruption column, as manifested by progressively violent ground shocks and heavy debris falling as far away as Stabiae, is perfectly consistent with a buildup toward an ever-widening and ever more lethal series of column collapses and surge clouds. Pompeii died about an hour and a half after sunrise, when the fourth Vesuvian surge cloud reached it, about 7:30 A.M. In the account of his uncle's death, Pliny the Younger supplies us with yet another time probe, with which we can compare eyewitness accounts against the story told by rocks, fossils, and artifacts: "Elsewhere it was daylight by this time, but [in Stabiae] they were still in darkness, blacker and denser than any ordinary night, which they relieved by lighting torches and various kinds of lamps. My uncle decided to go down to the shore and investigate on the spot the possibility of escape by sea, but he found the waves still wild and dangerous."

Pliny the Younger's own eyewitness account in Misenum, 24 miles (39 kilometers) west of Stabiae, across the Bay of Naples (and 15 miles west of Herculaneum), picks up the events of August 25 after a friend from Spain arrives at the house and scolds him for reading a history book when he should be evacuating further west. "Nevertheless," he recalls, "I remained absorbed in my book. By now it was dawn, but the light was still dim and faint [for the Sun had not yet broken the eastern horizon—which was higher now, on account of the monstrous black curtain from Vesuvius]. The buildings around us were already tottering, and the open space we were in was too small for us not to be in real and imminent danger if the house collapsed. This finally decided us to leave the town."

At dawn, Pompeii still has more than an hour left to live, but the eastern flag and lantern towers must no longer be transmitting signals. Chillingly, no further news is coming from the direction of Herculaneum.

As Pliny the Younger, his mother, and their servants leave town, following a northbound road that keeps the Bay of Naples within view for all of its first 2.5 miles (or 4 kilometers), they are "followed by a panic-stricken mob of people wanting to act on someone else's decision in preference to their own (a point in which fear looks like prudence), who hurried us on our way by pressing hard behind in a dense crowd."

The younger Pliny's account vividly records the sixth and final surge at about 8:00 A.M. He also gives the time of his departure from the villa as shortly after dawn, meaning that, with the Bay of Naples constantly within view, they are still plodding along the same 2-mile stretch of road when the sixth surge cloud rolls toward them. They have therefore advanced at a rate of fewer than 2, and probably less than 1, mile per hour.

Pliny's description of the Misenum exodus gives us a view (albeit only a fractional view) into what people must have experienced along the westward escape route out of Herculaneum (from which he leaves us no mention of survivors reaching Misenum), or during the even darker exodus, under constant ashfall, southward out of Pompeii toward Stabiae. Pliny the Younger's chronicle of the evacuation from Misenum, taking place in daylight and without the eruption column towering directly overhead, is dramatic despite the realization that it can barely furnish criteria for the manifestations everywhere along the Herculanean and Pompeiian exodus routes on those twenty-fourth and twenty-fifth days of August.

The slow progress made by Pliny the Younger is comparative and instructive, indicating that Haraldur Sigurdsson's belief in some eighteen thousand human skeletons strewn between Pompeii and Stabiae is a theory bearing currency.

Young Pliny's group, pressed hard from behind by a crowd of fellow refugees, is still within sight of his family's villa and its surrounding buildings, when the manifestations themselves compel the young naturalist to stop. "And there," his letters say, "we had some extraordinary experiences which thoroughly alarmed us. The carriages we had ordered to be brought out began to run in different directions though the ground was quite level, and would not remain stationary even when wedged with stones." This is the point at which Pliny observes the sea withdrawing, as often happens in advance of a tsunami. "[A]t any rate it receded from the shore," writes Pliny, "so that quantities of sea creatures were left stranded on dry sand. On the landward side [in the east, across the Bay of Naples] a fearful black cloud was rent by forked and quivering bursts of flame, and parted to reveal great tongues of fire, like flashes of lightning magnified in size."

Then, still looking toward the opposite side of the bay, in the direction of Pompeii and Stabiae, he witnesses the collapse of the eruption column and the spread of a surge cloud. What he describes to Tacitus is probably the surge of the final and widest-ranging of the six clouds, about 8:00 A.M.: "Soon afterwards the cloud sank down to earth and covered the sea; it had already blotted out [the island of] Capri [19 miles, or 30 kilometers, southeast of Misenum] and hidden the promontory of Misenum from sight."

As the cloud, though all but fractionally spent, spread its outermost boundary over Misenum and its northern road, Pliny the Younger's mother "implored, entreated and commanded" him to escape as best he could, for "a young man might escape, whereas she was old and slow and could die in peace so long as she had not been the cause of [her son's] death too.

"[But] I refused to save myself without her," Pliny writes. "And, grasping her hand, I forced her to quicken her pace. She gave in reluctantly, blaming herself for delaying me. Ashes were already falling, not as yet very thickly; I looked round: a dense black cloud was coming up behind us, spreading over the earth like a flood."

As the cloud approaches, Pliny the Younger quits the evacuation: "'Let us leave the road while we can still see,' I said, 'or we shall be knocked down and trampled underfoot in the dark by the crowd behind.' We had scarcely sat down to rest when darkness fell; not the dark of a moonless or cloudy night, but as if a lamp had been put out in a closed room. You could hear the shrieks of women, the wailing of infants, and the shouting of men; some were calling their parents, others their children or their wives, trying to recognize them by their voices. People bewailed their own fate or that of their relatives, and there were some who prayed for death in their terror of dying. Many besought the aid of the gods, but still more imagined that there were no gods left, and that the universe was plunged into eternal darkness forevermore."

A minute passes. Then another. And then another. And another. Pliny writes that, finally, "A gleam of light returned, but we took this as a warning of the approaching flames rather than daylight. However, the flames remained some distance off; then darkness came on once more and the ashes began to fall again, this time in heavy showers. We rose from time to time and shook them off, otherwise we should have been buried and crushed beneath their weight. I could not boast that not a groan or cry escaped me in these perils, had I not derived some poor consolation in my mortal lot from the belief that the whole world was dying and me with it."

Across the water, in the direction his uncle had gone, Pliny had no way of discerning, through the darkness, what was happening. He notes in his letters to Tacitus that after the admiral discovered that reeling and wild waves, and false tides, had made escape by sea impossible, "[a] sheet was spread on the ground for him to lie down, and he repeatedly asked for cold water to drink." Then the sixth surge cloud reached Stabiae. There came "the flames and smell of sulfur which gave warning of the approaching fire, drove the others to take flight and roused [the admiral] to stand up. He stood leaning on two slaves and then suddenly collapsed, I imagine because the dense fumes choked his breathing by blocking his windpipe which was consistently weak and narrow and often inflamed."

Near Misenum, so heavy is the downpour of ashes from the sky that it has not only softened the features of buildings, roadways, and push-carts; it has also covered the people with the same thick, feature-softening gray, so that as one by one they rise from the ash to sitting and standing postures, Pliny the Younger finds it impossible to discern slave from priest, man from woman. As the ashfall abates, he compares the return of daylight to what he knows to be a comparatively ordinary event—an eclipse of the Sun: "For at last the darkness thinned and dispersed into smoke and cloud; then there was genuine daylight, and the sun actually shone out, but yellowish as it is during an eclipse. We were terrified to see everything changed, buried in deep ashes like snowdrifts. We returned to Misenum where we attended to our physical needs as best we could, and then spent an anxious night alternating between hope and fear. Fear predominated, for the earthquakes went on, and several hysterical individuals made their own and other people's calamities seem ludicrous in comparison with their frightful predictions. But even then, in spite of the dangers we had been through and were still expecting, my mother and I had still no intention of leaving until we had news of my uncle."

The bad news was not long in coming. After Pliny the Elder collapsed in the arms of his two slaves, inside the southeast margin of the sixth surge cloud, the servants fled. They evidently survived to tell how he died and to bring searchers to the place where he fell. The younger Pliny recorded that the next day, "when daylight returned," the admiral's body was found "intact and uninjured, still fully clothed and looking more like sleep than death."

The Plinys, because their works were favored by (or at least not condemned by) what was evolving into the Holy Roman Catholic Church, would have the rare distinction of surviving Saint Cyril's burning of the libraries. Their books and letters would be copied and recopied almost forever—and, curiously, at least one contemporary Christian passage would echo the younger Pliny's experience of the sixth surge cloud: "And I beheld when he had opened the sixth seal, and, lo, there was a great earthquake; and the sun became black as sackcloth of hair . . . And the second angel sounded and as it were a great mountain burning with fire was cast into the sea—And he opened the bottomless pit; and there arose a smoke out of the pit, as the smoke of a great furnace; and thus I saw . . . men killed, by the fire, and by the smoke, and by the brimstone [by hot sparks with the smell of sulfur]."

During the centuries that followed, the legend of cities under the foundations of Herculano, Resina, and Naples faded into urban myth, then faded altogether from memory. When at last the Dark Age gave way to Renaissance and steam engine, and when archaeologists found skeletons in Pompeiian voids, laid out, seemingly, in the peaceful attitudes of sudden sleep, the account of Admiral Pliny's suffocation provided a basis for assumption: that all the human fossils of Pompeii and Herculaneum died in the very same way as Pliny the Elder. With such grace did the Roman naturalist and admiral, more exception than Vesuvian rule, become, by mistake, both model and rule for a self-perpetuating textbook dogma.

SARA BISEL, like the people she studied, had an affinity for the shadows. Almost without the world noticing, beginning with the discovery of the Herculaneum marina in 1982, she gave birth to the field of forensic archaeology. And it was not an easy birth, either—but it was, if anything, infectious. No matter how far her "students" sailed away from Vesuvius, they always came back, bringing newcomers, and strange new ideas.

In 1982, Haraldur Sigurdsson met Sara Bisel for the first time. Three years later, he sailed off to the deep-ocean volcanic springs of the East Pacific Rise, with Robert Ballard and the crew of *Melville*.

During that autumn of 1985, fresh from the robot Argo's reconnaissance of the *Titanic*, the first crude photomosaic maps of the lost liner were being assembled aboard the *Melville*. The world's first experiment in "deep-ocean archaeology" proved to be one of the easiest archaeological puzzles of all time (at first glance, if not in actual fact). Nothing had to be dug out of sediments or ashes. It was all laid out for us in black-and-white photographs. And within those photomosaic maps—in the hydraulic bulldozing of the officers' quarters, in the peeling outward of bulkheads, in the kicking outward of deck rails—we began to detect the signatures of a column of water that had funneled 2.5 miles (4 kilometers) to the bottom, matching the bow's terminal velocity of approximately 35 miles per hour; and when the ship struck the seafloor and ceased to move, the slipstream kept pushing toward the bed of the Atlantic, etching into *Titanic*'s steel—with tidal-wave force and with crystal clarity—a perfect analogy of collapse column, downblast, and surge.

Connections . . . within connections . . . within connections . . . From Pompeii to the *Titanic* to Thera, the field Sara Bisel pioneered was drawing in volcanologists, paleontologists, physicists, and slowly converting us all, by accident, into archaeologists. It was only natural, then (and perhaps even inevitable), that after a decade or two we would all come round full circle to Vesuvius.

They called Sara "the Lady of the Bones." When Haraldur met her in 1982, someone at the Smithsonian Institution had only recently asked her to go to the marina at Herculaneum to see what she could learn about the skeletons, which were then newly exposed by the digging of a drainage ditch. Already equipped with a background in the science of crime scene investigation, and with an ever-deepening interest in archaeology, the prospect of applying forensic methods to a large population of Roman skeletons excited her from the start. She had always regretted that the Romans of ancient times cremated their dead. Ashes could not tell anyone very much. So, stepping backward through time, from the crime lab into Vesuvian surge deposits, Sara began to tell anyone who would listen to her that it was through their teeth and their bones that dead civilizations really spoke to us—"Or at least," she would often say, "to those of us who know how to listen."

Not everyone was willing to listen. Several American and Greek archaeologists, acting upon territorial instincts, and perhaps upon their own insecurities, expressed very jaundiced opinions about Sara's theories, and about Sara herself. They had little tolerance for a detective—an outsider, essentially—intruding upon cities they had been excavating and studying for decades; and then, while barely pausing for introductions, "pretending" to teach them something new.

She became a scholar without a school, according to Haraldur. "Initially, she was working with some support from the National Geographic Society and from someone at the Smithsonian, but mostly, you might say she was freelancing. She did not have much backing. She did not go through normal academic circles. She was not based in a university or a research institution. But she was driven, more than most people, to simply see things no one had ever seen before. Her creed was 'Just do it.'"

More than 1,900 years under more than 65 feet (19.5 meters) of volcanic debris had protected the skeletons. But once exposed to oxygen, changing humidity, changing temperature, and a new bacterial assault, time would begin to catch up with the Herculaneans, all three hundred of them, and to beat their bones into shapeless powder.

Sara Bisel invented and tested her preservative techniques after only two weeks on-site, whereupon the directors of the Naples Museum put her in charge of preserving the Herculaneans and assigned to her a team of assistants—much to the chagrin of more than one of her self-appointed competitors, who considered themselves her seniors and therefore more worthy than her of prestige.

During the nineteen years that followed, for ten months a year, six days a week, ten to fourteen hours a day, Sara directed the lifting of each bone (and often the entire rock matrix that surrounded it), its cleaning with toothbrush and paintbrush, and its final sealing behind an acrylic membrane. In her spare time she studied the bones, pried secrets from them, and filled volumes of notebooks with her observations.

If it appeared to some that she was rushing to cram years of excavation, preservation, and observation into as little time as possible—to cram everything in at once—to Haraldur Sigurdsson, that was because, she was. From the time Haraldur first met Sara Bisel, she had been fending off the great "plague" of the late twentieth century: cancer.

"She had a brilliant project," Haraldur recalls. "She took notes, and collected huge quantities of information."

What Sara could learn about individuals from their bones was more subtle than what a volcanologist or an archaeologist would look for in the postures of the skeletons. She was not trying to reconstruct the moment of death. She was not interested in the last three seconds, or minutes, or hours of life. She was far more concerned with what the chemistry of the bones revealed about the whole person—slave or soldier, fireman or shop owner—throughout the *entirety* of life.

The teeth of the people were in better condition than those of Sara and her contemporaries—probably on account of the comparably lower levels of sugar in the Herculanean diet, combined with a water supply that contained three times the normal amount of tooth-strengthening fluoride. A slave girl's skull preserved a mixture of European and Asian features—"a lovely face of rare proportion," Sara wrote. Ridges on her teeth recorded a history of malnutrition and successive fevers during childhood. Her "current" owners had seen to it that she was properly fed, although the muscle attachments around her shoulder blades and her femurs revealed that she had routinely lifted heavy objects and bore them up and down stairs or over hilly roads. High levels of strontium in her bones spoke of a diet rich in seafood. Cradled in her arms, close to her cheek, was the object that rendered her one of archaeology's and paleontology's most poignant fossil finds: a baby wearing a golden cupid pin and bells.

Some of the other archaeologists had assumed, initially, that the two gently intertwined skeletons were mother and child. But Sara's examination of the girl's pelvic bones revealed that she had never given birth to a child. She determined that the beautiful girl, about fourteen to sixteen at the time of her death, was the family's nursemaid, and that the child was her wealthy charge. On the night of August 24, they must have become separated from the rest of the family in the attendant chaos; it was diffi-

As others in the Herculaneum boathouses attempted to shelter themselves against the back walls or hide their faces from the approaching surge cloud, a fourteen-year-old slave girl cradled another woman's child under her chin. The posture of her bones suggests an attempt to soothe—until, all in two-tenths of a second, their soft tissues were converted to incandescent gas and their skulls were exploded from the inside, by the pressure of vaporizing brain tissue and boiling blood.

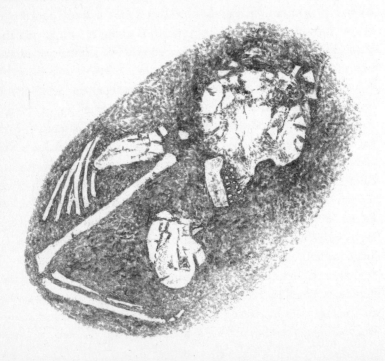

cult for Sara to imagine that a mother would willingly set off along a road, or out to sea, without her child. As the midnight surge cloud approached, the slave (only a child herself) lay down on her left side and cradled the infant under her chin in a posture suggesting that she was being simultaneously protective and soothing, giving her heartfelt love to another woman's child, as if it were her own.

The bones kept few secrets from Sara Bisel, but her ultrasaurian appetite for discovery was tempered by her one and only failing: a tendency toward writer's block. She kept meticulous notes (thousands of pages of them), but neither Haraldur Sigurdsson nor anyone else could get her to publish a paper about the sixteen-year-old boy whose bones recorded the markings of well-exercised chest muscles, from the time of early childhood. The development of upper-body strength from rowing in a standing position and hauling nets was identical to that seen in modern-day sons learning the fishing trade under their fathers in the very same Bay of Naples. The boy's teeth were worn deep into their enamel on the right side, in the very same manner that modern fishermen's teeth tend to become abraded and polished from holding fishing line in their mouths while mending nets. The only difference, Sara observed, was that the Herculanean boy's tool kit, though probably identical in appearance, must have been made of wood and bronze instead of plastic.

"A brilliant project," Haraldur laments, but there just seemed to be no power on Earth that could make her stop, and catch her breath just long enough to compile her dozens of notebooks into a series of fifty-page papers, or into a few books. Haraldur tried to get her to slow down and publish. He even offered to do most of the actual writing (or, rather, editing) for her, so that she would not have to pause for very long and the information would still get out to the world. "But she balked," he recalls. She just wanted to go onward and onward, exploring and recording new discoveries every day, for as long as she could, until she no longer could.

Some of Sara's discoveries did eventually get published; a tiny, tiny portion of them. By 2003 a new generation of archaeologists—*forensic* archaeologists—was arriving at Vesuvius, inspired by her and admiring her, and hoping to follow in her footsteps. But Sara Bisel did not live to

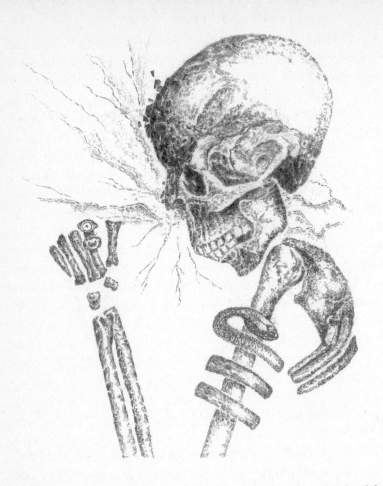

Embedded in a matrix of fused ash, Herculaneum's "Ring Lady" was felled with her collection of precious stones and two coiled shoulder bracelets, fashioned from solid gold, into snakes with matching jeweled eyes. She was about forty-five years old, taller than the average Roman, and in excellent health at the moment of her death. Her teeth, though crooked and "bucked," indicate a life history of good nutrition. By comparison, a slave girl who died nearby had ridges etched into several of her permanent teeth as they grew in. This indicated repeated episodes of malnutrition and/or illness that had interrupted calcium absorption while her "baby teeth" were being replaced.

see this. Carcinogen's angels had done their work: She died in 2001; and Haraldur Sigurdsson hopes that his friend's notebooks are still intact and being cared for somewhere. He hopes (as she had hoped) that they will eventually be studied, compiled, and published; for even though her discoveries are but fractionally revealed, fractional has proved remarkable enough. Fractional, in Sara Bisel's world, compares favorably to gazing through a time portal.

ITEM: A woman had been hurled to the beach by the surge cloud, apparently from one of the roads, balconies, or outdoor cafés above. Her skeleton was shattered so utterly that her pelvis was stamped flat and the bones of one leg snapped backward and impaled her head. Reading the coded language of the Herculanean's bones, Sara Bisel concluded that she was about forty-eight years old and postmenopausal, but her skeleton displayed no signs of arthritis, osteoporosis, or any other bone-wasting disease. She was not in good health, however. Though well-nourished throughout life, her skeleton differed from scores of others in having dangerously high levels of lead. She must have lived with acute symptoms of heavy-metal poisoning, including chronic fatigue, mental confusion, and violent mood swings. Lead decanters and warming vessels found throughout the city, with residues of their contents still intact, revealed that some Romans had an appetite for cheap, watered-down wine that was sweetened with syrup and then served like hot tea. Lead vessels tended to be the cheapest and least ornate kind, and boiling acidic wine in them was a guaranteed means of liberating lead into the solution. The woman with the smashed pelvis and broken neck had evidently fallen on unhappy times during the last years of her life. In the chemistry of the bones, Sara saw hints of a depressed and depressing personality that drank increasing volumes of toxin-laced wine. The lead, in turn, would have amplified feelings of depression and rage, and it was difficult for Sara to imagine that a woman in such condition cares very much whether she lives or dies. But in the end, the woman had gone down toward the marina, down to the place where people were being evacuated. In the end, she had chosen life over death, and was given death.

ITEM: A man trying to get the boats away died with an oar at his side. Muscle scars in his upper arms showed that he had labored at

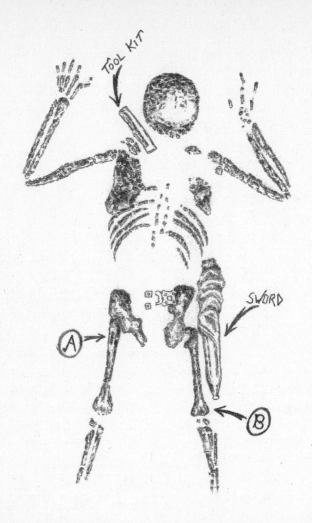

As he tended to the last of Herculaneum's "lifeboats," a Roman soldier was slammed onto the beach by the midnight surge cloud, his sword still at his side, a tool kit flung over his left shoulder. Forensic archaeologist Sara Bisel, "the Lady of the Bones," discovered a lump on the soldier's left femur (A), "where a wound [apparently a stab wound] had penetrated the bone and caused a blood clot that eventually had hardened." The lower extremities of both femurs (B) were unusually broad above the knee—which is consistent with the thickening seen among cavalrymen after years of gripping steeds between their knees. The midnight surge cloud pressed him into the sand with sufficient force to crack every bone, except those of the inner ear.

rowing, or at heavy construction work, or both, for many years. He was about fifty-five years old, and shorter than most of his contemporaries. Like those of the slave girl found clinging to a baby, his teeth bore scars of fever and malnutrition in youth. His bones, unlike the girl's, revealed that he was at least marginally malnourished throughout the remainder of his life. "He did not have good food, good treatment, good anything," Sara concluded.

ITEM: The force of the surge cloud, striking him from behind and pressing him into the beach, imploded a Roman soldier's lungs and cracked his ribs open. The impact of air and incandescent dust probably stopped his heart two-tenths of a second before it disintegrated. He was wearing two leather sheaths: one for a sword, the other for a dagger. When Sara first excavated the bones, his sword was still sheathed, but the dagger was missing. His money belt still bore three gold coins and two pieces of silver, reflecting Emperor Titus's recent increase in military salaries (as recorded by imperial biographer Josephus) to one gold coin per month. On his back, he carried a carpenter's kit, complete with hammer, wood-cutting tools, and chisels—which was consistent with Josephus's mention that legionnaires were expected to be efficient engineers and construction workers, and were required to carry on with a trade when on leave from soldiering. What fascinated most archaeologists were the tools, the sword, the coins. What fascinated Sara were the physical characteristics of the soldier's bones. The first thing she noticed was that he had stood taller than most people (at about 5 feet 10 inches, or 1.76 meters). At thirty-seven years old, he had been well exercised and well fed throughout life. He also had, without doubt, Sara noted, a high tolerance for pain: "When I examined the bone of his left thigh (the anterior ventral surface of his left femur), I could see a lump where a wound [apparently a stab wound] had penetrated the bone and caused a blood clot that eventually had hardened." About the time of the leg wound, three of his teeth had been knocked out. "He was a pretty tough character," Sara wrote, "[but] not at all good-looking. He lost those teeth, and his nose was really quite large." His face was rugged, even brutish in appearance. Bone growth had thickened his femurs, down near both knees, probably to accommodate the larger muscles needed to ride bareback—which suggested to Sara that he might have been a cavalryman. His arms were quite powerful, especially the muscles of his right forearm and shoulder, evidencing a muscular buildup developed during long sessions of practice with sword and shield. There is no way of discerning whether he was in Herculaneum on assignment or on leave, but when history found this experienced trooper, he was standing outside the shelters, in the open air, on the beach, doubtless trying to organize the rescue—manning the lifeboats until the last.

ABOVE THE SHORE, within the town of Herculaneum itself, the surge clouds (and the barely gentler mixtures of air and boiling dust that shifted lazily between surge deposits) left a record that is sometimes strange, other times merely disconcerting, and occasionally downright eerie. In the one-third of the city thus far excavated, fewer than a dozen skeletons (or skeleton parts) have been found outside the marina: Five bodies lying on a shelf in the Forum Baths . . . A man locked into an iron-barred cell in the Shrine of the Augustales . . . An adolescent boy in the gem-cutter's shop . . . A carbonized baby in a carbonized crib . . . Two skeletons lifted 25 feet (7.5 meters) above the city streets by an upwelling in the pattern of surge and flow, as if a tornado had occurred underground.

Tornadoes, whether made of air, or rock-laden air, or air-laden rock, have an inexplicable habit of completely exploding half of a home yet leaving the other half so intact that cups and napkins remain undisturbed on tables. The rock tornadoes of Herculaneum and Pompeii, like most tornadoes, seemed to express an inordinate fondness for contradictions.

At the marina, people vaporized more quickly and more thoroughly than if they had been located directly under the Hiroshima bomb. Yet in the House of the Christians (also known as the House of the Bicentenary), only a few hundred feet away, a testament against slavery, etched in wax, refused to melt.

The words are written in Latin; and they are court documents.

According to the Roman historian Gaius Suetonius (who was ten years old when Vesuvius erupted), the emperor Claudius had nurtured an intense distaste for the Greek language and, from the moment he ascended the throne in A.D. 41, endeavored to discourage its use by declaring Latin the official language of all government documents. In compliance with the still-extant Claudian decree, the wax tablets, the work of three different court stenographers, are recorded in Latin. They memorialize the struggle of a "hereditary slave girl" named Justa, who went to court and dared to declare her enslavement illegal and to prove her point by suing her master.

That this servile rebellion by legal memo instead of spears and catapults took place in the shadow of the Spartacan cliffs could not have escaped notice by the judges; nor could Justa's birth-given name— which, according to her mother, was derived from the Latin word *justitia,* "justice."

Justa's battle was recorded on tablets of wax-coated wood. The stenographers wrote on the wax with the pointed end of a pen-shaped stylus, and on several occasions they erased errors with the blunt end of the stylus, then wrote over their rubbings. The original wax engravings formed templates from which multiple copies could be made. (Wet clay, if allowed to harden against the wax letters, and if afterward baked, became something like a photographic negative, or a Roman-era photocopier, against which warm wax could be impressed to make multiple identical copies of the original . . . undoubtedly to be filed in triplicate somewhere.)

According to the wax, the story began about five years before the earthquake of A.D. 62 struck the Bay of Naples region. (According to Haraldur Sigurdsson, this quake was probably the first awakening of Vesuvius—which had been quiescent throughout all of Roman history.) About A.D. 57, a man named Gaius Petronius Stephanus had bought a woman named Vitalis—who would later give birth to Justa—as a wedding present for his wife, Calatoria.

The documents—which include subpoena dates, amounts of bail, property values of slaves, lists of witnesses, and transcripts of testimony— do not state how Vitalis came to be a slave in the first place. She commanded a "top shelf" price because she was educated, and was graded by the slave sellers as both articulate and highly intelligent. Surviving Roman records suggest that many born into slavery were barely fed by their owners and traders and were even less likely to be given expensive educations than good food. The contract of sale itself was claimed by Calatoria (the defendant slave owner) to have been destroyed during the earthquake of A.D. 62, but it was said to be (except for appropriate spaces to be filled in) identical to contracts used for the estate's cattle.

Calatoria acknowledged that Vitalis worked hard for her, was efficient and always courteous, and had gained such approval from Petronius that after only five years of ownership, he allowed her to go free. Apparently, in addition to working for the household, Vitalis was able to start and operate her own business. By A.D. 62 she had acquired enough gold to buy her own freedom. She gave her master a onetime lump-sum payment, plus a 5 percent "freedom tax" to the government, whereupon, as was the custom and the law, Petronius placed his hands upon Vitalis's head and said, in the presence of witnesses, "I declare this woman no longer bound."

Once free, Vitalis continued to work in Petronius's household (probably, though the court records do not say so, under salary). She also continued to live in the house and, in accordance with the custom of freed slaves, she even assumed her former master's name, becoming Petronia Vitalis.

In that same year, Justa was born. The court records do not name the father, but another slave, Gaius Petronius Telesphorus—who, like Vitalis, bought his own freedom, took the master's name as his own, and continued to work in the household—ultimately testified in favor of Justa and her mother and against an influential Herculanean family. Doubtless, this had a depressing effect on Telesphorus's career, as he must have anticipated it would. The impression from the testimony, and from the consequences knowingly accepted, is that there existed a strong bond of love between Telesphorus, Vitalis, and her daughter—possibly a family bond.

If there also existed love on the part of Petronius Stephanus for his former slave Vitalis, the records do not hint beyond a platonic or unrequited love. But we will never truly know.

Calatoria further acknowledged that until A.D. 72, when Justa was ten, Vitalis and her child dined nightly at the master's table, "as if they had been free-born Roman citizens and family members." A stenographer recorded a statement that Justa "was brought up like a daughter."

Calatoria added a complaint to this: she remarked that at some point Vitalis had forgotten her lowly post in life, had kissed her own hand, and needed to be reminded whence she came. Evidently, Calatoria was quick to perceive an insult and—whether real or simply imagined—once perceived, it was never forgotten.

Justa, meanwhile, had begun to grow up like her mother: brilliant, articulate, and fiercely independent . . . Or, as Calatoria would put it, and as at least one judge would agree, she was too smart and charming for her own good.

Calatoria had been tutored by Telesphorus, who had by A.D. 72 become the estate's administrator. He had further educated Vitalis when she was brought into the house as a gift for Calatoria, and it is clear from the transcripts in wax that Telesphorus and Vitalis had become very close.

Justa spent her childhood with two very good teachers, and by age five, about A.D. 67, she had learned to read and write. Calatoria's two children were born about A.D. 67, and Justa became their nursemaid, then their tutor. Nearly ten years later, Calatoria would claim that Justa had assumed these roles as a slave, not as a paid servant.

In A.D. 72, the internal human quake began. Petronius's health had started to fail. Simultaneously, as tremors overtook Petronius's hands, Calatoria ejected Vitalis from the house. Oddly, spitefully, Calatoria refused to let Justa depart with her mother and initiated proceedings to retain custody (initially as an adoptive parent, under the premise that Vitalis was somehow "unfit" to be a custodial mother). Petronius, growing progressively weaker as the battle lines were being drawn, sided with his wife.

During the next two years, Vitalis hatched a plan to either bribe her former owners to let her daughter go or, if requisite, to feed the prescribed sums of money into the legal system. Meanwhile, Telesphorus remained in Petronius's household and continued to watch over and tutor Justa—who, by A.D. 74, was growing into an adolescent of rare intellect, grace, and courage. By that time, Vitalis had acquired ownership of several shops (including, apparently, a dye shop and one of the local oyster farms). She had accumulated both gold and real estate and, in A.D. 74, she went to her former owners, hoping to resolve the issue peacefully by offering them her property in return for custody of her daughter. First Calatoria, and then, more adamantly, Petronius, refused to let Justa go.

By Herculanean law, a former slave was allowed every freedom except the power to bring a former owner before the judges. But Justa, as a free-born child, *was not* legally bound by the same law. By means of a war chest full of gold, deeds, and bank accounts, Vitalis was now well positioned to pay Justa's legal fees.

During the fifth year in the reign of Emperor Vespasian, in A.D. 74, Justa filed suit at the age of twelve. As hearings were about to commence in the Basilica of Herculaneum, Petronius Stephanus relented and allowed Telesphorus to broker an out-of-court settlement, "as a mutually-agreed reimbursement for Justa's upbringing." Vitalis signed several of her business interests over to Calatoria and Petronius, along with an unspecified amount of gold, in return for Justa.

Justa's happiness did not last long. In Graeco-Roman parlance, the Fates seemed to be against her. Vitalis was soon stricken by a mysterious wasting disease (possibly cancer). While tending to her mother (whose movements became increasingly bound to a chair, and then to a bed), Justa managed to build up—again—the family business (or businesses, as the case may be).

At age fourteen, in the year A.D. 76, Justa had become a wealthy Herculanean entrepreneur in her own right, but she might willingly have cast her wealth into the Bay of Naples if only she could create magic and somehow have her mother back for another year, or a month, or even a day; for early in that year, Vitalis had died.

Meanwhile, Petronius, too, had succumbed to illness and died, and Calatoria's business holdings began to fall on hard times. Soon after learning that Vitalis, in her will, had left all of her property to Justa— whose business holdings continued to trend upward—Calatoria firmed her earlier resolve that Justa was growing too smart and beautiful for her own good, "had stood too tall," and needed to be taken down a few pegs. What Calatoria, former stepmother and former defendant, had in mind for herself, and for her two awkward daughters, was a lawyer-assisted turning of the tables that would convert "defendant Calatoria" into not only "plaintiff Calatoria" but also "slave owner Calatoria." And if the process of bringing Justa "home" as a slave (and turning her into a Roman forerunner of Cinderella) also happened to transfer ownership of Justa's wealth, then all the better for Calatoria.

In the seventh year of Vespasian's reign, only a few weeks after Vitalis's will was read, Calatoria filed papers (or waxes) against Justa, alleging that the fourteen-year-old entrepreneur had been born during the month before her mother was freed by Petronius. The necessary proof of this claim (Justa's certificate of birth) was alleged by Calatoria to have been lost in her home during the earthquake of A.D. 62. The claim was at best a gamble but evidently a worthwhile one, for the court clerks admitted as evidence (on a provisional basis, pending further proof) Calatoria's sworn statement that Justa had been born while her mother was still a slave of the Stephanus estate.

Under Roman law, Calatoria's statement, if upheld as true, meant that while Justa's mother was undeniably free, Justa herself had belonged to Calatoria all along. Under this circumstance, the law was clear on one other point: As a slave, Justa was not permitted to inherit her mother's property or business holdings, meaning that everything owned by Justa via Vitalis automatically (and retroactively) reverted to Calatoria were it to be proved, "based upon a preponderance of the evidence," that Calatoria was Justa's rightful owner.

In A.D. 76, the magistrates and judges were called upon to determine whether or not fourteen-year-old Justa had a birthright to ownership of her own life. The stone columns of the Herculaneum Basilica were imposing structures, meant to convey the power of Roman law and to remind all who climbed the steps to the courthouse that they were as insects against the cyclopean scale of Rome. The pillars still convey a sense of frightful majesty, though few of them stand erect.

Before being cocooned in fused volcanic ash, the pillars of Roman justice were toppled like sets of bowling pins, and sections of roof crashed down around them. Today, only the westernmost part of the basilica is accessible to exploration, for the tunneling operation begun there was stopped long ago by the townspeople of Resina, who do not want their present-day living rooms and bedrooms undermined and brought down into the same courthouses that, during the last sunrises the building was ever to see, were being subverted as instruments of larceny and spite. In the years between A.D. 76 and 79, the halls of justice were undermined already, although to Calatoria and her attorneys just-seeming still.

The building, explored only fractionally by the tunnelers, extends more than 200 feet (60 meters) eastward, below the town of Resina. Near one of the entrances, a huge statue of Emperor Vespasian had fallen in pieces upon the marble floor. In a large, semicircular niche, two bronze figures stood relatively intact and in eternal struggle. One possessed a bull's head hybridized onto a human body—the result of a mythical union between Pasiphaë and the creature that had symbolized Minoan power more than 1,600 years before Vespasian was born. The second figure was Theseus, mythical slayer of the half-human, half-beast Minotaur.

Elsewhere in the courthouse, seeming to anticipate the paintings of Leonardo da Vinci and Michelangelo, frescoes of Theseus and Hercules copy Renaissance realism with such faithfulness that the only conclusion possible is that the Renaissance masters were directly informed and inspired by multiple unknown Roman works—which had survived more than a thousand years beyond Vespasian and Titus, much as tales of the Minotaur (and probably classical artistic renditions) had survived into Roman times. Many more works of Roman, naturalistic art must have been preserved into the fourteenth and fifteenth centuries than have trickled down to us through the subsequent Inquisitions, witch trials, and the burnings of cities and great libraries.

On the roof of the Herculaneum Basilica, four life-size bronze horses pulled a life-size bronze chariot. Together they formed a masterwork over which Michelangelo would have smiled approvingly. On the morning of August 25, A.D. 79, a surge cloud rolled impartially over them, blasted them from the roof, and scattered them in pieces over a broad shock front extending westward (and even southward and northward) through the city. Pieces of the three-dimensional jigsaw puzzle continue to be unearthed in Herculanean gardens and amid the remnants of collapsed rooftops. As each new piece fits into place, the rare beauty of the

This life-size, gilded bronze horse, still under reconstruction, stood with three others and the chariot-guardian Apollo atop the roof of the Herculaneum courthouse, or "Basilica." The statues were swept away in pieces by the "midnight" surge cloud and were scattered westward more than a sixth of a mile. At the time of the eruption, wealthy Christians, with apparently Gnostic roots, were lending their abolitionist support to the case of Justa—which had recently been tabled for an A.D. 80 hearing before the supreme court in Rome.

whole hints at a fairy-tale existence in a lost civilization. Like so much else about the remote past, it is an illusion, albeit a stubborn one.

For a real-life Cinderella in the year A.D. 76, the rooftop symbols of power and prestige must have instilled more fear than wonder, as Justa ascended the steps, knowing that her entire future was about to be foretold in the basilica. This was no Disney-esque wonderland in which fairy godmothers, singing mice, and magical steeds could be counted on to rescue Cinderella. This was a real courthouse filled with real magistrates and judges, to whom a search for the truth might or might not have any real relevance.

Truth, Justa understood, could be bought. Absolute truth might be meaningless if Calatoria hired convincing liars backed by a skilled advocate. Here, at the basilica, Justa knew that she faced more than the mere threat of enslavement under Calatoria's accusations. Here in Herculaneum, in the shadow of the mount upon which the Spartacus slave war had begun, the penalty was particularly severe for one judged to have been a slave who pretended freedom. First would come the forfeiture of all property to her accuser. And then the plaintiff Calatoria and her two young daughters would be given the choice of taking Justa to their estate as a slave or ordering her tied to a tree and crucified.

During the first hearing, Calatoria arrived with a witness prepared to give sworn testimony that Justa was indeed a pretender to her freedom, hoping for summary judgment. It did not go as Calatoria had wished. An attentive magistrate barred the way to the inner sanctum of the judges, noting that any witnesses brought against Justa would appear to be counterbalanced by Justa's previous status as "plaintiff" against Calatoria in the year A.D. 74. Because a slave was barred by law from suing either master or mistress, it stretched credibility, in the magistrate's eyes, that had Calatoria known all along that Justa were born as a slave into her household, she and her attorneys could somehow have failed to raise this as a defense against the lawsuit brought by Justa two years earlier.

Calatoria refused to admit that the contradiction amounted to anything more relevant than an innocent mistake. Her lawyer then begged the court, if it could not provide fair or timely relief, to hold Justa without bail until trial and to assign Calatoria and her children provisional stewardship over Justa's property.

The magistrate, in keeping with an old Greek saying about the mark of a fair decision, sent both parties away unhappy. He declared that the case, which involved complex legal (and political) questions, required "discovery" and evidentiary hearings before a judge. He released Justa on "affordable" bail in the amount of twelve gold coins (equivalent to a full year's salary for a Roman cavalryman). He then fixed bail for the appearance of Calatoria in the same amount.

At some time during the next three years, either Justa moved into Herculaneum's "House of the Christians" or one of the wealthy families who lived there simply sheltered copies of her case file within the house. The Christians were a puzzlement to most Romans, falling one day into disfavor, the next day into favor, and then into disfavor again. In moments of disfavor, one of the words used to denigrate the cult, and to cast its members as evil, translated to simply this: *abolitionists*. The Spartacus revolt of the previous century was essentially a civil war against slavery—Rome's second such war. But there never had been, nor would there be, a Roman Gettysburg.

Justa was fifteen years old and her city had two years left to live when her case came before a judge in the basilica. About this time, galleries were newly erected on both sides of the judge's apse, apparently to accommodate an increased number of law students and spectators. It seems likely, if not certain, that Justa's case was becoming a cause célèbre—a tale bound to spread beyond Herculaneum and to be told around cooking hearths and meal tables by the early Christians . . . Told, embellished, and retold for decades, and perhaps even for centuries to come.

About the year A.D. 77, a wax tablet from the House of the Christians records that a freed slave named Marius Calatorius Marullus gave devastating testimony against Justa. The court stenographer noted that Marius had only recently adopted the name Calatorius (in honor of his former mistress Calatoria), indicating that his freed status was a recent pretrial development.

Marius was illiterate; but the court reporter records, with a note of deliberate irony, that being unable to read or write was no obstacle to his showing up with a written and signed statement. Marius gave an oath that his "testimony" was true (which under Roman law required a man to grasp his testicles and swear by his progeny, an act from which the Latin word for witness—*testis*—is derived), and his statement was read for him: "I knowed Calatoria freed both the girl Vitalis and myself. So I knowed that this here girl is not a freedwoman of Calatoria."

Historian Joseph Jay Deiss believes that to any objective observer, reading Marius's statement after nearly two thousand years, it is plain that he and Calatoria had bargained a lie in return for his freedom. But to anyone who sat in that court and actually watched Justa's face respond to the lie and was able to see, in real time, the judge's expression and Calatoria's—it must have looked very bad indeed for Justa, if what happened next can be taken as an indication of how the court seemed likely to rule.

Exposing himself to scorn, ridicule, poverty, and perhaps worse (especially if he were to be judged ultimately a liar), a surprise witness stepped forward. In *this* Cinderella's world, there did in fact exist a princely rescuer after all.

The wax has recorded his name:

"I, Gaius Petronius Telesphorus, have written and sworn by the spirit of the sacred Emperor Vespasian Augustus and his sons that I know the girl Justa, defendant in this suit, was born free. She was the child of my fellow freedperson, Petronia Vitalis. It was I who arranged with Petronius Stephanus and Calatoria Temedis reimbursement for Justa's upbringing. It was I who helped restore her to her mother. From these facts, I know that the girl Justa, object of this suit, was born in freedom. This is the question at issue."

To Deiss and to other historians, it is clear that Justa's unnamed father had come forth, determined to rescue her at any cost.

For reasons never made clear in the wax, the judge declined a plea from Justa's attorneys for immediate dismissal of the case. Instead, the court adjourned for further discovery, further testimony, and new affidavits. For another six months, the case dragged on. Then A.D. 77 passed. A.D. 78 came and went. A.D. 79 came and Calatoria refused to go away. At the basilica, about the spring of A.D. 79, when Justa was seventeen years óld, it was decided that the case would have to go before the supreme court at the Forum of Augustus in Rome. A date for resolution was set for A.D. 80.

No resolution . . .

No absolution . . .

No survivors, either, according to Pliny the Younger. No one from Herculaneum was ever heard from again.

Save for the wax, no trace of Justa has come down through history. No one remembered her. Nothing of Justa lived on . . . except, perhaps, as the kernel of truth at the threshold of a fairy tale.

7

THE DAY AFTER

One of the most moving archaeological discoveries ever made took place in Israel in 1976, during a series of excavations carried out by scientists from the Hebrew University and the French Center for Prehistoric Research in Jerusalem. At a 10,000-year-old campsite, they uncovered the skeleton of a child, one hand pressed against its cheek. In that hand is another tiny skeleton: that of a puppy, about five months old. This is the earliest example we know of man and dog sharing the same grave. There must be many, many other ones.

ARTHUR C. CLARKE, *The Ghost from the Grand Banks, 1990*

When the fourth surge cloud reached Pompeii, about 7:30 on the morning of August 25, a man collapsed and was fossilized outside the city's northern gate, as he tried to pull his goat along by its halter. Behind him, a woman was autoclaved with an infant in her arms, while two little girls fell at her heels, still clinging to the hem of her gown. In the house of Publius Paquius Proculus, seven children were entombed during the night, when the roof of the entire second story imploded under deepening masses of pumice. Also dead, long before the fourth Vesuvian cloud arrived, were a man named Quintus Poppaeus and his ten slaves. Like Proculus's children, they died on the second floor of their home. The body of Poppaeus himself still held a bronze-and-glass lantern.

In one of Pompeii's warehouses, thirty-four people, having decided that the upper stories of buildings were unsafe, attempted to avoid the Proculus' and Poppaeus fates by sheltering in an underground wine vault. They brought bread and fruit to sustain them, but they were probably dead before dawn. Had they known all that science would one day reveal, they might have counted themselves among the lucky Pompeiians.

Throughout the two cities, only two creatures are known to have been alive after the passover of the sixth surge cloud. We have found them sheltered in the basement level of an apartment building near Pompeii's northern wall. In that sector, the buildings themselves rested against, and were shielded by, a natural scarp created nearly twenty thousand years earlier, when a glacierlike tongue of semimolten rock had crept down from Vesuvius, stopped, and hardened into the city's northernmost boundary. At the edge of this boundary, underground, a man managed to save both himself and his beloved dog.

Somehow, although buried under a story of partly collapsed building and a story more of volcanic debris, air continued to reach them, and they continued to live. They must have still been alive when Emperor Titus sent his rescue-and-recovery teams to the cities of Vesuvius, but the ground most certainly muffled the cries and the barks, if indeed any of the searchers even came near.

They lived long enough, the man and his dog, to digest whatever food the man had brought with him and to produce a layer of fossilized feces. The man must also have sheltered or tapped into an adequate supply of drinking water, for it was not thirst that killed them. That the dog was a beloved pet can be known from how the man died—evidently from slow starvation, more than two weeks after the eruption, to judge from the quantity of human feces within the tomb. It must have occurred to the man, during those weeks, that if he killed the dog and ate it, he might live long enough to finally succeed at what appears to have been hit-and-miss attempts at digging a route of egress. But he did not, or could not, kill the dog. And when at last death came to him, his pet—his beloved, faithful pet—gnawed the flesh from his bones and lived in the man's grave for a few weeks more.

Outside the grave, here in the twenty-first century, someone has scratched words on a rock. We call it "American Graffiti," for in English, and in "Yankee vernacular," these words appear: "He was a winner, he became the doggie's dinner."

Uncivilized, perhaps. Funny—but definitely mean and uncivilized. And it's nothing new.

Bury it for long enough, and even a bad joke may become priceless someday.

In the house of a wealthy patrician, on the Herculanean equivalent of a message board, was scratched a peculiar boast: "Here I, the physician of Emperor Titus, had a wonderful bowel movement!"

In a Pompeiian room, near the spot where a collapsed roof crushed a skeleton's upstretched arms, someone—possibly the very man whose bones are splayed on the floor—scratched a line of graffiti into a frescoed wall: "Nothing in the world," it read, "can last forever."

In Herculaneum's Suburban Baths, white walls in the waiting area seem to have been set up intentionally as graffiti boards. They are covered with hand-scrawled messages: "I Hermeros, slave of my mistress Primagenia, came from Puteoli to Timnianus Street and am looking for the bank messenger, the slave of Phoebus . . . Oh, touch me Titus . . . Primagenia, she thinks she's a Venus—but her nose, it is shaped like a . . . O wall, that you, who have to bear the weariness of so many writers, are still standing . . . Two companions were here. After the bad guidance of Epaphroditus in everything, they tardily threw him out. Then with the girls they joyfully consumed 105 and ½ sesterces: 12 offellae [12 thin-crusted baked breads, or pizza pies] with all trimmings."[1]

A sesterce is a unit of Roman silver coinage. In A.D. 79, 100 sesterces were equivalent to one-tenth of a gold coin, or one-tenth of a soldier's

---

[1] Take special note of the graffiti-writing slave Hermeros, who was looking for a slave bank messenger. Note also that Vitalis and Telesphorus, too, were literate, despite their slave origins. The cities of Vesuvius appear to be teaching us that even among Rome's lowermost castes, literacy was not such a rarity as to be unheard of, or even necessarily uncommon. A typical textbook view teaches us that writing in the first century A.D. was in the hands of the elite upper castes, including priests and government officials (much as in America into the nineteenth century). The Justa case, and the handwriting literally on the wall, suggest that the common textbook dogma is wrong, and that literacy at the time of Saint Paul's landing at nearby Puteoli was widespread if not prevalent. This, of course, addresses the question of whether or not sayings attributed to Christianity's founding prophet were likely to have been written down in the time of Paul, James, and other firsthand eyewitness participants.

monthly salary. According to the message board, Epaphroditus's companions stayed behind for a reasonably expensive feast (three days' salary for a soldier). What passed for pizza in those days—as revealed by Pompeiian and Herculanean restaurant menus (written on the walls, like graffiti) and by the fossilized food itself—was topped with cheese, anchovies, thin-sliced mushrooms, and (for an additional charge) thin-sliced, milk-fed snails. Fried noodles were another common staple, topped with either fruit-based sweet-and-sour sauce or a strongly flavored fish-and-garlic dressing. Most restaurants offered a wide assortment of pastries and cakes. The highest-priced of all desserts (up to 100 sesterces for a single serving of the white, fluffy treat) was widely advertised for its alleged medicinal value, and for being a food of the pharaohs. A plant-derived powder sprinkled on sugar and exported from the marshlands near Alexandria, it was called "marshmallow."

Several fast-food outdoor cafés offered ground beef—spiced, flattened into patties, barbecued, then topped with a "special sauce" and served between two bunlike pieces of bread. Cooked, homogenized pork was served in sausagelike skins on a long bun smeared with spiced beans. Romans living on the Bay of Naples in A.D. 79 enjoyed pizza, hamburgers, and chili dogs. On hot afternoons, the Pompeiians liked to dine along bay-view terraces or in gardens, where they usually washed the burgers and the occasional octopus or dormouse down with honey-sweetened wine diluted in sparkling mineral water. (One local brand of mineral water would still be in use, and indeed popular, more than 1,900 years later.)

"Here we ate heartily, a sunset meal," announces one graffiti writer, "and [we] talked with wonderful company late into the night."

Elsewhere, on the wall of the men's waiting room in Herculaneum's Forum Baths, letters of the Latin alphabet are written one after another, as far as "Q," as if by the hand of a father teaching his son. If so, then Q might mark the moment at which the first Vesuvian explosion intervened, and roused the Plinys from their studies, several miles west of the baths.

Compared with the other graffiti writers, it is the man identifying himself as physician to Emperor Titus (the one oh so proud of his "wonderful bowel movement") who fixed the cities of Vesuvius most firmly in time and space, by reminding us of their place in the succession of imperial dynasties.

"We have it from the Roman historian Gaius Suetonius that Emperor Vespasian died at the age of sixty-nine years, seven months, and seven days," says Haraldur Sigurdsson. "This was June 23, A.D. 79. Days later, Vespasian's son, Titus, became emperor in his place. So, the graffiti in the Herculaneum bathroom must have been written somewhere between July and late August. It seems very unlikely that the emperor's physician would have been traveling without the emperor himself. That Titus had a special fondness for Herculaneum is consistent with his behavior after the eruption. Titus actually made an effort [albeit a futile one] to rebuild the cities. He did much to help those who had survived [in Misenum, Stabiae, and other outlying areas]. He passed a law appropriating the [pre-Vesuvius, banked] funds belonging to families that had been wiped out, and he then redistributed those funds to help the survivors. So, history credits him with the first disaster-relief fund on record."

Suetonius wrote that Titus's reign was marked by a series of catastrophes, in which the eruption of Vesuvius was followed by an outbreak of plague and a fire that burned in Rome for three days, despite the recent introduction of fire hoses backed by twin-piston water pumps: "Throughout this assortment of disasters, [Titus] showed far more than an Emperor's concern; it resembled the deep love of a father for his children, which he conveyed not only in a series of comforting edicts but by helping the victims to the utmost extent of his [own] purse. He set up a board of ex-consuls, chosen by lot, to relieve distress in [the] Campania [Vesuvius region], and [he] devoted the property of those who had died in the eruption and left no heirs to a fund for rebuilding the stricken cities . . . And he appointed a body of knights to see that his orders were carried out."

As Josephus had "prophesied," Vespasian and Titus succeeded Nero, who died "young and hated by his own people." When all available historical accounts are compared and summed up, this really did not amount to very much by way of prophecy. One need not have had "words of knowledge" from God to see immediately that Vespasian and his son were determined to outlive Nero—who, as everyone knew by the time of the Josephean prophecy, had been busy inventing such "performance art" as tying men and women to stakes and devouring their genitals while dressed as a lion. Suetonius, who listed acts "worthy of praise" in equal measure alongside Nero's "follies and crimes," leaves the everlasting impression of a historical figure best summed up as Hitler with bad table manners. First, Nero burned and looted his own cities. Then he raped the Vestal Virgins and tried to have a boy named Sporus turned into a girl by surgery. Then, according to Suetonius, Nero started to get bad. He "practiced every kind of obscenity, and after defiling almost every part of his body finally invented a novel game." The object of his game centered on a growing fascination for cannibals. "He was eager," Suetonius reports, "to get hold of a certain Egyptian—a sort of ogre who would eat raw flesh and practically anything else he was given—and [the mad emperor would] watch him tear live men to pieces and then devour them. These 'successes,' as Nero called them, went to his head and he boasted that no previous sovereign had ever realized the extent of his power."

Tales of a cult whose members, it was said, ate the body and drank the blood of their founding prophet, led Nero to the followers of Jesus, James, and Paul. But the Christians disappointed Nero, for they were a pious lot who "at best" made an amateurish pretense at cannibalism as if it were only theater to them; so the emperor inflicted death upon these people, whom Suetonius characterized as "a sect professing a new and mischievous religious belief."

Of the surgically transformed "girl" Sporus, Suetonius recorded that Nero went through a wedding ceremony with him, "dowry, bridal veil, and all—took him to his palace with a great crowd in attendance, and treated him as a wife. A rather amusing joke," said Suetonius, "is still going the rounds: That the world would have been a happier place had Nero's father Domitius married that sort of wife."

Although Titus distinguished himself in battle against the Jerusalem garrisons, he had grown up in the court of Nero, and many Romans feared that he was in fact destined to become a second Nero. "He was believed to be profligate as well as cruel," Suetonius wrote, "because of the riotous parties which he kept going with his more extravagant friends far into the night; and immoral, too, because he owned a troupe of eunuchs [young boys castrated with the intention of preserving their prepubescent features], and he nursed a notorious passion for Queen Berenice."

However, Titus surprised the Romans, in both his personal and his public behavior; according to Suetonius: "So soon as everyone realized that here was no monster of vice but an exceptionally noble character, public opinion had no fault to find with him." He sent Queen Berenice (a particularly unpopular member of the Judean royal family) away from Rome, "which was painful for both of them; and [he] broke off relations with some of his favorite boys—[and] though they danced well enough to make a name for themselves on the stage, he never attended their public performances."

Josephus, who rode at the emperor's side, described Titus as a brave soldier—daring, and unusually regretful of having to kill people who proved too proud to surrender. He was also curiously merciful, even to his enemies. During the Jewish revolt of A.D. 66–70, Titus presaged Pliny the Elder's fate at Vesuvius—"Fortune favors the brave"—when he announced to his troops, "No great thing is to be accomplished without some danger." And yet, in book 7, chapter 5, verse 2, of *The Jewish War*, Josephus states repeatedly that Titus did not always sense victory in the slaughter of enemies and the destruction of architectural marvels. In the case of Jerusalem, he was particularly mournful: "So far was he from boasting that so great and goodly a city as that was, had been by him taken by force; nay, he frequently cursed those who had been the authors of their revolt, and had brought such punishment upon the city; insomuch that it openly appeared that he did not desire that such a calamity as this punishment of theirs amounted to should be a demonstration of his courage."

The cause of Titus's bad courage, according to Josephus, was that the Jordan Valley and its surroundings had always been inhabited by quarrelsome people who ultimately misinterpreted the Romans' tendency to build roads, and to increase the wealth of its subservient kingdoms, as signs of weakness. In book 6, chapter 6, verse 2, of *The Jewish War*, Josephus quotes a speech by Titus to the survivors of Jerusalem, in which the conqueror addressed the perceived weaknesses of the Romans, "who, in the first place, have given you this land to possess;

and, in the next place, have set over you kings of your own nation; and, in the third place, have preserved the laws of your forefathers to you, and have as well permitted you to live, either by yourselves or among others, as it should please you." What Titus found inexplicable, in this clash of civilizations, was his adversaries' belief that it was somehow acceptable for a state to bite the hand that fed it: "You sent embassies to those of your nation that are beyond the Euphrates [in Iraq] to assist you in your raising disturbances," said Titus. "And you made preparations for war against us with our own money; nay, after all, when you were in the enjoyment of all these advantages, you turned your too great plenty against those that gave it to you, and, like merciless serpents, have thrown out your poison against those that treated you kindly. I suppose, therefore, that you might [have] despised the slothfulness of Nero, and, like limbs of the body that are broken or dislocated, you did then lie quiet, waiting [to take advantage], though still with a malicious intention."

Thus reads a Roman-centric view of Jerusalem's destruction, penned by a general turned prophet, turned Roman mercenary, turned Roman historian. The Josephean books are an unusual window into the empire during the fall of Jerusalem, the burial of Pompeii, the disappearance of Herculaneum, and the origin of Christianity. The books are full of curiosities, not least among them Josephus's record of a prebattle speech in which Titus (according to book 6, chapter 1, verse 5, of *The Jewish War*) tells the soldiers what he believes to be true of the human soul and of martyrdom in battle: "As for myself . . . cannot I forbear to imprecate upon those who are of a contrary disposition, that they may die in time of peace, by some sickness or other, since their souls are condemned to the grave, together with their bodies. For what man of virtue is there who does not know, that those souls which are severed from their fleshly bodies in battles by the sword are received by the ether, that purest of elements, and joined to that company which are placed among the stars; that they become good demons, and favorable heroes, and show themselves as such to their posterity afterwards? While upon those souls that wear away in and with their diseased bodies comes a subterranean night to dissolve them to nothing."

The Titus speech, as recorded by Josephus, was ultimately preserved as hundreds of copies, published by Christian-era monks. Not coinciden-tally, the early Christians—"doing in Rome what Romans did"—bor-rowed, from a warrior-based theology dating back to the Etruscans, the idea that Roman soldiers martyred in battle were guaranteed a place in paradise.

So began the concept of rewarded martyrdom, inherited by Romans from Etruscans, by Christians from Romans, and eventually by Muslims from Christians. Two millennia later—and in a way that Titus and his legions could never have anticipated—it would come back to haunt their distant descendants.

Reiterating that death by old age or disease led only to the eter-nal peace of "a deep oblivion to take away all remembrance," Titus's address to his troops continued thus: "That [because] death is to come of necessity upon all men, a sword is a better instrument for that pur-pose than any disease whatever. Why is it not then a very mean thing for us not to yield up that to the public benefit that we must yield up to fate?"

In book 7, chapter 5, of *The Jewish War*, Josephus recorded remorse and (compared against the usual customs of his time) uncommon mercy on the part of Titus, at the very moment he appeared to have achieved the final rout of Israel's generals, high priests, and pharisees. As when Rome had snuffed out rebellious Carthage, finally, by salting the earth so that no crops could grow there and the survivors would starve, the massacre of Jewish civilization seemed close at hand. According to Josephus, there came to Titus messengers from foreign kings, accompanied by "a crown of gold upon the victory he had gained over the Jews." Titus accepted the crown, but when he arrived at Antioch (capital of ancient Syria), the continuous train of gift-bearing messengers "pressed him with [too] much earnestness," wrote Josephus, "[a]nd [when they] continually begged of him that he would eject the Jews out of their city, he gave them this very pertinent answer: 'How can this be done, since that country of theirs [Israel], where the Jews must be obliged then to retire, is destroyed, and no place will receive them besides?' Whereupon the people of Antioch, when they had failed of success in their first request, made him a second; for they desired that he would order those tables of brass [those sacred tables, or altars, upon which Syrian law was written in agreement with Rome] to be removed on which the Jews' privileges were engraven. However, Titus would not grant that either, but permitted the Jews of Antioch to continue to enjoy the very same privileges in that city which they had before. [He] then departed."

According to Suetonius, Titus had pleaded in the Roman forum as a barrister, for he was keenly interested in giving everyone (even the most downtrodden accused) "a fair go." Though it was generally considered below a monarch's status, Emperor Titus endeavored to practice law—and a particular species of law: the branch that would ascend into futurity as "constitutional law" and what Titus was beginning to perceive as the principle of "basic, unalienable human rights."

One of the most abhorrent legal practices in the days of Vesuvius, Suetonius observed (and the Justa documents memorialized this), was the extreme and sometimes poetic license enjoyed by paid informants—who were often slaves or prisoners, paid in freedom papers, sweetened with silver and gold. This "worst feature of Roman life" had become so pervasive that previously honest lawyers were finding lucrative second careers as "managers" for paid informants. When Titus discovered that jails, slave barracks, and gladiatorial schools were being filled with innocent and often wealthy property owners (whose property, naturally, was forfeited to their accusers under the "right" legal arguments), he became infuriated and resolved that under his reign the letter of the law would no longer be used to subvert the spirit of the law. Under the "letter of the law," false witness given by professional informants was perfectly legal. Titus put an end to this and steeled his resolve by making an example of the informants' agents and talent scouts, most of whom happened to be lawyers: "Titus had these well-whipped," said Suetonius, "—and clubbed, and taken to [the Colosseum in Rome], and paraded in the arena; where some were put up for auction as slaves and the remainder deported to the most forbidding islands. In further discouragement of any who, at any future time, might venture on similar practices, he allowed nobody to be tried for the same offense under more than one law."

What Titus invented, there, in Vesuvius-era Rome, were the legal protections against "double jeopardy" and "perjury." He also wrote statutes limiting the period during which one could be charged with an offense, and inquiries made—which passed across time as the "statute of limitations."

If Justa had survived the destruction of Herculaneum (and we cannot be 100 percent certain that she did not), her case would have been of particular interest to Titus. It was the right case, being referred upward to the right court, at just the right time.

As it turned out, however, instead of reading Justa's case, Titus probably visited her grave, without ever knowing of it.

When Titus began his disaster-relief program in the Campania region, he had hoped to rebuild the stricken cities. But only the tops of Pompeii's buildings protruded through the earth, hinting at where specific streets had once been and where tunnelers might begin to recover temple treasures and other valuables. Herculaneum had disappeared so completely beneath the new ground surface that it was difficult to guess within a mile where it had once stood. Oplontiae, located on the coast between Pompeii and Herculaneum, was another missing town. The opening decades of the twenty-first century would list the town (save for a perfectly preserved "palace" in approximately the right location) as still missing, along with the names Taurania, Tora, Sora, Cossa, and Leucoptera—each standing for a lost town or village.

During the decade that followed the eruption, the land over and around Pompeii proved to be very profitable for the winegrower's trade. The "Campo Pompeiano" vineyard, erected partly from bricks recycled from the upper stories of Pompeiian homes, represents the only rebuilding recorded there. Farther south, Stabiae recovered and, within a year, managed to take over the shipping routes that had previously belonged to Pompeii and Herculaneum. By A.D. 90, farming communities were springing up over the rooftops of Herculaneum, and a new shore road leading south to Stabiae and west to Misenum began to support the village that became Resina.

This was all part of a dirty trick played by nature and the Fates. The same volcanic dust that destroyed the humans and drove them out was rich in mineral nutrients and supported plant growth with unparalleled vigor. The same volcano that had killed, and would kill again, lured the people back to its foothills as farmers, sustained them as exporters and town builders, and finally as city builders. The humans were slow to be baited in and to rebuild, at first. Resina took more than two hundred years to evolve from vineyards into what anyone might call a fairly large town, and centuries more to become a city. But the volcano had destroyed everything within reach of its surge clouds, every millennium or so, scores of times . . . scores and hundreds of times . . . The volcano had existed for a quarter-million years before the first farmers and city builders arrived on its slopes, and it would exist for a quarter-million years after the Sphinx turned to dust. The volcano was (by human standards) ageless. The volcano could wait.

THE ENGINEERS who have examined the buried buildings can often be heard to say that Herculaneum's public sauna houses and baths—with their systems of metal pipes, valves, and boilers—were the work of a genius born ahead of his time.

When I hear this said, I often reply (and I do not believe it can be said too often): "History teaches us that there are no people born ahead of their times. There are only visionaries, and there are circumstances. Everything else is hindsight."

Were Benjamin Franklin or Thomas Edison born in A.D. 1000, they would probably have been executed simply for being themselves (even nine centuries later, Robert Hutchings Goddard was called "madman" and driven toward poverty in the time of Edison and Einstein, merely for proposing that rockets might kick open the doors to the new wilderness of space). Were the engineer behind Herculaneum's baths born in A.D. 1000, or even A.D. 1900, he might have faced the same fates as Giordano Bruno or Robert Goddard. Born into the time of Claudius, Vespasian, and Titus, he became a wealthy entrepreneur.

I've been following, like a kind of archaeological stalker, Herculaneum's Thomas Edison. Sorry to report that I've not had much success; he (or she) remains nameless and faceless. Several researchers have unearthed hints that the arts of bath building and pipe fitting evolved from (or at least applied the same technology as) oyster farming. So, by accident and then by habit, I have come to call "him" the "oyster farmer," though the name is probably erroneous. Still . . . Herculanean portraits of family life depict women wearing necklaces of gold and

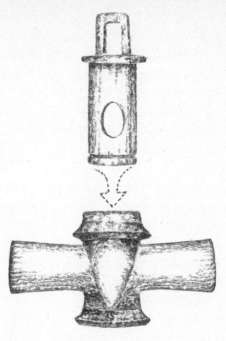

Household valves excavated from Herculaneum were still functional after nearly two thousand years. The city was honeycombed with indoor plumbing and underground sewage systems. Water pressure was maintained in multistory towers that were fed by filtration systems and other means of purification, including aeration. Such hydrotechnology was not seen again until the mid-twentieth century, by which time the widespread availability of germ-free drinking water, more than any other technological or medical advance, had contributed to the extension of the human life span.

pearl, and a golden choker excavated from a home in Pompeii is decorated with emeralds and artificially cultured (or "farm-grown") mother-of-pearl.

As the jewelers and historians tell it, the art of boiler and piston building really began to move forward in the time of Augustus (who ruled from 31 B.C. to A.D. 14), after an oyster farmer named Gaius Orata discovered that his "crops" grew more quickly if kept warm throughout the winter months. He made his fortune by harvesting oysters year-round, and he managed this feat by aid of pumps and furnaces—which fed hot air through a system of pipes underlying huge, saltwater tanks. Only one dynasty later, someone who may or may not have been an oyster farmer began building baths, boilers, and steam pumps in Herculaneum. Viewed through archaeological eyes, he moves ghostlike through the city, leaving behind only his machines, or strange historical accounts of them. (And, in flights of abstract fantasy, I like to imagine that Justa and her mother acquired their fortunes by finding newer, more practical applications for the inventions of Herculaneum's unknown genius.)

"Edison" (he or she) remains a phantom. But pipes and walls still stand, telling their story.

Herculaneum's Suburban Baths are so named because the surge cloud, and the material that drove behind it, like an avalanche of super-heated snow, swept away all but the foundations of nearby houses and yet—tornadolike—dislodged hardly a stone from the baths, and created the illusion that the building stood snug and alone in the suburbs.

The waiting room (a prebath "hot room" and possibly a winter warming room) was heated by pipes in the walls—part of an elaborate and very modern-appearing radiator system. The walls were decorated with stucco casts, identical in every way to the prefabricated impressions of floral and spiral trim mass-produced during the Edwardian period for Europe's luxury hotels, mansions, and ocean liners.

The surge clouds and pyroclastic avalanches buried the furnace room with all of its pipes, boilers, and valves intact. Wood is still piled neatly on the floor, and the unbroken wooden shutters on the boiler-room windows are identical to the shutters on houses of the Victorian era. Cold water was piped into the furnace room from the town aqueduct, then heated, then pumped at high pressure through the heating system. Elsewhere in the building, public latrines were flushed with semiclean wastewater piped from the baths and saunas, revealing that the engineer had given thought to the conservation of his city's resources.

The lounge was a postbath relaxation area—now filled with the incinerated remnants of round tables and wicker chairs. The architect-engineer had added three large picture windows overlooking the Herculaneum boathouses and the Bay of Naples.

The Suburban Baths were not the only building in which the weatherproofing qualities of glass were being used to create year-round picturesque views. Across town, in the Villa of the Papyri, someone had built an enclosed, windowed walkway—and one room, apparently a bedroom, had been provisioned with a sliding glass door.

In one of the Suburban Baths' hot rooms, the surge cloud, had burst indoors through broad glass windows. A round marble basin was lifted from its pedestal beneath the windows and pitched, on edge, against barriers on the far side of the room. The blast of pulverized glass and body-vaporizing ash appears to have fused instantly against the basin's inner surface, as if a film of vaporizing water had suddenly cooled the surge cloud's leading edge when it touched the basin—had dropped it 400 degrees, centigrade.

Inside Herculaneum's only slightly less luxurious Forum Baths, the cloud, as it jetted through the pipe-heated women's dressing room, collapsed the floor onto its pipes and underlying supports, yet left the mosaic floor design (though imploded onto a newer, deeper floor level) completely undamaged: a huge image of Triton (son of Neptune)—human in appearance, except below the waist, where his legs, curled and writhing, were the legs of sea serpents.

Gaius Suetonius made reference to a favorite circus and picnic ground of Emperor Claudius (who ruled from A.D. 41 to 54, just ahead of Nero and Vespasian). The main stadium was built of volcanic rock and wood, just like the amphitheater of Pompeii. Of the "picnic" displays, Suetonius mentions that the signal for a gladiatorial trial by water was given by a mechanical silver Triton—which, in the fashion of Disney-esque animatronics—emerged writhing and glistening from the bottom of an artificial lake, then (by either pressurized air or by steam power) blew a trumpet in the shape of a conch shell.

During the reign of Claudius's successor, Nero, someone, according to Roman legend, built, at the emperor's command, a yacht, or "barge," made out of (or faced with) white marble. This vessel was most often docked at Nero's Herculaneum estate, between the years A.D. 54 and 68. The mad emperor is said, by Suetonius, to have developed a myriad of fascinating obsessions ranging from boats and hot springs to steam power and all manner of poisons. And he had the means by which to spare no expense. On gold coins, he depicted himself as the robed sun god Apollo, with spokes of light radiating from his head and a flaming torch held high, in imitation of the colossal statue that stood at the harbor of Rhodes. (Known as the "Colossus of Rhodes," the earthquake-ravaged statue was melted down a millennium past Nero by Islamic conquerors who declared the spoked head "blasphemous." Surviving drawings and coin reliefs were later adapted to female form by a French sculptor. Known as the Statue of Liberty, a resurrected Colossus stands now in New York Harbor, draped in Roman robes, holding a Roman torch, her head adorned with the spokes of Apollo.)

Most Romans regarded Nero's sexual obsession with his mother (who might have fathered him by her equally mad brother, Gaius "Caligula") as a moral affront against the gods that might ultimately bring righteous ruin upon Rome.

They needn't have worried about the incestuous sideshow for very long.

Sooner or later, as seemed bound to become the fate of anyone who stayed too near Nero for too long, the emperor decided that his mother must die. He tried to poison her three times, but as Suetonius tells it, "she had always taken the proper antidote in advance." Turning next to technology, he had a steam-driven yacht designed to collapse the ceiling and walls of her cabin upon her bed, like a vise, while she slept. The boat was built to simultaneously sink itself with the evidence. According to Suetonius, "Under pretense of a reconciliation, he sent the most friendly note inviting her to celebrate the Feast of Minerva with him at Baiae, and then on her arrival made one of his captains stage an ostensibly accidental collision with the galley in which she had sailed. Then he protracted the feast until a late hour, and when at last she said, 'I really must get back to Bauli,' offered her his collapsible boat instead of the damaged galley. Nero was in a very happy mood as he led [his mother] Agrippina down to the quay, and [he] even kissed her breasts before she stepped aboard. He sat up all night, on tenterhooks of anxiety, waiting for the outcome of his scheme. On discovering that everything had gone wrong and she had escaped by swimming—when Lucius Agerinus, her freedman, entered joyfully to report that she was safe and sound, Nero, in desperation, ordered one of his men to drop a dagger surreptitiously beside Lucius, whom he arrested at once on a charge of having been hired to murder the Emperor. After this he arranged for Agrippina to be killed, and made it seem as if she had sent [the summarily executed] Lucius to assassinate him but [that Agrippina had] committed suicide upon hearing that the plot had miscarried."

Nero believed that the god Neptune had conspired with Triton to protect his mother during the sinking of his collapsible boat. He often admitted to his aides that he feared he was being haunted by his mother's ghost and that the Furies were pursuing him with whips and burning torches. And thus, Nero's paired obsession with water and furnaces: Near the end of his reign, he called upon the best engineers from Herculaneum, Pompeii, and the entire Bay of Naples region to build him a system of world-class baths connected by canals and stretching from Misenum to Lake Avernus. The volcanic hot springs of the Baiae district (where Nero had docked Agrippina's collapsible boat) would be tapped to feed the system. The emperor also planned extensive canal systems linking the Mediterranean to the Red Sea, and Lake Avernus to the port of Ostia—all in the hope of displaying, for all the world to see, his mastery over Neptune and the Furies. Prisoners from every part of the empire were ordered to be transplanted for employment on this task, wrote Suetonius, "even those convicted of capital crimes receiving no other punishment but this."

The mad emperor envisioned the canals and the seas filled, first with steam-assisted sailing ships, and then, inevitably, with completely sailless, oarless cargo carriers and warships (driven over Neptune and Triton by the fires of Hades). At least one prototype steamship, it is said, lies sunk in the Bay of Naples, near its home port of Herculaneum. Such was the state of Rome's resources, and its technology, in the time of Vesuvius.

"Nero's confidence in the resources of Empire was not the only cause of his furious spending," said Suetonius. "He had also been suddenly excited by tales of great hidden treasure, vouched for by a Roman knight who swore that the hoard brought by Queen Dido to Carthage centuries before, when she fled from Tyre, still lay untouched in certain huge African caves and could easily be retrieved. When this hope failed to materialize, Nero found himself destitute—and his financial difficulties were such that he could not lay hands on enough money even for the soldiers' pay or the veterans' benefits." It was at this point, there-fore—on the very verge of canals and steamships—that Nero sealed his own fate. He died badly: condemned by his own soldiers.

When, as Josephus "prophesied," Vespasian ascended the throne (and established the Flavian dynasty) in A.D. 69, it is easy to imagine the conquering hero calling aside the "oyster farmer" (or "Herculaneum's Edison," call him what you will) and then, after complimenting him on the efficiency of the Suburban Baths and the saunas, whispering, "But this steam-engine idea—for ships and for chariots or wagons driven over tracks—let this one go. Whatever would we do with all the slaves and horses?"

THE TECHNOLOGICAL SOPHISTICATION of the Herculanean and Pompeiian baths could scarcely be guessed at until they were actually excavated in the late twentieth century. Expertly engineered to provide the conveniences of central heating, hot pools, saunas, cold plunge baths, and exercise courts, they were better equipped and more luxuri-ous than most late-twentieth- and early-twenty-first-century country clubs. There were vaulted ceilings in the dining areas and mosaic land-scapes built, in some cases, from nearly 2 million individual colored tiles. The waiting areas, conversation pits, and dining saloons were decorated with carefully restored and preserved antiques dating back to ancient Greece.

And these were not rooms reserved for the monarchy or the extremely wealthy. The "graffitos" left on message boards reveal that these were places where average citizens and even slaves gathered. The houses beyond reveal, even in their smallest, least expensive quarters, wall decorations, balconies with bay views and hanging flowerpots, and perfume holders filled with oil of roses. The cities of Vesuvius reveal an extensive and thriving "middle class." The records left behind by Vitalis and Justa demonstrate that it was possible, in a single generation (so long as lawyers and paid witnesses could be kept out of the act), for a slave to become free, then middle class, then wealthy—all the better to feed and expand the empire's tax base.

Such technological and architectural luxuries as were seen in Pompeii and Herculaneum at this time (with their combined population of twenty-five thousand people providing us with only a narrow window through which we can glimpse, at a distance, Rome—population 1 million) were not seen again until nineteenth-century America and western Europe. Such standards of living for the average working citizen were not seen again until the mid-twentieth century.

As random snapshots of the past, the two cities yield up hints that even in the aftermath of Nero's reign (or perhaps even in response to his reign), the Romans appear to have been trending a little more conservatively, and perhaps even a little puritanically, when the volcano flash-froze some twenty-five thousand of them. Although paintings and sculptures idolizing the human form remained commonplace, and nudity continued to be accepted as a natural state, the youngest of the twin cities' walls reveal the beginnings of gender segregation in the baths, with separate dressing rooms and saunas. Paintings of women wearing light garments in the hot rooms, and of men wearing loincloths (corroborated by the volcanically preserved garments themselves), differ from earlier (and sometimes overpainted) images in which men and women bathed or saunaed together unclothed.

In A.D. 79, at the Pompeiian and Herculanean baths, men and women parted paths at the lobby and did not meet up again until fully clothed, where the exit corridors joined at the garden paths, and where they could stroll together among flowers, fountains, and musicians. Beyond the gardens were libraries filled with papyrus scrolls, and the reading tables were surrounded by statues and paintings.

The baths usually opened at midday, according to posted signs. The furnaces were probably lit a half-hour to 45 minutes before the lobby doors opened. The Herculanean Suburban Baths were wood-fired, but the Forum Baths (in both Herculaneum and Pompeii) had undergone conversion to coal-fired boilers during the end days. The midday timing for the lighting of the furnaces is consistent with the stacks of wood still piled neatly in the boiler room of the Suburban Baths, and with Pliny the Younger's testimony that the August 24 eruption began about lunchtime.

When it ended, the bones of four men and a woman lay preserved in Herculaneum's gender-segregated Forum Baths, near the city center.

As in the Suburban Baths, the lighting of the furnaces was probably interrupted by the onset of the eruption, and though the unearthing of 1,328 oil lamps within the complex sends a message that people were accustomed to visiting the baths at night, it seems unlikely that the five were merely trying to force the danger from their minds by mingling someplace comfortable and familiar. They were more likely stragglers who, some twelve hours after the eruption column formed, felt a terrible rumble in the ground, looked eastward, and witnessed the midnight surge cloud advancing toward them. The cloud gave them 90 to 120 seconds in which to respond, during which the thick, vaulted ceilings of the baths must have been perceived as the nearest and most resilient shelter. In the end, they climbed atop a concrete and marble shelf in the men's dressing room. Nineteen centuries later they still huddled together on the shelf, where on any normal night its marble dividers served as "lockers" for towels and street clothes.

According to Pliny the Younger, even on a more usual night, the visitors would have carried oil, perfume, and steel scrapers (for removal of oil-dissolved sweat and grime) instead of soap and washcloths, because soap-making technology was only then coming into existence. Pliny described the first bars of soap as "an invention of the Gauls [the barbarians] for giving a reddish tint to the hair." Manufactured from boiled beech ashes and goat's tallow, the soaps of the time were being used in the manufacture of hair dye and as an antiseptic treatment for sores and wounds, although there is no surviving written evidence that an understanding of germ theory had developed by this time outside of China, beyond the Roman observation that sores and gangrenous wounds sometimes healed after soap and/or very strong concentrations of alcohol were applied.

Farther afield, the Colosseum, commissioned ten years earlier by Vespasian, was a year from being dedicated by Titus. It represented a new construction method by which stone and concrete were braced together by iron bars and cross-beams. Aqueducts and bridges, then on the drawing boards, were to make increasing use of iron, until they evolved from iron-supported stone to structures of brick, concrete, and stone supported entirely on iron frames. Iron-supported stone and brickwork had already reached eight stories in the capital city, where a still-surviving legal transcript involving injury from a falling cow memorial-izes the origin of a city ordinance against the housing of livestock in high-rise dwellings. In the eight-story high-rises, according to court records, the lowest rents were on the top-floor walk-ups. But the best city views were also at the top, and already there was talk of correcting this contradiction (in order to exploit potentially higher property values at the top) by adapting elevators, then under design for the Colosseum's animal pits, for use in high-rise buildings.

When Titus ascended the throne and Vesuvius erupted, Rome was on the brink of erecting multistory towers of iron, concrete, and glass. Had the towers come into existence, steam-powered elevators (and large-scale steel mills) could not have been far behind.

Rome, in the year of Vesuvius and Titus, was in its golden age. No one would have believed, in those days, that the next two centuries would bring economic downturns, civil war, and ever-worsening inter-nal weaknesses, until any combination of external forces—plague, invad-ing armies, volcano weather—might trigger a downward spiral from which the civilization could not possibly recover.

Even after Vesuvius buried their cities, it must have seemed to the proud and daring Romans that they were masters of the world: It must have seemed as if they had all the time in the universe, as if even the stars, in time, would belong to their ever-ascendant empire.

As if . . .

8

THREADS

While stands the Colosseum, Rome shall stand,
When falls the Colosseum, Rome shall fall,
And when Rome falls—the World.

FROM A WALL INSCRIPTION ON
THE LOWER LEVELS OF THE COLOSSEUM

By A.D. 179, Christians and other increasingly common abolitionist groups were making gladiatorial death less and less popular, virtually guaranteeing the end of blood sport as a form of weekend entertainment, until witch burnings and public hangings came into vogue. Over the next decade, the Colosseum would fall into disrepair.

This was the time of Emperor Commodus, who in A.D. 190 began showing signs of Nero-like megalomania. A year later, he was robbing bank vaults, raping Vestal Virgins, setting multiple buildings afire, naming all the months of the year after himself, declaring himself founder of Rome, and renaming the entire city "Colonia Commodiana." He had also, by this time, developed a fondness for "Ambrosia of the Gods," which was in fact a chemically concentrated form of opium imported from the far east, and which might explain why he came to regard himself as a world-class gladiator on horseback. Sometimes he confused the issue and called himself "a god on horseback." In either case, in imitation of Caligula some 150 years before, he developed a habit of storming into the city's taverns, sword drawn, and demanding drinks for both himself and his horse.

Commodus's gladiator-deity delusions yielded two results: First, he repaired the Colosseum; second, in November of 192, he began performing there, usually dressed as Hercules and either shooting at wild beasts from the safety of a raised walkway or defeating gladiators who had already been stabbed for him. Somehow he believed such behavior endeared him to the other gladiators, and on December 31, 192, while celebrating New Year's Eve in the Colosseum's barracks, the gladiators, with the approval of several senators, poisoned and strangled him.

By A.D. 220, the Colosseum was beginning to rust and crumble again, and records show that Emperor Elagabalus was responsible for repairs, about five years before the empire resumed its fatal, Commodus-esque pattern of faltering, stumbling, regaining its footing, and stumbling again. In A.D. 282, to celebrate his victory over German invaders, Emperor Probus planted an entire forest in the center of the Colosseum and reenacted a victory battle by sending Roman gladiators, dressed as soldiers, against several hundred captive Germans, Isaurians, and Nubians. At this time, a half-century after Elagabalus, the Colosseum was once again falling into disrepair, and gladiatorial shows had long since become too expensive to be profitable even as a form of imperial public relations. Decade by decade, crowds were slowly but steadily diminishing.

In A.D. 307, Rome split in two, and Constantine became emperor of the Western Empire (which included Italy and Egypt). By this time, gladiatorial games were becoming so poorly funded that the Colosseum, for the first time in recorded history, was beginning to charge admission. The shows were mostly matinee slaughters of lions, leopards, and bears, followed by public executions.

Constantine became a Christian in A.D. 312, and in 325 he summoned the western and eastern bishops to attend the Council of Nicaea. There, under Constantine's direction, they were to lay down the principles of Roman Catholicism and to decide what should and should not become established, "once and for all time," as "canon." The gospels of Mary and Thomas were excluded; December 25 (Rome's winter solstice celebration) was declared the birth date of Jesus. Also to be dealt with was an increasingly divisive argument (advanced by

Egypt's and Italy's Gnostic Christians) that the sign of the cross was a symbol of torture and humiliation and should be replaced by the symbol of the fish, or by an ankh-cross hybrid. This argument was vigorously opposed by eastern Christians and those living in metropolitan Rome, who believed that the cross was the superior sign because it signaled that their founding prophet and savior had converted a symbol of humiliation into one of triumph. Constantine announced that this argument would be shelved until after the issue of reincarnation was resolved.

Most Christians of A.D. 325 believed in the enlightenment of imperfect human souls through successive reincarnations. Indeed, if the Nile River, or Gnostic, gospels are windows on early Christian beliefs—dominated, as they were, by visions of Isis, Orpheus, and seemingly infinite deaths and rebirths, and by stories of souls needing (and finding) enlightenment by falling to Earth—it seems likely that even if we possessed the ultimate archaeological tool, *a time machine,* we would not be able to recognize any modern church among the first Christians.

To settle the reincarnation debate, two votes were held in Nicaea. In the first vote, the bishops were asked to choose between afterlife taking place (a) in the kingdom of heaven or (b) right here on Earth, by cyclical rebirth.

The first vote weighed in against the earthly reincarnationists, whereupon Constantine ordered the immediate execution of those who had voted for a belief in an earthly kingdom of God.

He then held a second vote: (a) afterlife in the kingdom of heaven or (b) afterlife in an earthly kingdom of God?

The second vote was unanimous, of course.

According to the church historian Eusebius (who, we must bear in mind, was probably as careful about his words as Pliny the Elder in the time of Nero, during which the admiral had written only about grammar), the reincarnationists, who were settled mostly in Alexandria and along the Nile, were subsequently declared "heretics" and (except for one Gnostic community that still thrives, with its own pope, in modern-day Iraq) were purged from existence.

Ninety years later, in the early fifth century, Archbishop Cyril burned most of Egypt's Gnostic gospels, along with much of Alexandria's library. He then executed the last of Alexandria's resident scientists and philosophers by flaying them alive to the bone with oyster shells. After he died of natural causes at an advanced old age, the church made Cyril a saint. Constantine, the church's founder and essentially its first pope, was never elected to sainthood—which probably speaks volumes about what church historians did not write concerning him. As bad as Saint Cyril proved to be, the church fathers must have judged Emperor Constantine to be an even lesser human being.

Meanwhile, between A.D. 325 and 410, between Nicaea and Cyril, the church judged gladiatorial combats too violent a form of public entertainment to be any longer tolerated. By the first decade of the fifth century, the height of Colosseum entertainment had become betting on fights between roosters fitted with foot blades. There were occasional elephant and giraffe parades accompanied by trapeze and clown acts—in effect, a "circus," sometimes preceded by the beheading of a church "heretic" or by a burning at the stake in the center ring.

From A.D. 410 onward, Rome continued to weaken from within, inviting increasingly frequent incursions from outside. From 410 until his death in 423, Emperor Honorius was unable to fend off invasions by Germanic people from the north. Alaric accomplished in 410 what Spartacus could scarcely begin to dream a half-millennium earlier: The sacking of Rome. The Vandals took Spain from the Western Empire in that same year. Nineteen years later, in A.D. 429, they crossed from Spain into northern Africa and began moving eastward toward Carthage. The last of the western emperors, Romulus Augustulus, abdicated office at the age of sixteen, on September 4, 476, and retired to Misenum on the Bay of Naples. Not even the church historians bothered to record what happened to him next, or even to mark the year of his death. In Romulus Augustulus's place there stood an archbishop of Rome and a Germanic mercenary who declared himself king of Italy. The Visigoths and Sueve tribes divided Spain between themselves, while the Vandals kept North Africa, Crete, and the isle of Thera. Britain, and its Roman city Londinium, were protected by a natural moat and remained an isolated surviving outpost of first- and second-century Roman technology . . . for a while. At the end of the fifth century and the beginning of the sixth, the British Isles appeared to be evolving toward Roman-style monarchy. The climate was warmer than it is today, and the period's castles, if such existed, were large-scale Roman villas with guard towers. This was the time of mythical Camelot; but the knights had Romanesque faces, and Merlin might just as well have been an oyster farmer who knew how to conduct steam. And this "Camelot," as misty and vague as a lost Atlantis, lasted until about A.D. 535, when the British Isles met the Dark Age, and dissolved into infighting barbarian tribes.

In the east, Constantinople became the center of the Christian Roman Empire, the home of Byzantine emperors, or "popes." Aqueducts, streetlighting, libraries, and advanced metalworking survived there; and by A.D. 530 the Byzantine Empire had seemed on the verge of recovering a dying civilization's former strengths, and even moving forward again, toward steam and steel, antibiotics and gunpowder. Far from destroying the Eastern Empire, increased competition at its borders appeared to strengthen its technological and military prowess. The borders were hardening, trade routes were expanding, and 530 seemed to mark a decade of economic growth. Then the environmental calamity of A.D. 535 struck—apparently the product of a global canopy of volcanic haze—leaving its imprint of ash and sulfur in North and South Polar ice. The 535 catastrophe, the terminal Roman event, was recorded in Constantinople by Bishop John as a dimming of the Sun and a summer without heat. There followed massive crop failures, plague, and total collapse of the economy. Bishop John did not leave a record of how the Dark Age finally descended upon him. He stopped writing in 536, after the toll in Constantinople neared a quarter-million dead from plague and famine.

In Rome, as if to herald the fall of Byzantium and the world, the Colosseum lay vacant at last. As the halfway mark of the sixth century approached, the city's population (as recorded by church historians and supported by archaeologists and paleobotanists) had declined to twenty-five thousand from an empire maximum of 1 million people. Forests were actually creeping into a metropolis left suddenly and mysteriously to the rule of lizards, Germanic warlords, malnourished vagrants, and the occasional merchant. On the Colosseum's floor and in the seams of marble-faced seats, dark green foliage, interspersed by an extraordinary variety of wildflowers from all over the world, became the beginnings of a spectacular garden that would endure and enchant well into the nineteenth century. On the avenues outside, wildflowers and grasses were giving way to cottonwoods—which, in time, would give way to beech trees and umbrella pines. Where furnaces, steam pipes, and pistons had warmed baths or pressurized the fire department's water pumps, troglodytes hunted wild animals in the streets and roasted them over campfires. And the forest, as it crept up the avenues and climbed the Forum steps, commenced to wedge the steps apart with its roots, and occasionally brought mighty stone columns crashing in pieces onto the ground.

Eroded by vegetation, looted and stripped down by every civilization, by every warlord, by every person passing through, Rome and its Colosseum were worn down into mere shadows of their former selves. Yet miles to the south, in Pompeii and Herculaneum, scraps of paper and handwritten messages on walls were outlasting granite spires erected by Nero and Titus.

In time-present, the gladiators of Rome's Colosseum have disappeared without a trace; yet in Pompeii, those poor souls whisper to us still and speak for all those who faced their fate. The philosopher Seneca (Nero's reluctant tutor) was among the few voices raised against gladiatorial servitude. His words were evidently appreciated by at least one well-read Pompeiian gladiator, for on the dining room wall of the gladiators' barracks, these words were scrawled: "THE PHILOSOPHER ANNAEUS SENECA IS THE ONLY ROMAN WRITER TO CONDEMN THE BLOODY GAMES."

WHILE MORE THAN HALF of the Colosseum's stonework disappeared in Rome, the fossil impression of a dog belonging to a man named Vesonius Primus survived in a Pompeiian garden. The dog had been bound to a post by a chain and leather collar. All the members of the Primus family must have abandoned the city at the first sign of trouble, never looking back to free their dog. Like most of the other Pompeiians left behind, the dog survived by climbing on top of the deepening pumice, as if it were merely walking upon deepening snow—until the "snow's" depth exceeded the length of the dog's chain. Long before the surge clouds reached the city, the ash had surrounded the Primus dog and preserved him in the disquieting attitude of slow death.

This Pompeiian dog was already quite dead by the time the 7:30 A.M. surge cloud reached the city. Chained in an atrium (or backyard), the dog climbed on top of the deepening and mostly harmless "snowbanks" of volcanic ash and pumice stone. Sometime during the predawn hours of August 25, A.D. 79, the collar chain ran out and the forgotten pet faced agonizing death by suffocation, as the ash tide rose slowly over his nose and mouth. Interestingly, dogs and people were fossilized in great numbers, but no cats. One is reminded of stoker Jim Mulholland's Southampton interview with Paddy Scott on April 10, 1912. The stoker had resigned his position as a member of the *Titanic*'s crew after a cat he had been caring for carried each of its four kittens down the gangplank and never came back aboard. "That cat knows something," Mulholland said.

The bodies of horses, donkeys, and other pack animals are rare in Pompeii and Herculaneum, probably because those people who decided to heed the volcano's warnings, and to retreat, mobilized anything on four legs that could carry a sack or a pull cart. At Pompeii's "House of Menander's" delivery entrance, a cart packed with wine jars was left behind. The delivery had probably arrived around lunchtime; and as the first ashfall from the eruption column headed in a straight line toward Pompeii, the horses or mules were unharnessed and (probably) ridden out of town.

The surge clouds, fallout deposits, and avalanche-like deposits, as they left their marks within the cities, acted with a mysterious combination of total destruction juxtaposed against gentle touches that would not have riffled a child's hair. And with astonishing frequency, they exerted these opposing forces simultaneously against the same house. In Herculaneum, the entire front of a house was cleared away and dropped off, at intervals and in pieces, along the length of a single street—and yet an empty cradle appears not to have been displaced so much as an inch, in the nursery of this same house; and the household pots, when archaeologists found them, still hung undisturbed over the kitchen stove. Only steps from the place where the roof of poor Justa's basilica exploded, and where a bronze statue of a charioteer and his steeds was dissected in midflight and scattered over a sixth of a mile, a dining room table in the "House of the Relief of Telephus" was set with a serving of now-carbonized eggs—along with the rest of the lunch: bread, salad greens, fruit, and honey-sweetened cake. The owners of this house ran away at the first trump. This and several other served but untouched lunches throughout Herculaneum and Pompeii, when combined with evidence that furnaces in the Suburban Baths were still waiting for their lunchtime fire-up, reveal something about Pliny the Elder's habits—something trivial, perhaps, when considered against the larger scales of two lost cities and their place in the history of a lost civilization, but worthy of some small interest nonetheless. Pliny the Younger, in his letters to Tacitus, said that his uncle "had taken a cold bath, and lunched while lying down, and was then working on his books," when the younger Pliny's mother drew their attention to the eruption column. Either the eruption had been in progress for an hour before anyone in the Pliny household noticed (not likely), or Pliny the Elder, an early riser who, according to his nephew, was often working before dawn, took his afternoon bath and ate his lunch a lot earlier than most people. For Pliny the Elder, the daily routine was probably a matter of early to rise, early to work, followed by a late-morning bath and brunch, instead of breaking for midday lunch. A traditional time-stamping of "lunch hour" for the Plinys would suggest that the baths in Herculaneum and Pompeii should already have been heated for the arriving lunch-hour crowds. However, a closer reading of the admiral's work habits, as described by his nephew, appears to explain why the firewood for Herculaneum's Suburban Baths was still stacked and waiting to be used, when the volcano intervened. A nontraditional lunch hour in the Pliny household would fix the beginning of the eruption (the bottom of Pompeii's white pumice layer) between 11 A.M. and noon.

More than 16 miles (27 kilometers) east of Pliny, in Herculaneum's "Shop of the Drinking Priapus," samples of nuts had just been set out on the countertop, presumably for the usual lunchtime crowd. Lunch was also about to be served in the "House of the Philosopher," around the corner from the Priapus tavern. Silver cups had been laid beside napkins and spoons, apparently in preparation for the arrival of guests. Both the tavern and the house were abandoned before the customers or the guests could be seated and served.

Near Herculaneum's Temple of Augustus, the statue of a woman was thrown facedown onto the street, as lifelike as a Michelangelo sculpture, as lifelike as the flash-fossilized people of Pompeii. At first glance, it sometimes becomes impossible for us to discern once-living people from their statuary, as if the Greek myth of Medusa—whose gaze could turn men instantly into stone—somehow anticipated Pompeii by more than a thousand years. Closer inspection is no less disconcerting. Up close, I have discovered a woman sculpted in such spine-chilling detail that the Pompeiian custom of shaving the pubic hair to semicircular form has been rendered in polished white marble. On another side of the town, this same semicircular shape is plainly visible through folds of fine linen enclosing a woman sculpted in volcanic ash.

Herculaneum's "House of the Gem," though in its own right a grandiose structure with spectacular sea views, was all but surrounded by the even more grandiose "House of the Relief of Telephus," where the now-fossilized eggs, salad, and dessert had been set on the table for lunch, then abandoned. Only a portion of the Telephus mansion has been excavated from the solidified matrix. But this mere portion is more than enough for archaeologists attempting to pry stories from old walls, says historian Joseph Jay Diess: "In studying the irregularities of the ground plan [and the construction of "new" walls], one gets the impression that the owner had tried to buy the [nearby] 'House of the Gem' for its view of the bay, and frustrated, had built all around the 'House of the Gem,' almost swallowing it like a gigantic amoeba. As too-intimate neighbors, the owners must have greeted each other daily with a very testy 'good morning.'"

The "House of the Gem" got its name from a precious sapphire left behind, engraved cameo-like with the portrait of a beautiful woman. The larger, surrounding mansion of the Telephus sculpture was connected by a private passage to the Suburban Baths—which, in accordance with certain fractionally intact dedication marbles, were an apparent gift from Marcus Balbus, proconsul of Crete, to his beloved town of Herculaneum. The enormously wealthy Balbus (one of the John Jacob Astors or Bill Gateses of his day) had provided financial support to Vespasian during the civil war of A.D. 68–69 and was subsequently rewarded with proconsulship. That he was unable either to buy the property on which stood the "House of the Gem," or to move the courts to evict the stubborn neighbor, would suggest that the gem owner was sufficiently wealthy and well connected to resist such efforts. The idea of equal political connections gains support from graffitos on the Gem House's latrine wall (or message board), identifying Apollinaris, physician of Emperor Titus, as having moved his bowels there ("APOLLINARIS MEDICUS TITI IMPERATORIS HIC CACAVIT BENE").

The Telephus mansion appears to have taken the brunt of the first downblast and might even have served as a protective barrier for the neighbor it enclosed. A huge portion of it was completely uprooted, then shotgunned over the marina's boathouses and out to sea (while, naturally, a salad and napkins lay unmoved on a table).

In the House of the Gem, the stone for which the archaeologists have named it is not all that was left behind. A wooden cradle containing the carbonized and heat-fractured bones of an infant is still there, in the nursery. During the late twentieth century, before the nature and sequence of the eruption could be deciphered, one archaeologist, after examining the bones, speculated, "Perhaps the baby's parents were not home and the nursemaid fled when Vesuvius exploded, leaving the child." There were many cradles preserved in the two cities, but only one with a child still in it.

"It seems incredible that a baby could have been abandoned to Vesuvius," said another, "but it looks as if that is what has happened."

Even in a world where gladiatorial splatterfests were socially acceptable, it seemed, at first glance, incredible—and then, on second glance, precisely *because* of gladiator games (looked down upon with disdain by the twentieth-century "enlightenment")—that such abandonment became thinkable, perhaps even perfectly feasible. To the archaeologists, all crimes became possible under the spotlight of the games, despite the fact that within their own twentieth century (sometimes within their own countries) mob-inspired public lynchings had been cheered . . . and despite the fact that it had once been socially acceptable (even to a few who experienced the lockdown and lived to testify) to keep the "lower classes" down below on the sinking *Titanic*. Were the generations that saw Hitler, Stalin, and Pol Pot really any more (or less) human than the generations that saw Caligula and Nero?

(*Time will have its say.*)

The twenty-four thousand souls lost under the volcano were simply human beings, struggling to do the best that they could with whatever they had, in whatever time and place to which they were born . . . Some twelve hours after the eruption column surged into the sky, sometime between midnight and one, in the predawn hours of August 25, the infant still lay bundled in its cradle, in the House of the Gem. But it must not have been alone. The first downblast and surge was probably preceded by an avalanche within the throat of the volcano, or by some other nozzle-interrupting phenomenon that, 4 miles (7 kilometers) away, made itself known as a terrifying noise. Anyone remaining in the city who was tending to and protecting a child, would likely have gone outside to see what was happening, and to assess the danger. Logically, he or she had to.

There are some sights so cyclopean, so overmastering, that they can stun rational minds into inaction. The incandescent surge cloud was just that sort of sight. The adults who stepped outside probably watched for a time. In the final seconds, they might have turned and tried to run indoors—before being plucked from the street, vaporized, and swept out to sea, along with half of a neighbor's house.

In another part of town, another child died in the similarly named "House of the Gem Cutter." As in the "House of the Gem," the owners left behind not only precious jewels but their precious child as well. Here, too, archaeologists of the late twentieth century were quick to judge: The skeleton of a young woman found in the same room became, to them, "probably, a slave girl," and both were "abandoned, and left to die, by the child's father." But here, too, the child-abandonment theory fails to stand the test of time, if indeed it ever stood at all.

The child was an adolescent boy, aged twelve to fourteen. The young woman in the room with him was in her late teens or early twenties, certainly too young to be the child's mother, but about the right age for an older sister (though DNA tests are, in this case, inconclusive).

On close inspection, the boy's joints are revealed to be malformed. The muscle attachments to the bones are especially abnormal, in the manner of a disease rarely seen since the 1950s: polio. The nameless polio survivor was evidently too frail to be moved when the eruption began, so the gem cutter, his wife, and the rest of the family must have stayed behind, while the rest of the Herculaneans evacuated. Twelve hours later he still lay on a couch. Lunch hour was long past when the end came, meaning that the bowl of chicken soup lying near the couch

On a couch in Herculaneum's "House of the Gem Cutter's Shop," the skeleton of an adolescent boy was encased in a fusion shell of white-hot powder. Bone malformations bear witness to the child's fight against crippling illness at the time of the Vesuvius awakening. Not very far from the loom she might have been operating, a girl in her late teens was vaporized to ashes and chips of blackened bone in the space of a quarter-second. Expensive gems and finely crafted furnishings with inlaid wood designs were preserved in a neighboring room.

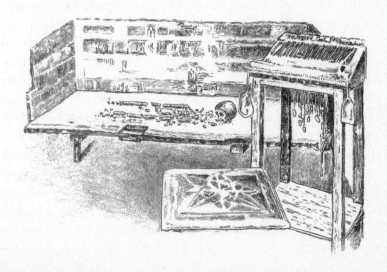

was probably a freshly heated late-night snack, for it is not likely that anyone who stayed in town slept easily that night. As in the House of the Gem, most of the family is missing, and probably for the same reason: Something quite loud, and more frightening than anything heard or felt during the previous twelve hours, must have drawn them outside. They lived long enough to see death rolling toward them from the east, and it had stupefied them. And then, doubtless, they wanted to run back to the children; but by then, of course, they could not.

THE SAME DOWNBLASTING and ground-surging eruption columns that cocooned the marina and the House of the Gem under a 60-foot-high (or 20-meter) canopy of airtight fusion crust, also piled up in the sea. A quarter-mile west of the House of the Gem's former bay view (for nearly three city blocks, or 656 meters out to sea), land now exists where once there was water.

And yet, groundwater rises so high that the marina and the lower terraces of the Suburban Baths would lie submerged if not for the constant action, day and night, of the archaeologists' water pumps. The beach, where the Roman soldier fell, lies 13 feet (4 meters) below early-twenty-first-century sea levels. The ground here has subsided, or the seas have risen, or the rising of the sea and subsidence of the land have combined to sink the city of Herculaneum 13 feet below the waves.

(Earth abides, and is never static, and time will always have its say.)

On the northern shore of Minoan Crete, I have followed the docks and foundation stones of the ancient harbor town of Heraklion— followed them underwater (on average, under 5 to 12 feet of water). Along some of the Greek islands, ancient stone roadways, traceable for miles and submerged 10 to 15 feet (about 3 to 5 meters) under the Mediterranean, are not uncommon. The same process that had been tearing down ice sheets and slowly raising sea levels hundreds of feet eight thousand years before the Minoans and ten thousand years before the Romans did not simply come to a halt in A.D. 79.

The very structures in which the Pompeiians and Herculaneans dwelled drive home the message of a world continually and perhaps even irrevocably in change. Outside of the public baths, heating appears (at first sight) to have been a severe problem for people living around the Bay of Naples. A closer look, a look beyond the baths and the saunas, reveals that none of the homes were equipped with fireplaces. Add to this the fact that most of the coal-fired braziers excavated from the living areas seem to have been designed more for heating wine and fruit juices (in their attached "cookers") than for removing the chill from Herculanean or Pompeiian reading rooms and dining areas during the winter months. Glass windows, even in the grander residences, seem rarely to have served as more than wind-and-rain breaks for residents wishing to study or dine in their gardens on stormy days, despite the fact that panes a quarter-inch (6 millimeters) thick could easily have been redesigned and repositioned to provide excellent insulation in the manner of present-day storm windows. And yet, though here and there panes framed in brass were inserted into walls, opening and closing on modern-appearing window pivots, most windows had only curtains or wooden shutters to keep out drafts, and many had ornate terra-cotta iron grilles, designed merely to keep out the birds.

In the twenty-first century, the months of December, January, and February can be uncomfortably and occasionally even bitterly cold along the foothills of Vesuvius. The mountain itself is often white with snow in mid-winter. Evidently, the houses within the earth are trying to teach us that when their roof tiles and balconies last greeted the sunrise, the Bay of Naples was shallower than it is today, and the winters were warmer.

Between Herculaneum's Fountain of Apollo (in the Suburban Baths) and America's Apollo missions to the moon lies an enigmatic period called the "Little Ice Age," at the conclusion of which George Washington's horses were buried up to their bellies in snow at Valley Forge.

The lessons from geology and bioarchaeology are clear: Earth and the Sun are unfinished. All that is, is transitory. Warming, cooling, and warming trends were (as rocks and even as human generations measure time) flashing over the land, long before the emergence of mechanized fishing fleets, automobiles, and global industrialization. Ever since we entered the last interglacial period (and it is, almost to a certainty, a mere *inter*glacial), temperatures have, quite naturally and of their own accord, been trending upward . . . two degrees forward, one degree back, two degrees forward—

The only guarantee given us (in accordance with cycles of warming and cooling displayed on the growth bands of Martian and earthly ice caps—which are likely identical cycles owing to an inconstant Sun), is that global climate is inconstant, almost as a matter of sheer definition. The only guarantee given us by the climate is that it will change. The solar constant may increase, or decrease. Simultaneously, a volcano may bring on a temporary global cooling. Human activity, including but not limited to a carbon-burning economy—may enhance a warming trend that has been in effect for ten millennia.

Humans, discovering now that the climate (as measured by the yardstick of their increasing life spans) may change quickly, are sometimes gripped by a combination of awe and panic. And then hubris sets in, expressed as the demand that something must be done to stop the change, to render Earth static again: steady and changeless, without chaos.

But Earth has never been static—

(Earth abides—)

And neither are living things static, or without chaos. Every electrocardiogram of a human heart is a graph of chaos with feedback, and with fractal repetition. We call the static, steady, and nonchaotic state "flatline," or "death." We may try, with the application of the right chemicals or legal restrictions, to render Earth's climatic trends static; our hubris may guide us toward molding weather patterns to a more stable, human view of life. We may even succeed, in the short term. But a half-billion earthly heartbeats from now, a half-billion Septembers from now, Earth will still be revolving around the Sun at its own planetary pace.

It should have cooled some, by then. Geologic heat, radiated away at the surface, shall slow the rate of continental drift, shall decrease the frequency of volcanic eruptions by several percent. The Moon, orbiting several thousand miles farther away, will no longer exactly match the apparent diameter of the Sun, and a coincidence so rare that it probably only occurs once or twice in an entire galaxy of stars shall pass; and no one on Earth will ever again see a total eclipse of the Sun.

But Earth abides, and does not know, or care, if something of our distant descendants still lives a half-billion Septembers from now, or if we shall be little more than broken roof tiles and scraps of skull sandwiched between interglacial fossil beds.

Earth abides . . . by its own rules—

Unknowing.

Uncaring.

Forever.

EXCERPT FROM SUPPLEMENTAL LOG,

KELDYSH EXPEDITIONS

DATE: *Tuesday, October 15, 2002*

PLACE: *Saint Paul's Chapel, Ground Zero, New York City*

Time is the fire in which we burn; or so the poets say. "Past, present, and future are only an illusion; albeit a stubborn one." Or so Albert Einstein used to say.

We who dwell too long in the past—we of archaeology, paleontology, volcanology, and astronomy—might do well to take heed of warnings from Einstein and the poets. We who trace the chain of cause and effect backward through time are bound to uncover unpleasant surprises; for as way leads onto way, and as the relics of the past kick open windows to both present and future, today becomes the yesterday you worried about tomorrow.

Downblast and surge physics . . .

It's easy in Herculaneum, even awe-inspiring. Of course it is. I did not know those people. Even Justa (though I can read her words), she's a stranger to me. She's part of another civilization—a civilization whose very light is now more distant than Orion and Ursa Major.

But could I ever have imagined, outside of science fiction, that I'd have ended up studying Herculanean-style surge cloud effects against artifacts from my own time—against window dressings, computer monitors, aluminum cladding, and an entire legal library shotgunned over the top of Engine 10/Ladder 10 House and into O'Hara's Tavern?

So here I sit, in a chapel on the edge of "WTC Crater," praying an agnostic's prayer to an agnostic's savior—

(Dear God—I don't believe in you; but if you're there, and I wish you were, don't let what's outside that back door be merely coming attractions for much of the world during the next forty years. No. Don't let us make any more artificial volcanoes . . . and half the world like Pompeiian dust.)

But enough of this. Enough for today. The only escape from the future is into the past, right? Time to go home to your lab, Charlie. Home to your library. Home to decipher Pompeiian dust. Vesuvian ash is easier than World Trade Center dust, always easier than present reality.

THE HOLLOW SPACE around her finger still enclosed bones when archaeologists began clearing the ash and dust away from Pompeii's "House of the Faun" (so named after a statue discovered in the house's garden). Further along her skeletal arm, behind the wrist, a coiled bracelet in the shape of a serpent gleamed with ruby eyes set in solid gold. During the last years of her life, Cassia had remodeled the atrium in which she died, and had decorated the rest of the house with antiques from Greece and India.

Cassia was descended from a prominent family that had built its mansion in Pompeii before Julius Caesar became dictator in 49 B.C. She was a woman of wealth and importance, but ultimately this made no difference. The volcano crushed her and the loan sharks of the Taverna Lusoria with equal ease.

Records buried inside taverns and bankers' houses preserve methods of banking and wealth-gathering in two different neighborhoods of Pompeii: Cassia's neighborhood and "Tavern Row." One neighborhood offered lower interest payments, detailed ledgers of all accounts, and modest penalties for failure to pay (ranging from an increased payment scale and foreclosure to sale of the borrower into slavery). The other offered higher interest payments, minimal bookkeeping, and penalties for nonpayment ranging from finger breaking or sale into slavery, to skull busting and death.

The safe in Lucius Caecilius Jucundus's office (in the Via Stabina, on Cassia's side of town) contained 154 wax tablets, buried on August 24 in a thick layer of pumice—which insulated the tablets from both the heat and the physical shock of the surge clouds that reached Pompeii about 7:30 A.M. the next day. At first, the archaeologists and "safecrackers" of A.D. 1875, as they began to read the safe's contents, were disappointed to learn that instead of the lost works of Plato or Saint Paul, they were slowly, painstakingly revealing scrawlings that might just as well have belonged in an accountant's or a banker's wastebasket. But excavators did, in time, come around to seeing treasure in the mundane.

The Jucundus ledgers revealed loans, repayment practices, and other monetary secrets of prominent Pompeiians, including the continually expanding popularity of the Scaurus family's recipe for bottled fermented fish paste into a sauce monopoly of international proportions. During the last years of Pompeii, the fish sauce barons became the Roman equivalent of overnight multimillionaires, or what Cassia's family would have looked down upon and called "new money."

Accountant Lucius Jucundus was, himself, the son of a slave-accountant who had bought his freedom and laid the foundation of the family banking business. The record shows that Jucundus, in his own turn, gave freedom to one of his own slave-accountants without accepting a payment in gold.

On the other end of town, near a V-shaped intersection that produced the Pompeiian forerunner of New York's "Flatiron Building," the Taverna Lusoria provided credit, gambling, heated wine, and legalized prostitution. The city's hotels and brothels ranged from cramped and cheap to the magnificent House of the Sallust, with its large rooms, garden restaurants, and availability to the city's highest-priced and most exotic "escorts."

Nearly two thousand years after four women—all wearing gold and pearls and one of them carrying a silver mirror—climbed out of the mansion to greet the fourth Vesuvian death cloud, historians liked to recount the tale of a famous freed gladiator and theatrical performer to whom the wealthy daughters of three cities were said to have offered hands of marriage. But he rejected them all, in preference for the company of prostitutes provided by the mistress of the Sallust's mansion. When asked why a man so handsome and so universally desired believed he needed to pay women to share food, wine, and his bed, he replied, "I do not pay women to dine with me and to sleep with me. I pay them to *leave* when I am finished with them."

ABOUT SIX HOURS after the last sunrise, just before lunch and the first trump, cakes and tarts were being removed from the baker Sextus Felix's brick ovens and set out to cool on a marble countertop. Several doors down the road, in a bakeshop that specialized in fresh bread and dog biscuits, flour was being milled by two donkeys whose bones reveal breeders in possession of an advanced knowledge of the genetic controls behind the shaping of animals. Through successive generations, someone had fine-tuned a breed of donkey to the specific purpose of turning millstones in small shops: The donkeys were, ounce for ounce of muscle, far stronger than dogs of average size, yet barely larger than dogs.

Elsewhere in the cities, brick-oven "flatbreads," or pizzas, were being baked. According to Apicius, the Roman chef who penned the world's first best-selling cookbooks, some of the pizzas, in addition to such usual toppings as goat cheese, anchovies, mushrooms, and sliced grilled octopus, might receive (for an additional fee) a generous helping of cream-fed dormice. This rare delicacy, like the miniature mill-donkey, was apparently the product of genetic fine-tuning: a special breed of hairless pink mouse (think of this as "crunchy mouse and octopus pizza").

Lunch at Vesuvius tended to be a light meal—essentially a midday snack of bread, eggs, cheese, or pizza. However, on that final August 24, some of the finer garden restaurants and bathhouses were preparing to serve more lavish fare. Entrails of mackerel were garnished with spiced and salted preparations of fermented fish sauce from the factory-style kitchens of Scaurus. Medallions of fresh ham were being oven-baked— honey-glazed with bay leaves and fig slices pressed into slits in the meat, and with the medallions themselves then folded inside thin, crisped pastry crusts.

On that fine sunny day, one local chef had garnished a sweet cheese-cake with poppy seeds. Then the mountain awoke and the cake was left unattended in an oven to overcook and to carbonize of its own accord, hours before the first grains of pumice and ash drifted indoors. Car-

A piece of Pompeiian bread, seared to ash and then fossilized, survived only as a hollow space in the ground—which was preserved by pumping the fossil impression full of plaster before the surrounding ash was excavated. Writing in the time frame of Emperor Titus's recovery operations, the historian Josephus appears to have mined discoveries from the first Pompeii excavations for his histories and his annotated bible, adding details to the Jewish apocalyptic tale of Sodom—"of which there are still reminders of that divine fire." Table settings and meals of the dead biblical city were preserved for all time—but merely as "shadows of the fruits." If plucked out of the ground, according to Josephus, the food, though giving the illusion of still being edible, would "dissolve into smoke and ashes."

bonization, the paradoxical preserver, reveals that even cheesecake was lightly flavored with (or contaminated by) Scaurus's famous fish sauce—broken jars bearing the Scaurus imprint, or "label," have turned up in first-century landfills as far away as France and Spain. Nearer to home, Pliny the Elder made special mention in one of his lists ("cities and their produce") of Pompeii's special fish sauce—a version of which, adapted to fermented shrimp, survives into twenty-first-century China, whence it has come full circle to the Bay of Naples, by way of Hong Kong's chefs. In August of 79, "Famous Scaurus" sauce appears to have been called for even in recipes for rabbit—and in one of Apicius's favorites: fish liver topped with flamingos' tongues and milk-fattened snails. According to Apicius, if the sauce was not quite spicy enough for a chef's individual taste, he should "kick it up a notch" with pepper and cumin.

On that final approaching lunch hour, on the first day of an archaeological deep freeze, a cooked mixture of beaten eggs and olive oil flavored with diced smoked ham, cracked pepper, and a dash of honey was being prepared in a Pompeiian tavern. A wall menu identified it as "OVA MELLITA." The name of the dish—pronounced "omelet"—was destined to outlive Scaurus, the Plinys, and the Empire.

ON A SILVER COIN discovered in the black sands near the Herculaneum marina, the deified emperor Augustus was proclaimed "Son of God" (presumably "son" of Jupiter, the Roman Zeus).

Augustus died in A.D. 14. Twenty-four years later, in 38, Gaius Caligula declared himself both a living son of Jupiter and the Messiah whose arrival had been prophesied by the Jews. In A.D. 41, he commanded that the Temple in Jerusalem be turned into an imperial shrine; but before the work could begin, he was assassinated by his own bodyguards. Caligula's uncle Claudius ruled from A.D. 41 to 54, and he was deified as a god after his death (his adopted son, Nero, was not). Claudius's childhood friend, Herod Agrippa I, was instrumental in sending Jesus to Caiphas to be judged for heresy, and then proclaimed *himself* Messiah in A.D. 44 (according to Eusebius)—whereupon he died suddenly of unknown causes. Vespasian, about whom Pliny the Younger's friend Tacitus wrote (in *Histories,* 1.50), "Unlike all his predecessors, [he] was the only emperor who was changed for the better by his office," ascended, like Augustus and Claudius before him, to deification after death, by senatorial decree. Titus, too—son of Vespasian—would become a posthumous "Son of God."

The worship of emperors (and kings) who had come to Earth from the heavens, lived as godly "spirits" or "sons" in human form, then ascended into the heavens and rejoined the other gods after death, was an idea with a long tradition by A.D. 79. At the same time, the Egyptian belief in mummifying or preserving body parts (or bodily "artifacts") was becoming popular throughout the Roman world.

In Herculaneum, the Shrine of the Augustales, established in A.D. 14

by senatorial decree, headquartered the priests who presided over the worship of Augustus, Claudius, and Vespasian. According to the temple record, Titus, the newly appointed emperor, had automatically assumed the title of high priest—*pontifex maximus*—of the Roman religion. In years to come, this very same title would be assumed by Roman Catholic popes.

The popularity of all things Egyptian in A.D. 79 would likewise live on beyond Vesuvius, in the Vatican's little-known practice of mummifying, and by other means preserving after death, the bodies (and bodily artifacts) of all popes. When an assassination attempt against Pope John Paul II required that a section of his intestine be removed in order to save his life, the body parts were dried and preserved for eventual burial with the pontiff. The would-be assassin's bullet, meanwhile, became the centerpiece of a jeweled crown.

Stepping six stories down into the earth, and backward in time, Herculaneum's Shrine of the Augustales has left us with a glimpse, perhaps, of Roman Catholic beginnings, and with a mystery. In a room adjacent to the great hall dedicated to deified emperors, the skeleton of a man lies facedown on a bed. The room has only one door and a tiny, iron-barred window looking out into the hall. Besides the bed, the room contains only one other piece of furniture: a table that is, like the bed, assembled from the finest-quality, most luxuriously worked wood. And yet, for the man in the bed, the room was a deliberately fashioned prison cell.

Evidently too important to be held in an ordinary jail, and therefore likely to be a priestly member of the imperial cult, the man is referred to by some archaeologists (either rightly or wrongly) as "the heretic." Some visitors have read, in that final, facedown attitude of the heretic's skeleton, a man who threw himself upon the bed in a last second of despair, although a last-second attempt to hide his face from the midnight surge cloud seems more likely.

What *can* be said, based on an analysis of the Vesuvian fallout and surge layers, aided by the Pliny account, is that nearly twelve hours passed between the beginning of the eruption and the moment the first surge cloud descended upon the temple. During those twelve hours, while Herculaneum remained entirely ash-free, most of the population, including (doubtless) the Augustale priests, had time to pack their valuables and evacuate westward along the road to Misenum. No other conclusion remains, except that the Augustales must have made a conscious decision to leave their prisoner locked in the temple, with absolutely no hope of escape.

In those final hours, as Herculaneum became a time capsule with people, buildings, and all the artifacts of everyday life "flash-frozen" at their last instant of use and existence, a murder was preserved in the shrine of the emperor worshipers.

In time-present, with more than two-thirds of Herculaneum still sealed in rock and unexplored, we cannot help but wonder how many similar mysteries wait to be discovered. The story of those last days is one that deserves to be reexplored, resolved more clearly, and told anew in every generation, lest we fail to remember whence we came, where we are going, and the sway that fate and random chance hold over us.

As the Augustile shrine slept within the earth, for two centuries, and then for three, whatever heresy had triggered the murder ceased to matter any longer. Between A.D. 79 and the start of Constantine's reign in 307, as the Christian faith grew in stature and numbers, emperor worship was put upon the wane (and ultimately was transformed, or partly borrowed, on Vatican Hill). Another casualty of the new religion was Epicureanism—which had, by 79, evolved from a philosophy (much like Buddhism) into a religion that would no longer have been recognizable to its founding philosopher-prophet.

Approximately 100 yards down the shore from the Herculaneum marina and the Suburban Baths, beyond a bridge that crossed a small and picturesque stream, lay the "Villa of the Papyri." In the center of the villa, a huge rectangular pond (217 feet, or 65 meters, in length) provided a showcase for ornamental fish, whose bones and scales reveal that they were cooked alive by the first surge cloud. More than a hundred years earlier, the Roman writer Cicero had deplored the increasingly common *piscinarii*: "These fanciers of fish, who give their finned pets names, weep when they die . . . And in their obsession for fish, the nobles neglect affairs of state, worrying only when their ornamental mullets refuse to eat from their hands."

Not very far from the fishpond—which was surrounded by pillars, and by statues depicting every manner of legend (ranging from the god

Apollo and mythical Amazons to an elflike Pan having intercourse with a she-goat)—there stood the main house, four stories tall. There, the midnight surge cloud had dislodged whole bookshelves of scrolls in wooden boxes, throwing some of them along hallways and outdoors, carbonizing them all, encapsulating them, then passing them like messages in bottles from a doomed empire with steam locomotives and even flight within three centuries' grasp to an electronic civilization with interplanetary and even interstellar flight within fewer than five decades' reach.

(Whatever we're coming to, we're almost there . . .)

Though discovered by tunnelers in the time of America's Revolutionary War, it was not until the twenty-first century (with the aid of the same digital-imaging and spectrographic scan technology that allowed space-probe *Odyssey*'s scientists to decipher the chemical makeup of Hellas Basin with cameras in Mars orbit) that scholars could actually begin to distinguish between burned black ink and burned black "paper." Not until the emergence of imaging technology derived from Hollywood computer-effects teams and NASA spacecraft could anyone actually read the Roman texts.

"They're whispering to us," says one of the papyrus scholars. "After all these years, the dead are whispering to us across time."

My own quest for the past began with paleontology—began three decades ago with the discovery that the marls of New Jersey's Big Brook Creek had preserved a tiny fossil crab that lived and scavenged in the time of the last dinosaurs. And from there, a paleontologist named Gerry Case led me to New Jersey's dinosaur-era amber beds, whereupon I became obsessed with unusual forms of preservation—amber, ice, oxygen-starved water, volcanic surge clouds—as Cicero's *piscinarii* had become obsessed with their pets.

And from among the strangely preserved fish bones, the homes, the human skeletons of Pompeii and Herculaneum, an Epicurean philosopher named Philodemus whispers clearly (and in ironic overtones) after almost two thousand years: "All this anxious love of life of theirs comes only from the fear of death. And they try to push all images of it away from them. And then, when it comes too close and [too near] to ignore, a strange thing happens to them. When [death] comes suddenly before their eyes, they—summing up with utter clarity as one sums up at the end of a long sentence—breathe their last. As gone as if their awareness of death had never failed them for the smallest interval of time."

Philodemus appears actually to have lived in the Villa of the Papyri (and to have tended, there, to his fish) in the time of Cicero and Julius Caesar, a century before the eruption. Born near the sea of Galilee, Philodemus had settled (for a time) in Rome, where he became personally acquainted with Cicero. In one of his surviving letters, the Stoic philosopher Cicero criticizes an unnamed Epicurean philosopher and "great friend" of Lucius Calpurnius Piso Caesoninus. Piso was the wealthy father-in-law of Julius Caesar. The dictator had actually financed Piso's construction of the Villa of the Papyri in Herculaneum. In "Philodemus' Herculaneum Library Document 1507," Piso dedicates his book, *On the King According to Homer*, to his dictator-benefactor: "Piso, which [illegible] it is possible to take from Homer for the correction of Monarchies."

According to Cicero, Piso and his Epicurean friend lacked the spirit of self-denial and discipline advocated by traditional Epicureans, because, far from advocating monogamy, simple meals, meditation, and study, they lived for sensual pleasure, for dining throughout the night, and for drunken group lovemaking with young Greeks of both sexes. Cicero also castigated them for having pillaged the great, already "antique" statues of Greece—hinting, perhaps, at the source of the Villa of the Papyri's scores of bronze and marble masterpieces.

In Greece, about 300 B.C., Epicureanism and Stoicism became the leading schools of philosophy. The Stoic schools were founded by Zeno, who believed in a deterministic universe, wherein a person's role in history was laid out (or determined) in advance, even before the births of parents and grandparents. In such a universe, a man or a woman had at best only a limited free will, expressed only in the way that a given part of the drama was perceived and played out. As Zeno saw the world, history's participants had no choice in what part to play. The Stoics, therefore, advocated a grim acceptance of whatever life had to offer, for better or for worse.

Epicurus, an Athenian disciple of Democritus (the father of the scientific method), believed, like Plato, that human beings could be (and would be) improved; but unlike Plato, he rejected the Greek pantheon of gods and a belief in "afterlife." The early, pre-Vesuvius Epicureans advocated the pursuit of knowledge above all other earthly treasures. In small universities, or monasteries, libraries were to be assembled and knowledge was to be shared over bland communal meals of bread and unsweetened wine. Building the mind, as one (simultaneously) builds the muscles in preparation for athletic competition, was the Epicurean goal in life, according to Epicurus, who wrote, "Let no one be slow to seek wisdom when he is young, nor weary to search for it when he grows old."

Not far from the place where Vesuvius ruptured the villa's library floor (and exposed evidence of a complex, high-pressure plumbing system that fed the garden's fountains and supplied the house's tanks with both hot and cold running water), the second century B.C. editions of Epicurean books, written mostly in Greek and scattered in fragments across the floor, advise Philodemus, Piso, and their distant descendants to preserve, always, one's childlike sense of wonder about Earth and Cosmos. One must never grow weary of cricket song at dusk, or cease to look in wonderment at the multitude of stars, according to the founding Epicureans. One must never let the child in him die as he grows older or allow his humanity to slowly drain away.

In twenty-first-century parlance, we might call this a "Peter Pan philosophy." Yet Epicurus would have been proud to have the inscription above his grave read: "He never grew up. But he never stopped growing."

Like most philosophies and religions, Epicureanism underwent reform and subsequent division (or speciation) into multiple expanding factions that guaranteed mutation throughout time. A result of this was that the more orthodox Epicureanism practiced by Cicero was different from the branch evidenced in the writings of Philodemus, as preserved in Herculaneum: "Demo and Thermian both sway me. One is a pro, the other still unversed [a virgin]. The one I can grope; the other I must not touch. I swear, goddess [Venus], I do not know which I want more."

Demo and Thermian were both young Greeks.

Time (which Epicurus once characterized as an "accident of accidents") has preserved, in the Herculaneum library, a changed and more materialistic, "easygoing" version of Epicureanism (certainly not Epicurus's version). No longer seeking austere freedom from desire and distraction ("freedom from pain")—which Epicurus called the ideal—the

In an era of valve, boiler, and piston, Herculaneum's seafront homes boasted sliding glass doors, pools, fountains, hot and cold running water, and garden dining areas. Reconstructed here, from tunnel-based exploration, the gardens of Herculaneum are viewed as if through the shadows of a Roman arch. A life-size bronze of the messenger god, Mercury, overlooks a pleasure garden in the Villa of the Papyri. Perfectly intact and largely unexplored, the villa and its extensive library still lie under the streets of twenty-first-century Erculano.

Philodemus theme became more closely akin to "Eat, drink, and be merry, for tomorrow you'll wish you were dead."

In a preserved "letter to Menoeceus," Epicurus, unlike Philodemus, advocated a simple, "travel lightly through life, with few possessions" philosophy. The orthodox Epicureans attempted to live unburdened by distraction, so that one's attentions could be more effectively concentrated on study. They had much in common with contemporary Buddhism—which was likewise a philosophy and not a religion.

"We consider it as a great gift even the fact of being happy with little," wrote Epicurus. "Not because we have to content ourselves with little, but because if we do not have a lot, we can content ourselves with little." Even in food, Epicurus generally recommended austerity—which is, again, at odds with the great Herculanean estate where the Epicurean scrolls are preserved, just steps away from a "Grand Dining Saloon." Epicurus himself advised, "Bread and water offer the supreme pleasure when received by one who really needs them. To have the habit of feeding oneself in a simple way instead of sumptuously not only guarantees good health and assures that man overcomes, without delay, life's unavoidable activities; it also causes us to taste more intensely the sumptuous banquets that turn up from time to time. It also makes us fearless in the face of destiny."

The original Epicureans fought to remove gluttony, lust, vanity, and other distractions from daily life, in favor of meditation and study. To Epicurus, the gaining of knowledge and wisdom and the teaching of what one had learned were like giving one's heart to life's true love. Like love, knowledge could be given to another and yet the giver still kept what he had given away freely.

In Rome, a century before the Villa of the Papyri went into the earth, Cicero had embraced "orthodox" Epicureanism. At Herculaneum, Piso and Philodemus had either joined or originated an Epicurean reformist movement that was (while building libraries and boasting the "trappings" of learned existence) neither austere nor centered on learning. Philodemus's own works, preserved as charred scrolls, seem to reflect this. They are notoriously dull and uninspired, becoming interesting only in those more creative moments when the vain and gluttonous philosopher passed, into futurity, what he believed to be either love sonnets or clever limericks but what were in fact closer in content and style to the local graffiti: "Philainion [my lady lover] is always ready for Anything, and often lets Me have it free. I'll put up with such a [mistress]—O, golden [Venus], until a better one is invented." And, said Philodemus to another, "So I am your 'darling girl'! Your tears say so, and the sleights your hands play—You are conventionally jealous, and your kisses suggest a lover who knows what he wants. I am the more confused, then. For when I whisper, 'Here I am, take me!' [illegible word] you fuss, cough, and adjourn the session. Are you a lover or a Senator?"[1]

Even the most nonjudgmental members of the archaeological community cannot help but look on with a sense of disappointment, when they pry the scrolls open and read how a once-noble philosophy of meditation, simplicity, and monogamous devotion was co-opted as an excuse for vanity and lust, sloth and gluttony (the excesses being excused, apparently, on the basis of priestlike authority seized in the name of a new religion, born of philosophy).

Elsewhere in the empire of Herculaneum's burial—the empire of A.D. 79—the secretive and "eccentric Christian cults" had already been accused in Rome (beginning with Nero, after the great fire that ravaged the city in A.D. 64) of professing, according to Suetonius, "a new and mischievous religious belief." Nero and his allies blamed the Christians for the Great Fire of Rome, and Saint Paul was crucified in Rome during that same year.

In *Annals XV*, Tacitus, Pliny the Younger's correspondent, wrote, "Nero substituted as culprits, and punished with the utmost refinements of cruelty, a class of men, loathed for their vices, whom the crowd styled Christians . . . Vast numbers were convicted, not so much on the count of arson as for [their alleged] hatred of the human race. And derision accompanied their end: they were covered with wild beasts' skins and torn to death by dogs; or they were fastened on crosses, and when daylight failed were burned to serve as lamps by night."

Derision was fueled by accusations that these "most eccentric of Jewish reformists" (as the first Christians were then known) formed

[1] Philodemus, *Epigrams VIII* (3203 ff.), *XIII* (3236 ff.), translated by K. Rexroth and D. Fitts (revised with bracketed reconstructions by C. R. Pellegrino).

secret cabals in which they practiced dark magic, poisoned wells, drank the blood of pagan Roman children, and bound their own sacred books of "witchery" in the skin of newly born infants. History seems determined, time and time again, to teach us that "the more things change, the more they remain the same."

And so, human behavior, tending to be what the human animal is (guided by instinct and not by civilization), tends also to be fractal and repetitive. As a species, we can be very slow learners. And so it came to pass—more than a thousand years after Nero burned Christians at the stake and Justa's house disappeared under a Vesuvian death cloud—that church authorities accused "witches" and Jews of secretly poisoning well-water, practicing "black magic," drinking the blood of Christian children and binding Bibles, upside down, in the skin of unbaptized babies. Here, the oppression was Christian rumor directed against alleged Pagan heretics and (to a lesser degree) against Jews and Muslims.

During the first years of the twenty-first century, Saudi newspaper editorials and the manifestos of scribes turned suicide hijackers leveled the ancient accusations of witchery and child vampirism against western synagogues, Christian churches, Rotary clubs, and Masonic temples (the last two being labeled "pagan"). Simultaneously, in America, a popular television evangelist named Falwell declared that God, "who will not be mocked," had permitted and even invited suicide hijackers to unleash the fires of September 2001 because his American brethren had descended to pagan witchery and "Romanesque" immorality. Here, the oppression was Muslim and Christian rumor directed against alleged pagan, Christian, and Jewish heretics.

All that actually changes, as the human population increases, is that the same accusations are repeated against a broader (and increasingly confusing) spectrum of targets, as if the cautionary tale of Babel's collapse were fated, from the dawn of history, to become a prophetic truth.

Sound observation of history, when combined with sound observation of human behavior, will often give rise to a stubborn illusion called "prophecy." The Christian scribes of A.D. 79 had already seen two lunatics named Caligula and Nero raised by their own people to positions of authority from which they could inflict the most harm. Among first-century Christians, it must have seemed logical to guess, based upon past acts, that the future of civilization would continue to be punctuated by Neros and Caligulas yet to be born. Herein, perhaps, lies another reason why the early Christian texts record what appears, in hindsight (and with selective reading of "standout" passages), to produce centuries of calamity foretold: That nation shall rise up against nation, brother against brother. Or, as in Matthew 24, Mark 13, Luke 21, and John 16: "Then shall they deliver you up to be afflicted, and shall kill you . . . And then shall many be offended, and shall betray one another, and shall hate one another. And many false prophets shall rise, and shall deceive many . . . They shall put you out of the synagogues: yea, the time cometh, that whosoever killeth you will think that he doeth God service."

Given our human tendency to follow charismatic or "prophetic" leaders, and to divide ourselves into groups hateful of other groups, the future foreseen by learned Christian scribes applies, with equal prophetic force, to the time of Nero, to the time of the Crusades and the Inquisition, to the time of Nazi occupation, and to the time we know best: our own.

Such readings of chapter and verse arise from an archaeological view of life, from tangible artifacts and texts transformed into hindsight. As to whether or not this view of time and human tide is mistaken, time itself is yet to have its say.

READING ONWARD and onward through digitally enhanced Herculaneum carbon, one finds a Roman poet and naturalist named Titus Lucretius Carus far more down to earth than Philodemus, easier to grasp, and a little more interesting as well. Portions of Lucretius's book, *On the Nature of the Universe,* have survived on two scrolls found in the Villa of the Papyri. Like Cicero, Lucretius believed in a more orthodox Epicurean philosophy. Like Cicero, he believed also in the science of Democritus. Like Democritus and Epicurus, he made no concessions to the Graeco-Roman pantheon of gods and wrote that he in fact did not believe any gods—or giants, or demons, or angels—existed. Because his books denied that emperors were sons of the supreme god Jupiter, Lucretius's works were becoming unpopular with the Augustales at the time of Herculaneum's burial. In the decades after Pompeii and Herculaneum were hidden in the earth, the Romans would mark Lucretius's books for burning, because they failed to advocate (and in fact precluded) the emerging state religion: the worship of Emperors Augustus, Claudius, Vespasian, and Titus as gods. The teachings of Christians, Jews, and Buddhists became unpopular for the same reason; but when Christianity evolved into the religion of the Eastern Empire, first Constantinople and then the Vatican marked most of Lucretius's books for burning because, by denying the existence of gods and saints, demons and devils, they failed to advocate (and in fact precluded) yet another state religion. Fortunately, his books burned first at Herculaneum. They were literally swallowed by the earth, simultaneously seared and preserved by the fires of Vesuvius.

As Lucretius saw the universe, not even souls existed. What some called the "soul" was simply consciousness, born of reactions made possible by atoms borrowed from the world and used during life. According to Lucretius, "The atoms of the soul and body, which are dispersed in death, reconstitute the material of the world."

And there, among such understandings, lay glimpses of a world to come. Already on the drawing boards, in A.D. 79, were designs for elevators in multistory, steel-supported buildings taller than the Colosseum. A factory equipped with water-powered millstones promised (or threatened) to grind wheat down into flour while freeing slaves and miniature donkeys from the task. Eight- and ten-story high-rises were recognized as a new challenge for fire prevention, so expansion of city fire departments was planned (newly equipped with horse-drawn tanks and hoses capable of reaching upper stories with the recently invented twin-piston pumps). Firehouses were staffed by conscripted or volunteered slaves, who were guaranteed freedom and Roman citizenship after six years of service. Lucretius, who made a study of fire, steam, and water, theorized that a system of regularly spaced firehouses, aqueduct-fed fire hydrants, and tank-fed sprinkler systems in tall buildings would render the cities virtually fireproof, but many thought his recommendations too extreme and far too expensive.

Most important was Lucretius's theory that all substance could be broken down into arrangements of chemicals (or molecules) and that the chemical basis of life resided in still smaller units of matter called atoms. The atoms, he theorized, differed from one another and could be arranged, with further study, into a periodic table of the elements, ranging from hydrogen and oxygen through iron and lead. He foresaw new metallic alloys, and explosive chemical powders. He also challenged the widely held belief that humans had evolved tongues because they spoke. He believed that humans had evolved tongues first—which enabled them to develop language.

Herculaneum, as it turned out, would be the first of the Vesuvian cities excavated, during the early 1700s. By the 1750s there arose, in Europe and in America, a thunderous excitement about the buried cities and a surging popularity of all things Roman. Texts long ignored in European monasteries, including a few "approved" scraps of Lucretius and the still-surviving theories of Justice and Constitution penned by Emperor Titus, were widely read and reproduced for the first time in many centuries.

Decorative cameos and ceramic vases depicting cherubs at play, women in flowing silk robes, and beautifully carved leaf-and-vine frames surrounding scenes of Pompeiian and Herculanean life reemerged in futurity as the finer details of Victorian architecture, leaving their distinctly Roman marks everywhere, from the Jefferson Memorial and Washington's Capitol Building to California's J. P. Getty estate (along with the "Spanish-style" estates that surround it), from Victorian houses to the *Titanic*'s Grand Stairway.

Thomas Jefferson designed silverware based on what he had seen recovered from Herculaneum and Pompeii during a visit to Italy. Queen Victoria, who ushered in an architectural era that bears her name, built Buckingham Palace's "Pompeiian Room" based upon notes and drawings from her 1838 pilgrimage to the Vesuvian excavations. She was drawn there by the increasingly popular Vesuvian architecture then being copied in vaulted ceilings, and in stunningly detailed flower, vine, and olive trails carved in oak trim, and in Mr. Wedgwood's ceramics.

The Wedgwood decorations, which became very popular after the American Revolution, had been created by Josiah Wedgwood specifically to reproduce frescoes and sculptural scenes from Pompeii and Herculaneum in general, and from the Villa of the Papyri in particular.

Lucretius's theories about evolution and "the sway of atoms" still lay undiscovered and unread at this time, but the Wedgwood fortune did, a century later, permit a young explorer who married Josiah's granddaughter to live by the orthodox Epicurean ideal of cloistered, nonstop study and contemplation. As way leads onto way, and as history fashions (from infinitely interacting events) unpredicted and unpredictable points of pivot, the many great works of art plundered by Piso and Philodemus, then copied by Wedgwood, afforded Charles Darwin the rare nineteenth-century luxury of being able to devote a life to pure thought. Independently, he reinvented Lucretius's theory of evolution, then refined it more fully into biology's version of $e = mc^2$.

And the world was never quite so simple again.

9

TESTAMENT

You see that mountain, down there on Earth? That's Vesuvius. A few years back, it really messed up a good liberty town.

ASTRONAUT JOHN YOUNG TO EUGENE CERNAN
AND TOM STAFFORD, AS *APOLLO 10* PREPARED FOR
TRANSLUNAR INJECTION, MAY 18, 1969

By the time Pompeii and Herculaneum began to grow from provincial villages into major Roman ports of call, their streets had evolved from randomly winding alleys into something that nature (outside the microcosmos of crystals) abhors: parallel and straight perpendicular lines. Walking the Roman streets of A.D. 79 was like walking through a city planned on graph paper, with the older, more colorful family names of streets replaced by numbers. A result of this graph-paper approach to city planning was that a first-century visitor would find Pompeii's Phoenix Tavern (identifiable by a painting of two peacocks and a phoenix perched above a slogan reading "YOU TOO WILL ENJOY THE HAPPY PHOENIX") located at the corner of 4th Street and 3rd Avenue.

The logic of the Roman grid system became so widely accepted that one might say they managed to clone the same city a thousandfold. Although most of the original buildings have been dismantled, or have fallen into ruin, Rome and Paris, London and Bonn, are still standing directly on the old Roman street grids. Across the Atlantic, the new American Republic was founded in the immediate aftermath of a surging interest in the lost civilization, brought about by the then-recent discoveries of Herculaneum and Pompeii. New York City and Washington became centerpieces for re-created Roman architecture, for the Founding Fathers believed no other shapes sculpted by the hands of architects and engineers seemed capable of conveying a more perfect image of power and order. Adopted and replicated, Roman buildings rose like phoenixes, on Roman-style street grids. A visitor to New York will find Grand Central Station on Forty-second Street, the New York Public Library at Fifth Avenue and Forty-second Street, and the General Post Office at Thirty-third Street between Eighth and Ninth Avenues. In this one city, museums, banks, courthouses, and the private homes of wealthy citizens—literally hundreds of different buildings—convey a distinctly Roman image. The Empire State Building (Roman in name only) does not; but it stands nonetheless on a Roman grid, at Thirty-fourth Street, between Fifth and Sixth Avenues. On Broadway and Vesey, George Washington's church, Saint Paul's Chapel, is essentially Pompeii's Temple of Venus, replicated with a steeple added, and with a few Colonial American touches inside.

In March of A.D. 1968, a *Star Trek* episode titled "Bread and Circuses" speculated about a parallel Earth (or alternate history) in which the Roman Empire never died but instead managed to survive into the twentieth century. Gene Roddenberry's fictional Roman Earth was really not far removed from what has actually occurred. Really. Not far removed at all . . . Aside from televised gladiatorial games (really not much more violent than televised WWE games or the evening news, and not quite as close-up as the simulated and computer-sanitized slaughter available to anyone with a fistful of loose change) . . . and aside from the fictional Earth's acceptance of twentieth-century slavery (really not much more science fictional than Sudan's policy of legalized slavery proving no obstacle to its appointment to the United Nations Council on Human Rights in the early twenty-first century). History, to be sure, has transgressed on Roddenberry's fiction. Even the episode's exterior scenes of twentieth-century automobile traffic passing before Romanesque buildings were simply shots of contemporary American architecture. If an old *Star Trek* episode or the alternate-history novels of Harry Turtledove have ever caused you to wonder what the world would look like today if something like the ancient Roman Empire actually had survived, take a walk down Fifth Avenue or Pennsylvania Avenue, and look around.

Stand before the old government offices you have seen a thousand times before and look again. You will discover that nothing is as it has always seemed—not the old Chinatown bank near Bowery and Grand . . . not the Lincoln Memorial . . . not the Philadelphia Museum of Art or the train station nearby . . . not the courthouses. Look around, and see these buildings for the first time.

IF THE ROMANS could have reached forward in time and grabbed Viking navigators for their ships, or if the architects of Erik the Red's Dark Age ships could have stepped back across time and made use of metal-clad hulls and other Roman innovations for Viking navigators, instead of the other way around, the Empire might have settled America on its own.

Like everything else about the lost Empire, its leap toward the New World came frustratingly near, and fell agonizingly short. As it turned out, the original settlers were able to move on without the intervention of Roman colonists, for better or for worse.

According to our genetic timekeepers (in particular those genes inherited only from our mothers, in microscopic bacteria-like "organelles" called mitochondria), the Plains Indians, the Aztecs, the Maya, and the Inca were descended from northern Chinese people. As indicated by the fact that long before 12,000 B.C. the first human seafarers had crossed the Exmouth Trench from New Guinea to Australia, the forebears of the first Americans must have developed sailing technology, no doubt to exploit abundant fishing resources (for Oregon and Washington State's oldest stone tools include, among the arrowheads, fish hooks and sinkers carved from flint). Most observers believe the immigrants followed now-submerged coastlines on foot, and while such overland (and over-ice) migration might occasionally have occurred, small fishing fleets are more efficient travelers, and I suspect that by accident, by human curiosity, and by a combination of both, fishing communities drifted east along the Aleutian shore to Alaska, then continued southward toward equatorial waters.

The ancestral history chronicled in our mitochondrial genes suggests that prehistoric people were more prone to wanderlust than most of us (watching smugly from time-present) were formerly willing to credit them.

Several descendants of North America's Plains Indians and South America's Inca carry in their blood genetic markers from as far west of China as Greece and Italy, dating back two thousand years and more. In Mongolia, European and Eurasian mummies (some dating back more than three thousand years) lend support to the idea that China's Alaska-bound wanderers (following an Asian-European genetic split dating back seventy thousand to eighty thousand years ago) carried with them some (relatively) recently contributed European DNA. Most of this genetic chatter was probably contributed by east-bound European wanderers, prior to the Ice Age departure of Alaska-bound boatmen from Asia.

Once Ice Age boats started arriving in Alaska, it is not likely that they simply stopped arriving. The occasionally striking similarities between Mayan and Chinese architecture, sculpture, and dragon-phoenix mythology, while far from conclusively drawing a link between distant cultures, is sufficiently compelling to make one stop and wonder. Certainly, there would be little cause for surprise if Chinese ships of the first century B.C. (and A.D.) were proved to have traveled east and then south, until they reached Mexico's west coast. Beginning with the first Qin emperor in 221 B.C., China's dynasties became so brutal that when a fleet of three hundred ships was dispatched to conquer Japan, the conquerors settled instead and never returned home to China. A saying had emerged—a saying that people still held true in China, at least into the end of the twentieth century: "A smart man must never stand too tall, and reveal himself too smart and truthful for his own good. If one stands too tall, above the rest of the crowd, they will make him as short as the rest, by cutting off his head." Given this environment, if a smart man saw an opportunity to sail away, never to return, he was quick to grasp it. And if on occasion ships continued eastward into the rising sun, it is reasonable to believe that, as occasion permitted, they carried to the New World snippets of European genome stitched into Asian DNA.

An additional pre-Columbian contribution of European DNA (and probably, also, African DNA) to South and Central American civilizations was first hinted at in 1982, when scuba divers located a Roman shipwreck, dating from the first century B.C., in Rio de Janeiro, Brazil.

(So agonizingly near . . .)

The wreck was dated to approximately the reign of Augustus Caesar by the style of terra-cotta handles on three distinctive, long-necked urns

This *Europa*-class merchant vessel of the first century A.D. is similar in size and structure to the two Roman ships discovered in Brazil (1982) and Venezuela (1987). Reconstructed from a plaster etching on a wall of Pompeii's "Europa House," the ship *Europa*, like the South American wrecks, was of average size, ranging from 50 to 100 feet in length (15 to 30 meters). *Europa* possessed a deep keel, characteristic of Discovery Period ships more than 1,500 years later. Larger ships, such as those built for Caligula and Nero, were multimasted, and were equipped with sophisticated systems of pipes fed by boilers that provided hot and cold running water and (possibly) supplemental, steam-assisted propulsion. The *Europa* was maneuvered by a combination of steering oars (protorudders) and modified lanteen rigs, fore and aft. The single mast held a square rig and a topsail (shown furled in the original Pompeii drawing). Because the reign of Augustus (31 B.C.–A.D. 14) began a period of accelerated shipbuilding, the probability of ships accidentally reaching South America via Mauretania and the Cape Verde Islands was not merely high, but statistically inevitable. Reaching the New World was the easy part. Going home? Nearly impossible.

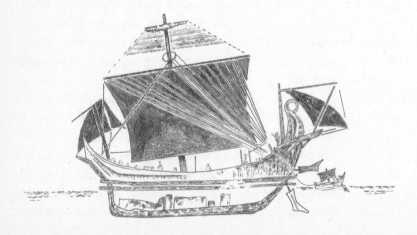

recovered from the wreck site. Several hundred identical urns (almost all that remained of the ship) were photographed lying in rows, where the decayed wooden ribs and planks of the ship's keel had been. Called "amphorae," the urns were used to carry water, wine, oil, and grain on long voyages.

As excavation and photographic mapping of the site began, a Brazilian magistrate suggested that the vessel had simply been blown off course, whereupon it drifted to Brazil with a dead crew; but historians from the Smithsonian Institution and Long Island's Air and Space Museum (among them curator Josh Stoff) argued that the ship's final resting place in a sheltered bay suggested that it was maneuvered there by a crew that had survived the voyage. The presence of so many amphorae gave credibility to the premise that the sailors had sufficient supplies of food and water. I was, at that time, less certain of the crew's survival. The presence of so many amphorae, still neatly arranged in rows when the ship sank in the bay, suggested to me a crew that had perished, either at sea or very shortly after landing and making first contact with local tribal warriors. Yet, even if the crew had been defeated in a very short-lived and localized war, it was difficult for any of us to suppose that native Brazilians would not have stripped the ship of any useful provisions before sinking it. The timbers and amphorae, all by themselves, were useful.

Conversely, if the crew had successfully settled, and been assimilated into local culture, containment vessels, even after they were eventually emptied, were of value in everyday use and should have been taken away. Adding to the complexity of the original problem, there was no reason to assume that the ship's final resting place was its first landing place. Even unintentionally successful settlers would continue to make use of, and to reprovision, their vessel.

A closer examination of the entire wreck, with particular emphasis on chemical traces of the long-vanished contents in hundreds of amphorae, might have solved the mystery. Unfortunately, a local dissenting lawyer took the mere mention of a pre-Columbian wreck as "a slander against [Christopher] Columbus," and he marshaled emotional support from several powerful politicians and industrialists. In 1983, the entire site was buried under sludge and landfill (which is not truly cause for despair, because, like the ash of Vesuvius, anoxic sludge provides a preservative service). The archaeologists were then persuaded (by death threats) to "bury [their] reputations elsewhere."

In 1987, a second European shipwreck was discovered in Venezuela, and before local tempers intervened, it, too, was identified by its contents as being Roman in origin, dating from somewhere between Julius Caesar (about 49 B.C.) and Titus (A.D. 79). As a crude estimate, only one out of every hundred wooden ships arriving in the Americas was likely ever to be preserved. Nature's probability curves were skewed overwhelmingly against any individual ship sinking where discovery was likely or (if it arrived with survivors) its entering the archaeological record before it grew old from a lifetime of use by its crew and, being judged eventually unseaworthy and unrepairable, being dismantled for whatever timbers and metal parts could be recycled into homes or new boats.

If two ships are found, and if the odds against preservation and discovery are estimated at ninety-nine to one, then there must have been hundreds of them. This should not surprise anyone, for over the course of two or three centuries we need only have a single ship go off course every year before more than two hundred vessels are America-bound. While it seems possible that scores and even hundreds of ships arrived from Rome; and while traces of European and African DNA have turned up in allegedly "pure-blood" descendants of Incan and Mayan temple builders; and while the world-famous giant stone heads of Mexico's Olmec people are curiously African in appearance, the ultimate fates of any would-be Roman settlers must have paralleled the Vikings' encounters with native peoples. Most of the Vikings were driven away from the North American mainland, while a few, according to the genetic record, were assimilated by intermarriage without, apparently, passing on their knowledge of iron and bronze technology.

After Rome fell in the east, the Aztec, Mayan, and Incan Empires continued to develop without leaving behind any *definitive* signs that they had inherited Iron Age metallurgy, either from pre–Dark Age Rome or from China.

But vague signs persist . . . vague, yet ever so slightly compelling signs . . . The earliest evidence of copper-based metallurgy in the Americas postdates the first-century Roman shipwrecks by more than half a millennium and postdates the fall of Rome by approximately two hundred years. During the eastern Dark Age, somewhere between A.D. 700 and 800, first in Ecuador, Colombia, and southern Mexico, copper tools began entering the archaeological record. Sometimes, the copper was alloyed with tin, to create bronze. By A.D. 800, the Maya were importing copper-based tools and weaponry from manufacturing centers located along Mexico's east coast. Interestingly, when we first see it preserved in tombs and ruins, this technology starts out highly evolved. One method of manufacture, the "lost wax" technique, was known in Europe, Africa, and Asia for nearly two millennia before it first appeared in the New World. This involved a shape carved from wax and packed in clay—which was then baked until rock hard, whereupon molten metal was poured into the space left behind by the vaporized wax. In an archaeological instant, the lost wax technique popped up throughout the Americas, fully developed. We may never know whether it was a Mayan or Incan invention, or something old introduced from "outside." In either case, the lost wax technique is not alone: Similarly, open mold casting and annealing were, seemingly by sudden proliferation, in common use in diverse places.

It is possible, and perhaps likely, that we do not see Central and South American metallurgy as archaeological artifacts until the science has become commonplace (after A.D. 700) and is, therefore, in the mathematical sense, certain to be preserved and to be found. As an indication of the random nature of archaeological preservation, and of a tendency for the record to be filled with gaps, a tomb in the great Mexican city of Teotihuacán contained a piece of smelted and refined platinum, memorializing high-temperature technology more akin to the Iron Age than the Bronze or Copper Ages. Mysteriously, the platinum was buried more than two centuries ahead of Mexico's Copper Age, about the time both Teotihuacán and Roman Byzantium fell, near A.D. 535, some five centuries past Augustus.

Rome, in the time of Julius Caesar and Augustus, had come out of an Iron Age civil war, culminating in the 31 B.C. battle of Actium between Octavian (later named Augustus) and Mark Antony. The naval defeat of Antony and Cleopatra had driven home, for Augustus, the message that sea power was of major importance for the care and maintenance of empire. After the war, within the time frame of two Roman shipwrecks in South America, Augustus built a "permanent" Roman navy (as opposed to the two-hundred-year-old habit of hastily constructing fleets in time of specific need). One of the first large permanent fleets was stationed at Misenum, sister city of Pompeii and Herculaneum. By the time Tiberius replaced Augustus in A.D. 14, other fleets were being established as far away as the Persian Gulf, the Danube, the English Channel, and in Mauretania, on Africa's west coast.

From Mauretania and its outlying Cape Verde Islands, the prevailing northeast trade winds (if they blew in the same direction as today) pointed like an arrow toward the mouth of Brazil's Amazon River, only 2,100 miles (3,444 kilometers) west. This is equivalent to a journey of approximately twelve weeks—which is comparable to sea voyages already being routinely made (during the years between Augustus and Vesuvius) from Misenum to western Mauretania, or back again (via a zigzag, typically upwind path) to Misenum.

Pompeii's "Europa House" has preserved a painting of the medium-sized merchant ship *Europa,* displaying a single-masted, square sailing rig, an aft lanteen rig (or steering sail), and a deep, Renaissance-style keel. Clues gleaned from the overturned boat in Herculaneum's marina, combined with studies of a dozen larger but less well-preserved Mediterranean wrecks, combined with surviving written records, provide, in reasonable detail, a picture of shipbuilding methods in the time of Vesuvius and the South American wreck sites.

The frames (or skeletons) of Roman ships were typically fashioned from oak. The hulls were softer pine, fir, cypress, or Lebanon cedar. Below the waterline, the outer hull was often sheathed in lead, held in place by lead-dipped bronze nails. The metal-clad hulls served a dual function of toxifying the wood against "marine worms" and helping to ballast the ships. Above the cladding, the exterior and interior hull surfaces were protected by a more lightweight mixture of pitch and beeswax, sometimes pigmented with lead-based paint.

The larger ships were double- and triple-masted square-riggers,

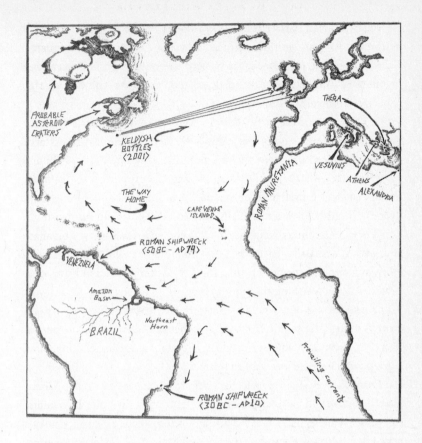

The Mauretanian fleet, centered in Caesarea, was based far west along the African coast, projecting Roman power southward to the Canary and Cape Verde Islands. After the battle of Thapsus in 46 B.C., Julius Caesar expanded Roman borders along most of Mediterranean North Africa. Under Augustus, Tiberius, and Claudius (between 27 B.C. and A.D. 54), the Mauretanian territory was extended westward through present-day Morocco to Cape Verde (in present-day Mauretania). About A.D. 42, Mauretania was split into east and west imperial provinces: Mauretania Caesariensis (Mediterranean Africa) and Mauretania Tingitana (Atlantic North Africa). Between A.D. 284 and 305, after the Hispaniae Armada brought the breakaway "British Empire's" War for Independence to an end, Emperor Diocletian made Mauretania Tingitana a "diocese" of Hispaniae, also known as Roman Spain.

steered by double, oarlike rudders working in combination with lanteen and spirit sails (mounted fore and aft, perpendicular to the square sails).

The *Europa,* like most midsized merchant vessels, measured between 50 and 120 feet (15 and 37 meters) in length and had a cargo capacity between 150 and 350 tons.

An example of the larger Roman metal-clads—twice as long as the *Europa*—was found lying perfectly preserved in the oxygen-starved waters of Italy's Lake Nemi during the 1920s. The hull was 239 feet (73 meters) long and 79 feet (24 meters) wide, with a carrying capacity above 700 tons. Raised and then carefully preserved, it was bombed out of existence during World War II. Both Josephus and the Roman historian Lucian mentioned ships with 1,200-ton capacities—carrying, from Alexandria to Ostia, grain and Egyptian-made obelisks (turned by Augustus into the needles of giant sundials, and replicated in America as the even larger Washington Monument).

In the second century, Lucian described what was then one of the world's largest ships—the *Isis*—widely believed in her day to be "unsinkable" but forced nevertheless to shelter in Piraeus after almost sinking during a storm. The *Isis* was 182 feet long and 45 feet wide (55 by 14 meters). Most significantly, she was 42 feet deep (four stories, or 13 meters). According to Lucian, she carried, in her hold, 1,300 tons of grain. Lucian also recorded that the only vessels with any resemblance at all to regularly scheduled passenger ships were in fact the giant grain carriers—which traveled direct routes from Alexandria to Ostia, Misenum, and Rome, and were usually fitted with cabins and upper-deck "tent space" for hundreds of passengers.

A Roman ship starting out from Caesarea in northern Mauretania, heading west toward Cape Verde through the Strait of Gibraltar, could be carried astray of Cape Verde by the northeast trade winds and the North Equatorial Current—astray toward Venezuela (location of the 1987 find) or a little farther north to the islands of the West Indies (which is where Columbus landed after heading out west from Gibraltar). A journey from southwestern Mauretania (heading westward from the coast of North Africa), into the northeast trade winds, tends to push sailing ships toward northern Brazil and the Amazon River. To move from this most likely landing site (near the Amazon) to Rio de

Janeiro requires a journey *eastward*, 1,000 miles (1,640 kilometers) along Brazil's northeast "horn" and against prevailing oceanic currents (requiring skilled use of the sails), then 1,400 miles (2,296 kilometers) south to Rio—a total distance of 2,400 miles (almost 4,000 kilometers), which exceeds, by some 300 miles, the initial trans-Atlantic crossing. Assuming that the ship was not blown out to sea from somewhere far south of Mauretania—from Angola or Namibia, where the southeast trade winds and the South Equatorial Current can point a "drifter" toward Rio— then, if the 1982 find did indeed land first at the Amazon via West Africa's Roman port of Mauretania, its crew must have arrived in America quite alive. In this case, the newcomers would have commenced a long journey, restocking their amphorae with food and fresh water as they went, mile by tedious mile, in the wrong direction.

Had they traveled (from the Amazon) in the opposite direction— *following* the currents northeastward instead of resisting them, they would have, in the same 2,400-mile distance, passed Trinidad, Martinique, and Puerto Rico before reaching the Bahamas, just short of Florida. Following the Gulf Stream and making occasional landfalls for supplies, the next 2,400 miles would have pointed them into the North Atlantic Current—which, with the precision of a crossbow, directs all drifters, whether Roman or Columbian, toward the English Channel. In August and September of 2001, I tested this portion of the path by launching messages in bottles from the research vessel *Keldysh*. (Among these: a letter to someone very kindhearted and very special in New York. The letter ended with a proposal of marriage—which was received via "squid mail," and accepted.)

The bottles went from the thirteenth *Titanic* expedition to England, Scotland, Ireland, and the Channel Islands of France. To judge from the dates of release and the earliest dates of recovery, they covered the 1,700-mile (2,788-kilometer) distance at approximately 10 miles (16 kilometers) per day. A Roman ship with sails, and with men experienced at their control, would certainly have been capable of doubling or quadrupling the speed of bottles.

But Roman mariners, arriving from Mauretania, could not have known that the Gulf Stream and the North Atlantic Current would have carried them home. Nearly 1,500 years later, these same currents pointed the way home for Columbus (who probably knew, from Viking sagas, that the North Atlantic Current existed, for he followed it homeward from the West Indies and Grand Bahama, as if with foreknowledge of its existence). Instead of traveling in the direction of the currents, along a more circular but ultimately easier path home, the pilots of the 1982 find appear to have pushed instinctively against the currents and the prevailing winds, sailing initially eastward along the Brazilian horn— which would have been, in terms of mere physical geography, the most direct path home. If the proposed Mauretanian origin of the Rio wreck is true (and this is, when all is said and done, still an "if"), then their "wrong," eastward path is also the most logical path.

For a crew displaced westward of Cape Verde and into the Amazon basin, lost in a strange land, their awareness of having come from the east would have been a major driving force in their thinking. The theory that they turned the ship around and headed whence they came is both logical (on the crew's part) and, for us, archaeologically instructive. East, along the horn and against the currents, was the shortest distance between a (likely) Amazon landing point and Mauretania. A combination of likely points of origin (centering on Cape Verde and Mauretania), likely initial landing places, and an unlikely final resting place suggests that Rome's Rio wreck arrived with a live crew, able to work the sails. Unfortunately, if and when they reached Brazil's eastern tip, there was simply no direct route to Mauretania. The currents (probably then, too, as in Columbus's time and now) divided north and south at the tip. If the ship turned north, it would have been swept back again toward the Amazon and Venezuela, or toward Martinique and Cuba (and toward the circular path home). South of the tip, the currents drove along another path, farther and farther from home, toward Rio de Janeiro. There was simply no way a sailing vessel could have moved against the powerful South Equatorial Current and reached Africa . . . which brings us, again, to Venezuela and Rio: Wherever two vessels from any given time period enter the archaeological record, they are invariably indicators of others—perhaps hundreds of others from the same three-hundred-year period—because so much more is lost to history than is ever discovered.

Given scores or even hundreds of individual crews trying to voyage home (given so many throws of the dice) it becomes likely if not inevitable that one or more captains gave up the difficult eastward route and followed the currents north (as Columbus did some fifteen centuries later): The only way home was to sail north, until the sea grew cold, and then—only then—to turn toward the rising sun. Indeed, it is possible that Columbus (and the Vikings before him), having access to maps and historic accounts that no longer exist, planned their own voyages based upon tales of returning Mauretanian sailors. If it should turn out to be true that any of the Mauretanian ships returned, the failure of Rome, like the failure of the Vikings, to launch a successful colonization of the Americas produces a rare and fascinating pivot point in the parade of colonization and conquest that has shaped most of our species' history. Two or three centuries after its first ships began arriving in Venezuela and Brazil, the Roman Empire was crumbling and on the brink of extinction because it had failed to plant a distant, surviving offshoot. Rome's Christopher Columbus (if one existed) was either unwilling or unable to follow through on what he had discovered.

A strange lesson, a strange swerve of history—but perhaps (to historians and archaeologists of our own future) no stranger an irony than the Mauretanian, Viking, and Columbian explorers of the twentieth century. After naming their fleet "Apollo" and christening their lunar orbiters and landers *Columbia, Eagle,* and *Challenger,* after putting their footprints upon the Moon from July 1969 through December 1972, they retreated to the confines of near-earth orbit (and almost retreated altogether from the frontiers of the night), as if they had failed to see any further advantage in the exploration of deep space. Like the Romans, they appear simply to have looked away.

AT LENGTHS OF 200 FEET (62 meters), with average carrying capacities of 1,000 tons, Roman ships were the largest that would ever be seen on saltwater until Spain's Manila galleons of A.D. 1600 and the Atlantic steamers of the nineteenth century. Throughout the Empire, aqueducts, water towers, and networks of lead pipes provided city dwellers with gallons of clean water per person per day. This was a luxury not widely equaled again until the 1950s, a time in which American physicians were coming to realize that access to clean drinking water, flush toilets, soap, and showers had contributed more to the lengthening of the human life span than all the combined medical advances of the twentieth century.

Two centuries earlier, during the 1750s, the western world in general, and America in particular, were embracing and obsessing about ancient Rome. Aqueducts and Pompeiian baths were being measured, dissected, and sketched in photographic detail. The ancient classics, the writings of philosophers, and records of Roman laws were being studied. Josephus and Titus, Pliny and Plato, Cicero and Epicurus, Cincinnatus and Tacitus were of intense interest to men named Franklin, Hamilton, Washington, and Jefferson.

"In designing the Constitution of these United States of America," wrote Thomas Jefferson, "we have at various times sought precedent in the history of that ancient [Roman] Republic, and endeavored to draw lessons both from its leading ideas and the tumult and factions which finally brought it low."

In the New York Public Library's Jefferson Archive, one can read a Jeffersonian paragraph removed from an early draft of America's Declaration of Independence. In that paragraph, Jefferson had proposed the abolition of an increasingly entrenched colonial tradition introduced under British rule, but his compatriots (who, like Jefferson himself, were slave owners) thought it would read all too hypocritical to "cry freedom" and to decry the king's slave ships while at the same time being slave owners. Those with abolitionist leanings were persuaded to agree: "Independence first. We will deal with slavery later." Jefferson's paragraph against slavery was deleted from the final draft, but the line "We hold these Truths to be self-evident, that all Men are created equal" assured that it would indeed be dealt with later.

Later, when the Constitution was written, its authors decided again that slavery would be dealt with at a later date, and as America prepared to face the nineteenth century, it had decided to preserve the same grim practice that in Herculaneum had brought nothing except tumult into the life of a brilliant and daring young woman named Justa.

Almost eighty years after the Declaration and the Constitution, the unwitting resurrection and preservation of the old Republic's slave culture would finally be dealt with. The debt would be paid with interest, in the blood of more than seven hundred thousand Americans.

For all its human faults, for all its moments of human daring and genius, the new Republic was rooted by its founders in the philosophy of the Stoics and the orthodox Epicureans, to whom self-sacrifice ("wherein the needs of the many outweigh the needs of the few, or the one"), discipline, and valor formed the three essential virtues.

To George Washington, in particular, adherence to the three classic Roman virtues meant discovery of the most important virtue of all: the exercise of power with restraint. Washington meant to fashion this virtue into a uniquely American ideal, and though he, Franklin, and the others knew that the Republic would err and from time to time stumble or inflict unjust wounds (upon itself and upon others), they also knew that if they could pass this single ideal—*power with restraint*—if no other, forward to the generations unborn, it would build America into something the world had never seen before: a nation with the power to appoint new kings and to build itself into a global empire . . . but chooses *not* to.

Endeavoring to draw lessons from the past, so that he might build a better future, Washington saw tomorrow in a pre-Epicurean Roman general named Cincinnatus, who lived in 450 B.C. Cincinnatus had pointed the way to the path that Rome should have taken. Washington was choosing for his own people the road not traveled by Imperial Rome, or by any other nation. This time, it was all going to work out quite differently.

In 458 B.C., the Celts had invaded from Gaul (from present-day France), breached the gates of Rome, and set the city aflame. Under the Roman constitution, the Senate was given authority to appoint a temporary dictator in times of grave crisis. They appointed Lucius Quinctius Cincinnatus, a nobleman and plantation owner who loved nothing more in the world than to plant wheat stalks and to work the fields with his own hands. He was also a lucid writer and much-admired public speaker; but most important, for Rome's Senate in exile, Cincinnatus was a brilliant military engineer and strategist who won the loyalty of his soldiers by riding with them at the leading edge of battle.

Fourteen days after Cincinnatus's victory over the Celts, the Roman Senate voted in favor of declaring him dictator for the duration of his life. The idea that the people wanted him to be king of Rome, and the realization that the obvious next step was for his children to form the basis of a never-ending Roman monarchy, horrified Cincinnatus. The general immediately resigned the office of dictator and announced that he was returning to his farm, so that he could tend to the next season's crop.

The exact contents of his resignation speech have not been preserved, for they were recorded by latecomer historians only as second- and third-generation word-of-mouth recollections. But the essential elements survive: Cincinnatus vowed that he would never be king because he, and the Senate, "shall pledge allegiance to the Republic, for which we must stand." By example as well as by eloquent words, he emphasized that upholding the republic meant Rome must elect its leaders, "[i]n order to build a more perfectible government based on restraint, trust, and the rule of law." Under the Cincinnatus Doctrine, so began the Roman experiment: Everyone would have a say in how government was run. The republic worked in principle, and sometimes even in practice, for approximately four centuries, until Julius Caesar declared himself dictator in 49 B.C.

Cicero was in his fifties when Julius came to power, and like Cincinnatus he was a writer, an orator, a brilliant military leader, and a farmer. He preferred to live a simple, Stoic life, scorning people who (in the manner of Piso and Philodemus) sought opulence, who scoured the Mediterranean for rare jewels, "like hunting dogs sniffing down every trail." Nevertheless, a letter written to his brother, whose Pompeii estate Cicero "house-sat" while the brother was away in France, provides the clearest written account we have of the Vesuvian pleasure gardens after the Spartacus War and before the surge clouds of August A.D. 79: "All is right on your estate. Nothing left [for me to repair] but the aviary . . . The [stone] columns have been polished and . . . your landscape gardener has won my praise; he has enveloped everything in ivy—even the Greek statues seem advertising it. It's the [thermally] coolest, greenest retreat. Statues, wrestling ground, [pretentious] fish pond, water system—all are fine."

Like Cincinnatus, Cicero was a vocal Roman "Republican"—which probably explains his sudden disappearance in 43 B.C.

Several months after Julius Caesar's assassination (in March of 44 B.C.), Cicero delivered fourteen violent orations against Mark Antony and demanded a return of the republic. Evoking "Cincinnatus and the ideals of self-restraint and self-sacrifice he embodied," Cicero wrote, "the key to the Republic's future is in her past."

Cicero's younger brother, owner of the Pompeii estate, was executed in 43 B.C. Cicero, too, seems not to have survived the year. The republic was dead, and along with it freedom of speech.

More than 1,800 years later, after they defeated the British army, the American Revolutionaries wanted to appoint General George Washington "king" of the New World. The thought horrified him, as it did Jefferson, Franklin, Hancock, and all the cosigners of the Declaration of Independence. Washington took the road least likely for a victorious military leader, the road traveled by few in all of recorded history, except Cincinnatus and Washington.

("to the Republic, for which we must stand . . .")

Picking up the Cincinnatus Doctrine where the Roman republic had ended, Washington set in motion the American experiment.

("In order to build a more perfectible government based on restraint, trust, and the rule of law . . .")

And after his work was done, he led a prayer service in Saint Paul's Chapel in New York City. He offered up thanks to his God, and returned to his farm.

(Discipline, valor, and power with restraint . . .)

South of New York, in the city named after the American general and president who would not be king, the sculptor who memorialized George Washington rendered him as Cincinnatus, holding a plow instead of a gun or a sword. Then, before Washington's death in A.D. 1799, America's first city in the new Ohio Territory was named, at his request, after the Roman visionary who had embodied the doctrine of power with restraint.

Two centuries later, America still struggles with its growing pains, but the Republic does not hide its pains by imprisoning or executing its Ciceros. Instead, its pains and its scandals, no matter how embarrassing, are displayed on the front page for all to see. And the concept of power with restraint still lives. Say what you want about the American experiment (you're free to do so); the single event that speaks loudest for what Cincinnatus started, and for what Washington revived, came at the dawn of humanity's nuclear adolescence.

Once upon a time, only one nation on all of Earth possessed the atomic bomb—the ultimate, unstoppable weapon. Four months after the nation of Washington, Jefferson, and Lincoln ended a terrible war at Hiroshima and Nagasaki, America had assembled five new Hiroshima-class fission bombs, and Dr. Edward Teller (aka "Dr. Strangelove") was already pointing the way toward a Vesuvius-class explosive. That quickly, America was absolutely invincible and absolutely powerful.

The most probable next step for any other nation on Earth, or at this same technological crossroad anywhere else in the cosmos, would be the immediate subjugation of every other nation.

Instead, America chose the most improbable of all possible roads. Rather than seizing Tokyo, Berlin, and Rome, then moving onward to the takeover of Russia, China, Australia, and so on, until Earth was united by unbeatable power into a universal empire, the Americans behaved in a way contrary to the actions of every victorious nation that had gone before them. They rebuilt Japan, Germany, and Italy, and then turned them over to their own self-government. They thereafter refused to be led by the temptations of nuclear conquest and global empire building.

"Absolute power corrupts absolutely," or so the philosophers say. Usually this is true. But in post–World War II America, something unusual occurred. For nearly half a decade after Hiroshima, no one else on Earth held sway over the thermonuclear inverse to the Golden Rule—and the one nation that did hold sway over such energies could easily have seen to it that no neutron-articulate competitors arose and survived the challenge for very long. Something unusual occurred, something extraordinary.

Moving against human nature, guided by civilization and not by instinct (as if to prove that what is natural is not always good), the Americans approached nuclear adolescence with a single governing principle, articulated by Cincinnatus, resurrected by Washington, and adopted as the unbreakable habit of power with restraint. This is a habit so contrary to nature that, at a guess, it is likely to have occurred only once among all the civilizations that ever have, or ever will, exist on our little island of 600 billion stars.

(Power with restraint . . .)

Humanity's greatest evolutionary change was not the one that occurred in its genes, but in its way of thinking.

IMPERIAL ROME, in A.D. 79, was a study in gold and scarlet: a world of enlightened intellects pitted against blackened hearts, of incomparable splendor and incomparable squalor, of political savagery and lofty ideals, of freedom and slavery, of law as a search for the truth and professional perjurers peddling their services to lawyers, of state religions that preached the sanctity of life and gladiatorial sacrifice as state religion, of genius against madness, logic against riot, and starlight against bible black.

In the year before his assassination in A.D. 41, Emperor Gaius Caligula stood on the roof of Rome's Basilica and flung thousands of gold coins onto the main plaza, deliberately inciting a stampede whose casualties he meticulously recorded: 247 women, 32 men, and 1 eunuch.

The Empire of A.D. 79 was populated by 50 to 70 million Romans. In the capital city alone, a million people lived. According to one surviving census, 16 million human beings—between 23 and 30 percent of the Empire's population—were either slaves or slave-born. This ratio would still hold true a century later when, during the civil war that followed the death of Commodus, Pertinax Augustus, the son of a slave turned wealthy wool merchant, ruled briefly as emperor. In Pertinax's footsteps soon followed Rome's first African emperors.

Slaves and emperors, like the rest of the population, exhibited a blend of all national origins and all races. The Silk Road had brought both merchants and slaves from as far away as Tibet and Mongolia. In the streets of Rome, Ostia, and Pompeii (according to the Roman census takers), a traveler could meet people of Egyptian, French, Syrian, and Indian descent as well as Greek and native Italian. All of these people were in fact Roman citizens. Except for occasional German and Judean uprisings, there are few records of ethnic or racial tensions within the Empire. Suetonius, Josephus, Tacitus, and Dio Cassius recorded that their rulers understood the concept of moving economic power, as well as armies, along well-maintained roads and shipping routes. Realizing that economic and military strength were equally important, Rome adopted the motto "Out of many, one"—*e pluribus unum.*

And so it came to pass that in A.D. 161, Marcus Aurelius, born near Córdoba Spain, south of the Lusitania Province in Hispania, became the first of Rome's "Hispanic" emperors. According to the *Historia Augusta,* Aurelius was "forced by the Senate [actually against his will] to assume the government of the State after the death of the Deified Pius." Written in approximately A.D. 380, the *Historia* records that Marcus Aurelius adopted Stoic philosophy at an early age, rejecting all the trappings of status and wealth in favor of a simpler, more cloistered existence of perpetual learning and writing: "He studied philosophy with ardor, even as a youth. For when he was twelve years old he adopted the dress and, a little later, the hardiness of the philosopher, pursuing his studies clad in a rough [and simple] Greek cloak and sleeping on the ground; at his mother's solicitation, however, he reluctantly consented to sleep on a couch strewn with [woolen blankets]."

During the centennial of Pompeii and Herculaneum's disappearance, Marcus Aurelius, in his *Meditations,* brooded over the transitory existence of all that seemed permanent to Romans. He, more than most anyone alive in his time, realized that the marble on which great temples and columns had been raised, the gilded bronze monuments to Augustus and the other deified emperors, would be eroded and weathered down into sand and metallic ore, then returned to the earth until some distant future civilization dug it up again, and built something new, expecting it to last forever. "But substance is like a river in constant flow," Aurelius warned. "The cycle is never complete. And there is hardly anything that stands still."

Seeing dissolution and rebirth as part of the natural parade of events, he advised his readers to accept Rome's ultimate insignificance against time's vastness, for "the first rule is, to keep an untroubled spirit;

[because] all things must bow to nature's law, and soon enough you must vanish into nothingness, like Hadrian and Augustus."

The Roman Catholic Church, when it came into existence after Constantine, did not look back kindly upon Marcus Aurelius and regarded him as both a bull-worshiping pagan and an atheist. Church historian Eusebius noted (about A.D. 300–330) that in Aurelius's time at least two bishops were martyred in Rome while trying to settle an internal and increasingly violent dispute (between eastern and western churches) over the proper date to celebrate Easter (literally, Passover). When the governor of Gaul (France) wrote to Aurelius, asking for a ruling on Rome's feuding and rioting Christians, the emperor, who was more than a little distracted on the Danube (being, as he was, engaged in battle against a German revolution for independence), wrote, "Those who recant are to be set free; but those who persist are to be condemned to the beasts or, if they are Roman citizens, beheaded." The governor of Gaul took this as a nod to persecute Christians in his own territory, and similar persecutions are recorded (by Eusebius in book five of *Historia ecclesiastica*) in Africa during the final year of Aurelius's reign (A.D. 180).

Although the "martyrdoms" were instigated by localized Roman mobs and were not, at that time, empire-wide policy, the church fathers (150 years later, after the conversion of Emperor Constantine to the new faith) laid the blame at Aurelius's feet; and in centuries to come the church would pull down and either pummel to dust, or remelt, every statue bearing the Spaniard's name, just as Aurelius had said it would be: "Ponder the life led by others long ago, the life that will be led after you, the life being led by the uncivilized races; how many do not even know your name, how many will very soon forget it, and how many, who praise you perhaps now, will very soon blame you."

Before he died, before he was blamed, Marcus Aurelius left behind, in the Han Court, the earliest official record of contact between Rome and China. The chroniclers of the Han dynasty reported an ambassadorial visit, in A.D. 166, of emissaries bearing gifts of ivory and rhinoceros horn from "A," the king of the western empire of Rome.

Aurelius's predictions of blame and oblivion turned out, at least in his case, to be wrong on several counts, and for reasons that he would not likely have anticipated. His *Meditations* were copied and preserved as far away as China and Japan (and on occasion by Jesuit priests in those faraway lands). Nearer to home, the very same Christians who despised him during later centuries exerted herculean efforts in preserving, beneath protective layers of the purest gold leaf, one of the great masterpieces of Roman imperial art. Mounted atop his horse, the gilded and bearded bronze Aurelius extends his right hand in a gesture of command, his index finger pointed heavenward. In his left hand he holds the globe of Atlas (the earth) surmounted by a winged angelic woman (interpreted by the church as an angel but actually the Roman goddess Victory). The church of Rome preserved the golden image of Aurelius through the Dark Age, through the Renaissance, through the Inquisition because, for one reason or another, the bearded figure with its right hand extended toward heaven, and an "angel" in its left hand, was believed to depict either "the Savior" or the Christian emperor Constantine.

Posterity was less forgiving of Aurelius's son, Commodus, about whom Dio Cassius wrote, "Our history now descends from a kingdom of gold to one of iron and rust." The civil war that followed Commodus's assassination in A.D. 192 ended with the accession of Septimius Severus a year later. In keeping with the motto "out of many, one," Severus was of African birth, a black Mauretanian emperor in a kingdom whose slaves (some 18 million of them) were typically fair-skinned Europeans. Against slavery, from the time of Justa in Herculaneum, were the Christian abolitionists. Some of these monotheist radicals had been sentenced to slavery specifically because of their mischievous, "all men are created equal" preachings. And yet, more than a thousand years later, in England and on the far side of the Atlantic, from Georgia to Chesapeake Bay, the distant descendants of Rome's oppressed and enslaved abolitionists would reinterpret, convolute, and misuse their own Bible to argue that God "wanted" humanity to enslave humanity.

Septimius Severus, "the African," arrived in Rome at the age of eighteen, during the reign of Marcus Aurelius, and was appointed to the Senate under Aurelius. Of him, Dio Cassius wrote, "Severus was small of stature but powerful, though he eventually grew very weak from gout; mentally he was very keen and very vigorous. As for education, he was eager for more than he obtained, and for this reason was a man of very few words, though of many ideas. Towards friends not forgetful, to enemies most oppressive." During this time, Decimus Clodius Septimius Albinus, also of African descent, ruled as governor of both Britain and the southern half of a divided Germany.

Severus's son, Caracalla, became emperor in A.D. 211. His mother, Julia Domna, had been a Syrian sun worshiper who associated with astrologers and "mystery cults." Caracalla was grim, brooding, and, according to Dio Cassius, evil. To enhance his image as a merciless emperor of rare and dark design, "[h]e invented a costume of his own," wrote Dio—a long, caped cloak, black and close-fitting, with a hood. Originally of Celtic origin, Caracalla made the costume more intimidating by lengthening it, so that the cloth reached down to his feet. In time, the cloak, which would be adopted by future "evil and foreboding" emperors and then by Inquisitors, came to be called the "Caracalla," the name by which it would still be known 1,763 years after Caracalla's death, when a filmmaker named George Lucas would use it, to intimidating effect, for a fictional emperor he had in mind.

In A.D. 217, the year of Caracalla's death by assassination, there existed approximately 250,000 Christians within the boundaries of the Empire. They had, as far back as archaeologists and historians can see, both mystified and irritated the Romans with so-called "good news" that the heavens, or human civilization, or some blend of both would eventually bring about the end of the world.

The apocalypse of John, as preached by the Christians, with its visions of great cities destroyed by a fiery blow from the heavens, and with "wailing and gnashing of teeth," had a precedent in Pliny's and Dio's descriptions of Vesuvius in A.D. 79—which in turn had a precedent in the apocalyptic verses of Sibylline oracles. These had been collected into at least fourteen books (most of which still survive) by Emperor Augustus, around 4 B.C.

More than eight decades before Pompeii, about a century before archaeology's earliest known drafts of the Revelation of John (sometimes called the Nile River gospels), Sibylline books in the Temple of Apollo, on Rome's Palatine Hill, prophesied to Augustus: "And on thee one day shall come, O' hardy Rome, a deserved blow from heaven. You will be plundered and destroyed and with a wailing and gnashing of teeth, you shall pay . . . And you, daughters of Rome, clothed in gold and luxury, drunk with the attention of [illegible]—you shall be made a slave and a whore because men forgot the good; gave themselves to greed and unrighteous living."

The Sibylline apocalypse, in turn, has literary precedent in Plato (whose *Republic,* albeit fragmentary and poorly transcribed, was bound together with the Nile River gospels and buried in Nag Hammadi with an entire Gnostic-Christian library). In 347 B.C., Plato penned a cautionary tale about a once-noble civilization whose people had forgotten goodness, and become debased, and thus incurred a devastating and deserved blow from heaven. In his *Critias* (117–121d), Plato warned, "When this divine portion [their enlightenment] began to fade away in them . . . and human nature got the upper hand, they then, being unable to bear their [good] fortune [of gold and other property—and the largest of their harbors full of vessels and merchants coming from all parts], they behaved unseemingly, and to him who had an eye to see, grew visibly debased . . . tainted with unrighteous avarice and power. Zeus, the god of gods, who rules according to law, and is able to see such things, perceiving that an honorable race was in a woeful plight, and wanting to inflict punishment . . . collected the gods into their most holy habitation." In *Timaeus* (22c–24e), Plato described how the blow came down to Earth: "The stream from heaven, like a pestilence [came] pouring down . . . Afterward there occurred violent earthquakes and floods, and in a single day and night of misfortune all your warlike men in a body sank into the earth, and the island of Atlantis in like manner disappeared into the depths of the sea."

The eighteenth chapter of John's Revelation seems to echo Plato's caution: "For [the city's] sins have reached into heaven, and God hath remembered her iniquities . . . Therefore shall her plagues come in one day, death, and mourning . . . for strong *is* the Lord God who judgeth her . . . and the merchants of the earth shall weep and mourn over her; for no man buyeth their merchandise any more: The merchandise of gold, and silver, and precious stones, and pearls . . . the merchants of these things, which were made rich by her, shall stand afar off for the fear of her torment, weeping and wailing . . . And [cry] when they [see] the smoke of her burning—for in one hour is she made desolate . . . And a mighty angel took up a stone like a great millstone, and cast *it* into the sea, saying, 'Thus with violence shall the great city Babylon be thrown down, and shall be found no more at all.' "

IN AD 307, 654 YEARS after Plato, approximately 311 years after Augustus assembled the Sibylline verses, and between 200 and 250 years after the Revelation of John began to appear in written form, Emperor Constantine came to power. The sun god Apollo, with a halo of radiant spokes surrounding his head, continued to be represented on Constantine's coinage until at least the year A.D. 320. According to the church historian Eusebius (who, having been born about A.D. 260, was a contemporary of the emperor), "Constantine the Great" was converted from the Apollo cult to Christianity in 312 by a vision of the cross in the sky, shortly before his victory at Milvian Bridge. A later historian named Zosimus theorized that the miraculous conversion more likely came about because Constantine had behaved so badly (for example, by murdering his wife and son) that pagan priests expelled him from the Temple of Apollo and refused him forgiveness. Damned by Jupiter and Apollo (or so the temple priests had said), the emperor found forgiveness in the only religious alliance remaining open to him: among Eusebius and the other Christian bishops.

Writing about A.D. 470 (sixty-five years before the 535 Byzantine catastrophe), Zosimus was a Greek historian whose *Historia nova* attributed the then-current decline of the Empire to punishment by Zeus for the acceptance of Christianity and the widespread rejection of pagan gods.

WE ARE HARD-PRESSED to name a more fascinating year in all of Roman existence than the year in which Vesuvius chanced to flash-freeze two cities and all their organic furnishings.

"Justa's House," also known as the "House of the Christians," also known as the "House of the Bicentenary," is located on "Main Street," about two city blocks northwest of the marina, on the northernmost extension of the Herculaneum excavation. None of these house names

Past is prologue. The discovery of Herculaneum and Pompeii in the 1700s was met with such universal excitement that all things Roman, from ancient law to the Latin language, were soon adopted by an emerging industrial civilization. A dozen centuries past its extinction, the Empire exerted its influence everywhere: from the ceramic designs of Josiah Wedgwood to the architecture of the Victorian, Georgian, and Edwardian eras. Roman cherubs (such as the one above, right) were a common motif on the Bay of Naples, often crafted to hold oil lanterns or candlesticks. The cherub on the left, inspired by the furnishings of the lost cities, once held an electric lamp at the base of the *Titanic*'s Grand Stairway.

were known to the Romans of A.D. 79; they came into existence only after the building was discovered in 1938. The oldest of the modern names—House of the Bicentenary—came into use because the red tile roof was uncovered exactly two hundred years after the exploration of Herculaneum began. The later names came into use after the remains of what appears to be the world's first-known Christian shrine (or chapel) were discovered in a small second-story room—in an adjoining room, the story of Justa was found.

Originally a large private mansion, "Justa's House" was remodeled, during the decades before the eruption, to accommodate tenants and/or an extended family on the second floor—where balconies draped in ivy and flowering vines overlooked a luxuriant central garden framed with white marble columns. The shaded walkway encircling the columns was painted, mirrorlike, as a reflection of the marble architecture, and of the garden itself—in decorative panels and cornices displaying vines and all manner of flowers.

On the ground-floor dining and living areas, one fresco depicts a pastoral setting in which the god Mars is attempting to seduce an only scantily clothed Venus. In another country landscape, Daedalus and Pasiphaë stand before a bull, planning, together, the creation of the Minotaur. According to a legend already ancient when the child Plato first heard it told, the imprisoned scientist and architect Daedalus was forced to design the Labyrinth for King Minos of Crete, and to create for it a pitiless monster, half-man, half-bull. Pasiphaë was King Minos's wife. After falling under Daedalus's spell, she provided her own egg, from which the inhuman hybrid was conceived, and in this manner Pasiphaë became, according to legend, the mother of the Minotaur.

A small second-story room of this same house, located between two bedrooms, was uniquely painted (compared with the rest of the house): Its walls were bare white. No landscapes. No wall designs. Just white paint, with not a single splash of color anywhere. Nothing except an unusual mark left in the wall plaster, above the room's only piece of furniture: In a room where wood was perfectly preserved, a wooden object in the shape of a cross is missing—pried with a tool from the wall, sometime during that last August day. The tool marks, the grain pattern of the wood, and the holes from the four nails that originally held it in place are impressed in the plaster. The mounting nails were driven into the top and bottom of the longer, vertical strip of wood—which is not where someone striving for sturdiness would have driven the nails into, say, an unusually shaped, weight-bearing shelf. (In accordance with the logic of bringing up alternative explanations and attempting simultaneously to support them and to explain them away, the shelf reigned for a time as the only reasonable substitute for a Christian cross. Eventually, this explanation fell away, and what remained was the mystery of the cross.)

The Herculaneum cross. A room of "Justa's House," furnished only with a Romanesque household shrine (adapted, apparently, for kneeling), preserves a mark in the wall plaster, left when a wooden, cross-shaped object was hastily pried loose for rescue. Excavators have found a plate of incense intact atop the shrine. Against twenty-first-century stereotypes of impoverished martyrs in the time of James and Paul, the owners of this oldest known Christian-like chapel were wealthy. Court records in a nearby room suggest that they were also against slavery. Elsewhere in the house, paintings of Daedalus creating the Minotaur and of the god Mars seducing Venus suggest that they practiced a polytheist version of Christianity known as Gnosticism. Exterminated as heretics in A.D. 325 by what later became the Holy Roman Catholic Church, the last surviving branch of orthodox Gnosticism would be found north of Baghdad in the twenty-first century. The Gnostic prophecies of apocalypse, which grew in stature and became sacred after the Vesuvius holocaust, also survived into the twenty-first century in the Book of Revelation.

In a home where, during the first minutes or hours after the lunchtime concussion of August 24, precious legal documents and items of silver were left behind, a cross-shaped ornament appears to have been hastily pried loose and spirited away, much as the priests whose bodies became fossilized at the Temple of Isis, in Pompeii, were clutching and apparently trying to save religious icons when the surge cloud caught up with them.

Immediately below the cross stands a small wooden cabinet, or "oratory," built in the same shape (with the same apparent function) as household Roman shrines found throughout the city and dedicated to Roman gods. It differs from pagan oratories, or altars, in being considerably shorter, apparently to accommodate the cross mounted above it at eye level. The cabinet is fronted by a hinged compartment door (but the storage compartment, or "holy of holies," is empty), and below the door a padded, floor-level ledge had been added, most probably to accommodate a kneeling worshiper or priest (or, if they were Gnostic Christians, a priestess).

Like small pagan chapels and alcoves in other homes, the room appears to have been set aside specifically as a place of worship. The cabinet under the "cross" is the sole piece of furniture in the "chapel," which has no windows and only one door.

The Christian Bible records that the apostle Paul landed in the Bay of Naples in A.D. 61, during the seventh year of Nero's reign. Archaeologists, Jesuits, and historians have proposed that after Paul's visit, a small group of Christians began meeting to worship in the upstairs room of "Justa's House."

Maybe . . . and maybe not. Something Paul's early Christian sect had in common with the Jews of A.D. 79 was the rejection of all but one God. They universally abhorred all pagan images. In decades to come, disciples of Paul would chisel away the faces of Egyptian and Roman idols, wherever they could be found. The images of Venus, Mars, and the Minotaur creation myth on the ground floor of Justa's House indicate a sect rather more tolerant of polytheism.

Something the various Gnostic sects (later condemned as "heretics" by the Pauline sects) had in common with the Romans of Pompeii and Herculaneum was acceptance of the goddess Isis and several other Egyptian / Roman deities (but not the deified Roman emperors). While

A cabinet-sized Roman shrine was preserved in the atrium of a Herculaneum home.
The intense heat of the surge cloud, as it carbonized decorative wood columns and
panels, inflicting "alligator skin" burns, sealed the shrine and acted, paradoxically, as
both destroyer and preserver. Family members prayed here, before their "household
gods," and made burnt offerings on ceremonial plates. The shrine preserved frankincense, items of food, and a chalice from which wine was either poured or consumed,
evidently as part of a religious rite.

St. John's, Newfoundland, A.D. 2001: A portable Christian shrine with apparent resemblance to the Herculaneum shrines. Ancestrally, the resemblance may be more real than apparent.

it is possible that Pauline Christians, as a matter of survival, might have maintained and openly displayed pagan images on the ground floor while secretly worshiping in an upstairs chapel, this does not seem likely. Though under Nero, open refusal to accept Roman gods, resulting in public martyrdom, had already become widespread for the followers of Paul. There is no record suggesting (or even hinting) that followers of Paul made such open pretensions of pagan belief.[2]

More likely (perhaps only slightly more likely), the chapel in Justa's

---

[2] Writing in the time of Constantine (about A.D. 330), and after a two-hundred-year enmity between church and synagogue, Bishop Eusebius described Nero and the early Christians thus: "Once Nero's power was firmly established, he plunged into nefarious vices and took up arms against the God of the universe . . . He was the first of the emperors to be declared an enemy of the Deity. To this the Roman Tertullian [in *Defense 5*] refers, 'Con-

House belonged to Gnostic Christians, whose Nile River gospels are brimming with polytheistic references: "Now Sophia, who is the Wisdom of Afterthought and who represents an eternal realm," according to John, in codex 2, chapter 6, "wanted to give birth to a being like herself." Then, in a tale that makes the Minotaur's secret origin seem unimaginative by comparison: "When Sophia saw what her desire had produced, [her creation] changed into the figure of a snake with the face of a lion. Its eyes were like flashing bolts of lightning. She threw it away from herself, outside of that [eternal] realm, so that none of the Immortals would see it. For she had produced it ignorantly . . . Then [her offspring] left her and moved away from the realms where he was born. He was strong, and created for himself other realms by means of a bright flame that still exists. He mated with the Mindlessness that is in him, and produced his own authorities: Cain . . . Abel . . . Pigeradamas appointed a son, Seth, to the second eternal realm, along with the second star, Oroiel . . . These things were communicated to John [by the Savior] as a mystery, and afterward the Savior disappeared at once. Then John went to the other disciples and reported what the Savior had told him. Jesus Christ Amen."

Cain and Abel, like Rome's legendary founding brothers, Romulus and Remus, are the basis of an ancient cautionary tale in which one brother, consumed by jealousy, rose up against the other and killed him with a rock. The story of Cain and Abel, as mentioned in the Gnostic Book of John, must therefore have resonated with the Romans. In cities where a Temple of Isis already existed, mention of the fallen god Seth must also have struck a familiar (and comfortable) chord. Like Romulus and Cain, Seth murdered his brother (Osiris, husband of Isis, father of the falcon-headed god Horus). Osiris was afterward resurrected—phoenix-like, from his own ashes—while Seth was cast down to Earth to live for-

---

sult your own records: there you will find that Nero was the first to let his imperial sword rage against this sect [Christianity] when it was just rising in Rome. We boast that such a man was the originator of our pruning, for anyone who knows him can understand that nothing would have been condemned by Nero unless it were supremely good. So it happened that this man [Nero], the first to be announced publicly as a fighter against God, was led on to slaughter the apostles. It is related that in his reign Paul was beheaded in Rome itself and that Peter was also crucified, and the cemeteries there still called by the names of Peter and Paul confirm the record.' "

ever (like Cain) and to seek redemption for his sin. The Gnostic "Gospels of the Egyptians," in a manner very similar to the New Testament Gospels about the life of Jesus, describe Seth's arrival on Earth, where he sets out from Sodom on his work of salvation (for himself and for others, conducted mostly through baptism). Ultimately, the redeemed and once evil Seth gives all of his love to, and is willing to suffer for a noble race endangered by "temptations and a falsehood of false prophets."

The Gnostic book of "The Great Invisible Spirit" proclaims: "This is the book which the great Seth wrote, and placed on high mountains on which the sun has not risen, nor is it possible. And since the days of the prophets, and the apostles, and the preachers, the name—[Seth]—has not risen upon their heads, nor is it possible . . . The great Seth came and brought his seed. And it was sown in the eons which had been brought forth, their number being the amount of Sodom. Some say that Sodom [the lost city] is the place of pasture of the great Seth, which is Gomorrah. But others [illegible] that the great Seth took his plant out of Gomorrah and planted it in the second place, to which he gave the name Sodom . . . To this [human] race which came forth . . . through the word to Truth and Justice—a conflagration will come upon the earth . . . Because of this race famines will occur, and plagues . . . and their error, that they acted against themselves . . . [Then, as the revelation of things to come showed the terrors of Sodom approaching, the great Seth saw the gift of salvation.] Then the great Seth saw the activity of the devil, and his many guises ["a falsehood of false prophets"] . . . Then the great Seth rejoiced about the gift—which was granted him by the incorruptible child . . . Christ whom the [great] invisible Spirit had anointed . . . Then everything shook, and trembling took hold of the incorruptible ones. Then the three male children came forth from above down into the unborn ones, and the self-begotten ones, and those who were begotten in what is begotten."

Like most things biblical, the story of Seth is strange, hauntingly poetic, and subject to all manner of interpretation. The Gnostic apocalyptic books date back at least to the first and second centuries A.D., and were carefully buried outside of Alexandria, probably as soon as the Egyptians received news that Emperor Constantine's Council of Nicaea had declared the texts "heresy," and that he was commanding that all existing copies be collected and burned, along with anyone who attempted to protect them.

In A.D. 79, the various Christian sects probably faced enough scorn and ridicule just on account of being Christian, without having to expend their energy and their lives fighting Christian against Christian, in the manner of Egyptian Gnostics and Roman Catholics in A.D. 325 or Irish Protestants and Irish Catholics in the nineteenth and twentieth centuries. In the House of Justa, therefore, we should not be surprised to discover clues hinting at the presence of Gnostic Christians who displayed both the symbol of their savior and images of Roman gods. The Gnostics were, after all, living under first-century Roman rule, and they did, after all, have a whole book devoted to Seth and the family of Isis. The Nile River gospels (some of which can be dated with reasonable certainty, to the first and second centuries A.D.)[3] are teaching us that the chapel worshipers of Justa's House, though favoring the symbol of the cross over the symbol of the fish (apparently not a point of contention until Constantine's time), were, if not overtly Gnostic, at least Gnostic-influenced.

While it is true that Paul visited the Bay of Naples in A.D. 61, he was by no means the sole potential source of early Christian influence in Herculaneum. The Gnostics were a distinctly Egyptianized branch of Christianity, and there existed, in the embryonic stages of the Byzantine faith, in the last days of Pompeii and Herculaneum, constant ship traffic between Misenum on the Bay of Naples and Alexandria in Egypt.

What the Gnostics had in common with the rest of the Egyptians, and with the rest of the Romans, was a belief in more than one god. What they had in common with the followers of Paul was a belief in the

---

[3] Dating by such measures as carbon-14 analysis and referenced passages outside the Nile River texts brackets much of the Nag Hammadi library within the first and second centuries A.D.: On the Origin of the World (50–200); the Gospel of Thomas (50–200); the Gospel of Truth (40–180); the Apocryphon of James (100–150); the Gospel of the Savior and the Gospel of the Egyptians (dated 180–200 by external quotation by Clement of Alexandria); the Apocalypse of James, Parts I and II (80–200); Plato's Republic, a Greek-Gnostic hybrid version (100–200); The Sentences of Sextus (50–150); the Gospel of Mary Magdalene (90–200); The Teachings of Silvanus (180–220). Curiously, Silvanus and related texts include distinctly Buddhist passages among early Christian writings: "The opposite of love is not hate. It is fear. Fear leads to hatred. Hatred leads to darkness."

Hebrew Testament, in Jesus, and in resurrection. The Gnostics believed, too, in many of the same sayings and philosophies attributed to Jesus by Paul, Matthew, James, Mark, Luke, and John.

Throughout what evolved, by Shakespeare's time, into the King James edition of the New Testament, the Constantine-approved sayings of Jesus were reinforced by repetition in texts attributed to Paul and the other disciples. Interestingly, if all the repeated sayings of the canonical, post-Nicaea New Testament are written down and spoken only once, then a single recitation of every saying attributed to Jesus would last approximately an hour and fifteen minutes. The sayings attributed to Jesus in the Gnostic, pre-Nicaea gospels (what some scholars call the "unedited" gospels, or "the secret teachings of Jesus") would add more than an hour of sermon, parable, and instruction. In the Gospel of Saint Thomas, "the doubter," the Jesus of the Gnostics spoke of "enlightenment." He spoke of the quest for knowledge, wisdom, and discipline much as Cicero the Epicurean spoke of these same virtues, and in much the same manner as monks from India spoke of truth, enlightenment, and humane behavior: "His disciples said, 'Show us the place where you are, for we must seek it.' He said to them, 'Whoever has ears ought to listen. There is light within an enlightened person, and it shines on the whole world' (saying 24) . . . Jesus said, 'Show me the stone the builders rejected: that is the cornerstone' (saying 66) . . . Jesus said, 'If you bring forth what is in you, what you have will save you. If you do not have that within you, what you do not have within you will destroy you (saying 70) . . . It is [better] for you to be defeated [while speaking the truth] than to be victorious [through deceit]. He who is victorious through [a lie] is [defeated] by the truth (writes Sextus, in proverb 165) . . . The sins of those who are [ignorant are] the shame of those who have taught them (Sextus, 174) . . . You will use [great] property if you give to the [needy] willingly (Sextus, 330) . . . If you take on the guardianship of orphans, you will be [the] father of many children [and] you will be beloved of God (Sextus, 340) . . . A man who does evil to someone will not be able to worship God (Sextus, 370) . . . It is a faithful person fond of learning who is the worker of the truth (Sextus, 384) . . . Guard yourself against lying: there is he who deceives and there is he who is deceived' (Sextus, 393)."

The apostle Paul shared a belief in Jesus (and little else) with the Gnostics. While Christians of both sects believed in "a common brotherhood of man," and in sharing worldly goods, Paul (and later Constantine) did not believe in empowering women and did not question the ownership of slaves. Herein lies, perhaps, another clue to the Christians of Justa's House.

Justa was a young woman faced with the threat of enslavement. Her legal transcripts reveal that she and her mother were both brilliant and powerful women who had embarked on their own business ventures and prospered greatly. The Gnostics, like the Jews with whom the Romans often associated them (as in the term "Jew Chrestus"), were against slavery. Unlike the Jews and the followers of Paul, the Gnostics, according to their scriptures, believed that a man and a woman could somehow inhabit the same body (whatever that was supposed to mean). This allowed them to believe, also, in the empowerment and the essential equality of women—as might be expected of an Egyptianized Christianity that had seen, within recent memory, Queen Cleopatra, and within its Golden Age, the female pharaoh Hatshepsut (whose divinity, according to Egyptian scripture, was heralded by a bright star, and whose divine trinity as a "man," a "woman," and a "living spirit" was declared by Isis and Horus). Though it is unclear precisely when the various early Christian sects "drew lines in the sand" over reincarnation vs. resurrection, over the symbol of the cross vs. the symbol of the fish, over the empowerment of women vs. their oppression, the people of Justa's House appear to have gravitated toward the cross, pagan gods, and empowerment of women. And, most interestingly, they appear to have taken, under their collective wing, an independent "hereditary slave" girl fighting valiantly for her freedom.

A Gnostic identity for the chapel builders of Justa's House is consistent with the Gospel of Thomas, sayings 113 and 22. According to the Gnostic chroniclers, Simon and Peter said to the congregation, "Let Mary leave us, because women are not worthy of life." And Jesus, according to Thomas, disagreed. Echoing Hatshepsut's divinity as both man and woman—by which, under Isis and Horus, she had been empowered to rule simultaneously as king and queen of Upper and Lower Egypt (such declaration was a necessary response to priests who had said that Hatshepsut, because she was a woman, must be stricken down and made to leave)—Jesus said of Mary: "Behold! I shall guide her so as to make her male, that she too may become a living spirit like you men. For every woman who makes herself male will enter the kingdom of heaven (the kingdom which is within you, which is your own responsibility) . . . When you make the two into one, when you make the inner like the outer and the outer like the inner, and the upper like the lower, when you make male and female into a single one, so that the male will not be male and the female will not be female . . . then you will enter the kingdom."

In A.D. 325, Emperor Constantine, speaking from highest authority and with self-professed "[f]oreknowledge granted by God himself," burned every available copy of the Gospels of Mary Magdalene and Thomas and "struck Mary down from amongst the apostles." Ever after, Mary Magdalene is portrayed as a fallen woman, a former prostitute uplifted by Jesus, when in fact Gnostic scripture identifies her as Jesus' "most beloved," and possibly his wife (from the time of a wedding feast—traditionally supplied by the groom—which was defined by the miracle of water and wine). Constantine struck Mary down on the basis of absolute enlightenment, by which he claimed to have cleansed himself of all ignorance.

In chapter 5 of the Gnostic Book of Thomas, when Jesus addresses the equal and opposite powers of ignorance and enlightenment, he seems to reiterate the teachings of India's Buddhist philosophers, dating back almost to 460 B.C.: "And the Savior said, 'Some of those who rush into this madness do not realize they are foolish, but think they are wise.' "

And the wise men from the east said, "To recognize knowledge as ignorance is noble; but to regard ignorance as knowledge is evil."

"I DON'T KNOW" is always a good place to start. And if you happen to be conducting your scientific explorations properly, every new answer you think you've come up with should be kicking the doors open to a half-dozen new questions.

I do not know for certain that the Christians of Justa's House belonged to a Gnostic sect. Nor do I know, all household evidence considered, that they were necessarily Christians.

Viewed in reduction isolation, all by itself, Justa's House provides only a single archaeological snapshot. Fortunately, Vesuvius has preserved a rather broader picture. In the city next door, in the atrium of "Number 11 House," on Pompeii's "Street of the Overhanging Balcony," someone identified himself (or herself) on a wall inscription, with the word CHRISTIANOS.

Biblical scholar Paul Berry, who has made a study of the inscription, the house that contains the inscription, the city that contains the house, and the empire that contains the city, recalls the words of a Dominican priest and teacher of Latin who once told him, "Any attempt to read the New Testament without reference to the Roman Empire would produce an imperfectly focused view of the text." A page can hardly be referred to in the post-Constantine canon or the pre-Constantine extraneous (or "heretic" Gnostic) texts—"which," according to Berry's mentor, "[does] not place the reader at some point along the Roman road."

Echoing what Constantine rendered canon, the Gospel of Thomas, saying 98, reads: "They showed Jesus a gold coin and said to him, '[Tiberius] Caesar's people demand that we pay taxes.' He said to them, 'Give Caesar what is Caesar's, give God what is God's, and give me what is mine . . . Woe to the Pharisees, for they are like a dog sleeping in the food trough of cows: the dog neither eats nor lets the cows eat.' "[4]

Within a Roman time frame, the New Testament (within the approved Constantine version) seems to position the origin of the word *Christian* with considerable precision. In Acts of the Apostles 11:26–27, the dearth (or famine) that occurred during Emperor Claudius's reign (A.D. 41–54) is prophesied in the church of Antioch (the ancient capital city of Syria, presently located behind the southernmost extension of Turkey's border). It is here that we read of an early Christian tradition of sharing worldly goods—and here, too, that an early Christian event is placed firmly in time and space: "And when [Barnabas] found [Saul], he brought him to Antioch.

---

[4] Mentioned only by Josephus and in canonical New Testament and Gnostic texts, the Pharisees were a sect of Temple high priests who claimed direct "words of knowledge from God" in their interpretation and observance of Jewish law. Unlike the much stricter Sadducees, they believed in resurrection, charismatic healing, and "magic." By the second century, however (and probably by A.D. 79), in the aftermath of a divide between Judaism and Christianity, both Egyptian and Roman gospels began portraying the Pharisees as hostile opponents of Jesus.

And it came to pass, that a whole year they assembled themselves with the church, and taught [many] people. And the disciples were called Christians first in Antioch. And in these days came prophets from Jerusalem unto Antioch. And there stood up one of them named Agabus, and signified by the Spirit that there should be a great dearth throughout all the world: which came to pass in the days of Claudius Caesar. Then the disciples, every man according to his ability, determined to send relief unto the brethren which dwelt in Judea."

According to Dio Cassius (whose histories of approximately A.D. 230 record that the dust from the eruption that buried Pompeii and Herculaneum darkened the sky in Rome, more than 100 miles away), Egyptian grain had once been routinely carted to Rome by road from docks at Puteoli and Misenum. Claudius launched a giant engineering project at the port of Ostia, so that a greater number of ships could be accommodated closer to the city of Rome, at the mouth of the Tiber River. Dio noted that Claudius redesigned and expanded the Ostia port in response to a famine (or "dearth") that had brought riot to Rome, and near-widespread revolt throughout the Empire.

Tacitus, with whom Pliny the Younger corresponded about the Vesuvius eruption, also provides an extrabiblical view of the Claudian famine. Tacitus attributed the mob violence in Rome to the fact that the capital city had, out of long-standing tradition, stored only a two-week reserve of grain. In A.D. 51, the emperor safely escaped from a mob at the Forum only by the quick action of his Praetorian Guard. Although Claudius was, in reality, far from the timid and all-too-forgiving monarch depicted in Robert Graves's *I, Claudius* novels (a basis for the incomparable BBC miniseries of the same title), rather than responding with military reprisals against the rioters, he at once provided government subsidies to all grain producers and importers, insuring them against the possibility of price destabilization, should "a glut of supply decrease demand in the marketplace."

Evidently, the market-price assurance worked, despite the fact that grain production throughout the known world was being reduced by what Gaius Suetonius recorded as a widespread and long-continued drought (corroborating some details of the famine prophesied, in Claudius's time, in Acts 11, but limiting the prophecy, perhaps, to a prediction that an already years-long episode of crop-ravaging weather might continue).

According to Suetonius, Claudius was a man haunted by his belief in omens; he not only "revived obsolescent traditions but invented new ones." If a bird of "evil omen" perched on a building, Claudius would go to the Basilica in his capacity as chief priest and lead the populace in prayer. But evil premonitions did, in the end, get the final hand: "The main omens of Claudius' death included the rise of a long-haired star, known as a comet," wrote Suetonius. "There is also evidence that he foresaw his end and made no secret of it: While choosing the Consuls he provided for no appointment after the month in which he died."

Suetonius's chronicles of the fortunes and misfortunes of Claudius's time mention, in passing, an apparently Jewish sect, not yet distinguishable from Jews, yet clearly followers of a martyred "revolutionary," known to the Romans as *Chrestus*: "Because the Jews at Rome caused continuous disturbances at the instigation of Chrestus, [Emperor Claudius] expelled them from the city."

Tacitus (in his surviving work, *Annals*) also uses the name "Chrestus," in reference to a sect that had appeared in Rome by the time of Claudius and Saint Paul. "The founder of that sect, a certain Chrestus," wrote Tacitus, "had suffered execution in the reign of Tiberius, during the procuratorship of Pontius Pilate. Held in check only for a time, the wicked superstition broke out once again, not only in Judea, the birthplace of the malady, but even here in the city [of Rome] itself."

Claudius became emperor in A.D. 41, having emerged from a fifty-year period of fratricide, patricide, and even infanticide, in which members of the royal family poisoned, slandered, stabbed, or otherwise attempted to claw their way to the height of power. To freeze-dry a half century of history down to its bare essentials: The Claudians essentially eliminated one another but ignored the future emperor because he was a pratfalling stutterer who walked stiffly, twitched, dribbled, and wrote histories that, according to his family, no one ever did read. According to Suetonius, Claudius's books were in fact "learned works." While still a boy, Claudius had started penning his "Story of Civilization," encouraged by the historian Livy. During his life, he published more than seventy volumes, including an autobiography in eight parts (which, according to Suetonius, proved "liable to criticism more for their lack of taste—that is to say, their shocking honesty—rather than for any lack of style"). The city of Alexandria responded to Claudius's works by adding a new wing to the world-famous library and museum, and then naming it in the historian's honor.

Despite praise from the likes of Gaius Suetonius, none of Claudius's works survived the fourth-, fifth-, and sixth-century library burnings or the Dark Age that followed the fires. And, despite the apparent merits of his work, Claudius's own family members had failed from the start to understand that he was not the fool they believed him to be; they had failed even to read his books before mocking them—which was, per-haps, the reason Claudius survived. Had his sister, his uncles, his nephews, or "Grandmother Livia" recognized him as intelligent instead of merely feeble and harmless, he would not have remained the last man standing after the rest of the Claudians had removed every real and imagined contender to the throne.

Suetonius described the afflicted emperor (prone, not surprisingly, to conspiracy-theory paranoia and associated bloodletting), in his mother's words, as a twitching and stumbling monster of a man "whom Nature had not finished but had merely begun." But the Suetonius chronicles contain a hint that in an effort to keep his books (and everything else he produced or thought worthy of producing) invisible to those nearest to him, Claudius might have exaggerated his afflictions, sensing correctly that seeming half-witted was better than dying with all of one's wits intact; that being ignored in *this* family imparted a Darwinian survival advantage. So, through the perilous reigns of Tiberius and Caligula, Claudius continued to dribble and stumble and crash into both animate and inanimate objects, perpetuating the opinion that he might wreck the Empire simply by strolling through it. In reality, he might have defined "survivor type." According to Suetonius, "His health was wretched until he succeeded to the throne—when it suddenly became excellent!"

In his extrabiblical account of the Claudian famine of Acts 11, Suetonius explained that in response to the Forum riots, Claudius "took all possible steps to import grain, even during the winter months—insur-ing merchants against the loss of their ships in stormy weather, and offer-ing a large bounty for every new grain-transport built, proportionate to its tonnage." At Ostia he constructed a new harbor by creating protective breakwaters—which projected into the sea like the "arms" of a giant scorpion. Forward of the entrance (between the arms), Claudius built an island—an additional breakwater capped by a very tall lighthouse, "like the Pharos at Alexandria that guided ships into the harbor at night by the beams of a lamp." The foundation of the island was a huge ship in which Claudius's predecessor, Caligula, had transported a giant Egyptian obelisk from Heliopolis. The ship was moored in the desired place and sunk, then secured with piles, then built upon, buried, and preserved.

Caligula's private boats were engineering marvels in their own right. His "Nemi Palaces" were precisely that: floating palaces. The Suetonius chronicles describe "[h]uge spacious baths, colonnades, banquet halls, and even a great variety of vines and fruit trees, that on board of them he might recline at a table from an early hour, and coast along the shores of Campania," where preeruption Misenum, Puteoli, Herculaneum, and Pompeii still flourished in sunlight.

Twenty-first-century excavation has revealed that Suetonius might have understated the imperial luxury liners' fittings. Between the years A.D. 37 and 41, boilers had been mounted belowdecks to provide steam for the saunas and to pump hot and cold running water to first-class staterooms through hundreds of yards (or meters) of lead pipes.

All of the mechanical elements necessary for Nero's steamship were already present in Caligula's pleasure fleet, two decades before Nero and the mysterious "Thomas Edison" or "Merlin" of Herculaneum. The multiple-gearshift Antikithera devices (mechanically operated analog computers) were also present; and there existed iron-reinforced concrete, and the explosive black powders reported in the books of Lucretius . . . And the first trans-Atlantic voyagers (no matter how unintentionally) were, by all archaeological indications, landing Roman ships in South America.

And yet, during the next 250 years, the Empire would become distracted and fragmented, stepping up to the very edge of economic collapse, backing away from the precipice, then stepping forward again and again (with slavery providing the ever-present twin threats of internal rebellion and long-term economic suicide). The end was a probability curve, awaiting only some combination of natural, economic, and political stressors to split the Empire, then push Roman Byzantium too far, then usher in, finally, a dark age.

After Thera and the Minoans, the world had waited nearly 1,500 years for the reintroduction of dams, aqueducts, internal plumbing, and clean drinking water on a national scale. After the fall of Rome and Constantinople, civilization waited another 1,500 years.

And again, a question intrudes upon our imaginations: How could they have been so close to steam power—so close to an industrial revolution, and to the understanding of electrical power that was so soon, so inevitably, to follow—and yet failed to grasp it? What went wrong?

And we are forced to wonder if, 1,500 winters from now, someone will look back upon a civilization on the verge of unlocking the secrets hidden in the ganglia of a fly and applying those secrets to the at-once wondrous and obscene technology of self-replicating robotics; a civilization close to building a genetic Rosetta stone and applying it to the treatment and reversal of all disease—including aging—and artificially boosting human intelligence while they were at it; a civilization capable of throwing open the doors to the universe.

Will our distant descendants look back, through an intervening dark age, upon a civilization that already had designs for relativistic, star-crossing rockets on its drawing boards as early as 1984; and will they shrug at us, and ask, "How could they have come so close and yet failed to grasp it?"

Will they look back upon tools that at this very moment may lie before our eyes, not yet recognized by us, not yet connected to produce the next obvious breakthrough (so obvious, as most of history's giant leaps are, when viewed with twenty-twenty hindsight); and will they wonder, then, how we failed? Will they ask themselves, then, perhaps with a sense of pity, perhaps with a sense of relief:

"What went wrong?

"What went wrong?"

DOWN THERE, in the shallows of time's backward abyss; down there in Pompeii's "Number 11 House," archaeology's first physical appearance of the word *Christianos* wades us into the deeps of empire and enigma.

VINA

MARIA

ΛDIA ΛV

BOVIASAYDI CHRISTIANOS

8X SICVOSO ONUS

Reading the handwriting on the wall of Pompeii's "House of the Christian Inscription" is a journey into the mysterious, doomed to frustration. To begin, the left-hand portions of the top three lines appear to be missing. The remainder is reconstructed as a hybridization (crp, 2002) of the 1862 cleaning and the 1995 optical enhancement of carbon-stylus particles retained in the wall surface. The lower left portion of the inscription (or poem) appears to include numerical shorthand, exemplified by an "8" (which represents "1,000" in surviving Pompeiian accountants' books). "X" may represent "10," in association with "1,000." Above the numbers, "BO" is Latin for "cry aloud." Reference to a journey or a path may be indicated by "VIa" (alternatively, this may represent the Roman numeral 6, "VI," and the symbol "alpha"). "SAY" has no known meaning. "DI" can be either "God" or "the answer to the meaning of life in the Cosmos" (or the Roman numeral "501"). "SIC" probably means "So" or "Thus," while "VOSO" represents power, force, violence, and havoc. "ONUS" has several possible meanings, chief among them, "to bear a great burden," or "to bear an adversary." With some repetition, sampling, and remixing, a best guess at the meaning of the most intact lines translates, roughly, to this: "To havoc, O, God's Christians. Cry havoc. A great number [of people, or of years?] Great power is thy burden. So, cry aloud, O, Christians. Thy strength is thy enemy. Thy strength is thy weakness." A hundred years after Vesuvius buried the inscription, the Christian writer Tertullian (in *Apologetics*, 40-1 and 8) seemed to echo the power, or "witchery," with which the growing faith was seemingly destined to be associated in blame: "They take Christians to be the cause of every disaster which befalls the State . . . but no complaint of Christians when the fires from Heaven drenched the Volscians out of the mountains of Pompeii." Of the dozen words and word fragments now revealed, only the name MARIA and the plural noun CHRISTIANOS speak clearly, just as they had been written around the time of Paul—who, according to Acts 28:13, had stayed at Puteoli, west of Pompeii, on his path to Rome.

Bakeries and dye houses surround Number 11, and the neighborhood's crowded boardinghouses and market stalls convey a sense of absentee landlords, poorly kept tenements, and occupation by a transient class. Yet Number 11, a spacious and well-cared-for home, stands apart from its surroundings. The House of the Christian Inscription has more in common with Justa's House, in Herculaneum, than with its neighbors.

The New Testament stories of the austere fishermen who traveled with Jesus, and the impoverished, downtrodden, and generally illiterate Christians depicted in post-Constantine church histories, teach us to expect first-century Christians among the transient neighbors of Number 11's residents, not among the Number 11 residents themselves. Against the expectations of Scripture and Eusebius, the two earliest samples we have, indicating resident Christians—Justa's House and Number 11—suggest that the emerging faith was attractive not only to the poor and downtrodden, but to people of wealth and influence as well.

Number 11 was a piece of property 200 feet (60 meters) long, with windowless walls of stone and concrete that blocked the outside world from view. Inside, the residents enjoyed two large open-air gardens; one of them a grape vineyard, the other an olive grove, both of them (as revealed by fossilized trunks, roots, and pollen) enhanced by herb gardens and decorative flowers.

The inscription itself, the plural noun CHRISTIANOS, was painted on stucco with a carbon-based pigment, in letters 3 inches (7.5 centimeters) high, at eye level, in the atrium, or "living room," of Number 11's ground floor. Far from being a secretive or cryptic inscription, the word could not have been spelled out in a more heavily trafficked or conspicuous room. Perhaps the persecutions that began with Nero were more sporadic and localized (to the city of Rome, for example) than the writings of Rome-based historians have suggested; or perhaps a piece of furniture covered the inscription (for the furnishings of Pompeii have decayed more completely than those of Herculaneum and could easily have vanished without a trace). Much has been lost, and we do not have (and may never have) all of the clues.

Six blocks east of Number 11, in another private house, another Latin inscription was discovered in 1874. On a dining room wall, with the letters of one word placed exactly above the letters of the other, these words appear:

SODOMA GOMORA

Tracing the writer's reference to the Old Testament account of Sodom and Gomorrah's destruction (in Genesis 18–20), or to Luke's account (in 17:29), or to the Gnostic's Seth-Jesus accounts (as in the book of The Great Invisible Spirit) is an intractable problem. The inscription can be dated anywhere between A.D. 79 and a hundred years before, with a lingering possibility that it was penned during the afternoon or evening of Pompeii and Herculaneum's burial.

In Acts (28:13–14), Paul is quoted as stopping for seven days at Puteoli, between Misenum and Herculaneum, on the Bay of Naples. This was during Nero's reign, approximately two decades before the eruption. The Bible makes no mention of the volcano, towering dormant-still, across the bay. In a letter to his brother Atticus, Cicero (15.13.60) wrote that he was retreating, for a while, from the hyperactivity of Rome to the shadow of Vesuvius. The philosopher perceived only tranquillity in the shadow; he hinted at not even the vaguest suspicion that something ominous lurked beneath: "I am hurrying to Pompeii, so I may [relax and] write a book. I should be less troubled by interruptions there."

Pliny the Elder, too, retreated to Vesuvius and the Bay of Naples, and for the same reason: "I should be less troubled by interruptions there."

Pliny's contemporary, the poet Martial, in his Epigrams (4.44.7), wrote of once red-tiled roofs, brilliant white sea-front façades, and colorful gardens, "drowned now in fire and melancholy ash"—much as the Sibylline oracles had said it would be.

Although the church leaders of Paul's time, and of Constantine's time, were openly opposed to such clearly paganistic verses as the Sibylline prophecies, the Vatican preserved all of the Sibylline books; and the pre-Christian Sibyls sing to us still, in the rhyming Latin triplet that begins the Roman Catholic Requiem Mass:

DIES IRAE, DIES ILLA,
SOLVET SAECLUM IN FAVILLA,
TESTE DAVID CUM SIBYLLA.

Day of wrath, O, on that day,
Dissolve the earth in ash and clay,
David and the Sibyl say.

SIBYLLA . . . CHRISTIANOS . . . SODOMA . . . GOMORA . . .

The linguist Paul Berry has observed that by the time of Claudius, Titus, and Vesuvius, Latin had come to mean the essence of everything Roman: "Simple to the point of rigidity, straightforward to the point of woodenness, direct to the point of inflexibility, it was the Mediterranean's first irreducible tongue, and fragmentation was not possible." As indeed it was not. Latin lived on as the unchanged and unchanging language of the church, and of genus and species, and the language of evolution. Though the church and the evolutionists were, for more than a century after Darwin, poised galaxies apart, their common language was such that, aboard the oceanographic research vessel *Keldysh*, in 2001, it was helpful but not always necessary for Russian and American scientists to speak each other's language, for in our shared Latin we were already communicating the entire phylogeny of Gorgon colonies that had been growing for more than fifteen years on the *Titanic's* prow.

According to Berry, the Roman language never contained more than a third the number of words found in the English vocabulary of the twenty-first century; and yet to eliminate from the English language every word derived from Latin would be to burn half the dictionary. Down there in the abyss of time, down there in Pompeii, the utterance in carbon and Latin seems to stand apart from the rubble of Number 11. The word CHRISTIANOS breaks out unconditionally, says Berry: "The image has been borne to us on history's most enduring transport vehicle, the Roman alphabet. A translator is not called for, a statement from the scholar is not required. The inscription is read by a schoolchild from the child's own primer. Steadfast across two thousand years of human experience, the Roman alphabet, now a world standard, remains a wonderment of history. The child, holding its exercise tablet, copies the same incomparable script, lithe and spare, sinuous and stately."

IN THE YEAR 2001, Sir Arthur C. Clarke, known to the world for a film with that year as its title, became increasingly disheartened by my reports from Ground Zero in Manhattan. One day, he made the leap from agnosticism to atheism, then wrote to me from Sri Lanka: "Perhaps we should thank the Taliban for finishing the task that the Crusades only half-completed nine hundred years ago—proving that Religion is incompatible with Civilization."

At that time, with Christmas approaching and with the fires of September still burning under the earth, it really did seem as if the history of civilization was all fire and killing in the name of God. Again and again, as a child's Beanie Baby doll—downblasted undamaged through the roof of a flattened car—came again into my dreams and jolted me awake . . . Again and again, I came back to wondering if all of history might simply be freeze-dried down to five thousand years of people maiming and murdering one another over who had the one and true imaginary friend.

"Imagine no religion?" Or so the poet had asked. No religion. I hear they tried that experiment in cold war Russia. It did not work out very well. And yet, there in the deep, hellish abyss of New York, someone had erected a cross. Someone else had left a Star of David in the ruins; someone else, a tiny crescent moon. Near Saint Paul's Chapel, I found candles and incense at a makeshift Buddhist shrine. And I met a fireman who said that when he saw the first plane nose slightly downward and shift course from off-center to dead center on the North Tower's ninety-sixth floor, he knew immediately that it was a suicide attack. Thinking "Islamic jihad," he had uttered these words: "Please don't tell me this was done in God's name. Please don't let anyone tell me . . ."

(That religion is incompatible with civilization?)

After a time, I replied to Arthur Clarke: "*Extremism.* That is the qualifier I would add to your thesis. I would revise it thus: 'Perhaps we should thank the Taliban for finishing the task that the Crusades only half-completed nine hundred years ago—proving that religious extremism is incompatible with civilization.' Religious extremism is the sincerest form of intolerance. There, within intolerance itself, and not within religion itself, lies civilization's Pandora."

Arthur replied that there were no qualifiers: "[R]eligions are (by definition) extremist, even if some of their adherents aren't!" By "some of their adherents," he was referring, in particular, to our kindly and ever-tolerant friend, Father Mervyn Fernando.

Father Fernando, who for more than two decades had been building a teaching center and orphanage connected by a bridge to Sri Lanka's Arthur C. Clarke Science Center, had gotten into a little trouble some years ago on account of me and Arthur. During 1989's "God, the Universe, and Everything" sessions, through which scientists and theologians were gathered around the common watering holes of physics, astronomy, paleontology, and biblical archaeology, Arthur and I had carried the simultaneity question a bridge too far: "In a universe where every photon of light manifests simultaneously as a self-contradictory particle and wave, why can't all faiths—including even lack of faith—be simultaneously correct? That ought to be child's play in God's universe, in a universe already inhabited by the 'impossible' photon."

Father Fernando thought about that for a while, and one day he told me that I could no longer call him "Father," because when he began embracing Buddhist philosophy, studying the Bamboo Annals, and writing about "quantum spirituality" and the "oneness of all humanity," the modern-day Inquisitors responded with unimaginable rapidity.

"You and Arthur," he said, "*cannot* call me 'Father' anymore because I have been *defrocked.*" But we refused to stop calling him "Father," refused to recognize church (read: human) authority to say that one who so devotes his life to helping other human beings and to asking new questions about the nature of human existence is neither enlightened nor holy.

As I hear it, Rome coerced Father Fernando into recanting his "heresy." Rome did much the same to Galileo, and I'm certain that Galileo, after he renounced his theories, privately whispered, "But Europa *does* orbit Jupiter, and the earth *still* goes around the Sun." I do not know for a fact that Father Fernando whispers similarly. The fact is, we do not talk about it.

In 2001, Father Fernando wrote: "To Pontius Pilate's question, 'What is Truth?' the answer of Christ was silence, not unlike the silence of Buddha to questions about the 'truth' of the Cosmos. Are the Buddha and Christ telling us that truth can be found only in silence—in openness and receptivity to the silent voice of reality? Can it be that the human mind is 'condemned' to the word? Still—it is a blessed 'condemnation.'"

"Condemned to the word," Father Fernando had said. In the Nile River Apocryphon of James (codex 1, 4-16; 4-8), Jesus is quoted as instructing humanity, "Hearken to the word; understand knowledge, love, and good works—for from these comes life. Then no one will persecute you and no one will oppress you, unless you [human beings] do this to yourselves."

(Hearken to the word . . .)

As Father Fernando has pointed out, the answer to Pilate's question, "What is Truth?" was silence. In the fourth chapter of Genesis, Cain cries out to God, "Am I my brother's keeper?" And, as the biblical scribes told it, God never did give Cain an answer.

"What is Truth?"

"Am I my brother's keeper?"

Twice in the Bible, human beings demand an answer, and are left with their questions. The rest of the Bible (in all its various forms), and the rest of history, might be described as humanity's attempts to answer those two questions.

According to the church, in the time of Constantine, the word *Gnostic* was defined to mean "heresy," and the Gnostic Christians were declared Byzantium's heretics. To the Gnostics, the word meant "knowledge." The word *agnostic*, reduced to its original Latin, defines one who "lacks knowledge," and who seeks it by asking questions.[5]

Seekers were not well tolerated in Constantine's time. After his A.D. 325 conference at Nicaea, books spanning a half-millennium were placed

---

[5] Before Emperor Nero called him to Rome for execution, the apostle Paul came upon an altar in Athens inscribed with the Latin phrase *Agnosto Theo:* "To the Unknown God."

in a large ceramic jar by people who understood the preservative qualities of Egypt's dry sands. The books were buried in Nag Hammadi, about the time bonfires of books began to spread throughout the stillcivilized but Dark Age–bound world.

The Nile River Gospels were written in Coptic—which defines letters of the Greek alphabet used to translate the Egyptian language. The end of the Prayer of the Apostle Paul is inscribed with a hybrid symbol drawn from the Egyptian ankh (the hieroglyph of "life") and the Christian cross. Elsewhere, this same book is inscribed with the symbol of the fish, referring to the Christian expression "You will become fishers of men."

In the Old Testament Book of Jeremiah, the faithful are told that burial in a jar will preserve a book—"Thus sayeth the Lord . . . Take these evidences . . . and put them in an earthen vessel, that they may continue" (32:14)—while a fire is the way to destroy it—"When Jehudi had read three or four leaves, he cut it with the knife, and cast it into the fire that was on the hearth, until the roll was consumed in the fire that was on the hearth" (36:23). Much as the Dead Sea Scrolls were sealed in jars and buried in the time of Vespasian, Titus, and Josephus (as Rome's Tenth Legion approached), the Nile River Gospels, too, appear to have been buried during the approach of the Romans, who by then had become orthodox Christians. The Gnostics already had a clear sense of preserving theology and prophesy by casting it into the future, in much the same manner as one might cast a message in a bottle onto the North Atlantic current.

The Gospel of Seth and the Egyptians states that a copy of Gnostic scripture had already been hidden in a mountain by Seth, "in order that in the end of times and the [future] eras, [these writings] may come forth . . . when something dreadful this way comes [something dreadful, toward this race], which came forth through Edokla; for she gave birth through the word to Truth, and Justice, the origin of the seed of the eternal life which is with those who will persevere because of the knowledge of their emanation. This is the great, incorruptible race . . . But because of this race, a conflagration will come upon the earth."

The Nile River Gospels lay undisturbed in the earth for a millennium and a half, and then for a century and a score of years more, until the end of the Second World War, in 1945. They were discovered by a young man named Muhammad Ali, from the town of al-Qasr. Ali brought the manuscripts home on camelback, straight into the center of one of Egypt's most notorious blood feuds. Some months earlier, Ali's father had been murdered. As if by some strange fulfillment of destiny, something in the Nile River Gospels seemed to have prophesied what happened next.

About a month after the discovery of the books, according to James Robinson (a translator of the Sethian gospels), a jealous neighbor pointed to a sleeping man named Ahmad—"pointed him out to Ali as the murderer of his father. He ran home and alerted his brothers and widowed mother, who had told her seven sons to keep their mattocks sharp. The family fell upon their victim, hacked off his limbs bit by bit, ripped out his heart, and devoured it among them, as the ultimate act of blood revenge."

As it turned out, the victim was the son of a local sheriff. It becomes difficult to keep count of the obituary reports that followed. At one funeral procession, a half-dozen attendees were shot and killed, and the feud was still very much alive more than a half-century later.

Meanwhile, the books themselves had been divided and sold, sometimes for little more than pennies, sometimes for enough money to enable a merchant to open new shops in both al-Qasr and Cairo. During the 1960s, the government in Cairo recognized the library as a national treasure and for a total compensation of four thousand pounds managed to buy back all privately owned Nile River Gospels and to reassemble the library in Egypt's Coptic Museum. Not all of the gospels had survived, however; and as it turned out, if not for dispersal from the Ali household and into private collections, none might now exist. Most of the twelfth codex and four to eight pages from the Gospel of Mary Magdalene were burned in an oven by Ali's mother, who is said to have believed the books were a source of bad luck, comparable to the release of a "jinn" that had been closed up inside the ancient jar.

Ali's mother could not read the words; and yet by the oddest of coincidences, the unread library had come into a family driven by fury and blood oaths to hack out the heart of another human creature, and to devour it in vengeance. What they would have thought, we can only wonder, if afterward they had been able to read the texts, and if afterward their eyes had settled, by chance, upon these words in the fifth chapter of the Book of Thomas: "The Savior said [of the intentionally cruel, and the vengeance-driven among human beings], 'Do not think of them as human beings, but consider them as animals. For as animals devour each other, so also people like this devour each other. Moreover, the kingdom is taken from them, since they love the delights of fire, they are slaves of death . . . They fulfill the lusts of their parents.' "

The family into whose possession the Nile River Gospels had originally fallen happened to be—as the Romans would have understood it—driven by the three Furies: Anger, Jealousy, and Vengeance.

The Gnostic Book of John carries on with the Graeco-Roman myth of the Furies, naming four principal demons, one of whom is called Fear, from whom arise anguish, shame, and slavery. Much in the manner of the canonical Book of Revelation, some of the John passages are utterly nonsensical, as if penned by someone not at all in his right mind; as in Codex 13: "I am Mother and I am Father since I copulate with myself." And yet, within a maze of incomprehensible and astonishingly garbled pages, as if hidden there by design, one comes across a paragraph in which a Savior says, "The opposite of love is not hate. It is fear." According to John, fear arises from misplaced desire, leading to jealousy and anger. Anger leads to vengeance, and vengeance leads to evil—to a sincere interest in wickedness, and finally to eternal damnation.

The Gnostics believed that Seth had been seduced to his darker side by the Furies of Desire, Anger, Jealousy, and Vengeance. He murdered his own brother, and for this crime he fell (with his legions) to Earth. But instead of committing Seth to eternal damnation, the gods left him with a hope (albeit a faint one) of redemption. Sensing that there was still a glimmer of goodness in him, they allowed Seth to wander the earth, and to seek. As century gave way to century, and then to millennium, Seth worked for the betterment of humanity, eventually putting the needs of the many above his own. Along this path, he achieved both enlightenment and redemption, and became revered by the Gnostic prophets and scribes as an equal to Jesus (and in fact occasionally so indistinguishable from him as to possibly even *be* him).

Of his wanderings on wilderness Earth, The Second Treatise of the Great Seth records: "After we went forth from our home and came down to this world, and came into being in this world in bodies, we were hated and persecuted, not only by those who are ignorant, but also [now] by those who think that they are advancing the name of Christ." According to the Second Treatise, Seth, haunted by wrath and fear, "stole" human form by the taking of human life, only later to embark on the road to redemption: "I visited a bodily dwelling. I cast out the one who was in it first, and I went in [to the body]. And the whole multitude of archons became troubled . . . For he was an earthly man, but I am from above the heavens. I did not [in later times] refuse them even to become a Christ, but I did not reveal myself to them in the love which was coming forth from me. I revealed that I am a stranger to the regions (of the lower realm, on Earth) . . . I am the Son of Man, the one from you who is among you. I am despised for your sake . . . lest you give birth to evil, and [its] brothers: jealousy and division, anger and wrath, fear and a divided heart, and empty, non-existent desire. But I am an ineffable mystery to you . . .

"Neither (Moses) nor those before him, from Adam to John the Baptist—none of them knew me nor my brothers (we [who] went forth from our home and came down to this world)—[f]or they had a doctrine of angels . . . and bitter slavery, since they never knew the truth, nor will they know it."

(What is Truth?)

In the Asclepius codex of the Nile River Gospels, an initiate to the sect of Hermes (the Roman god Mercury) confuses the "holy matters" still further by arguing that man creates gods in his own image: "Since we have entered into the matter of the communion between the gods and men, know, Asclepius, that . . . just as the Father, the Lord of the universe, creates gods, in this very way man too, this mortal, earthly, living creature, the one who is not like God, also himself creates gods . . . Are you astonished Asclepius? Are you yourself . . . like the many?"

(Am I my brother's keeper?)

"Do not put maliciousness in your judgment," says the Stoic teacher and Nile River Gospel scribe Silvanus. "For every malicious man harms his heart." Sextus (in codex 12) agrees with the Stoic philosopher and characterizes the love of one's brothers as the beginning of godliness: "For it is God's business to save whom he wants; on the other hand, it is the business of the pious man to beseech God to save everyone. It is better for [a] man to be without anything than to have many things while not giving to the needy."

It is clear that Josephus, a contemporary of the Plinys, Titus, and Vesuvius, knew of the Gnostics, though he evidently did not recognize them as a sect entirely separate from the Jews, for he went so far as to consider part of their biblical history his own. In chapters 2 and 3 of *Jewish Antiquities,* Josephus described the generations of Seth from the time of Cain and Abel. For a century or two, according to legend, they proved to be pious and of good dispositions. "They were also the inventors of that peculiar sort of wisdom which is concerned with the heavenly bodies and their order."

In agreement with the Gospel of the Egyptians, in which Seth is said to have hidden books of knowledge inside the mountains, Josephus recorded that the Sethians, concerned that Adam's predictions about a coming world destruction might come true, inscribed their accumulated wisdom and hid it in pillars of stone and brick, "that the pillars might remain, and exhibit those discoveries to mankind." Eventually, the posterity of Seth lost their virtue and began to inflict malicious judgment against their brothers, and they came to despise all that was good, "on account of the confidence they had in their own strength; for the tradition is, that these men did what resembled the acts of those whom the Greeks call giants." As a punishment for their turn to the dark side, God "turned the dry land into sea," sparing, according to Josephus's version of the Old Testament, only one Sethian descendant, a man named Noah. The Babylonian *Epic of Gilgamesh* (published on clay tablets from 2800 through 2400 B.C.) describes the Sethian deluge thus: "And the seven judges of hell . . . raised their torches, lighting the land with their livid flame. A stupor of despair went up to heaven when the god of the storm turned daylight into darkness, when he smashed the land like a cup."

"And again he shall provide," according to the Nile River Apocalypse of James, "[an] end for what has begun, and a beginning for what is about to be ended." According to James the Just, for every beginning there must come an end; and from every end there shall arise a new beginning.

As if designed to confound the receivers of so many "glad tidings," something the Nile River Gospels and the Dead Sea Scrolls (but not the New Testament) have in common is that they speak of *two* apocalyptic teachers of righteousness, two messianic Jewish figures martyred in Jerusalem. Both, at times, appear so interchangeable as to be a single person, but ultimately they are referred to as brothers. One is identified as "Jesus," and "Lord," and "Rabbi." The other is called, by Jesus, "the brother of Jesus," and "James the Just," and "the Righteous One."

The first decades of the Jewish reformist movement that became Christianity saw the crucifixion of Jesus, during Tiberius's reign (about A.D. 30), the execution of James by Temple high priests (called Sadducees), about A.D. 66, the invasion of Jerusalem two years later under Vespasian, the burning of the Temple Mount by Titus in A.D. 70, and the A.D. 79 disappearance of whole cities under a smoking mountain. Collectively, these were first-century terrors crying out for explanation.

"Thy faith is upon the earth the whole day," says Shem, in the Seventh Nile River codex—which, though aimed at prophecy, appears to have been written after the sudden passings of the "Lord," the "Righteous One," Jerusalem, and the cities of Vesuvius: "Nature takes herself to the Righteous One, for Nature is burdened, and she is troubled . . . Evil times will come, and a demon will come up from the power who has a likeness of fire. He will divide the heaven (the sky will split and) he will rest in the depth . . . and the world will quake." The Silvanus codex adds: "To be sure, it is He (God) who touches the earth, causing it to tremble and also causing the mountains to smoke."

Writing from a post-Vesuvius perspective, the first-century faithful, as they evolved toward Christianity, came forth already intensely messianic and, to one degree or another, increasingly focused on the end of time. The disasters of that century, the near-incomparable disasters, likely strengthened the priests' and scribes' taste for apocalypse. The impacts of calamities both natural and man-made have a way of resonating upward through the ages. In the Minoan world, more than 1,100 years after Babylon's Sethian-Gilgamesh deluge, the years of earthquake, tsunami, and eruption that preceded the Theran explosion had graduated the once-peaceful civilization from bullfighting to human sacrifice. "There but for the grace of God, go I," or so the Christians say.

When we enter Crete's Akames Temple excavation, and look upon the skeleton of a boy tied in the manner of a sacred bull, his cervical vertebrae showing the marks of a slit throat, let us not pretend for a moment that we, as a civilization or as a species, are necessarily any better (or worse) than the last Minoans. It is a lamentable fact of history (but a fact nonetheless) that ancient and depressing visions of destruction, transmitted as scripture and prophecy, can easily be misused by modern-day deceivers who cloak themselves in the guise of religion, and who turn their backs on the fundamental messages of strength and restraint, charity, and reverence for the peacemakers, as preached by prophets named Solomon, James, and Muhammad.

Ignoring every ancient plea for mutual human tenderness, driven by the Furies of Jealousy, Vengeance, and unceasing Anger, the deceivers (what James might have called "a falsehood of false prophets") use religion, not as a tool for enlightenment but, rather, as a weapon of unspeakable hatred. The Crusades were but one example of this, culminating in the third Great Fire of Jerusalem. The fires of September were another.

Ben Peiser, a social anthropologist at England's John Moores University, warns that such deceivers, by obsessing their followers with visions of apocalypse, martyrdom, and the promise of a new world for the "chosen," provided the legs on which twenty-first-century terrorism rose: "Once you believe that the end is imminent and that your direction will hasten the coming of end-times, every atrocity is sanctioned."

These strange swerves of history, the legs on which "end of time" belief rose, do not appear to gain strength until the time of Jesus, James, and Vesuvius.

Up to the first century A.D., the widespread Jewish belief in the coming of a Messiah and a new kingdom was sometimes apocalyptic, but not obviously or intensely so. This changed during the decades of war, famine, plague, the burning of Jerusalem, shape-shifting of mountains, the burial of cities, and the splitting of the sky.

The Pauline and Gnostic scriptures, written in the aftermath, describe Jesus as a Jewish apocalyptic prophet who foretold the end of history. One day God would intervene in human affairs by overthrowing the forces of evil in a cosmic act of judgment. He would destroy cities and rivers and huge masses of humanity, abolishing political and religious institutions and replacing them with a new kingdom—either on Earth or in heaven.

Between A.D. 30 and 79, prophets were murdered, a holy city burned, a mountain exploded; and history swerved, sending forth a cascade of consequences, like ripples through time.

Seven decades after the A.D. 535 catastrophe and the fall of Roman Byzantium, the Prophet, Muhammad, began his ministry as a member of the still young and turbulent Christian faith, as a devout visionary who bowed in prayer toward Jerusalem. According to the Koran, the Christians rejected him and chased him into the desert, and he brought with him to Arabia, in A.D. 610, the equal and opposite traditions of paradise and apocalypse. In this context, the lost city of Iram, "The City of Towers," became the Koran's Sodom and Gomorrah: a preview of the world to come if humanity did not follow the Prophet's example of self-evolution, from anger toward mercy. For Iram, the mountains shook and the sky was split, and the towers were swallowed by the earth, as if summoned to hell. The Prophet had warned that the city would reemerge before a time of great tribulation, on a day when men climbed a rope into the far sky and looked back upon the disk of the earth. In 1983, special cameras carried aboard the space shuttle *Challenger* revealed a network of ancient roads under the deserts of Oman, leading to the lost oasis of Iram. The city and its towers had in fact collapsed into the world's largest known "sinkhole," had in fact become what Christian monks of the ninth century began referring to as "the Atlantis of the sands." As the Koran told it, the tower builders of Iram were punished for their impious living and their sin of overweening pride. It was an old story, often applied to dead cities, and long antedating the Koran, the Old Testament, and Plato's *Critias*.

One way of reading (and summarizing) all apocalyptic texts is: "And God said, 'Remember that part about *Love thy neighbor as thyself*? Well, I *meant* it! Don't make me have to come down there.' "

But of course, the legacy of ancient scribes leaves great latitude for interpretation, and even for intentional distortion.

A man driven by fury and hatred will interpret religion in his own way. He may attempt to twist faith into apocalyptic fear, binding his followers into an army by hiding fear in the smoke of hatred.

A more benign religious leader will suggest that sayings attributed to the prophets paint a picture of horrors that might be avoided by good and humane behavior. In this view of legend, Sodom and Iram were filled with people who had been forewarned, by past generations of scribes, simply to live righteously under the Golden Rule. With those legendary warnings, free will entered the universe. The future of the Sodomites (if such people actually existed) never was cast in stone.

Similarly, the Apocryphon of James can be read as a cautionary message from the past—worth reading and considering even if one happens to regard it in the same manner as Greek mythology and philosophy. After pointing out that every end has a beginning, every beginning an end, every end a new beginning (as if to echo the oscillating universe of Big Bang cosmology, or the extinction of dinosaurs and their replacement by birds and mammals, or the rise and fall of civilizations), James says: "We heard with our ears and [we] saw with our eyes [the revelation] of wars, and a trumpet blare, and a great turmoil [in Jerusalem]."

Josephus, who lived in the time of James and the burning of Jerusalem, attributed the holy city's destruction (in book 6 of *The Jewish War*) to warnings that went ignored, and to (as cited in Origen, *Against Celsus,* 1:47; and in *Eusebius,* 2:23) the murder of James: "These things happened to [Jerusalem] as a retribution for James the Just, who was the brother of Jesus who was called Christ . . . Impostors and false prophets deluded the pitiable people, who, as if moonstruck, blind, and senseless, paid no attention to God's clear portents and warnings of the approaching desolation. A star stood over the city like a sword, and a comet that lasted for a year. Then, prior to the war, when the people had gathered for the Feast of Unleavened Bread, on the eighth of Xanthicus at 3 A.M., a light shined on the temple and the altar so brightly that it seemed to be mid-day, and this lasted for a half hour. To the inexperienced this seemed a good omen, but the sacred scribes gave the true interpretation. During the same feast a cow brought for sacrifice by the high priest gave birth to a lamb in the middle of the temple."

As a guide to where James the Just stood among the first-century prophets and apostles, Eusebius, the Bishop of Caesarea (in book 2 of his church history), spoke clearly: "James was called the brother of the Lord since he was called Joseph's son, and Joseph Christ's father . . . This same James, whom the early Christians surnamed 'the Just' for his outstanding virtue, was the first to be elected to the bishop's throne of the church in Jerusalem." Eusebius then quoted a now lost work by Clement of Alexandria, in which James is said to have received "gnosis," or higher knowledge. "To James the Just and John and Peter," wrote Clement, "the Lord transmitted the *gnosis* after the resurrection. They transmitted it to the other apostles. And the other apostles transmitted it to the Seventy, one of whom was Barnabas. Now there were two Jameses: one, James the Just, who was thrown down from the parapet [of the temple] and beaten to death with a fuller's club; the other, the James who was beheaded [in Acts 12:2]."

Of himself, according to Gnostic scripture, James was not quite so clear as his biographers: "It is the Lord who spoke with me: 'See now the completion of my redemption. I have given you a sign of these things, James, my brother. For not without reason have I called you my brother, although you are not my brother materially . . . But my father has become a father to you . . . Therefore, your name is James the Just . . . [And] a multitude will arm themselves against you, that [they] may seize you . . .' And James said, 'Rabbi, you have said they will seize me. But I, what can I do [afterward]?' He said to me, 'Fear not, James. You too will they [try to] seize. But leave Jerusalem. For it is she who always gives the cup of bitterness to the sons of light. She is a dwelling place for a great number of [dark angels, called] archons.'"

Again, the lesson of human free will enters into prophecy. As the scribes record it, a warning comes to James from Jesus himself: "Leave Jerusalem." However, James ignores the warning, remains in Jerusalem, and is seized there, exactly as foretold, despite the fact that the prophecy of his martyrdom appears to have come with a specific instruction for avoiding it, or at least forestalling it.

The Apocryphon of James attests that Jesus appeared to the disciples nearly a year and a half after the resurrection, whereupon he told them that the prophecies he had given were meant, not for the disciples of Jesus, but for the children who would be born much later—"after bidding [us] love them, as we would be saved for their sakes." The Gospel of Mary communicates much the same message: The prophecies are meant to be fulfilled in the very distant future. While the disciples believe this "revelation," they are angered that it is not meant for them, or for their children, or even for their children's children's children. James therefore dispatches the apostles to other lands, angering them still further with an insistence on distant future time frames and explaining, perhaps, why Gnostic writings professed to be letters from James and Mary were deleted from canonical Scripture.

THE GENEALOGY of Christianity's founding prophet and the nature of his relationship with James the Just and Mary Magdalene, manages to outdo even the most fanciful family tree. The Gospels approved under Constantine portray Mary as an acquaintance of Jesus (a former prostitute who found redemption), while Gnostic scripture names her as the most virtuous and favored of the disciples, and suggests that she might have been a sister of Jesus, or even his wife. Matthew (in 13:55–56) names James and Jesus as sons of the carpenter Joseph and adds brothers Simon, Joseph, Judas, and sisters Salome and Mary. In his letter to the Galatians (1:18–19, written during Claudius's reign, about A.D. 50), Paul wrote, "Then after three years did I go up to Jerusalem to visit Cephas and stayed with him fifteen days; but I did not see any other apostle except James the Lord's brother."

The Gnostic scriptures identify James as the Lord's brother in more a spiritual sense than an actual genetic brother (as in codex 5:4): "And as I [James] raised my face to stare at him, [my] mother said to me, 'Do not be frightened, my son, because he said My brother to you. For you [plural] were nourished with this same milk. Because of this he calls me his mother. For he is not a stranger to us. He is your [illegible] . . .' Jesus said (to James), 'Hear and understand—for a multitude, when they hear, will be slow-witted. But you, understand as I shall be able to tell you. Your father is not my father. But my father has become a father to [you] . . . Your father, whom you consider to be rich, shall grant that you inherit all these things that you see.' "

Evidently, the Gnostic Christians were referring to an adoptive,

יעקוב בר יוסף אחוי דישוע

diYeshua akhui Yosef bar Ya'akov
James (Ya'akov/Jacob),
son of Joseph (Yosef),
brother of Jesus (Yeshua).

From the moment its existence was made public, late in 2002, the "ossuary of James" was the center of controversy. Initial tests by Israel's Geological Survey (under the direction of Drs. Rosenfeld and Ilani) revealed that the patina (a thin, calcium carbonate film produced by mineral accumulation over long periods of time) was indeed ancient and overlay some of the scratched-in letters. Inexplicably, discussions of the James inscription quickly degenerated into accusations and counteraccusations, name-calling and food throwing. Not surprisingly, the ossuary, made of a brittle limestone known as "chalk," was shattered into pieces. During shipping to the Royal Ontario Museum, it was tightly shrink-wrapped in expandable plastic bubbles, placed in an ordinary cardboard box, and loaded with tons of mail and freight onto a trans-Atlantic cargo plane. The plastic bubbles alone (manufactured at 14 psi and sure to expand at 8 psi when a pressurized aircraft ascends to 30,000 feet) guaranteed that the priceless artifact would be destroyed before it reached North America. Subsequent reassembly and restoration of the surviving inscription fragments removed much of the patina, and all but invalidated the ossuary's previous authentication. Even in the original Geological Survey report, pre-shatter cleaning by curators had proved to be a paradoxical restorer and destroyer. "The same [CaCO$_3$] patina is found within some of the letters," Rosenfeld and Ilani reported, then complained, "although the inscription was cleaned and the patina is therefore absent from several letters."

stepbrother relationship between James and Jesus—which, in first-century Rome (as in twenty-first-century Italian families) was not regarded as being in any way different from an actual blood bond. Even in the Roman monarchy, the historian Gaius Suetonius noted examples of adopted sons inheriting the throne (as in the case of Nero, who was favored, in Emperor Claudius's last will and testament, over his own genetic heir, Britanicus).

In October 2002, a limestone ossuary, or "bone box," was brought forth in Jerusalem. Dating from approximately the seventh decade of the first century A.D., it appeared to shed new light on the existence of a brotherly relationship between James and the historical Jesus—but no archaeologist would endorse such a claim without first trying to explain it away, even if the inscription on the tomb did read, in unmistakable Aramaic letters: "JAMES, SON OF JOSEPH, BROTHER OF JESUS."

Again: Religion is based on faith, whereas archaeology, like the other sciences, is based on doubt. The very process of scientific investigation dictates that we approach virtually everything with a raft of questions. By explaining away every likely alternative explanation for a remarkable inscription (as, for example, by asking whether or not it is a forgery), what remains standing, no matter how remarkable or improbable, is (theoretically) walking us closer to the truth. Scientific skepticism does not arise from sourness or arrogance; it's simply a means to avoid tricking oneself.

The box in question is 20 inches (51 centimeters, or 0.5 meter) long. Approximately three hundred such boxes have been discovered in the holy city, most of them with inscribed names. Unfortunately, most of Jerusalem's portable limestone tombs have come to the attention of archaeologists through Israel's technically legal but at the same time technically illegal antiquities market—with illegality often entering the picture when the exact site of discovery is known, especially if there is any chance that said site might be considered "hallowed ground," as in the case of a grave. A result of the technicalities is that every ossuary coming to market in Israel, in order to remain "legal," must do so with all knowledge of where it was found (beyond "within Jerusalem or its environs"), and with all bones and associated tomb contents "lost to the ages." Much as the Gospel of Matthew ends with the tomb of Jesus

Queen Hatshepsut, the *I, Claudius* of Egypt's Eighteenth Dynasty, survived a horrible spasm of imperial assassinations, evidently because, as a woman, the throne's contenders had overlooked her. As it turned out, she led Egypt into a golden age, though contemporary law required that she be deified as both man and woman and wear a false beard of gold. The Hebrew Hyskos merchants of Memphis utterly rejected the idea of a woman pharaoh, and they were among the first to be exiled into the eastern desert around 1628 B.C. by Hatshepsut's stepson, Tuthmosis III, when a period of Exodus-like plague and famine followed the volcanic eruption of Thera (modern-day Santorini) and triggered history's first known rationing. This episode of mutual rejection may explain why the Old Testament leaves nameless the pharaoh of the Exodus. During the decades following Thera and the woman pharaoh, Egyptians became uniquely receptive to the idea of empowering women, and the temples of the goddess Isis grew in both stature and grace. Echoing the Hatshepsut period, Egypt's Gnostic gospel of Thomas quotes Jesus preaching that a true living spirit resides in one whose divinity is "both woman and male."

being found empty, the tomb inscribed with the words "JAMES, SON OF JOSEPH, BROTHER OF JESUS" is empty, but only because, at the urging of human law, the bones of "James" were probably tossed on a suburban roadside or into a garbage pit.

People of faith believe the tomb of "James" might have been empty for a very different reason, dating back some two thousand years. Some of the faithful have suggested that the emergence of the artifact into the troubled beginnings of the twenty-first century was a warning sign, or an omen, and not merely a chance happening. At Saint Paul's Chapel in Manhattan, one of the volunteers who had ministered to Ground Zero recovery workers and family members emphasized for me that the future was never preordained, that she believed humanity was being called upon to confront "a third great shaking of the earth"—a shaking that "would probably occur, but did not absolutely have to occur." She said that God, or the universe, or the evolution of the human mind ("or whatever you want to call it") had given man free will and the ability to anticipate the future in reasonable detail and to detect (or to create) warning signs.

"A third great shaking of the earth," she had called it. About this same time (late in the year 2002), another woman, while recalling the prophecies of her tribal elders, used a hauntingly similar phrase: "Twisted Hair raised his voice so all could hear: 'You live in the shadow of the third great shaking of the world.'" Holly McClure, a Cherokee descendant, said that the legend of the here-again, gone-again prophet

Rome owed much of its architecture and religion to its Egyptian and Greek predecessors. Egypt's Isis and Osiris cults had temples in Pompeii and Herculaneum, and Isis was worshiped by Rome's Gnostic Christians. The Gnostics, like the Egyptians, were more accepting than Roman Gentiles of women in priestly and even political authority. They were also, like Egyptians, believers in resurrection, baptism, and a hierarchy of winged, humanlike angels.

Abydos, Egypt
August, 1988 CRP

Western civilization owes much of its architecture, law, and religion to its Roman pre-decessors. Saint Paul's Chapel in New York City is a replica of Pompeii's Temple of Venus, with a steeple on top and an Egyptian obelisk on one side. America's first president prayed often at Saint Paul's; and after his death, the world's largest Egyptian obelisk—the Washington Monument—was erected in his name.

dated back before the time of her grandfather, who had died at the age of 108. As Holly McClure records history, "Strange things were foretold that caused wonder even to the holy people. It was said, 'Look to the Eagle, for you will see her fly her highest in the night, and she will not stop until she sits on the moon. When this sign is seen—when the Eagle has landed—it will mark the [time] . . . in which we must learn to live [correctly] . . . as one human family, or the [third] shaking of the world will begin.

"Strange things." And stranger, still, to be reading about the "shaking of the world" in a chapel on the crater rim of what two man-made volcanic collapse columns had wrought; to be reading, in George Washington's chapel, of great shakings foretold before Washington and Jefferson were born: "Visions showed other signs of the third shaking. A house of mica was seen, built in a great city in the east. It rose higher than the tallest tree and gleamed in the sun as if made of mica. Representatives of all the people of the four doors were to come together in that great house and talk of peace . . . in a prairie of houses [each] so tall that they must block out the sun . . . We would look into the sky and see stars in a different place—and a star displaced, as if it had strayed from its path to the other side of the world. This was the final omen [of] the beginning of sorrows . . . On the third shaking, only human beings can prevent the world from shaking apart. The keepers of wisdom watched as the warning of the first shaking was forgotten. The second shaking has come and gone and still, there is hatred among the family of human beings. They spoke of the warriors in the sky who dropped the gourd of ashes upon the land. The nation who dropped it must be warned, for in the third shaking, it will fall upon its makers . . . Visions showed the great city: The houses, so tall that when you stood among them you could not see the sky. At sunrise they—the tall, tall houses of people from all the lands—will still be standing. But by midday, there will be nothing but ashes, and smoke rising from barren ground. That will be the first thunder of the third great shaking of the world."[6]

***

[6] In the year 2002, the elders called Twisted Hair's House of Mica the "United Nations Building." The Eagle on the moon had long been interpreted as the *Apollo 11* lunar module, which had been christened *Eagle* by its crew. (Indeed, among the first words spoken from Tranquillity Base, at the moment of engine cutoff, on July 20, 1969, were: "The *Eagle* has landed.") The first shaking of the world became World War I. The second shaking, with its prophetic inclusion of sky warriors dropping the "gourd of ashes," became World War II, and the gourd, the atomic bomb. Ahead of the third shaking, fallen towers in a great city were interpreted as the World Trade Center attacks of 2001. According to the final omen of Twisted Hair, in the time of a house on the other side of the sky, and a displaced star, the House of Mica would threaten disintegration into a Tower of Babel; and as the House of Mica failed or succeeded, stood or fell, so too would stand the world.

Words such as this cannot help but chill the bones on autumn mornings in Saint Paul's. Had I not spent many of childhood's summers near a reservation, and heard some of these words before, I'd have tried to explain them away as some sort of hoax. So the words chilled me more than ever, as 2002 inched toward 2003. But I am not a Cherokee, or a Christian, or a Jew, or a Muslim. On the subjects of gospels, and prophecies, and the ossuary of James being found "when the world required a sign," I maintained a militant agnosticism.

(Agnostic. *Read:* lack of knowledge.)

"JAMES, SON OF JOSEPH, BROTHER OF JESUS" . . . The French epigrapher (or "reader of inscriptions") André Lemaire was the first to attempt to explain away the inscription on the Jerusalem ossuary. Much as the careful penmanship of Charles Dickens and Mark Twain was distinct from the script of Arthur C. Clarke and Stephen King a century later, Lemaire was able to discern, from the subtle curve of each line (compared against his knowledge of Hebrew and Aramaic inscriptions spanning many centuries), that the James inscription was perfectly consistent with writing styles of the Herodian-Claudian period.

The next trial was geochemical: to explain the box away by searching the limestone itself for signs of recent inscribing. All the primary clues lay in the patina, a thin chemical film deposited on the ossuary surface, over long periods of dissolving and redeposition of calcium and silicon, governed by moisture and the life spans of bacteria. If scanning electron microscopes (equipped with electron-dispersive spectrometers, which reveal specific elemental compositions on the surfaces scanned) exposed twenty-first-century dye pigments, or if the patina on the inscribed letters differed from the patina on the rest of the limestone, then a "painted" surface would have been revealed.

The patina, uniform except where cleaned for study, was consistent everywhere with development over many centuries in a cave environment. Amnon Rosenfeld and Shimon Ilani, of Israel's Geological Survey, discovered that silicon had actually evaporated from the sand upon which the ossuary lay for two millennia and had then been literally "breathed" onto the limestone, a molecule at a time, until the letters and the entire ossuary surface acquired a silica-enriched skin (about 5.0 percent relative to 1.5 percent in the original limestone). No modern elements (indicative of modern pigments, or "paints") were detected anywhere on the silicon skin.

Having passed the first two trials, a third was needed: the test of identity, and of numbers. In his December 2002 report to the *Biblical Archaeology Review*, the epigrapher André Lemaire noted that the James inscription, while passing the tests of authenticity and while at first glance provocative, does not confirm an identification with "James the Just" or "James the Righteous," for he is called by neither of these names in the inscription itself: "JAMES, SON OF JOSEPH, BROTHER OF JESUS." The names James (Jacob) and Joseph were as common in the first century as in the twenty-first, and all three inscribed names are found scattered among other Jerusalem ossuaries. But those other inscribed ossuaries—all 233 of them—move James from the language of Aramaic letters to the language of mathematics.

For a relatively brief interval of time, from the reign of Augustus (31 B.C.–A.D. 14) to Vespasian and the burning of Jerusalem (A.D. 70), the practice of *ossilegium* became widespread among the Jewish people. The deceased would be dressed in white linen, covered with flowers, and sheltered from dogs, birds, and other scavenging creatures, in sealed burial caves. The caves were usually carved into the perimeters of stone quarries—which were invariably located beyond the city walls. In the centers of the quarries, Jerusalem's rubbish was burned. About a year after primary burial, the bones of the deceased were removed and placed in a chest or ossuary, typically hewn from Jerusalem limestone. Some, like those found in the family vault of Caiaphas in 1990, were finely polished and ornamented with geometric and floral designs.[7]

As if in keeping with the Stoic and (reportedly) early Christian traditions of austerity, simplicity, and humble origins (as in the birth of a savior in a manger), the James ossuary is roughly hewn, without ornamentation or polish, in stark contrast to the Caiaphas tombs.

Of the 233 inscribed ossuaries known to Lemaire in 2002, the name Joseph appeared nineteen times. Jesus appeared ten times, and James / Jacob

---

[7] In one of the Caiaphas ossuaries, a Roman coin minted in the time of Claudius was found inside the skull of an adult woman. Although this was a Jewish burial, the coin is indicative of the Roman polytheist custom of placing money in the mouth of the deceased to pay the ferryman Charon for safe passage across the river Styx.

five times. A colleague of Lemaire, Rachel Hachlili, enhanced and more or less confirmed the statistical trend with a census of names used during the first century in hundreds of other inscriptions: Joseph appeared 14 percent of the time, Jesus 9 percent, and James / Jacob 2 percent.

Using these percentages as a mathematical guide, approximately 0.14 percent (barely one-eighth of 1 percent) of the male population were named "James, son of Joseph." Working from the likelihood that each male had two brothers, Lemaire concluded that approximately 18 percent of the men named "James, son of Joseph" also had a brother named Jesus—which brought to 0.05 percent the members of the population likely to be called "James, son of Joseph, brother of Jesus."

The estimated population of Jerusalem, during the generations between Augustus and Vespasian, was about eighty thousand people. Of this number, forty thousand were presumably male. If 0.05 percent of this forty thousand were, by the guideposts of probability, likely to be called "James, son of Joseph, brother of Jesus," then this statistic accounts for about twenty people.

In his report, Lemaire pointed out that it is impossible to estimate how many of these twenty people were buried in ossuaries and how many of these ossuaries would have been inscribed.

Does the fact that the James inscription names not only the entombed, but also his father and his brother, narrow down or confuse the identification? Lemaire wondered. It was common, on other ossuaries, to see the name of a man's father inscribed. But among the others, among all 233 of them, there existed only one mention of a brother in this context. For the brother's name to be identified with the deceased, Lemaire decided, probably means that *this* brother Jesus was a well-known figure, and that the deceased had a special connection with him.

"When we take into account that this [James] had a brother who was by this time well known," said Lemaire, "and that [the biblical James], leader of the Jerusalem church, had a special relationship with [his brother Jesus], it seems very probable that this is the ossuary of the James in the New Testament. If so, this would also mean that we have here the first epigraphic mention—from about [A.D. 63–66]—of Jesus of Nazareth."

WRITING NEARLY FOUR DECADES after the death of James, the burning of Jerusalem, and the eruption of Vesuvius, the Roman historian Tacitus evidently found Jesus sufficiently well known to be worth mentioning in his *Annales* (15.44.3). Tacitus was a friend of Pliny the Younger, who by the early second century had become an elderly governor. The letters of Tacitus and Pliny preserve not only their discussions of the Vesuvian apocalypse, but also Pliny's concern that the Christians of A.D. 110 had grown alarmingly in number. The governor's concern was mingled with puzzlement over a revolutionary movement that forbade adultery, murder, theft, and dishonesty, a movement whose members in every way conformed to the law (save for the refusal of some sects to accept Roman gods), and whose founder, in response to his followers' questions about violence against the Romans, had replied with an extension of the Golden Rule: "Whatsoever you do to the least of my brothers, that you do unto me."

That the mysterious founder had preached nonviolence and that his disciples had not committed acts of lawlessness or sabotage against Romans were considered, by some of Pliny's political overseers, as "ominous developments" requiring further investigation, and perhaps punishment. Tacitus noted that punishment for nonevents seemed to be the lot of the early-second-century Christians, and he recorded that their leader, Jesus, had been executed by Pontius Pilate in the time of Tiberius (between A.D. 14 and 37). According to Hegesippus (a Christian writer who wandered between Jerusalem and the Sea of Galilee in the time of Tacitus and Pliny), after the crucifixion of Jesus, James became the leader of the Christians in Jerusalem. Preaching that Jesus was a messianic prophet who descended to Earth in human form, James won many converts, including, wrote Hegesippus, some "among the wealthy Romans" (which is, again, consistent with the obvious wealth of the two Vesuvian homes bearing signs of Christian habitation in A.D. 79: Justa's House in Herculaneum and the House of the Christian Inscription in Pompeii).

Clement of Alexandria (writing in approximately A.D. 190, in

Outlines, book 6) recorded that the apostles, "after the Savior's ascension, did not contend for the honor because they had previously been favored by the Savior, but chose James the Just as Bishop of Jerusalem."

Although the Gnostic Christians and the Pauline Christians had diverged by the time of Clement, and probably had been mutually antagonistic as early as the first correspondence between Tacitus and Governor Pliny (about A.D. 103), James the Just remained an important figure to both groups.

After the death of a messianic religious leader, the most likely outcome would have been for the man considered (either spiritually or by actual family bonds) to be the "brother of Jesus," to take on the mantle of Messiah in Jesus' place. But thirty years after the crucifixion of Jesus, the apostles of A.D. 60 did not act as the probabilities of human behavior would have directed. Acting contrary to human probability, they did not put "the brother of Jesus" in Jesus' place. They did not follow James as "Messiah." According to the Hegesippus account, till his dying day James insisted "that Jesus, the Rabbi, was indeed the Christ," and that he, James, was himself but a follower, a mere "bishop," and a witness, and (notably) a Jew.

What strange event could have brought this improbable, history-molding outcome?

(I don't know . . .)

If Constantine's historian, Bishop Eusebius, is to be believed, there was magic in the world, between the time of Claudius and Vesuvius. In book 2 of his church history, he describes a Roman of Claudius's time (A.D. 41–54) who "ravaged the [earliest] church, entering the houses of the faithful, dragging out men and women, and committing them to prison," until the day he was struck by a thunderbolt in an open field, surrounded by a multitude of witnesses who stood unharmed. Emerging from a "revelation," he converted to the new faith and became known to later generations as Saint Paul.

In this same time frame, Eusebius spoke of Saint Philip's meeting with a wizard turned Gnostic heretic named Simon Magus, the Samaritan: "So great was the divine grace at work with [Philip] that even Simon Magus [was] captivated by his words. Simon had gained such fame by the wizardry with which he controlled his victims that he was believed to be the Great Power of God. But even he was so over-whelmed by the wonders Philip performed by divine power that he insinuated himself [into the faith], hypocritically feigning a belief in Christ even to the point of baptism." According to Eusebius, such feigned belief, by witches and wizards, was perceived in A.D. 325 as a clear and continuing threat against the Christian faith. Expressing the policies of an increasingly warlike and intolerant Byzantine church, the bishop spoke of false Christians fastening themselves to the faithful like noxious insects, "destroying all whom they succeed in smearing with the dreadful, deadly poison hidden within them." With the faith beginning to spread, a figure identified by Eusebius as "the enemy of salvation" planned to capture the imperial city of Rome in advance by sending Simon Magus there ahead of Paul and Peter.

Bishop Eusebius reinforced his case by quoting a passage from the subsequently lost works of Justin Martyr, who was a contemporary of James, Vesuvius, Simon Magus: "After the Lord's ascension, the demons presented men who claimed to be gods, and they not only escaped being persecuted by you but even became objects of worship. Simon, a Samaritan from a village called Gittho, worked wonders through magic in Claudius' time, thanks to the demons who possessed him. He was deemed a god at Rome and honored as a god with a statue in the River Tiber between the two bridges . . . nearly all Samaritans and a few in other nations also acknowledge him as their chief deity and worship him."

Josephus, too, believed in magic. In book 6 of *The Jewish War,* he describes the Jews of A.D. 60 as still adhering to a belief in the sacrifice of sacred cows in the Jerusalem Temple. He also describes warnings from two men named Jesus (one is "son of Ananias," the other "Jesus the Christ")—foretellings of Jerusalem's impending fall and the utter destruction of the Temple. The priests were said to have heard a distur-bance in the Temple, and the abandonment by God himself with a thun-derous cry, "Let us leave this place!" During one of the last feasts the Temple would ever see, according to Josephus: "A cow brought for sacri-fice by the high priest gave birth to a lamb in the middle of the temple, and at midnight the eastern gate of the inner sanctuary opened itself—a gate of bronze fastened by iron bars and secured by long bolts so massive that twenty men were required to shut it each evening. Not long after the feast . . . a demonic apparition of incredible size was seen . . . before sunset . . . in the sky over the whole land, chariots . . . [perhaps meteors] speeding through the clouds."

Dio Cassius had claimed that giant demonic apparitions were seen moving busily to and fro within the smoke of the Vesuvius eruption; and according to Gaius Suetonius, when Julius Caesar faced the critical decision of whether to cross the river Rubicon, or to draw back, "an apparition of superhuman size and beauty was seen sitting on the river." Rising before Caesar's men, it blew a thunderous blast from a trumpet, and crossed the Rubicon. Suetonius records that Caesar responded (to his own tall tale, or to this mass hallucination): "Let us accept this as a sign from the gods, and follow where they beckon, in vengeance on our double-dealing enemies. The die is cast."

The belief in magic was strong in those days; just as the belief in science is strong today. The principle "I lack knowledge, and I will seek out what lies hidden" is a kind of enchantment in its own right: pure magic, though we call it science.

IN OUR OWN TIME, the mushroom cloud of Hiroshima remains, decades after the fact, an apocalyptic image that our civilization is not likely ever to forget. The two atomic bombs dropped at the end of World War II produced results so nightmarish that human beings, once they glimpsed the streets of ashes, and the cloud—once their minds began to surround the thermonuclear inverse to the Golden Rule, and what it meant—frightened themselves into the longest strategic peace the world had ever known.

And yet, Hiroshima and Nagasaki, together, were five hundred times weaker than the volcanic apocalypse that had descended upon the Romans in A.D. 79.

Vesuvius could not have failed to leave at least some small impression on a once-obscure Jewish reformist movement whose writings were evolving by about A.D. 120 from intensely messianic toward intensely apocalyptic. The Sibylline verses, collected and preserved by Emperor Augustus around 4 B.C.—"And on thee shall one day come, O' hardy Rome, a deserved blow from heaven"—suggest that the Romans among whom the first Christians moved and who would eventually assimilate them had an affinity for end-time scenarios, even before Vesuvius.

Again: Any attempt to read the gospels, whether the King James version or the lost episodes of Nag Hammadi, cannot succeed in a vacuum. There is neither a page nor a paragraph that does not require us to broaden our focus to the entire Roman landscape against which these stories, as they became sacred, were first written and edited.

Writing in about A.D. 250, Dionysius, bishop of Alexandria, believed that the Book of Revelation, with all of its descriptions of miracles and magic, and all of its omens of Vesuvius-scale destructions, was a fiction and not an actual foretelling given by his founding prophet. Dionysius noted that, according to the epistles then available to him, Paul had hinted at receiving news of many revelations, but did not record them all. Eusebius (in book 6 of his church history) quoted a now-lost manuscript in which Dionysius expressed his doubts about the authenticity of John's Revelation. "Some of our predecessors rejected the book altogether," wrote Dionysius. "They criticized it chapter by chapter as unintelligible, illogical, and its title false. They say it is neither John's nor a 'revelation' in any sense, since it is veiled by its thick curtain of incomprehensibility, and its author was neither a saint nor even a church member." Bishop Dionysius recorded that many believed the writings to have originated with the Cerinthian and Menander sects that succeeded the "wizard" Simon Magus in the time of Emperor Nerva (A.D. 96–98).

In book 3, Eusebius defined these sects as heretical and identified Menander (whose revelations survive, under his own name, in the Nile River Gospels) as a disciple of Simon Magus who was similarly driven by demons: "He appeared in Antioch and deluded many—[for he was] a second tool of the devil as evil as his predecessor. Having risen to the same heights of sorcery as his master, [he] reveled in still more miraculous pretensions." He taught, according to Bishop Eusebius, "[t]hat no one—not even the angels who made the world—could survive unless resurrected through his magic skills and baptism."

Approximately seventy-five years after Dionysius, in the time of Constantine and Eusebius, John's Revelation, in edited form, entered the Bible as officially approved canonical Scripture. Bishop Dionysius, though he had his doubts, had written earlier that he would not dare to reject the book, "since many brethren hold it in esteem, but since my intellect cannot judge it properly, I hold that its interpretation is a wondrous mystery." Putting his reliance on faith rather than on his own comprehension, he concluded, "I do not reject what I have failed to understand but am rather puzzled that I failed to understand."

As it turns out, the Revelation of John appears to be a fossil remnant of Gnostic "heresy" that survives as the final chapters of New Testament canon.

IN THE NILE RIVER Dialogue of the Savior, penned somewhere between the Vesuvius eruption and the end of the second century, there are hints of a future apocalypse, an Egyptian understanding of rapture (in which chosen people are "taken up to the light," as a terrible wind approaches), and the beginnings of Ptolemic astronomy—all weaving their way into church doctrine: "The Lord said, 'So I tell you [missing words]—Light is the darkness . . . In that place [there will] be weeping and gn[ashing] of teeth over the end of [all] these things . . .' Then he said to his disciples, 'Have I not told you that like a visible voice and a flash of lightning will the good be taken up to the light?' [. . . And] he said to them, 'That which supports [the earth] is that which supports the heaven, When the Word comes forth from the Greatness, it will come on what supports the heaven and the earth. For the earth does not move. Were it to move, it would fall. But it neither moves nor falls, in order that the First Word might not fail. For it was that which established the cosmos and inhabited it and inhaled fragrance from it.' "

A somewhat clearer understanding of nature (as regards the ecological principle of preserving resources, if not an understanding of Lucretian or Galilean astronomy) is preserved in the Nile River Gospel of Thomas, in which Jesus is quoted as observing, "The man is like a wise fisherman who cast his net into the sea and drew it up from the sea full of small fish. Among them the wise fisherman found a fine large fish. He threw all the small fish back into the sea and chose the large fish without difficulty. Whoever has ears to hear, let him hear."

"An environmental ethic based on enlightened self-interest," Stephen Jay Gould had called it. "Christians call this the principle of the golden rule; Plato, Hillel, and Confucius knew the same maxim by other names." A voice from the remote past seemed to understand that if one killed all the small fish in, say, the Sea of Galilee, that little corner of Earth would bleed, starve the humans out, bandage up, and go about her business whether the humans lived or died. As Gould interpreted the passage: If the fishermen treated the sea nicely, she would keep the towns going for a while. The advice seemed as relevant to twenty-first-century civilization as it must have been to the Romans.

Elsewhere in the Gospel of Thomas (in saying 95), the apostle reveals that by the time of Tiberius, Titus, and Vesuvius, the Roman banking system had evolved a system of loans with interest payments. The saying—"If you have money, do not lend it at interest, but give [it] to someone from whom you will not get it back"—also hints that some of what Jesus is quoted as saying (including the advice to "turn the other cheek" if slapped by an adversary, showing him where next to slap) might have been spoken with an undertone of wry humor and was not always to be taken literally. "For the earth does not move," Jesus said. "Were it to move, it would fall." Humor? (Why not?) In Dialogue of the Savior, Jesus topples Galileo even before the scientist is born. In Origin of the World, his Gnostic scribes evoke Einstein, Hubble, and the physics of an infinitely oscillating universe.

As if to recollect the idea of "laughing Buddha," the Nile River codex On the Origin of the World begins: "Seeing that everybody, gods of the world and mankind, says that nothing existed prior to chaos, I, in distinction to them, shall demonstrate that they are all mistaken, because they are not acquainted with the origin of chaos, nor with its root." From chaos we came, the unnamed author of codex 13 claims, and to chaos the universe shall return—repeatedly. The chaos from which all things were created was not the once-only beginning of everything but the outcome of something that had existed, and lived, before. "It is, moreover," says Origin's scribe, "clear that it (viz., the product) existed before chaos came into being and that the latter is posterior to the first product." The laughing Buddha, indeed—and a glimpse, perhaps, of the scientific tale of an oscillating Big Bang universe, created and destroyed, and created anew—infinitely.

Just ahead of the Origin's final Gnostic revelation, an element from the far east enters the history of the world: A new species of spirit-life arrives on Earth—"A soul-endowed living creature called PHOENIX. It [this suffering servant] kills itself and brings itself back to life as a witness to the judgment against them, for they did wrong to Adam in his generation." There are, accordingly, three phoenixes in the image of man: the spirit endowed of eternity, the soul-endowed, and the earthly. "The first [is] immortal; the second lives one thousand years; as for the third, it is written in the *Sacred Book* that it is consumed." The trinity of the phoenix undergoes three baptisms: "The first is spiritual. The second is by fire. The third is by water. It is written [that] the just man will blossom like a Phoenix. And the Phoenix first appears in a living state, and dies, and rises again, being a sign of what has become apparent at the consummation of the age. It was only in Egypt that these great signs appeared—nowhere else—as an indication that it [the Nile] is like God's Paradise."

Then, speaking in past tense of beings who discovered an incomparable truth and "put to shame all the wisdom of the gods," only to find all their wisdom and glory turned to emptiness and condemnation, the Origin shifts ominously to future tense: "Before the consummation of the age, the whole place will shake . . . Their kings will be intoxicated with the fiery sword, and they will wage war against one another, so that the earth is intoxicated with bloodshed. And the seas will be disturbed by those wars. Then the sun will become dark. And the moon will cause its light to cease." And then, after a thunderous force shakes the world from above, "She will put away the wise fire of intelligence and clothe herself with witless wrath . . . for they will come to be like volcanoes and consume one another until they perish."

(*"On the third shaking [of the world], only human beings can prevent the world from shaking apart," the prophet said. "The keepers of wisdom watched as the warning of the first shaking was forgotten. The second shaking has come and gone and still, there is hatred among the family of human beings."*)

In the Nile Asclepius "gospel," an initiate is told that there have been many destructions of the world, sometimes by submergence in great floods, other times by "a great fire, and crystal water, and furrows of fire." The references to crystal waters (beautiful, calm seas) and furrows of fire seem to echo the calm, wind-sheltered Bay of Naples at the feet of Vesuvius. Then, looking to the future, the initiate of Asclepius is told that Egypt and the world will be led into atheism, dishonor, the disregard of noble words, and the teaching "of things contrary to nature." In that distant future, the earth will not be stable, men will cease to sail the sea, and they will forget their knowledge of the stars in heaven (a probable reference to Egyptian astrology). Finally, in a vision that appears to forecast, with equal fidelity, Egyptian civilization after the burning of Alexandria and / or the biblical apocalypse, Egypt is destroyed: "And Egypt will be made a desert by the gods and the Egyptians. And as for you, River [Nile], there will be a day when you will flow with blood more than water. And dead bodies will be [stacked] higher than the dams. And he who is dead will not be mourned as much as he who is alive . . . And it is proper for you not to be ignorant that a time will come in [our land when] Egyptians will seem to have served the divinity in vain, and all their activity in their religion will be despised. For all divinity will leave Egypt and will flee upward to heaven. And Egypt will be widowed; it will be abandoned by the gods. For foreigners will come into Egypt, and they will rule it. Egypt! Moreover, Egyptians will be prohibited from worshipping God. Furthermore, they will come into the ultimate punishment, especially whoever among them is found worshipping [and] honoring God. And in that day the country that was more pious than all countries will become impious. No longer will it be full of temples, but it will be full of tombs. Neither will it be full of gods but it [will be full] of corpses. Egypt! Egypt will become like fables. And your religious objects will be [missing passage] and your words are stones. And the barbarian will be better than you—O Egyptian—in his religion, whether [he is] a Scythian, or the Hindus, or some other of this sort."

In the Gnostic Gospel of Mary Magdalene, the actual revelation of how the world will end is missing (burned in an oven by the family that found it), but it is probably similar to both canonical and noncanonical descriptions of the apocalypse, including those found in the Revelation of John, Origin, and Asclepius. Originally written in Greek, somewhere between the second-century reigns of Emperors Trajan (A.D. 98–117) and Severus (A.D. 193–211), the gospel recounts Mary's vision of Jesus, and a private dialogue with him, more than a year after the crucifixion.

For a time, Mary keeps the dialogue secret, but the apostles urge her to tell what was hidden from them: "Peter said to Mary, 'Sister, we know that the Savior loved you more than the rest of women. Tell us the words of the Savior which you remember—which you know [but which] we do not, nor have we heard them.' " [As a possible reflection of Jewish tradition, a man cleaves to a wife, more than to a sister, or to a mother, or to "the rest of women."]

Mary quotes Jesus: "Where the mind is, there is treasure," and when she elaborates on what her Savior meant, she confuses and actually enrages her listeners. She describes the seductive powers of the dark half, the power of desire, the power of "wrathful wisdom," and how an enlightened soul (after lifetimes of phoenixlike reincarnation on Earth) eventually overpowers the dark side with her "gnosis" (knowledge) and attains eternal, silent rest: "And my desire has been ended and my ignorance has died—I was released from a world . . . and from the fetter of oblivion which is transient. From this time on I will attain the rest of the time, of the season, of the eon, in silence."

Andrew turns to the other disciples and challenges Mary, for these teachings are strange: "Say what you [wish to] say about what she has said. I at least do not believe that the Savior said this. For certainly these teachings are strange ideas."

Mary, like James the Just, has further angered the disciples by telling them that the prophecies of apocalypse and a great world change (which, to many of the disciples, means the final passing away of Rome) are meant not for their children, or even for their grandchildren's children, but for people living in a very distant and unattainable future.

Peter, too, according to the Gospel of Mary Magdalene, challenges Mary's vision: "Did he [Jesus] really speak with a woman without our knowledge [and] not openly?" Peter asks the disciples. "Are we to turn about and all listen to her? Did he prefer her to us?"

"Then Mary wept," the gospel reads, and she said to Peter, "My brother Peter, what do you think? Do you think that I thought this up myself in my heart, or that I am lying about the Savior?" Whereupon Levi stands in Mary's defense and admonishes her inquisitor: "Peter, you have always been hot-tempered. Now I see you contending against the woman like the adversaries. But if the Savior made her worthy, who are you indeed to reject her? Surely, the Savior knows her very well. That is why he loved her more than us. Rather let us be ashamed . . . and acquire him for ourselves . . . And preach the gospel." And they began to go forth, according to the scribes, "[to] proclaim and to preach."

According to biblical scholar and Nag Hammadi translator Karen King, the confrontation between Mary and Peter (which is echoed in the Gnostic gospels of Thomas and the Egyptians) reflects some of the tensions prevalent in second-century Christianity: "Peter and Andrew represent orthodox positions that deny the validity of esoteric revelation and reject the authority of women to teach. The Gospel of Mary attacks both of these positions head-on through the portrayal of Mary Magdalene. She is the Savior's beloved, possessed of knowledge and teaching superior to that of the public apostolic tradition. Her superiority is based on vision and private revelation and is demonstrated in her capacity to strengthen the wavering disciples and turn them toward good."

("What is Truth?")

The ancient texts can be interpreted in many, many ways. After nearly two thousand years, they invite conclusions and other types of meddling from a civilization that is a stranger to the complex and mostly hidden social systems from which the preachings and writings emerged. What does it mean, then, when Mary, in her dialogue with Jesus, learns that the heavens will one day ask the souls of man, "Whence do you come, slayer of men, or where are you going, conqueror of space?"

More often than not, interpretation exists in the eye of the beholder only, and not in reality. Interpretation is a way of meddling, and meddling is a way of causing trouble.

"Whence do you come, slayer of men?" the powers of heaven will ask, and will demand an answer, according to the revelation of Mary. Read any document, late at night, just before sleep, and a passage is likely to remain with you in your dreams, and to jump out at you when you awake. Scratch any cat, and will you not chase out a flea?

Two thousand years pass, and we read, from the Gospel of Mary Magdalene, "Where are you going, conqueror of space?"

ON THE MORNING of September 11, 2001, I was 800 miles (1,312 kilometers) east of New York, in the communications "shack" of the

Russian research vessel *Keldysh,* when word came down from the bridge that America was under attack. A decade earlier, during a human misadventure called the cold war, some twenty-five thousand nuclear-tipped rockets were aimed from the United States into Russia; and a similar number were aimed by Russia against the United States. Jointly, our people were capable of unleashing a Thera-class eruption, spread over the entire planet, against all of humanity.

Where were we going, then, we conquerors of space? And the visionaries of centuries and millennia past—what did they really believe? And how can we pretend to really know? The message from Jesus to his brother James—*leave Jerusalem and escape your fate*—would seem to suggest a belief that, even when "words of knowledge" came from the founding prophet himself, the lessons of things to come were never meant to exclude human free will. In the time of the Gnostic and Pauline scribes, in the immediate aftermath of the Jewish War, the burning of Jerusalem, and the Vesuvian upheaval, it must have been easy to foresee apocalypse. But the question— *are these things that must happen, or things that may happen?*—the disciples and the scribes seem to have answered this question with the same silence as: "What is Truth? . . . Am I my brother's keeper?" And strange to think that, in time, we really did become a civilization capable of unleashing miniature suns and miniature volcanoes in the hearts of our cities, thus rendering the Gnostic prophecy of rivers flowing more with blood than with water something that, in the twenty-first century, may actually be brought about, by our own hand.

Coincidence. All is coincidence. Or so the scientists say.

During the last weeks of the old world, we former adversaries, Russians and Americans, went together into the coldest, darkest recesses of the North Atlantic. I brought with me an old letter dating back to the Apollo-Soyuz program, during which academician Mstislav Vsevolodovich Keldysh (the Russian scientist after whom our ship was named) had expressed hope that by learning to survive together in the depths of the ocean and the depths of space, we might one day discover our common humanity. At the beginning of the joint scientific and filming expedition, in August of 2001, the last threads of the cold war lingered still, at least from where I stood. We were working together, yet there was still a paper-thin barrier between us—not easy to see, but definitely felt. At the hour of the attack, the Russians took away our communications with the crews aboard the *Mir-1* and *Mir-2* submersibles. I was reminded, in that hour, of a film called *2010*, in which a Russian-American expedition to Europa received word of a war breaking out at home, and the joint expedition split in two, with Russians and Americans moving to opposite sides of the ship.

But in recalling that particular film, I had underestimated the Russians.

During the hour (maybe two hours) in which we Americans had no contact with the *Mir*s, I received an E-mail message from the space station, which was also crewed by Russians and Americans. It was brief, only about four sentences: The three men had drifted to a viewport as "Alphatown" passed over New York. From an altitude of more than 200 miles (328 kilometers), they reported that they could see a thin black cloud stretching toward us, stretching more than 150 kilometers (nearly 100 miles) out to sea. The message ended with the observation that tears just did not flow the same way in microgravity.

Later, Anatoly Sagalevich came down from the bridge, clutching a piece of paper. He apologized for taking our "coms away" and explained, with tears reaching down to his chin, that protocol had required such measures until they heard the official position from Moscow. The message, hastily translated into English, said, "Your misery is our misery." (Actually, the word *misery* had been translated as "mischief." No matter—it would turn out to mean the same.)

A decade or two earlier, there was no imagining that one dark day, with America under attack, I would be standing in one of the most isolated places on Earth when a Russian commander would throw his arms around me and proclaim, "We are all Americans, now."

The Russians raised an American flag on the stern of their ship, and over the speaker system they played Ray Charles singing "America the Beautiful" (unable, apparently, to find, anywhere aboard, a recording of "The Star-Spangled Banner"). And the last threads of the cold war truly died there on the decks of the *Keldysh*. And that song has been my personal national anthem ever since.

On September 12, we were ordered to "pull the plug" on the expedition and return home. Somewhere, more than a thousand miles west, some bureaucrats had decided that bioarchaeology and science documentaries were irrelevant, that even discovering new medicines and new kingdoms of life on the bottom of the ocean did not matter anymore, and might not matter again for a very long time. But we took a vote, we of the American crew, we of *Keldysh,* and decided that we could not leave the job unfinished. In addition, something strange—something good, even—was happening between us and the Russians. The American restaurateur and historian, "Big Lew" Abernathy, had been trying to tell me all along that the Russian people were the best friends we "Yanks" never knew we had. The bonding that was taking place on the decks, the disintegration of old walls, was instant and heartfelt. (A month later, we did not want to leave the Russians, and they did not want us to leave them. The ship's photographer recalled that I had boarded the *Keldysh* as an only child, with no brothers or sisters, and he assured me that I had at least forty of them now.)

So, on September 12, we took a vote, we "Yanks," we of *Keldysh*—a vote for "mutiny" against our American sponsors who were calling us home. We would not leave our job unfinished, no matter how insignificant that job might have seemed against the cyclopean scale of everything else. We had decided that *Keldysh* was one changed and changing little piece of planet Earth over which evil was not going to be allowed to grab a foothold. *No,* we voted. Not after we former enemies, round the Arctic rim, had begun to discover in the weight of deepest darkness, our common humanity, and hope.

And a month earlier, in August of 2001, something else happened aboard *Keldysh*—which, by aid of such meddlings as the calculation of odds against coincidence, can be bound in the meddlings of hindsight and (rightly or wrongly) interpreted as having heralded the fires of September.

I remember Lew marveling over the "rust-icicles" hanging down the sides of the *Titanic.* "There must be millions of them," he said. Microbiologist Lori Johnston and I had corrected him: "Not them, Lew. *It.* They're all one organism." A Consortial life-form, totally new to science, was turning *Titanic* into one of the largest "creatures" on Earth. By September 5 we had raised—as "in situ" rusticle sources—a section of railing from Boat 8's launch point, and a davit bit (also from Boat 8's location, where *Titanic*'s band had calmed the crowds). These were the

The return. Dive 8, launched 9:00 A.M., *Titanic* time; 7:30 A.M., New York time, September 11, 2001. Two metal samples (one draped in rope from the lifeboats) are sent back to *Titanic* via the *Mir-1* submersible. When both samples, upon recovery, broke into the shapes of crosses, a Russian crew member had lamented, "A third cross is coming. And it will be big. Terrible big." As the "*Titanic* crosses" were being returned home, the "Ground Zero cross" was forming, atop the crater's central peak.

only samples raised from *Titanic* that year; and both of them broke into the shapes of crosses.

"When Lew held [the broken railing] up," I had e-mailed my friend Rip Mackenzie, "it played havoc with the crew's imaginations, and with some of their beliefs." I explained that cross-hatching was a very common architectural form, and that I'd have been more impressed had the metal broken into the far less probable shape of a fish, or a Star of David. Nevertheless, the Number 8 davit bit had come up with a piece of rope attached to it, and thus had brought an unusual comment from one of the Russians: "Two were hung on their crosses with rope . . . on that hill, that day. Three were crucified on that hill. A third cross is coming. And it will be big. Terrible big."

I asked Rip: "Isn't this a strange thing to be hearing—coming, as it did, from a woman who grew up in a country officially without religion?"

Late on the night of September 10, 2001, I ascended from *Titanic*'s stern in *Mir-2*. I had been without sleep for more than two days; but I was not tired, and there was something I had to do. Had to.

About 2:00 A.M., as the line of shadow that bisected Turkey and Egypt retreated toward us from the east, one of the Russian biologists found me in the lab, working on the two "crosses." They had, days earlier, been stripped of their rusticle "roots," and I was carefully cleaning and oiling the "*Titanic* crosses" for their return to the deck—making them appear, wherever the metal allowed this, shiny and new. The scientist thought I should be in my cabin resting, and he explained that there was no "use or purpose" in what I was doing.

"Why this?" he asked.

I did not know why. I said that I just wanted to return something to the *Titanic* in better condition than we had found it. He gave a nod, and replied that he understood.

Hours later, as the attacks were under way, the Number 8 rail and davit bit were being returned whence they came. Afterward, Rip e-mailed, to *Keldysh*, photographs of a Franciscan chaplain standing with a group of firemen and recovery workers beneath a metal cross that had been found standing atop the "Ground Zero hill" on the morning of September 12.

"Here's your third cross," Rip said.

At the expedition's start, Rip had asked a question that, e-mailed around the world, went through the personal computers of a hundred physicists and generated more than a thousand pages: "How much does darkness weigh?" Some respondents spoke of the 6,000 pounds (3 metric tons) per square inch that compressed styrofoam coffee cups (tied outside the submarine) down to the size of shot glasses, in the sunless abyss into which *Titanic* had fallen. Others spoke about the mass of a single photon of light against the vastness of time and space. And others spoke of the infinitesimal mass of the ghostly neutrino, of "dark matter" (incapable of interacting with the force of electromagnetism, and therefore unable to either reflect or absorb light), and of "dark energy"—words which meant that 95 percent of the universe was made of "I don't know what," and the rest (only 5 percent) consisted of the atoms and energy of stars and planets.

But aboard *Keldysh,* that year, I found a simpler and more direct answer. Aboard the good ship *Keldysh,* I began to see:

"How much does darkness weigh?"

Not as much as light.

VESUVIUS IN NEW YORK

It's easy to forget, amid the distractions of artifacts and great structures, that archaeology is about people.

JAMES CAMERON

Ground Zero was west of Van Dam Street . . . From the helicopter, Tam had seen evidence of the mysterious "shock bubbles" in which certain objects inexplicably survived a tornado, or a plane flying into a mountain, or a nuclear explosion, while all around them was total disintegration . . . The [sides of] the old Twin Towers of the World Trade Center . . . looked much like mowed grass spray-painted black . . . Richard's world, too, was tilting . . . irrationally, like a dish, and he felt as if he were standing on its edge. Every new frame of video showed streets of broken glass, overturned trucks, and debris that included smashed t.v. screens . . . office buildings [were] still smoldering, their former executives with a look of madness in their eyes . . . He had spent a fair portion of his career digging in ruins, often finding civilizations stacked on top of each other like the layers of a giant cake; the oldest, most romantic, and mysterious of them always lying at the bottom of the mound, naturally. But now, for the first time, he saw the youngest, uppermost layer of ruins still gleaming in the daylight—the beginning, perhaps, of the next Atlantis legend . . . This time it was his own home, and the homes of friends . . . that were becoming the substance of archaeology. It was a painful and belittling picture to behold. There was no romance in it. No dignity either.

EXCERPTS FROM A SHORT STORY BY RICHARD SINCLAIR, 1998

Foreshadowing forensic physics at "ground zero," the volcanic collapse columns and downblasts of A.D. 79 gave dust and air a power rarely seen outside of tornadoes and atomic bomb blasts. When archaeologists began clearing layers of glass-hard ash from the neighborhood of Herculaneum's "Suburban Baths," they discovered that several nearby cliff-top buildings had been uprooted and dissected in midflight, as if struck by walls of water instead of air. The Suburban Bath hot room was sheltered from the full force of the blast—which shot over the top of the building toward the sea, on which a large picture window gave panoramic views. Within seconds, the underside of the surge cloud reversed course and came landward, in the direction of a low-pressure eddy of its own creation. It is possible that the windowpane began to crack outward, in a chip of time before the surge burst indoors. The ash-laden air overturned a white marble basin and hurled it across the room. Though restoring the basin to its presurge position, excavators have left the original fossil impression exactly where the basin came to rest before subsequent ash flows and surge clouds encased it and the entire room.

In late September 2001, I did not want to leave *Keldysh*. I did not want to return home to New York City, for I had a very clear picture of the kind of work that lay ahead, in the crater behind Saint Paul's Chapel. Already, the strange physical phenomena captured on video and in photographs of the Tower collapses, were acquiring names familiar to volcanologists and deep-ocean archaeologists: Collapse column, downblast, out-splash, pyroclastic flow, shock cocoon, and surge cloud. Even before we reached shore, the physics and structural forensics of "WTC" promised to be everything like *Titanic* and Pompeii, and nothing at all like *Titanic* and Pompeii.

At intervals over the preceding years, Detective John Murphy (of the NYPD), George Skurla (of Grumman/NASA), and several other old friends had attempted to coax me (first out of the field of entomology, then out of paleontology and archaeology) into the fields of plane-crash analysis and crime-scene investigation. Vain efforts. I never wanted such responsibility. If I made a mistake with the interpretation of an archaeological artifact, or a trail in rusticle dust, or the manner in which a skeleton came to rest on a Herculanean beach, no actual harm could result. If I pointed the finger of blame at a man who died a hundred years ago, or two thousand—no harm was done (or so I once believed). If I made that same mistake in modern dust, an innocent might go to jail or a monster from whom the world needed protecting might be declared innocent and released. And there was another factor involved, a purely emotional factor: I was utterly repulsed by the idea of working with artifacts from my own time, and trying to extract truth from them.

In 1996, aerospace engineer George Skurla had wanted me to look at the central fuel tank and engines of a jumbo jet that had mysteriously exploded offshore of Long Island. He explained that more than three hundred other reviewers of the evidence had arrived at the same conclusion, and had essentially eliminated, as "erroneous," some thirty eyewitness claims that the plane had been brought down by a terrorist missile attack. The former Lunar Module engineer explained that everyone else was arriving at a group opinion; but George knew that I would "go at it lone wolf," following bends in the metal and in eyewitness accounts, ignoring the consensus view until after I saw where the evidence was leading. George Skurla wanted that four-hundredth opinion from me, but I let my emotions decide my actions.

Although time divides the Romans from us like an alien civilization, if we apply the tools of archaeology to reconstruct their homes, their faces, their joys and sorrows— there is no escaping this: The abyss of time is a mirror, and the children of Vesuvius are us.

If not for a sudden crisis in my family, in July of 1996, if not for a change in what should have been my normal routine, I would have been on that plane. Instead of stopping in France to reexamine artifacts at the IP-3 Laboratory, before joining the research vessels *Nadir* and *Ocean Voyager* in the Azores, I was on the beach with my little girl Amber when Flight 800 passed overhead and, minutes later, exploded on the horizon. Amber called my attention to the explosion: "Oh, Moon! Pretty!" she had said . . . And I knew where I would have been sitting; and I did not want to touch that part of the plane, or any other part.

Emotion got the upper hand. I turned away from the job, and I will never know whether or not I could have touched something, or seen something, or asked something new—which, as the shadow war loomed, might have turned out to be important. By 9/11, I knew that I had probably, in Skurla's test-pilot parlance, "screwed the pooch."

It's not making mistakes that so often counts against us; it's the frequency with which we repeat those same mistakes. Though I had lost family and old friends in the North Tower and therefore did not want to go anywhere near the site, did not want to touch the dust and the steel, did not want to interview surge-cloud survivors (for such "data collecting" was never without deep emotion), a man named Patrick Brown, of Ladder 3, kept me from "screwing the pooch" again.

Much as I had missed Flight 800, owing to a change of routine, my beloved Mary had missed her appointment with the Towers. Her friend Captain Patrick Brown did not. Mary believes that she felt the moment of his death; and I, for one, believe her.

"Paddy" had an understanding of engineering—as did many of the firefighters who arrived on site that morning. One of the staging-area discussions he had, before ascending the North Tower, was whether or not the remaining beams would soften, and slip, and allow the upper floors to jackhammer down in more or less than four hours. The principle of mass and acceleration had been recently (and graphically) demonstrated in several army recreation rooms. New recruits had discovered that by tilting vending machines forward, just a few inches off center, cans of soda could be coaxed to drop into the receiving trays, free of charge. A rash of injuries (at least one of them fatal) involving young soldiers crushed beneath falling vending machines proved beyond all serious dispute that the power of any moving object lay in its mass. A quarter-ton soda machine (weighing approximately 500 pounds) could easily be pushed across the floor by a man or lifted off the floor by three men. But if a man tipped the machine toward himself, so that it became unbalanced and began to gain momentum, it need only slip 2 feet (0.6 meter) and achieve a forward velocity of 5 miles per hour (7 feet, or 2 meters, per second) before it exerted more than a ton of force. At this point, no man, no matter how strong (if he continued to stand in the machine's way and tried to push against it), could exert enough opposing force to prevent the object from sledge-hammering him.

Pat Brown, and many of the others who ascended the stairs that day, were aware of the soda-machine principle (for a firefighter, in order to save lives, and to keep himself alive, has to be part chemist, part engineer, part physicist, part tactician, and part psychologist). They knew the temperatures at which jet fuel and office furnishings burned (and they understood the chemistry of the toxins released by burning carpets, plastics, and containers of transformer fluid). They knew the expansion ratios of steel beams, in inches per hundred feet, per hundred degrees Fahrenheit. And they knew that once the steel softened, like clay—once it weakened to the point that a single floor of supporting beams could slip uninterrupted for just a half-second—the rescue was over. All that was necessary for the triumph of evil was for floors 95 through 110 to drop just 7 feet (2 meters). In that tiny interval of slippage, the scale of everything was the soda-machine principle multiplied by the mass of a fifteen-story office block dropped on top of a skyscraper at 7 feet per second—and a half-second later, at close on 30 feet (9 meters) per second. After that first half-second slip, no power on Earth could prevent the beast from jackhammering all the way to the ground. It was destined to become, from that moment, an unstoppable and continually swelling hammerhead of dust and steel.

As soon as Pat Brown and the other captains saw the damage that Flight 11 had wrought, the overriding question became simply this: How bad will the jackhammer effect be, and how long until it kicks in? Was the jackhammer really inevitable, or just theoretical—and, if real, did they have more than four hours, or less?

According to preliminary, on-the-spot estimates, they had four hours, perhaps more. But they were entering uncharted territory. Miscalculations were inevitable. Jackhammer, collapse column, downblast, and the first surge clouds were scarcely an hour away.

When Mayor Giuliani arrived at the Fire Department's command post on West Street, he asked Chief Pete Ganci if he thought it was possible to send helicopters up to the roof, to evacuate people trapped above the fires. Ganci replied, "I have men inside, about halfway up the North Tower. We should be able to save everybody below the fire." The mayor understood, then, what his friend was telling him: There would be time only to evacuate people below the fires, *if only* the World Trade Center could stand strong enough for long enough. Ganci advised the mayor to evacuate north of Vesey Street. They shook hands, and wished each other luck. Mr. Giuliani never did see Pete Ganci again.

Ladder Company 3 was a relative latecomer to the scene, as near as anyone can tell. Someone had shouted at Captain Brown, before his Ladder 3 group moved toward the North Tower stairwell—"Paddy, don't go in there!"

"Are you nuts?" he hollered back. "We've got a job to do!" They had clear communications with him all the way to the end. At 9:59 A.M., when the South Tower jackhammered and downblasted, Ladder 3 group was on the forty-fourth floor of the North Tower. They had located approximately three dozen burn victims in the sky lobby, none of whom were able to stand and be moved. Although the true extent of the damage, when science reconstructed the fall, would reveal that the Towers, as if by miracle, stood against impossible abuse long enough for fifty-five thousand people below the fires to escape, the collapse of the South Tower became a time probe for the minutes remaining to Tower One. With nothing except a (constantly weakening) Roman arching effect—formed by interlocking girders above the Flight 11 wound—keeping the North Tower from becoming a collapse column, the order went forth from a command post near the Winter Garden dome: "Everybody out of Tower One! The South Tower is down! North Tower—evacuate, now!"

Ladder 3 received and acknowledged the evacuation order. Pat Brown sent his men downstairs; but, though a half-hour remained, none of them managed to escape the second collapse. For his own part, Pat Brown refused to leave the burn victims he had found on the forty-fourth floor. His driver, Mike Carroll, stayed with him, keeping the lines of communication open.

"I'm not going to leave these people to die alone," said Captain Brown. His friend Captain Richard Meo, insists that there was nothing even remotely suicidal in Pat's decision to stay with the burn victims. He knows (*knows* for a fact) that "Paddy," until the very last minute, was struggling with his driver to get two, or three, or just one of those people to stand, and to move with him toward the stairs. "If he could have saved just one life, then and only then would he have felt right to save his own."

At 10:10 A.M., eighteen minutes before the North Tower surge cloud formed, Pat Brown called out a "Mayday." That was the last anyone ever heard from Ladder 3.

They say that in New York no fewer than fourteen hundred women swooned over "Paddy Brown's James Cagney looks"—and *that* was only south of Fourteenth Street. His girlfriend, Olinda, was convinced that he more closely resembled Eddie Munster than James Cagney, and that he often behaved like the little wolfen Eddie all grown up. As if to drive home the point, the crews of Ladder 3/Rescue 1 had awarded her a silver Medal of Honor on the anniversary of their third year together. Like any pair of human beings, they had their good years and their bad years. But no matter how many continents of physical distance separated them, Paddy always made contact with Olinda on her birthday. I guess you could say they ended on a good year. The recovery workers found Pat Brown and his driver in the same stratum, with the burn victims of floor 44, on Olinda's birthday, in December of 2001. Along with red dust from one of the two "*Titanic* crosses," his ashes were scattered in New York City, in the shadow of the "Ground Zero Cross."

And during the months that followed, on those days when I found it difficult to examine surge-cloud dust, or to interview survivors—on those days when I simply wanted to walk away, never to return—it was Pat Brown's words that stiffened my spine, and gave me focus:

We've got a job to do . . .

THOUGH SIXTEEN YEARS under the *Titanic*'s spell should have taught me this, I'm not sure I ever really knew the meaning of hallowed ground until Ground Zero. I do know that I was always careful never to pollute the *Titanic,* or any other archaeological site, with objects from my own time. Injunctions against such contamination (to avoid confusing archaeologists of the future) were always a cardinal rule in the field . . . And then Haraldur Sigurdsson and the volcanologists were drawn to the crater in Manhattan, where they became forensic archaeologists. Officially, the focus of our work was purely scientific, for the collapse columns and "WTC surge clouds" were in every way identical to the physics (the hitherto poorly understood physics) seen in *volcanic* collapse columns and surge clouds.

Our initial examination of metal from the stairwells and elevator cores, when compared with data obtained from the Bikini Atoll atomic bomb tests, indicated that the forces acting in the center of the North

Tower collapse column ranged between 3 and 9 tons per square inch. This meant that some of the steel beams had been subjected to forces ranging from one-third of a .38-caliber bullet, upward to a complete .38, exerted against a single square inch—which was approximately equivalent to standing within 50 yards (or meters) of a 10-kiloton atomic bomb blast (such as the one that stamped the city of Hiroshima flat). Under such force, even cold steel can sometimes behave like a semi-fluid, twisting and warping like warm taffy. And yet, inside one of history's largest known "shock cocoons"—more than ten stories deep and, throughout most of its length, less than 20 feet (6 meters) wide—sixteen people survived in the hollow tube of the North Tower's B stairwell.

Sometimes the safest place to be when facing an overwhelming force is dead center, in the line of fire. As near as physics allows me to guess, the genesis of the stairwell B shock cocoon required but a single piece of metal, breaking or twisting in just the right way, and jutting upward at precisely the right angle, so that it became like the point of a supersonic jet breaking through hypersonic wind, and the stairwell B survivors became like fighter pilots, located safely behind the diverging shock wave, in a fuselage ten stories tall.

Elsewhere, in the core of this same collapse column, diamonds and jade pendants shattered—yet somehow, simultaneously within the column, leather fire helmets, wallets, and plastic-laminated drivers' licenses survived. Chains and rings fashioned from soft gold were sometimes found, in the collapse core, completely undamaged—where all else had been pounded to dust. Near Liberty Street, not much more than 100 feet (30 meters) from the grave of Ladder 4 Truck, two phone books had descended from a great height, somehow staying together even as they were collapse-columned and downblasted five stories underground and were impressed into the roof of a flattened car. Much as tornadoes have been known to drive speed-slung blades of grass, like nails, into the trunks of trees, the two books were literally hammered into the car, producing a single rectilinear depression in the shape of a book. The books themselves looked only a little frayed for their travels.

In this same region, where cars from the street ended up five stories underground, recovery workers came upon two casualties entombed

Field notes: The unsolved mystery of shock cocoons. Ejected from the Titanic's stern section, a jar of olives, discovered amid downblast ejecta. And, 9-11 (2001): a paper-thin birthday card "charm" (width=1cm.) fell out of the South Tower surge cloud — scratched; yet with none of its four plastic candles broken. Recovered on September 5, 2002, at the bottom of an ejecta blanket, inside Firehouse 10's rooftop vents.

only paces from a shock cocoon. The destruction, there, was so all-encompassing that the largest piece of concrete over which the excavators walked was no larger than a hen's egg—and yet, incredibly, they came upon an area some 15 feet (4.5 meters) in diameter with its ceiling intact, and (echoing Herculaneum) a table and chairs with soda cans and other items set as if for lunch. It occurred to one of the Port Authority police officers who came upon this scene that if the two dead men outside the cocoon had merely seated themselves at the table, they might have survived when the collapse column struck.

Amid such devastation, archaeologists and volcanologists learned (for better or for worse) to break the cardinal rule. We began to leave flowers on every visit. For the first time in our careers, dust samples—bagged, numbered, dated, and identified by location—were stored with dried roses. At the *Titanic*, at Thera, at the Herculaneum marina, it had sometimes been possible to bury our thoughts completely in science, as if we were merely children with exciting new puzzles to solve. But the Towers would not let us bury our minds in science and technology, would not let us lose our imaginations in the puzzles of collapse column, shock cocoon, downblast, and surge cloud—would not let us forget, even for a moment, that we were in a "hall of souls."

And then, for the first time in the recorded history of archaeological endeavor, when we left the Towers and returned to the marina of Herculaneum, we placed roses among the skeletons and shed tears for the soldier, and for the young slave girl protecting her master's child, and for Justa.

Archaeology's cardinal rule was broken, and to this day, it seems gone beyond recall. We "pollute" now, and probably forevermore, with roses. Perhaps someone in futurity will puzzle over the transition of habit—never guessing that, after the Towers, even a site two thousand years old had become hallowed ground to us. I know that I, for one, will never cease polluting. If you love science and technology, as I do, you can sometimes lapse and forget humanity. Ladder 3, Ladder 4, 10 House, and Donna (and a man named William Murdoch, and another named Patrick Brown)—they've seen to it that I, for one, will never forget.

FOR ME, the first revelation of the *Titanic* was the downblast—which had resculpted her decks the moment she impacted the bottom of the sea. It was all physics for me, at the start; and then I came, bit by bit, to understand (and occasionally to misunderstand) the people. When I first stood on the edge of Ground Zero, on November 3, 2001, I thought that the *Titanic* had prepared me by teaching everything she could about downblast and surge effects. As it turned out, downblast was among the least of her lessons. As the *Titanic* herself had pointed the way toward understanding the physics of collapse columns, downblast, and surge at Vesuvius and the Twin Towers, her first officer had (in a manner of speaking) given me a promise to keep and pointed me (in a manner of speaking) toward the wrongly maligned crew of Ladder 4.

It was mostly my fault that much of the historical debate about the

Titanic, during the first years of the final decade of the second millennium, had focused on whether or not the ship's first officer had really shot two passengers and then himself. The historian Walter Lord had argued that the shootings must have occurred exactly as passenger George Rheims described them, but other historians had objected loudly against the possibility. I'm the arrogant blunderer who then gathered every published and unpublished firsthand eyewitness account of those last moments on the starboard boat deck, near the ill-fated Boat A, and then endeavored to follow wherever the evidence led. From multiple eyewitnesses, from multiple points of view, the story of William Murdoch's last five minutes played out the same: "Earlier, during the loading of the collapsible boat on the starboard side," said steward Thomas Whitley, "there was a bitter panic. The officers had to use their revolvers. The Chief Officer shot two men but three others attempted to get into the boat. Later, I saw the Chief Officer shoot himself."

(The last five minutes of Murdoch's life . . .)

On September 10, 2001, I crouched in *Mir-2*, upon the very same patch of deck on which Mr. Murdoch made his stand. By aid of ten eyewitness accounts, my imagination went back to the past, and conjured ghosts out there, on the deck. Murdoch was giving everything he had to the task of getting the women and children away, against repeated and ultimately violent "mob-runs" on the Boats C and A. He wore no life jacket, and though the air temperature was below freezing, his uniform was drenched in sweat. Survivors recalled that even on this coldest of North Atlantic nights, the steel bulkhead (off to Murdoch's right) still smelled of fresh paint. And it occurred to me that, from where Murdoch stood, the ghosts of the abyss lay neither in his time-present nor in our time-past, but rather in his time-future.

On that September evening, marine archaeologist John Broadwater, pilot Victor, and I were (from a Murdoch point of view) the *Titanic*'s ghosts—the shape of things to come, descending from the heavens in contraptions of steel and blazing light. In shadowy, silent futurity, we dispatched deep-ocean robots—which passed through the space occupied by the first officer and by everyone else gathered round the last lifeboats, passed through them as if they were not even present upon the deck, as if our machines regarded them with contemptuous indifference, on their way to more important concerns in the dining saloon, the crew's infirmary, the Ismay and Russell suites.

I had wished it were possible, as one ghost to another, for me to tell Mr. Murdoch that as a scientist looking backward along the stream of time and trying to form, for myself, an image of what had happened to him (sometimes with the assistance of robotic eyes), I regretted that I had gotten only a small part of the picture right, and that I had done him a grievous wrong.

J. Bruce Ismay, one of the *Titanic's* owners, had testified that when he left the ship, in Boat C, there had been no pandemonium at all, that the people on the deck "could not have been quieter or more orderly if gathered in a church," and that anyone who spoke otherwise was lying. Seventeen-year-old Jack Thayer had said that he did not blame Ismay for leaping into the lifeboat, and declared that he would have done so himself if not for the utter pandemonium between his position and Boat C—and then he heard the gunshots. In my attempts to gather and sort every eyewitness account for credibility, and to discern whether the evidence supported the Ismay account or the passengers' accounts, I spent, in the final analysis, an inordinate amount of time scrutinizing the last five minutes of William McMaster Murdoch's life. I had failed, therefore, to consider those minutes within the context of the rest of his life, or even within the context of his behavior during the last two and a half hours leading up to those last five minutes.

I had no way of knowing this, but on the starboard Boat Deck, eighty-nine years after he died, Mr. Murdoch was preparing me for the Towers. Eighty-nine years after he made his stand, on a ragged patch of deck where hermit crabs now roamed, he was teaching me about keeping a faith with people who were dead and could no longer defend themselves . . . with people who, 800 miles away in the west, and 2.5 miles overhead, had but hours left to live.

Shortly before the expedition, historian Paul Quinn had done the much-required homework of following, through an exhaustive study of the British and American hearings, Murdoch's movements throughout the night. The first officer was seen forward starboard, launching boats and making sure they were filled to capacity—and he was seen aft starboard, and aft port, doing the same thing. He was, in fact, seen here, there, and everywhere that the lifeboats were being successfully launched—departing little if at all from the tradition of the Roman soldier at the Herculaneum marina, whose skeleton was still launching the city's last lifeboats into the Bay of Naples. Murdoch was, as demonstrated by the Quinn analysis, directly responsible for most of those souls who survived that incredible night.

In the end, amid what began (according to Thayer and the others) as warning shots, Boats 1 and C were launched in quick succession, while crowds gathered around the last set of "live" davit heads and the forward deck came down level with the sea, finally on the verge of dunking under. Murdoch had so far launched three-quarters of *Titanic*'s survivors away, and yet historians had often called the launchings of Boats 1 and C—only minimally filled, from "A's" davits—acts of incompetence on Murdoch's part. However, given the details of the Quinn chronology, combined with multiple eyewitness accounts of panic near the last set of boat-bearing davits, even the launch of two partly filled lifeboats became consistent with a cool and sensible logic: Get as many people loaded as you can—quickly—and fire the last boats off like shotgun shells, before the (strengthening) mobs attack and nothing can be launched at all. This was logical, if one knew that an attack seemed likely at any moment, and if one had made a decision not to enter one of the boats himself. The next logical move was to see the last boat loaded with as many women as could be seen—loaded fast, and as completely as possible— and to keep back the rest of the people (the hundreds of them still on the upper decks) with examples of deadly force, if requisite.

All these actions seemed clear, as I crouched for a long time at *Mir-2*'s starboard viewport, bringing to life, in my imagination, the specter of William Murdoch, doing whatever was necessary, as the deck threatened to slip under, to give the women at his back a few seconds more cutting time to get the ropes undone and to push off in Boat A. There were, at that moment, fifty seats at Murdoch's back, for fifteen hundred people remaining aboard.

The deck was, in the replay of history, alive-seeming still when I turned away from the viewport and penned (on the title page of Susanne Stormer's biography of William McMaster Murdoch) a promise that was fated to bear no less meaning in the shadow of Ground Zero than it had under the davits of Boat A:

September 10, 2001; 6:30 p.m.
On Board R.M.S. Titanic
To First Officer William Murdoch

A wise archaeologist named Trude Dothan once told me that we (we who stroll through the cellars of time) are the biggest story-tellers in the world—that we are become speakers for the dead; simply that. Nothing more. Nothing less. But we are more than that and I believe [my friends] and I have done you wrong, William McMaster Murdoch— done you wrong by focusing on the last five minutes of your life without realizing that 75% of the people who got away from this place owed their lives to you. I, especially [dealt you a wrong]—for I painted less than half of your face and asked the world to guess from that the measure of the whole man. [Someday], I will correct this picture. Trude was wrong. [Archaeology] is not so simple as telling stories about the dead. We must keep a faith with the dead—and I've a faith to keep with you, Mr. Murdoch.

—Your friend, in time. C.R.P.

PAST IS PROLOGUE; or so the poets say. I remember being astonished by row after row of unbroken stained-glass windows inside the *Titanic*— astonished to the point of becoming misty-eyed. The artist Ken Marschall and I both remarked about how it looked so like a chapel in there—driving home to us (as if we needed to learn it again, again) the lesson of hallowed ground, and perhaps, too, the dawning awareness that we really did have a faith to keep with those who could no longer speak for themselves.

Hours later, and hundreds of miles away, New York City Police Officer Timothy O'Neill had his own encounter with unbroken glass. He more felt than saw his way out of the fog of smoke that completely obscured Vesey Street. As far as he could see into the fog, Manhattan had been converted into a moonscape, complete with craters and dust. He thought he was dreaming when the smoke suddenly pulled apart to reveal tombstones near Broadway—covered, like everything else, in a layer of dust 6 inches (15 centimeters) deep. Then he saw footprints leading to Saint Paul's Chapel, and he followed them inside.

"It was pitch dark," he reported. "Eerie silence. And I'm looking up, and looking at the windows and not even a single window is broken in there. And I said, 'I can't *believe* that.' It was right behind the graveyard—behind the Twin Towers. I mean, the rubble wasn't 30 feet [9 meters] away!"

As I later explained it, the squat, nine-story building known as 5 World Trade Center—which stood between the Towers and Saint Paul's—had taken the brunt of the collapse column and its ground-level surge cloud. As my physics told it, Number 5 had acted somewhat like a giant air bag. The chapel had, in effect, been shock-cocooned.

Officer O'Neill had a different explanation. For him, as he swung a flashlight beam across a plaque commemorating George Washington's church pew, and across row after row of unbroken stained-glass windows: "It added a little spirituality and a little reminder. To me, at least—it was protected. It was immediately designated a sanctuary by a higher power."

Saint Paul's Chapel was more than a hundred years older than the *Titanic,* more than two hundred years older than the World Trade Center. And ahead of the chapel's construction lay the long and often troubled history of a civilization's growing pains. From the time of Vesuvius and Justa's House, and Pompeii's House of the Christians, there had come the split between Christians and Jews, between Gnostic Christians and Pauline Christians. Witch burnings came and went, and there came the split between Pauline Christians and Muslims. The Crusades came and went, and the practice of witch burning came on again stronger. There came a split between Catholic Christians and Protestant Christians, and in some quarters the enmity between Protestants and Catholics seemed never to go away.

In the wake of the September attacks, all the nonsense of centuries past died forever in the chapel of Saint Paul's—died as surely (and as permanently) as the last shreds of the cold war died on the decks of *Keldysh.*

I do not know for a fact that it died anywhere else on Earth; but it died, definitely, in that chapel. What can you say about a nondenominational island of peace and hope that sprang to life on the rim of an abyss? For Ground Zero recovery workers, for friends and family members of the lost, for crime-scene investigators and volcanologists—even for the agnostics among us—it became "the chaotic hotel of radical hospitality."

With no thought of race, creed, or gender orientation, hundreds of volunteers gathered there, helping in any way they could. "I guess you know I'm a Buddhist," said one of the new permanent members of Saint Paul's. "The person most pleased when I came to Saint Paul's and Trinity was my rabbi," said another. And they are still part of the parish. I never believed, before the attacks, that I would see an openly gay couple embraced by a Christian church. Even a Doubting Thomas like me was welcome, and no one there has ever tried to "convert" me. *E pluribus unum* ("out of many, one") truly was the creed at George Washington's chapel. When I first stepped inside, late in the winter of 2002, it was already a global neighborhood on the rim of despair. So, in the same way that the *Keldysh* became my extended family, Saint Paul's became my church.

During the spring and summer of 2002, I discovered that one or two of the women at the door always knew when someone had been through a bad day. They sensed from a look in your eye, or from your gait, when you had found a birthday card or a teddy bear in the dust, and you were a tad unsteady, or angry, and you needed a tissue or a hug. Each bend in Ladder 10 House's steel doors, each surge-cloud survivor's account, each impossibly compressed or impossibly intact artifact brought out of the crater, sharpened or reedited the little movie picture playing in your head—adding a detail here, subtracting one there. After you had replayed, in your brain, the collapse of the North Tower eight hundred different ways, with your cousin still inside, you sometimes began to wonder if you would ever be right again.

("We've got a job to do," Captain Brown had said . . .)

The volunteers arrived at the "chaotic hotel" from all points of the compass. Massage therapists, chaplains, people who wanted to cook food or carry supplies into the crater—they came from as near as Battery Park City or flew in, at their own expense, from as far away as Seattle. The story that stuck most in the minds of the volunteers was the one about the old lady, "infirm, hardly able to walk," who rode all the way down from the Bronx by subway, then hobbled up to the gates of Saint Paul's: "And she said that she wanted to give us her cane. It was all she had to give, but she said she wanted the church to give it to someone who might have been injured."

(Am I my brother's keeper?)

And from all around the world, children sent colorful cards and banners—which were hung everywhere within the chapel. An oasis of bright color in a field of grayish white dust: a thousand paper cranes from the children of Hiroshima . . . flags of all nations, including an American flag more than a story tall, made from the handprints of schoolchildren. One of the children's cards read: "I think you should build the Towers back, but next time don't tell anyone where they are." It was an epitaph, a modern-day Pompeii graffito.

The fires burning beneath the ruins were the strangest any firefighter had ever encountered. They burned for more than three months, making lava, fusing steel and concrete and glass into the disquieting sculpture of holocaust. The ground burned through the thickest protective boots, sometimes requiring medical attention; and it occurred to one of the chaplains of Saint Paul's that the idea of a podiatrist setting up office in George Washington's pew had been thoroughly unimaginable in August of 2001. Food was being cooked and served in the aisles. They broke every rule, in that church, for the preservation of a Colonial landmark.

It was there, in the chapel, about three o'clock in the morning, that I met a young medical student who wanted to volunteer for the "dirty bomb protocol." She was twenty-four years old, and she knew exactly what she would be getting herself into, and it did not matter to her. (Just the same, I had said she did not belong there, but she will never know how much I needed to be reminded, that night, of what a child had written in a card: "More people have more nice in them than mean.") During the worst of times, good people really do seem to come out of the woodwork. They're not necessarily generals or mayors or presidents, either. Most of them are standing right next to us, and they just seem to step forward when they are needed. When I explained to one unit of firefighters—the group most likely to be a radiologic weapon's first responder unit—that I believed it would be possible to save lives but that a professionally built "dirty bomb" should render the responders very grave men, they merely bowed their heads, uttered the appropriate curses, and resigned themselves to the new reality. They had been advised that anyone under age forty-five, or with very young children, should transfer to another unit. A year passed. And not one of them transferred out. Not one of them. This told me 99 percent of everything I needed to know about the FDNY.

I've seen human beings at their best, in the aftermath of 1.6 kilotons. And I've seen the worst: The minority of inhuman vultures who unfolded tables on the crater rim, where they sold bootleg postcards, books, and photo albums of the buildings burning, of the people falling . . . And the mercifully even smaller minority of inhumans who (armed with a legal determination that "no one can sue on the premise of slandering dead men") chose to ignore the evidence of videotape, physics, and forensic files, in order to make a controversial claim. Through books, magazines, and television interviews, they proclaimed the image of the heroic 9/11 firefighter a twenty-first-century myth. They then stood this claim upon an accusation of looting, leveled against the men of Ladder 4. It was well known, within the publishing industry, that if a book were to suggest UFOs probably do not exist, or that Lee Harvey Oswald acted alone, or that in July of 1969 Neil Armstrong and Buzz Aldrin walked on the moon, it could not sell nearly so many copies as a tall tale accusing the White House of sanctioning alien UFO abductions, or the CIA of killing President Kennedy, or NASA of faking the Apollo missions to the moon.

(What is Truth?)

At Saint Paul's, Timothy O'Neill had said, "You run [the entire gamut] from total sadness and sorrow, [to] rage and anger—and joy. I met true heroes, people who were true heroes. And I saw people who were the worst I'd ever seen: taking pictures of dead bodies and stealing firemen's gear and going down into the pit and trying to film them trying to recover [the lost]." O'Neill had personally ferreted out several vultures—at least one of whom had scavenged a dead fireman's hat and gear and filled his pockets with rings and watches from a jewelry store while impersonating a recovery worker—

(Trude Dothan was right about many things. But, again, I think she was wrong when she said that archaeologists are speakers for the dead. We've got a job to do. And we've got to get it right. A faith to keep. A job to do. And a faith to keep with the dead. And a faith to keep with the truth—)

Some of those who believe in the motility of consciousness (and I'm not one of them) have told me that they think it was William Murdoch and Patrick Brown who, "somewhat like guardian angels," directed my attention toward Liberty Street. Months before anyone fashioned a literary box cutter (with its indictment against Ladder 4), Captain Paul Mallery, of Ladder 10/Engine 10 House, on Liberty Street, had told me that there must have been a "reason" why he had been allowed to live through the downblast and ground surge when so many others had died so near. He said that he had not yet discovered the reason; but he knew that the truth was out there, somewhere, and that it would come to him eventually.

"There had to be a purpose," he said, "why I lived to see all of this. Why I lived to tell it."

Ten House was located 250 feet (75 meters) from the South Tower's southeast corner and, much as Saint Paul's Chapel had been air-bagged by 5 World Trade Center, the nine-story frame of 4 World Trade Center protected 10 House by taking the brunt of the 120-mile- (197-kilometer-) per-hour collapse column. Nevertheless, the dust-laden air—the air alone—as it entered the open truck bay where evacuees had gathered, ballooned steel doors outward from the center of the bay, then shot a hundred feet aft and "blew" one of Paul Mallery's friends out through the back wall. The fireman found himself and one of the evacuees in a world turned suddenly blacker than a mine shaft, in which he was unable to see his own hands through the dust. As the rescuer felt a familiar brick wall, the evacuee told him, "We've got to get out of here! Let's go outside!"

"Friend, we already *are* outside," the fireman said, and the stranger replied, "We gotta get back inside! Let's go inside!"

Behind them, in the kitchen, refrigerators, cabinets, and other heavy objects were torn from the north (Tower-side) wall and piled in the center of the room, as if by a whirlwind. In the hallway leading to the kitchen, a man running with fireman Sean O'Malley was lifted off the floor and thrown 50 feet (15 meters) down the hall. Sean O'Malley

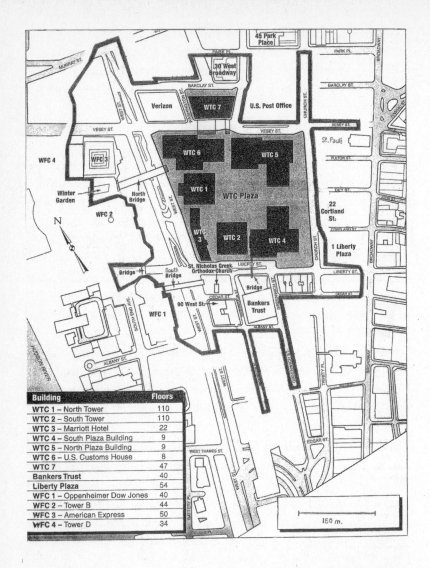

Building	Floors
WTC 1 – North Tower	110
WTC 2 – South Tower	110
WTC 3 – Marriott Hotel	22
WTC 4 – South Plaza Building	9
WTC 5 – North Plaza Building	9
WTC 6 – U.S. Customs House	8
WTC 7	47
Bankers Trust	40
Liberty Plaza	54
WFC 1 – Oppenheimer Dow Jones	40
WFC 2 – Tower B	44
WFC 3 – American Express	50
WFC 4 – Tower D	34

Key: Perimeter of Twin Tower downblast; zone of greater than 95 percent mortality for unsheltered persons.

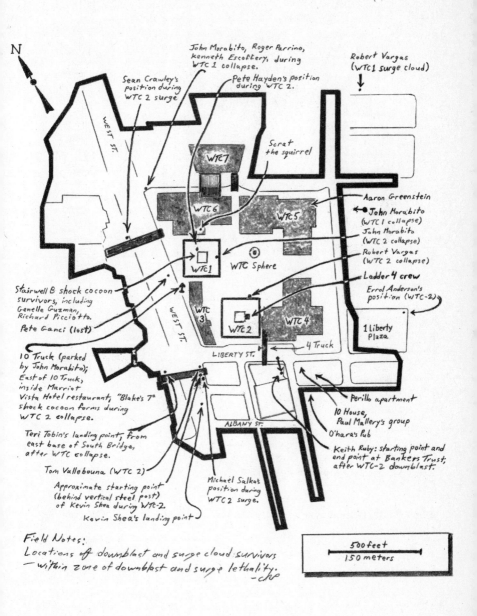

N

John Morabito, Roger Parrino, kenneth Escoffery, during WTC 1 collapse.

Sean Crawley's position during WTC 2 surge

Pete Hayden's position during WTC 2.

Robert Vargas (WTC1 surge cloud)

WEST ST.

WTC 7

Scrat the squirrel

WTC 6

WTC 5

Aaron Greenstein

John Morabito (WTC 1 collapse)

John Morabito (WTC 2 collapse)

Robert Vargas (WTC 2 collapse)

Ladder 4 crew

Errol Anderson's position (WTC-2)

WTC 1

WTC Sphere

Stairwell B shock cocoon survivors, including Genelle Guzman, Richard Picciotto.

Pete Ganci (lost)

WEST ST.

WTC 3

WTC 2

WTC 4

4 Truck

1 Liberty Plaza

10 Truck (parked by John Morabito); East of 10 Truck, inside Marriot Vista Hotel restaurant, "Blake's 7" shock cocoon forms during WTC 2 collapse.

LIBERTY ST.

Perillo apartment

Teri Tobin's landing point, from east base of South Bridge, after WTC collapse.

Tom Vallebouna (WTC 2)

ALBANY ST.

10 House, Paul Mallery's group

O'hara's Pub

Michael Salka's position during WTC 2 surge.

Keith Ruby: starting point and end point at Bankers Trust, after WTC-2 downblast.

Approximate starting point (behind vertical steel post) of Kevin Shea during WTC-2.

Kevin Shea's landing point

Field Notes:
Locations of downblast and surge cloud survivors
— within zone of downblast and surge lethality.
—chp

500 feet
150 meters

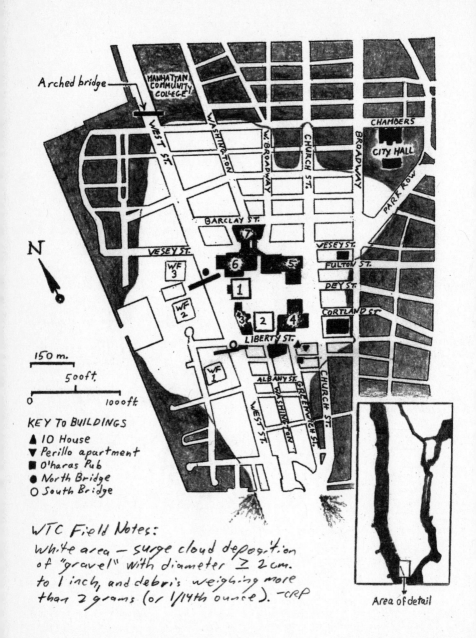

Arched bridge

MANHATTAN COMMUNITY COLLEGE!

WEST ST.
WASHINGTON
W. BROADWAY
CHURCH ST.
BROADWAY
PARK ROW

CHAMBERS
CITY HALL

BARCLAY ST.

VESEY ST.

N

WF 3

6 7 5

WF 2

1

3 2 4

VESEY ST.
FULTON ST.
DEY ST.
CORTLAND ST.

LIBERTY ST.

WF 1

ALBANY ST.
WASHINGTON
GREENWICH ST.
CHURCH ST.
WEST ST.

150 m.

500 ft.

0   1000 ft

KEY TO BUILDINGS
▲ 10 House
▼ Perillo apartment
■ O'haras Pub
● North Bridge
○ South Bridge

WTC Field Notes:
White area — surge cloud deposition
of "gravel" with diameter ≥ 2 cm.
to 1 inch, and debris weighing more
than 2 grams (or 1/14th ounce). —CRP

Area of detail

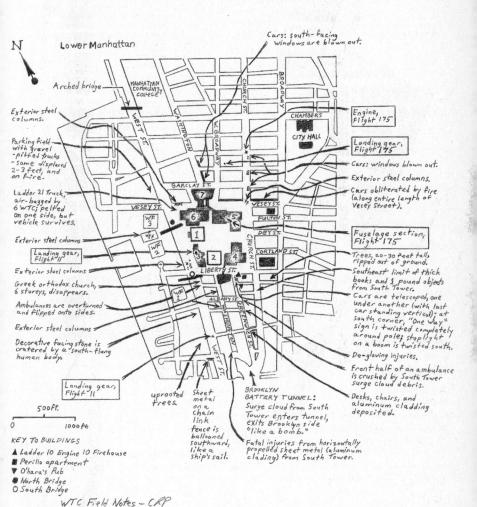

N

Lower Manhattan

Cars: south-facing windows are blown out.

Arched bridge

Exterior steel columns.

Parking field with gravel - pitted trucks - some displaced 2-3 feet, and on fire.

Ladder 21 Truck, air-bagged by 6 WTC; pelted on one side, but vehicle survives.

Exterior steel columns

Landing gear, Flight 11

Exterior steel columns

Greek orthodox church, 6 storeys, disappears.

Ambulances are overturned and flipped onto sides.

Exterior steel columns

Decorative facing stone is cratered by a "south-flung human body.

Landing gear, Flight 11

uprooted trees

Sheet metal on a chain link fence is ballooned southward, like a ship's sail.

BROOKLYN BATTERY TUNNEL: Surge cloud from South Tower enters tunnel, exits Brooklyn side "like a bomb."

Fatal injuries from horizontally propelled sheet metal (aluminum cladding) from South Tower.

Engine, Flight 175

Landing gear, Flight 175

Cars: windows blown out.

Exterior steel columns.

Cars obliterated by fire (along entire length of Vesey Street).

Fuselage section, Flight 175

Trees, 20-30 feet tall, ripped out of ground.

Southeast limit of thick books and 1 pound objects from South Tower.

Cars are telescoped, one under another (with last car standing vertical); at south corner, "One Way" sign is twisted completely around pole; stoplight on a boom is twisted south.

De-gloving injuries.

Front half of an ambulance is crushed by South Tower surge cloud debris.

Desks, chairs, and aluminum cladding deposited.

MANHATTAN COMMUNITY COLLEGE

CHURCH ST.

BROADWAY

CHAMBERS

CITY HALL

WEST ST.

WASHINGTON

W. BROADWAY

BARCLAY ST.

VESEY ST.

7

WF 3

WF 4

WF 2

6

1

5

VESEY ST.

FULTON ST.

DEY ST.

CHURCH ST.

CORTLAND ST.

3

2

4

LIBERTY ST.

WF 1

ALBANY ST.

GREENWICH ST.

WASHINGTON ST.

WEST ST.

500 ft.

0   1000 ft.

KEY TO BUILDINGS

▲ Ladder 10 Engine 10 Firehouse
■ Perillo apartment
▼ O'hara's Pub
● North Bridge
○ South Bridge

WTC Field Notes - CRP

managed to avoid being thrown, by ducking down the west stairway and making a dive for the generator room. He recalled vividly a precursor wave striking the backs of his ears—"Yes, this powerful gust of clear air definitely came before the darkness hit"—and the picture that came to mind, as the air pressure increased, was of the atomic bomb test films from the 1950s. When the blast wave and the dust struck him, it was as he expected, based upon his recollections of those films.

O'Malley had noticed that the kitchen's steel door was open when he made his dive. When he reemerged, seconds later, it had slammed shut (from the direction of the hallway and the blast), sealing off the kitchen and bending in the middle. The seal had formed, behind the two who were "blown" out of the kitchen and onto Cedar Street, before they could actually be "pushed" out the back of 10 House. With the room sealed, the collapse column's base surge, as it shot over the roof of the firehouse, created, in the street between 10 House and the four-story apartment block atop O'Hara's restaurant, something akin to a tornado turned on its side: a horizontal whirlwind. The kitchen's two occupants, along with the window frame and part of a brick-and-cinder-block wall, were *sucked* out the back of the firehouse.

Eight stories above 10 House, two tons of office memos, law books, telephones, strips of carpet, a photograph still in its frame, and fragments of office furniture—most of it out-splashed from the outermost fringes of the South Tower collapse column—jetted into Mary Perillo's apartment through only three windows, each 27 inches wide by 54 inches long (0.7 by 1.4 meters). When a recovery worker escorted her into the apartment, a computer monitor only slightly narrower than one of her windows was lying on the floor. Pointing to a large crack, the worker told her, "I'm afraid that monitor of yours will never work again."

She shook her head in disbelief. "I don't own a computer," she replied.

In the core of the collapse column, almost nothing at all familiar seemed to survive. Near the center, powdered concrete and microfibered paper became major components of WTC dust. The core was near-perfect nothingness: not a single doorknob, or chair leg, or file cabinet—little except shock-cocooned gold necklaces and plastic-laminated cards. "Shock-cocooned," in such cases, did not quite apply or explain. Sometimes the phrase was simply a dumping ground for what we did not yet understand. Objects outside the core, objects nearer the Tower windows, met an equally strange fate: They were jetted away from the center, sometimes in extreme disorder, sometimes with inexplicable order.

Outside the collapse columns, at a radius of more than 200 feet (or 60 meters) from the stairwells and elevator cores, the manifestations at 10 House and the Perillo apartment reproduced themselves—prodigiously. In every direction, the strange contradictions of tornado physics: One half of O'Hara's restaurant and bar looked as if it had been H-bombed by the surge cloud; and yet just a few feet east of total devastation, glasses and bottles had not been tipped over or displaced a single inch. We had seen this effect before, in the ruins of Herculaneum.

A car on Liberty Street had followed the curb five stories under Building Number 4. An incredible anthology of the World Trade Center appeared to have been tornadoed inside the vehicle before it was crushed shorter than knee level. There was a piece of concrete curb in the company of twisted shreds of venetian blinds, part of a bathroom urinal, and a huge, industrial-sized container of Poland Spring water, crushed Frisbee-flat and emptied. As these objects entered through one side of the car, the front and rear seats appeared to have been squirted out the opposite side. Like the seats, the motor was nowhere to be found; but jeans from 4 World Trade Center's Structure store warehouse—still neatly folded and sometimes compressed and frayed into stacks of two and three—seemed to be everywhere under the eastern half of the Liberty Street excavation. Law books and phone books had gone underground in much the same pattern as the jeans: two by two and three by three. Much as a stream of running water will deposit gold nuggets of approximately the same size in the same place, objects of the same mass and grain size traveled together within the WTC clouds. Gravity currents may be chaotic, but chaos is not without a certain order.

Anyone who spent twenty minutes surveying the crater rim could not help but notice the signatures of chaos. I could spend the next decade trying to reconstruct the forces acting against a single car, or a fire truck, and still I would be raising more questions than answers. Every twist and snap in the metal, every inexplicably intact piece of paper, seemed to reinforce, archaeologically, the Reverend Milton Williams's eyewitness account: "If you can imagine the little brown paper bag you took to school when you were a child . . . If you were to take a tornado, a typhoon, an earthquake, and a major volcanic eruption: Put all of that into your little lunch bag. Shake it up. And open the bag. That's what we saw." He paused and thought about it for two seconds. "That's what we saw," he repeated.

To date, Reverend Williams has given the most apt description I've heard of the strange physics that took charge when 10 to 15 percent of a *Hiroshima* descended into the heart of Manhattan on twin collapse columns. The reverend from Saint Paul's, or anyone else who truly lived on the rim, understood how a memo from Marsh and McLennan Insurance Company could travel a seventh of a mile south of the North Tower's ninety-eighth floor and become jammed with floor tiles and bits of window dressing inside an air vent on the roof of 10 House . . . how a hundred law books could travel together and land in a heap at the Battery Park City Marina, a sixth of a mile from their starting point in the South Tower . . . how a computer monitor could be catapulted from the South Tower, a tenth of a mile east and through Mary Perillo's window . . . how, across the street from the Perillo apartment, in the fire escapes above O'Hara's pub, part of a legal library could land and still retain its alphabetical order . . . how 4 Truck, as it was hammered five stories below street level with a force approaching three tons per square inch (the same pressure exerted against a submersible's hull 2.5 miles under the sea) passed hundreds of *unbroken* wine bottles. Above 4 Truck's final resting place, under the southeast corner of the South Tower lobby, most of a wine cellar survived in a shock cocoon. In every direction, chaos and order stood side by side.

Still . . . none of this knowledge could discourage the publication of public indictments against the crew of Ladder 4, entirely on the basis of folded jeans from a clothing warehouse coming to rest in orderly piles, near (but in fact not on or in) 4 Truck. At first glance, it had seemed impossible, to some, that order could arise within such chaos without the intervention of human hands. If the work of gravity currents was an inkblot test, in which one sees what one wants to see, there were certainly those who (perhaps acting out of rage against the ruins themselves) saw something more sinister at work in nature's physics. It was hard, so a writer claimed and so his editor upheld, to avoid the conclusion that Ladder 4 was at the center of "a widespread pattern of looting that started even before the Towers fell."

Here are the facts, to the best that our science can tell them. This is what happened, when a tiny ember of Vesuvius fell upon New York:

Ladder 4 Truck arrived on Liberty Street, within clear view of 10 House, between twenty and thirty minutes after the South Tower was struck by United Airlines Flight 175. At that time, the top thirty stories of the Tower were leaning eastward, toward 1 Liberty Plaza, dropping glass and steel and groaning audibly. Every man in every fire team knew, then, that he was entering his worst nightmare.[1]

Paul Mallery, who was calling World Trade Center evacuees inside the open bay doors of 10 House, had a clear view of Ladder 4 Group from the moment their truck turned the corner from West Street and worked its way gingerly down Liberty Street, over and around steel beams, over smashed computer terminals, and over airplane parts from

---

[1] Some of these crews took last rites from chaplains before they went in. Firefighter Michael Lynch is sometimes cited by Ladder 4's detractors as having left the Ladder 4 crew and died away from his team (on a looting search for jeans, they seem to suggest), but the citing results from confusion with Engine 40's Michael Lynch, a firefighter lost from the same Battalion (Number 9), who had the same name. Captain Dave Wooley, who *did* die away from his team, was normally assigned as company commander of Ladder 4, but on that day he deployed with Engine 54 (from the same firehouse, at Forty-eighth Street and Eighth Avenue). He was last seen near the lobby of the Marriott Hotel (3 World Trade Center), with one of the Engine 54 crew, and it is believed that during the minutes before the South Tower fell, Captain Wooley was headed toward the Ladder 4 crew (for they were in need of extra manpower and a water supply in the main lobby). This would have put Wooley near or behind a group of firemen that Port Authority Police Sergeant Robert Vargas saw walking toward him seconds before a shock-cocoon event rendered him the South Tower's sole, moment Zero survivor. Officer Vargas also had a clear view, across the glass-enclosed lobby, toward Liberty Street and 10 House. In the lobby, firefighters "seemed to be working with something" at the elevator doors. Only one other man is believed to have separated from the Ladder 4 crew: Joseph Angelini Jr., who has on occasion been confused with Joseph Angelini Sr., who worked with Terry Hatton's Rescue 1 team but had, on that day, been detailed to one of the Special Operations command posts. The younger Angelini survived the South Tower collapse (possibly in a Vargas-type shock cocoon, but no one knows for sure). By all accounts, his most immediate concern was finding his father—which, in fact, he did. Both father and son appear on a surviving video-tape recorded after the South Tower collapse. As near as anyone can tell, they died together in the North Tower base surge. Joseph Angelini Jr. had been detailed to Ladder 4 early on the morning of September 11, to replace a crew member who had been injured the night before and who had been sleeping in the firehouse on medical leave. As 4 Truck received the call to the South Tower, the injured crewman jumped aboard. "Maybe that fella needed to stock up on Gap jeans," says 10 House's Paul Mallery. "Sorry. You just gotta keep some sense of humor, here, or the terrorists win."

Flight 11's North Tower exit wound. They parked near the doomed South Tower, and Paul's little knot of survivors observed that the crew had a terrible time maneuvering into the building. They scurried, first, under the footbridge that had connected 4 World Trade with Bankers Trust Plaza. Using the bridge for shelter, they crossed Liberty Street to the south side of the South Tower. During the first five minutes, they separated into two groups near the south entrance: The main group assessed what was needed, and a second smaller group of "about three men" returned to 4 Truck for the Hurst tool. Their backs hugging the south wall, their Hurst cutting tool in tow, they made their way toward the entrance. The Hurst was not a simple or light piece of equipment: It had a motor, and it was usually carried on wheels.

"They *had* to keep their backs against the wall," Paul reported. "Eighty floors up, people were swarming out of the windows like bees. Some of them struck the ground like firebombs, and the men from Ladder 4—they were hit [by "ejecta"]. They were hit by something bad, and they kept on going."

Ladder 4 happened to be one of the teams that had clear communications and line-of-sight contact throughout its mission. As "4" drove to the site, they received word that there were people trapped in elevator banks on the ground floor of the South Tower. Ladder 4's driver acknowledged the message and reported that they were bringing a Hurst tool—the same piece of equipment that Paul Mallery observed them carrying into the building, between 9:30 and 9:40 A.M., some twenty to thirty minutes before the first collapse column formed.

Inside the South Tower, KBW research associate Linda Rothemund and approximately eight of her coworkers had survived a fly-wheel-cushioned elevator crash from the 78th floor.[2] The crash was not the end of their troubles, however; for the elevator was being heated from below, apparently by burning jet fuel that had trickled down neighboring shafts. Being the smallest member of the group, Linda was able to squeeze through what she described as an eight-inch rupture near the

---

[2] The main impact zone of United Flight 175 was between the 78th and 84th floors. Linda Rothemund and several of her co-workers had decided to disobey loudspeaker instructions indcating that the first explosion at 8:46 a.m. was limited to the North Tower, that the South Tower was secure and "occupants should return to their offices." Rothemund entered the 78th floor express elevator and closed the doors just seconds before the impact of Flight 175.

START TIME	EVENT
8:46:26 A.M.	North Tower (WTC 1) impact, American Airlines Flight 11; 767 at velocity 470 miles (771 km) per hour.
9:02:54 A.M.	South Tower (WTC 2) impact, United Airlines Flight 175; 767 at velocity 590 miles (968 km) per hour.
9:59:04 A.M.	South Tower begins to form collapse column, 0:56:10 after Flight 175 impact.
10:28:31 A.M.	North Tower forms collapse column, 1:42:05 after Flight 11 impact; surge cloud impacts Tower 7 (47 stories) and initiates multiple fires.
17:20:33 P.M.	Tower 7 (WTC 7) collapses at maximum velocity 50 mph, 6:52:02 after being struck by WTC 1 surge cloud; fails to form true collapse column and downblast but nevertheless sends out surge clouds of its own.

Chronology of major WTC events, New York time, September 11, 2001, based on seismic recordings made by the Lamont-Doherty Earth Observatory of Columbia University.

elevator's floor. She emerged into Tower Two's ground-floor lobby, and had attracted the attention of firefighters and police officers who were evacuating people through the north wall's revolving doors, into the WTC concourse. Linda brought a whole team running to her friends' rescue, with axes and fire extinguishers. One of those rescuers was firefighter Timothy Brown, that day's supervisor from the Mayor's Office of Emergency Management. About this time, Tim had been trying to verify the availability of military air cover for New York. He had already received the 9:16 A.M. announcement (which came thirteen minutes after the South Tower impact of Flight 175 and the severing of cable connections to Linda Rothemund's elevator) that Flight 93 was now a third cruise missile believed heading for Washington or New York. He also received the 9:24 A.M. announcement that Flight 77 was a fourth missile, and that they "should be prepared to get hit again."

Then his connection with Washington was lost, and an operator told him that the Pentagon had just exploded. As Flight 77 impacted the Pentagon, the clock touched 9:38 A.M. About the time of this third impact, 4 Truck had arrived near the Liberty Street entrance to the South Tower—approaching from West Street (as memorialized on surviving video) and parking on the sidewalk, with its cab partly sheltered under a footbridge that connected WTC-4 to the Banker's Trust Building. The truck was in a direct line of sight with a second command post then being set up inside the lobby, next to the glass doors at the South Tower's southeast corner. About this same time, Tim Brown noticed that more and more of the office workers emerging through the stairwell doors appeared to be from the floors directly below the second impact: Many were severely burned. Three or four of the Ladder 4 crew were already at work on the fallen elevator, and had pulled Linda's equally thin friend, Lauren Smith, to safety. The clock, now, was at or beyond 9:40 A.M.—twenty minutes (and probably less) from Zero.

Linda and Lauren's friends in the elevator were not as thin, and not as lucky. "These people were getting smoked and slowly cooked," Tim reported. While a group of men worked at the elevator, he set off in search of Emergency Medical Service specialists—wondering, at every step, about the warning: "Be prepared to get hit again." He wondered if the next plane might strike the already weakened skyscraper hard enough to bring it crashing down instantly upon survivors and rescuers. And then he discovered that he might soon die even without a third impact: "I stepped out the doors, onto Liberty Street. There were things crashing all around. Deadly things. Pieces of burning furniture. Sheets of glass. People."

Corroborating the observations of Paul Mallery's 10 House rescue team (across the street from Tim's position, in direct line of sight with 4 Truck), Tim noted that near the end, probably as the upper floors began to tilt and slip and to crack open, people were indeed swarming out of windows above the fire. One of them had fallen upon Dan Suhr of Engine 216, killing him in an instant. Looking to his left, Tim saw 4 Truck parked on the sidewalk, just east of the Liberty Street entrance. Its driver, Michael Lynch, was struggling with a Hurst tool—trying to free the "jaws of life" from the rig, so he could pry open the doors of the crushed elevator, and free Linda's friends. He was having difficulty with the heavy, motor end of the tool, so he called to Tim for help. Tim started running toward the rig, but another man beat him to it, and saved his life.

"Never mind," Michael called out. "We've got it."

Considering the danger that was raining down and exploding all around them, Tim would recall later that the exchange was extraordinarily calm and confident. The men had known, on first viewing of the inferno, what they were stepping into. When Tim met his friend Terry Hatton, from Rescue 1, they had hugged, and kissed on the cheek, and Terry had said, "I love you, brother. It might be the last time I see you."

The last time Tim saw Michael Lynch, the driver was towing his Hurst tool into the lobby with two other firemen. Tim then sprinted west along Liberty Street, as fast as he could, to the shelter of the pedestrian bridge at West and Liberty, in search of an EMS crew. There, he began assembling a team, to return with him to the South Tower lobby and help him to evacuate the growing number of burn victims he had seen gathering there, and falling from exhaustion. He would need fifteen minutes to pull a team in; but time was getting away from him. The clock had, by now, touched 9:50 A.M.

At 9:59:04, the upper thirty floors of the Tower snapped eastward, like the initial side snap of an ax-felled tree. During the first second and a half, its horizontal velocity reached 35 miles (49 kilometers) per hour; but three seconds after that, its vertical velocity was nearing 120 miles (197 kilometers) per hour, quickly exceeding all horizontal momentum, so that the structure seemed simply to implode. Gathering mass and strength as it compressed earthward, the precursor wave passed through the Ladder 4 crew in a chip of time measurable only in hundredths of seconds. The rescuers might have heard its approach, but they had ceased to exist before their nerve endings could begin to feel the wave, much less to actually transmit any sensations from it. An alarming roar, a burst of pressurized air, a surge of adrenaline—and, then, instantaneous nonexistence.

Outside, 4 Truck was swallowed by the collapse column. It came to rest five stories below its starting point: on the B5 level of the South Tower parking lot. On December 17, 2001, excavators reached the flattened wreck of 4 Truck. A few paces west of the wreck, hundreds of unbroken wine bottles survived intact and in clusters. Dozens of yards east of the wreck, hundreds of still-folded blue jeans from the Structure store also survived intact and in clusters; but the base surge had scattered the clothing store's warehouse more severely than the South Tower's wine cellar—had scattered the jeans as far east as Church Street, in patterns perfectly consistent with downblast and surge. Though the direction of scatter clearly began east of and continued *away* from the wreck, the curiously ordered nature of some of the clothing—still folded and tagged and sometimes still stacked—led to puzzlement among some observers. To a few, it did not seem possible that order could occur in the midst of total chaos, without the meddling of human hands. Puzzlement led, evidently, to embellishment. And embellishment led, months later, to a firsthand eyewitness participant's account—at once strange and cruel—professing that the cab of 4 Truck, when it was opened by excavators, was *"filled* with dozens" of those "tagged, folded, and stacked" jeans.

As it turned out, the grave of 4 Truck (as a result of lying within what became the nearest thing to an orderly archaeological transect through the crater) was filmed and photographed throughout the three days of its exhumation. The FEMA (Federal Emergency Management Agency) video made two facts clear: First, the "firsthand participant journalist" who "saw" the jeans in the cab was never present in the first place (an absence later, and reluctantly, acknowledged by the "looting event's" sole eyewitness of record). Second, there were no jeans in 4 Truck's cab.

FEMA cameraman/archivist Patrick Drury noted that when he was brought to the southeast corner of the site, at about 3:00 A.M. on December 17, the firemen were hoping that the driver, Michael Lynch, had returned to or stayed with 4 Truck, and that they would recover his body from the cab: "I stood in the rain and the Trade Center muck with the firemen," Drury reported, "and we all looked on as a few of their own dug with their hands and small tools in order to get into the truck's cab." All that remained were a few shreds of spare bunker gear (a fireman's usual jacket, pants, boots . . .). "A glove was pulled out and then a few scraps of cloth that looked as if they might have once been a pair of pants or a jacket. Shortly thereafter a fireman on the other side of the cab popped his head up over the vehicle and said that there were no remains to be found. The mood was very somber and I could feel the strain on the men around me." Later, when the hoax began circulating in the press, Drury found it impossible to believe that someone had reported seeing the cab of 4 Truck stuffed to the gills with stolen jeans. "If this had been the case," he said, "I would have had one of the biggest stories to come out of the World Trade Center since its destruction." Drury added, "There is to be no bias or censoring of what I shoot. If there had been Gap jeans in the cab of Ladder 4 and all around it as it laid six stories below street level I would have gladly shot them."

In April of 2002, the helmets and boots of Ladder 4 team—Michael Brennan, Mike Haub, Michael Lynch, Dan O'Callaghan, Sam Oitice, John Tipping II, and Frank Callahan—were unearthed near a South Tower elevator bank, along with the Hurst tool that they had been using to free the people trapped inside, up to that final split second of life.[3]

Surviving firefighters and Port Authority police officers reported that there was no shortage of heroic efforts that day—especially after the collapse of the South Tower, when the fall of the North Tower became inevitable and imminent. In the ground-level concourse of the

---

[3] As the summer of 2003 approached, I was headed out to sea again, to a live deep-ocean volcanic zone where animals entirely new to science were beginning to offer up the possibility of new antibiotics that also worked against cancer. I took with me, to the bottom of the sea, the patch of Ladder 4 crew (to be returned to the firehouse, with my dive patch, at the end of the voyage). Out at sea, I had a sudden recurrence of what had become known as "the WTC cough," severe enough to cause ripped abdominal muscles and minor abdominal bleeding. The ship's surgeon cleared me (just barely) for a deep-ocean submersible dive—what we all understood might be the last clearance of my career. It was a memorial dive, dedicated to the wrongly maligned crew of Ladder 4. A month earlier, on the day I picked up the patch at the firehouse, a stranger had walked by and shouted through the engine bay doors, "Scum!" I watched one of the Ladder 4 replacement crew, a United States Marine, choke momentarily with tears. The cloth patch he handed me was stitched with words that highlighted the firehouse's location in Midtown's theater district. On September 11, those words had become a prophetic motto, and they work equally as epitaph: "Pride of Midtown. Never missed a performance."

North Tower, the rescuers had no trouble calling civilian volunteers out of the stream of evacuees to carry the injured to safety, sometimes on makeshift stretchers made from broken panels. In the main lobby, fire-fighter John Morabito grew suspicious of the number of civilians who so unreservedly followed his orders to evacuate those who had been burned or otherwise rendered unable to move. It occurred to him that the seemingly obedient civilians might simply be dropping the victims on the ground and making a dash for safety as soon as they rounded a corner and were beyond sight. So he followed after them and discovered that, at risk to their own chances of escape, they were carrying on with their assigned missions.

"I was more proud of the civilians than anybody else, that day," Morabito recalled. "They *all* had to get out of there, and they were scared; yet every single one of them was listening to every single direction I was throwing at them. They were helping. They were New York-ers. That's all I can say."

One of the last groups of firefighters and police officers to evacuate alive, down the stairwells of the North Tower, met two civilians running up. The "civvies" were carrying flashlights and walkie-talkies. They identified themselves as building security and announced that they had made contact with people trapped in an office on the sixty-second floor. The security guards acknowledged a warning that the building would soon collapse, but they refused to leave. The last time anyone saw them, they were climbing toward Floor 62. No one knows their names, and no one ever will. The North Tower's security guards suffered 100 percent mortality.

The firefighter who followed, by suspicion, the rescuers he had assigned, spoke often, during the coming year, about the heroism of the civilians. But others corrected him; others pointed out that the Towers, like Gettysburg, were a battlefield, that day.

There were no civilians.

HERCULANEUM WAS THE FAIREST of cities, and beautiful even by twenty-first-century standards. Or so the ruins say. And then one night it was all gone, and an evidence of evil—in the guise of giant demonic faces—was said to have leered out at the dying citizens from within the smoke. Or so Dio Cassius's contemporaries say. And for decades thereafter, for *centuries* thereafter, people tried to make sense of the evil that had descended from the mountaintop. Or so the Christians say.

The civilizations have changed, over the course of two thousand years, but the essential questions have not. The "reason" for senseless evil in the world seems as timeless a mystery now as in the time of Vespasian and Pliny, Justa and James. Two thousand years before Vesuvius, according to biblical scribes, a man named Job probed the mystery with his god directly, and the conclusion he reached, as the scribes told it, was that the universe will not easily yield up answers, or even necessarily make sense.

Doubting Thomas? Again, that's me. If I need to invent a reason (or "use") for our species' dark half, perhaps in a world without night we would take the light for granted, until at last we failed to even notice the day. Many of us live without ever appreciating the goodness in ordinary people all around us—not because we are self-absorbed or ignorant, but because most of us have never seen our neighbors contrasted against, and brought to the fore, by the worst behavior of others.

At Zero, late one night in the early spring of 2002, shortly after the recovery operation had ceased and all the equipment had been temporarily shut down, I stood on the crater rim with a Port Authority police officer and a man who had lost his wife. It was two in the morning and, strangely, there was no traffic out there on the opposite rim, and not a soul was stirring in the pit below. It occurred to me that lower Manhattan had not known such silence as we three were then experiencing—had not known such peace—in probably more than two hundred years, probably not since a deep winter snow in George Washington's time. If a kitten were moving down there, I believe we would have heard her. It was peaceful, even mournfully beautiful, and yet disturbing.

Earlier that evening, fireflies had appeared in the crater, at least a month out of season and miles out of place. Thousands of fireflies. Someone was reminded of a Japanese film about children trying to survive World War II: *Grave of the Fireflies*, he had called it, and said, "Why do fireflies have to die so young?"

I walked away to Saint Paul's that night, and I stayed until sunrise.

THE MAN-MADE COLLAPSE COLUMNS of 2001 crashed to Earth at about 120 miles (197 kilometers) per hour, then surged out radially at approximately this same speed. This is also the approximate velocity at which the Herculaneum Basilica and the buildings clustered around the Roman boathouses were struck by the Vesuvian surge cloud of A.D. 79. Square inch by square inch, the forces exerted were the same. At 120 miles per hour, air, made more massive by dust, is equivalent to (or greater than) a gust of sea-level air at 160 miles (262 kilometers) per hour. This is also equivalent to being struck point-blank by an F3 or greater tornado, or by a category 5 hurricane. In meteorological or storm-chaser slang, such destructive potentials are called "The Hand of God."

The main difference between the Herculaneum surge cloud and the World Trade Center surge clouds was that while wax tablets and other delicate objects survived in the Herculaneum shock cocoons, people could not, because the air outside the cocoons was exceedingly hot. Another difference was that the 120-mile-per-hour surge was exerted over far fewer square miles in New York City than in Herculaneum and Pompeii. A result of these differences was that Vesuvius produced eye-witness accounts only from very far away—from, say, a Plinean vantage point. Partly because the Twin Tower collapse columns, downblasts, and surges were next of kin to room-temperature pyroclastic flows, the Towers sometimes permitted survival at close range. Never before had so many survivors' accounts been made available from so many different places in and around massive gravity currents. In the slang of the scientific journal (the slang of Sigurdsson, Carey, Pellegrino, and the National Science Foundation), the survivors' accounts were "multiple data points transecting the various effects of a phenomenon that has a parallel with volcanic eruption column collapse." At Saint Paul's Chapel, the Reverend Milton Williams had another name for "multiple data points." He urged us never to forget that they were "people."

The reverend was perfectly correct to remind us that this was a hall of souls, and he was right about another thing: His initial impression, when he saw the first collapse column forming, was that it appeared to be a tornado and a major volcanic explosion rolled into a single, evil entity.

"Volcanoes," he thought. "And terror . . ."

The accurate forecasting of terrorist assaults is probably (ever so slightly) easier than predicting exactly when and how a volcanic collapse column will form. As the twenty-first century opened, Mounts Rainier, Vesuvius, and a handful of other volcanoes were known to be "corked and building pressure from below." Rainier and Vesuvius in particular appeared to be building toward Pompeii-class eruptions . . . "in about ten or twenty years, give or take ten or twenty years." Despite the installation of laser measuring devices, which could detect even anthill-sized bulges on mountainsides (and which did occasionally detect new anthills), the science of eruption forecasting was more art than science, and there were bound to be (and already had been, by early 2003) several false alarms.

A half-century earlier, hurricane forecasting had been in a similar embryonic state of development. For most people, the first indication of a storm's approach was a rising tide and strong winds, and by then, of course, it was all so clearly too late. On the East Coast of the United States and in the Gulf of Mexico, hundreds of casualties in a single storm were not unusual. Many of the first, pre–weather satellite predictions of hurricane paths turned out to produce false alarms—which proved fatal when the science and art of weather forecasting merged, and generated the first reliable warnings. Unfortunately, many people, accustomed to inaccurate warnings, did not understand that weather prediction was a constantly evolving skill; and the first accurately predicted hurricane paths killed many, unnecessarily, because they were largely ignored.

The history of the hurricane should not repeat itself at Vesuvius or Rainier, in Naples or Seattle. Evacuation warnings, though at first likely to be inaccurate, should never be disregarded, especially when considered in the context of the strange physics that manifested in virtually every corner of America's Pompeii. The phenomena reported by Manhattan's collapse-column and surge-cloud survivors are fantastical and even, at times, incomprehensible. But the overriding lesson is that the Manhattan collapse columns were directed at a relatively small area, and that the only way one might reasonably expect to survive a "full-grown" volcanic surge cloud is simply to be very far away. As spectacular and obscene as the New York surges were, what people experienced beneath them was but one ten-thousandth of Vesuvius in A.D. 79, and only one ten-thousandth of the forces still lurking beneath Naples and Seattle and waiting to hatch out.

PORT AUTHORITY POLICE OFFICER Aaron Greenstein thought often, during the months and years to come, of the men who chose to stay beneath the surges, in the World Trade Center generator rooms. When he and Robert Vargas descended from Church Street to the concourse level of Number 5 World Trade Center, the second plane had already struck, and the South Tower was already approaching forty-five minutes to "Zero Hour," though still it stood defiantly against the sky, with almost everybody on the streets below ignorant of its destiny. Three and a half thousand million years of life had preceded the first molding of bricks, the first forging of steel. But even against the cyclopean perspective of deep time, what happened there that morning mattered, and would live on . . . for at least a little while . . . Because against time's vastness, only deeds can live forever.

When Greenstein and Vargas reached Building 5's concourse, one story beneath Church Street, the World Trade Center lights still prevailed. The escalators were dead, but all the cafés, jewelry stores, and clothing stores along the underground mall still had full power. A PATH mechanic approached and asked if he could help, and Greenstein asked him if he had the keys to restart the escalators—which had shut down during a recent loss of power. The men below, in the generator room, had pulled the right switches and were feeding power back into the buildings; but the escalators' fail-safe systems required a manual, on-site restart in the event of power loss, or a snared sandal strap, or other interruption. Greenstein directed the mechanic to turn both escalators to the "up" position, so that he could more quickly send the crowds of evacuees and wounded up to street level, and leave the stairwells clear for rescuers coming down.

Officer Vargas headed west along the underground concourse,

thankful that at times such as this, a dozen or more electricians and engineers were staying at their posts, and keeping the lights on. He followed, to its beginnings, a thousand-foot (300-meter) trail leading from the main lobby of the North Tower, northward under 6 World Trade Center, then east under Number 5, and up to Church and Vesey Streets. The reason for this subsurface ant trail, over a fifth of a mile long, was that debris and swarms of people were raining from the upper floors. The glass showers alone were deadly: Patent attorney Paul Hoffman described windows above and around the fires popping fully intact from their frames, every half-second, popping from above like a continuous volley of gunfire. It seemed to him that the rapid-fire glass storm was being caused by heating and shifting of the steel. Hoffman spent a long time ("maybe thirty seconds, maybe a full minute") wondering how the steel could shift so, and still hold the Towers up.

Robert Vargas would be astonished, later, by the strangely irrelevant thoughts that popped into one's mind during moments of incomparable danger. At forty minutes to Zero, he had passed evacuees with singed hair and hideous burns. The emergency sprinkler system had produced ankle-deep ponds along the concourse, and he realized that he was damaging a perfectly new pair of shoes. "I'm ruining my patent leather shoes," he lamented to himself. And his next astonishing thought was, "I'm going to *die* in these shoes."

At thirty minutes to Zero, he passed a commotion in the North Tower lobby. Officer John Perry was on a cell phone, talking with his sister; and another officer named Lucas was trying to block his path to the stairwells. Perry's sister was above the fire, in the offices of Cantor Fitzgerald.

At twenty minutes to Zero, as two other officers threatened to put handcuffs on Perry to keep him from running up to the fires, Vargas exited the Tower lobby and began searching the southern concourse. Somewhere beneath the Golden Globe sculpture, he located stragglers and directed them toward Greenstein's position. He noticed that the lights occasionally flickered; but always the power was restored. Always.

FDNY Battalion Commander Richard Picciotto also noticed that the lights, though strained, always prevailed. Even after the South Tower collapsed and surged, he would recall, the North Tower had lights again after only twenty seconds. He realized that the generator and switch rooms must have been a "real horror show" throughout the attacks. But the men, he knew, were still there.

The World Trade Center was truly a city within New York City, with its own shops, lodgings, electrical company, and police force. A person could commute to the office by subway from New Jersey or the Bronx, shop in the concourse after work, and return home without ever stepping aboveground. There was a whole building, 60 feet under, that most people never even knew existed: a housing for turbines and cooling systems, two stories tall and more than 400 feet (120 meters) wide.

Officially, the city within the city was being abandoned; but engineer Frank DeMartini and his team remained behind, commanding the lightning, as it were, and keeping alive the engineer's tradition of never leaving the machines, until or unless their machines left them. According to Port Authority estimates, fifty-eight thousand people were inside the WTC complex when the first plane struck. More than fifty-four thousand people who were below the fires—a population comparable to that of Pompeii and Herculaneum combined, then multiplied by two—were able to safely evacuate, due in part to the stubborn persistence of the lights and power grids. Robert Vargas would never forget how, on a day when monsters took wing—mad with the intoxication of spite—the men behind the grid also existed, on that same day, and outnumbered the monsters. He would always remember DeMartini's team, who perished, every one of them, in the collapse columns.

At about thirty seconds to Zero, Vargas came to the revolving doors at the southern boundary of the concourse. He was looking through the lobby of the South Tower, past firefighters and other rescuers, to Liberty Street. He was able to see right through the glass-enclosed lobby to the Banker's Trust Building, across the road. And he was, at that moment, located on the northeastern side of the South Tower. He was standing literally on the edge of the Tower, and of all those standing on or in the Tower's footprint, he was about to enter history, as the sole survivor.

Less than five minutes earlier, Ladder 24/Engine 1's Lieutenant Blake McLouglin had walked into the Marriott Hotel restaurant, approximately 150 feet (45 meters) from Vargas and the South Tower, whereupon the newly arriving teams were directed to the Tower lobby. Some of the men walked into the concourse, toward Vargas's position; but the lieutenant was suddenly overcome by a certainty that he had somehow seen this awful morning before, and that he would not be returning from the Tower alive. He asked for a minute to himself, and some of his men lingered nearby while he called his wife from the restaurant to say, "I love you," one last time. This happened about twenty seconds to Zero. Lieutenant McLouglin was still on the phone with his wife, twenty seconds later.

A man running onto West Street in flames. That is what put Ladder 10's John Morabito 300 feet (90 meters) north of Robert Vargas. He had stopped the truck in front of the Marriott's north end, and had seen that the man, whose clothes were mostly burned off, was carried safely to an ambulance; and this became the random event that sent the rest of the team ahead of Morabito, and put him at the east end of the North Tower's lobby, where he was directing a steadily diminishing stream of evacuees into the concourse and toward Greenstein's position in Building 5 when, all too near in the south, the sky opened.

At a staging area near the North Bridge, approximately 750 feet (225 meters) from the core of the South Tower collapse column, Pat Cullen saw the top of the building yawn open along a huge, horizontal line. As the chasm widened, his first impression was that more than thirty floors were being hoisted gently into the heavens—as if the entire top of the South Tower were lifting away from him—and then he realized that it was only the west face lifting away, that he was really watching the entire top canting east, toward Long Island. Then, more quickly than it had opened, the chasm closed, swallowing a score of stories and ejecting them instantly as mountains of seemingly liquid skyscraper; and the air was split by a sound that Cullen believed would have credited Dante's hell itself.

To Fire Commissioner Thomas von Essen, watching from a vantage point 700 feet (210 meters) north of Pat Cullen's position, 1,200 feet (360 meters) from Robert Vargas, it really was the sound of Dante's *Inferno*. He was both surprised and captivated by how much it reminded him of the video footage he had seen of Mount Saint Helens exploding.

At moment Zero, Commander Picciotto was standing outside an elevator bank on the North Tower's thirty-fifth floor, some 400 feet (120 meters) from the center of the South Tower's collapse column. For him, it started as a rumble from somewhere above and far away yet at the same time near enough to vibrate the walls and floor. He felt for a moment as if this were really just a scene in a Stephen King horror novel, rather than a horror he was living for real. For long seconds the lights stayed on, but no one near him dared move. They just stood in the hallway, looking up toward the ceiling, trying to understand whence the sound came and what it might mean. Picciotto envisioned a rock-slide, gathering force and gaining speed—still hundreds of feet above him but coming down fast—"like a thousand stampeding beasts, a thousand inconceivable terrors, and then a thousand more. Hell! Make it ten thousand and still that wouldn't have covered it, that's how impossibly loud it was!" A new picture flashed into his mind, completely formed, of the building in which he stood collapsing toward him from above. He braced for instant death, and it would occur to him in later years that thoughts were being flashed up from his subconscious fully gestated and crystal-clear, landing one on top of the other and all at once: "It's amazing, the things you think about when there's no time to think." And as the sound passed through him—passed, actually, through his body—what he believed would become his last vivid recollection, in a barely begun near-death life review, was the freshly toasted and buttered bagel he had left on the kitchen countertop, back at the firehouse.

At 9:59:11 A.M., three seconds before the collapse column reached Robert Vargas and Blake McLouglin, its air shock passed through Commander Picciotto. Slightly more than a half-second before that it had passed with equal ease through Pat Brown's team on Floor 44. And now, seven seconds into Zero, it continued on its path, becoming rapidly more distant, roaring down to the plaza below, then six stories deeper into the earth itself. "And the strangest, most unsettling part," according to Picciotto, "was [that] we couldn't see a thing to correspond to the ridiculously loud noise." It seemed to him that the closer you were to the throat of the eruption, the less you knew about what was happening. But across the river in Jersey City, and on television screens a thousand miles away, your relatives and your friends saw, too clearly, what you were hearing.

Sergeant Vargas thought, at first, that he was hearing the explosion of a generator. But it kept growing louder, and nearer. (Another plane?) He stepped back from the revolving doors, still looking across the South Tower lobby, and across Liberty Street to the Bankers Trust building— just looking, during the seven seconds the source of the noise took to descend to Picciotto's level, just thirty-five floors (and three seconds) above Vargas's head. Before him, in the South Tower lobby, most of the rescuers had stopped what they were doing, and were looking at the ceiling.

At 9:59:11 A.M., Vargas turned away from the lobby and looked to his right: down the long, shop-lined corridor that ran westward along the northern border of the South Tower, to the Marriott Hotel. He saw a team of firemen walking toward him, from the direction of a con-course ice cream shop and the Marriott restaurants—where, more than 150 feet away, Lieutenant McLouglin was on the phone, saying good-bye to his wife.

Nearly two thousand years earlier, from a perspective far safer, Pliny the Younger had described the behavior of dust-heavy air—collapsing to the ground under its own mass, then spreading over the earth explosively.

During the three seconds the collapse column needed to descend from Floor 35 to the concourse level, the firemen continued walking toward Vargas. One or two of them might have glanced up, but they did not break into a run. Sometime within that three-second interval, Vargas felt the air pressure ratcheted up so quickly that the precursor struck him like a blast from a rocket engine. So sudden was the wind from above that the firemen did not have time to look back, or to duck for cover, before the "tidal wave" appeared behind them.

Vargas did not know this, but he was about to be shock-cocooned, and he would live to provide history's first detailed account of a means (one, probably, out of many possible means) by which such miracles form. In his immediate vicinity, a dozen floors were being compressed, within the space of a single second, to a horizon of dust no thicker than an average man's height. Within this horizon, the oak from which an executive's desk was carved scattered northward as something less than individual wood fibers, sometimes less than individual cells. On average, the forces acting within the collapse column exceeded the peak pressure exerted against a space shuttle's hull, burrowing through hypersonic air.

Here and there within the collapse column, those pressures soared above 3 tons per square inch, peaking as high as 9 tons, or even 10. Objects manufactured to receive abuse—someone's golf ball, the barrel of a policeman's gun, the sole of a shoe, an artificial ball joint, half of a stapler, Ladder 4's Hurst tool, part of an artificial heart valve—these would turn up battered but still recognizable in the compression layer around Vargas's cocoon. And there were coins, too, outside the cocoon—loose change that had been in people's pockets—buckets upon buckets of loose change.

The collapse column, as it reached the South Tower lobby and broke through the concourse roof, was traveling earthward at 120 miles per hour (53 meters per second; 5 meters in a tenth of a second; the height of a man in only one-thirtieth of a second). The human brain makes a complete scan of its surroundings and recharges for the next scan approximately thirty times per second. A result of this is a most remarkable effect in which information originally registered and recorded as wide-screen high-definition snapshots and clips of sound or sensation are stitched together, by the brain, into vivid reconstructions of the world's natural, fluid motion. Vargas's mind, between 9:59:13 and 9:59:14 A.M., was on maximum overdrive, and therefore recharging and firing a little faster than usual.

The "tidal wave," when it appeared behind the firemen, was approximately 80 to 100 feet (24 to 30 meters) west of Vargas's position. It was moving straight down, into the earth, at 176 feet per second. Within the collapse column, every grain of pulverized concrete and every fragment of steel, every golf ball and every dime, trailed a tiny slipstream of air. The camera crews outside were memorializing the cumulative effect of 6 trillion individual slipstreams, as recorded in the paths of hundreds of aluminum sheets (and even steel beams), sprayed outward from the sixtieth and seventieth stories—which abruptly reversed course as the collapse column descended between Picciotto and Vargas, and were suctioned into the downblast, toward Vargas.

Had the hammerhead of air and dust merely stopped at Vargas's level, the downblast would have exploded toward him at the very same speed it was descending. It would have covered the 80-to-100-foot distance in ten to fifteen scans of his brain, in an interval of less than half a second. Certainly there would have been no time for him to turn and run; to say nothing of sightseeing.

But that's not the way it happened.

The "tidal wave," as it approached Vargas, was indeed violent, but nowhere near as deadly as simple mathematical formulae would have predicted. "The only thing I could equate [the cloud] to," Vargas would record later, "is those fast, crashing and foaming waves in Hawaii." And it was moving at almost the same speed as one of those waves, according to Vargas—30 to 40 miles an hour, about one-third the speed of the collapse column, maybe even a little less: "And you look and you see the tidal wave of water coming at you, but it was billowing. You could actually see the billowing. I'm looking and I can actually see the pieces of debris, the cement, and pieces of metal—and it was coming down—and it picked up the firemen. As soon as I saw it coming, it picked them up . . . like rag dolls. And I started running."

Starting about 100 feet (30 meters) from Vargas, and reaching westward to the center of the Marriott Hotel, the collapse column plunged six stories underground. At this time, it took Ladder 4 Truck and everything fore and aft of it on Liberty Street (including the street itself) all the way down to the basement bedrock. The hole in the concourse, beginning almost where Vargas stood, was a roughly circular crater whose farthest fringe cut through the southern boundary of the North Tower's lobby. It spread 250 feet (75 meters) wide and six stories deep, and that was just the north rim of the South Tower collapse column. The downblast that followed the column into the earth, six stories below Vargas, is probably what saved him. The hammerhead took nearly a half-second to reach the basement level, and during that half-second, the downblast trailed it, drawing air behind itself and slowing—literally retarding, from behind—the progress of the cloud that was simultaneously trying to burst away from the center, toward Vargas. The downblast continued pushing, at the same velocity with which it had entered the basement, for another half second, perhaps even a whole second or more, until the underground surge clouds, spreading radially, began to encounter barriers and to recoil, and to produce backfire.

Six stories higher, on the concourse level, Sergeant Vargas was granted a three-second respite.

The corridor down which he fled, during those added seconds, ran eastward from the Marriott, under the north passage of the South Tower, and into Building Number 4. He had advanced only a few steps, when a new picture flashed suddenly into his mind, replacing the tidal-wave analogy. He thought of a shotgun barrel aimed at the east wall—which dead-ended under 4 World Trade Center—and he was an insect located inside the gun barrel, and the firemen coming up behind him were living buckshot. During that last second before the recoil from below accelerated the blast from 40 to 120 miles per hour, Vargas dove into a side corridor pointing north, toward Greenstein and Building Number 5. By a chance of one in billions, as one shock cocoon ceased to exist, he found another.

By his own, perfectly correct description of the physics involved, "The blast was coming up behind me and it was looking for spaces—for open spaces—just to attack. I believe that when I made that left turn [into the corridor], the blast kept going in a straight line [east] . . . so, it basically shot right past me. It was coming out [from the collapse column] so fast that it couldn't just make that left turn, so I believe it came down that east corridor, hit that back wall, bounced back westward—hit a dead end, built up pressure, and then fire-hosed me north."

Vargas had run only 5 or 6 feet (1.5 to 1.8 meters) into the north corridor when the blast bounced off the east wall. Less than a third of a second after he turned north, the cloud struck him from behind, turned his world black, pitched him on his stomach, and dragged him along the floor at (he believed) 40 or 50 miles an hour (up to 22 meters per second). The sergeant felt as if, all around him, the air literally flowed liquid: "It was like being wiped out by a wave at the beach and dragged against the sandy bottom, but at a speed that's unbelievable." And during those seconds, he believed that every tenth of a second would be his last—but the surge abated without hammering him headfirst into some immovable object, and after the blast died away to nothing, he began to realize, with a mixture of surprise and joy, that he wasn't dead yet. He shook rubble from his back and stood up, but he couldn't see anything. He suspected that he had been shotgunned 200 feet (60 meters) closer to Aaron Greenstein and Building Number 5; but there was no way of measuring distance, for when he opened his eyes, it was dark—"As if someone threw me in the middle of the Atlantic at three in the morning, during a new moon." His mouth was dry, and he was coughing up something that felt like wads of cotton.

"I'm having a really strange day," he said to the cave; and he dared not ask how it could get any stranger.

Approximately 500 feet (150 meters) north of Vargas's landing spot, on the concourse level of 5 World Trade Center, Aaron Greenstein had just gotten a gnat's-eye view of an air bag's interior. The easternmost out-splash from the South Tower's collapse column spread out 600 feet (180 meters) and fell vertically upon the southwest half of Number 5, some two or three seconds ahead of the blast that propelled Vargas toward Greenstein. (Indeed, it was probably the slightly earlier Greenstein shock wave, racing south toward northbound Vargas—racing toward Vargas from the world's largest air bag—that met and overpowered the northward wave front, stopped Vargas from being propelled any further, and saved his life. Vargas would record later that, near the point where he stopped, even storefront windows had ceased to break, though in every other direction, the concourse looked as if it had been swept by a tsunami.)

During the moment Number 5 became Saint Paul's air bag, Aaron Greenstein was standing at the bottom of the escalator, directing evacuees up to Church Street. The lights flickered, the escalator stopped, and a woman, glancing south over Greenstein's shoulder, screamed. An instant later the cloud struck him from behind and the woman screamed again, more loudly. The leading edge struck him "like a fluffy avalanche, or wave," not quite strong enough to knock him down.

Two seconds later it felt like a heavy, driving snow; but it was *hot*, and thick, and Greenstein discovered that it was almost impossible to breathe. He thought later that he had managed not to be thrown by the cloud because a wall had intervened, and placed him in a relatively calm eddy; but his gun, when he took it apart the next day, would tell another story: "The only part of the gun that the holster exposed to the cloud was the handle. And yet the air pressure, entering from behind, was so great that it forced concrete dust through the magazine into all the inner workings of the gun, fully encasing all twenty-six pieces."

Greenstein thought that being underground, and more than a city block away, should have been the safest of places during the formation of a collapse column, but the damage to his gun would become a tangible and chilling reminder of the forces he had survived that day.

Approximately 250 feet (75 meters) west of Vargas's starting point, the collapse column had taken the entire center of the Marriott Hotel into the basement. The missing pieces looked as if they had simply been sliced away, as cleanly as one might slice a sausage with a knife. Inside the Marriott restaurant, another shock cocoon had formed, more resilient than the Vargas cocoon. The same premonition of impending death that had compelled Lieutenant Blake McLouglin to make a last-minute phone call to his wife had placed Blake and the men who stayed with him inside the Marriott cocoon. Their corner of the restaurant was completely unharmed. Napkins still lay undisturbed on the nearest tables, beside glasses of water that had neither broken nor spilled. "Uh-huh," Blake said, still holding the phone. "This is different."

"Different" and yet eerily like the shock cocoon that had preserved plates of eggs, fruit, and honey-sweetened cake—still set out on a table-cloth for a family lunch that had been waiting for 1,922 years in Hercula-neum's "House of the Relief of Telephus."

At 9:59:11, three seconds before Vargas made his acquaintance with the collapse column, Battalion 21's Tom Vallebuona was standing near a vertical support beam, under the Liberty Street side of the South Bridge, some 450 feet (135 meters) southwest of the collapse column's core. For seven long seconds, the column had held him spellbound: "It spreads out like a fountain—resembling somewhat those giant Grucci fireworks fountains. And I think for a moment of how beautiful it looks. I actually stop to stare, thinking, 'Boy! That really looks pretty!' And in [that] instant I think I really must be at the firehouse sleeping. It's like I'm dreaming it, or watching it happen to somebody else. And then I under-stand that this is really happening to me and that I'm not in the firehouse dreaming this whole thing up—and *damn* I'm really close to this thing. RUN! And then, of course, I can't. It hits fast. And it's hot. I see a weird glow near me, and then it's gone—a fireball in the cloud came close, then shot away, and the wind stops and I'm crawling around in the black—at least 50 feet from where I started. I was picked up by the cloud. Thrown. Thrown south."

And for all of this, Vallebuona was in a shock cocoon. The vertical beam parted the wave to either side of him, much as the prow of a speedboat throws water off to port and starboard. Vallebuona and a half dozen other people in the shadow of the beam were buffeted but survived almost as well as water-skiers behind the wake of a boat. Those standing just a few steps to the right or left of the South Bridge shadow shield were blown 200 feet south of Vallebuona's position and were, with few exceptions, killed instantly. Some of them exhibited de-gloving injuries, in which the skin was turned inside out and pulled from their hands, as one might remove a rubber glove. De-gloving requires such extreme force that most physicians and coroners have never seen such injuries, outside of F4 tornadoes, or the Hiroshima and Nagasaki archives.

Vargas, McLouglin, and Vallebuona were spared much by shock cocoons. Ladder 10's John Morabito was not. When the first collapse column began to form at 9:59:04 A.M., he was standing 375 feet (113 meters) north of its center, on the east side of the North Tower's concourse level. He was, at that moment, sending people through the lobby's revolving doors, into the concourse and toward what was about to become Greenstein's air bag. The North Tower had always been a fascination to Morabito: wider than a cathedral, with open spaces reaching six stories high. In those final seconds before the sky opened, he noticed people milling about on the mezzanine level above. They actually appeared to be posing for pictures, as if either completely oblivious to the possibility of danger, or hoping to become finalists for next season's "Darwin Awards."

"Let's go!" he hollered, waving for attention. "Let's go! We gotta get out of here! Move your a—" And then Morabito's world went turtle. He swore that it had to be a new phase in the attack: A nuclear explosion. Something like that. Something huge. From the south, through the six-story windows, a shadow came out of the sky, like a world-engulfing Niagara—its water, black. Glutted with debris, the waterfall struck Earth and appeared to bore right through it, for a half-second or so, perhaps more; and then it ceased to fall vertical and swelled out horizontal—and all Morabito could sense was its speed, and its expanding dimensions—and then there were beams—giant networks of steel beams flying intact through the south wall—like missiles—And the fireman saw a woman on the other side of the revolving glass door—trying to run to him—She leapt toward the doorway but she never made it through—Morabito watched a beam slide across the concourse floor and smash her against the north wall—And the lights snapped out, and the cloud struck him— Twenty feet, maybe only fifteen, he was thrown, until he pitched up against a mound of steel and marble—The wind continued to push from the south, pinning him against the mound—And the missiles continued to crash through—He could hear steel beams impacting nearby . . . The wind stopped after ten seconds, maybe fifteen, according to Morabito's maximum overdrive accounting of time, and when the first light filtered through, he found it impossible to believe that he was still alive.

One hundred fifty feet (45 meters) northwest of Morabito's position, on the opposite side of the North Tower's elevator banks, firefighter Pete Hayden was also lifted up and thrown by the surge cloud. But when the debris came around the central elevator and stairwell core, he was shadow-shielded and did not get Morabito's full CinemaScope experience of downblast and base surge. "There was a great blast of hot air," he would recall. "*Hot* air. And then it quickly subsided. We were very lucky to be alive."

Outside, on West Street, at a radius 800 feet (240 meters) northwest of the collapse column's core, the surge cloud reached Pat Cullen and blew him more than 100 feet (30 meters) northwest, into the parking garage under 2 World Financial Center. He traveled on his back, actually on a cushion of dust-laden air. He said it felt like the surf at Coney Island, except that this was much faster; and it occurred to him later that if he had known in advance that he was going to survive the ride, he might even have called it "fun."

About 50 feet north of Cullen's landing point, NYPD Captain Sean Crawley characterized the South Tower surge cloud as anything but "fun." At 9:59:09, five seconds into the collapse column's formation, he ducked behind a pillar, under the west side of the North Bridge. When they first arrived at the site, Sean Crawley and Ed Aswad had parked their cars at the pillar's south side—"So we had the pillar for protection," Crawley would record. "And the cars were protecting the pillar (sort of). So we had a reasonably safe view, behind a shield, and from a sixth of a mile [a quarter-kilometer] away."

During the next seven seconds, the collapse column struck West Street and bounced forth as a surge cloud. What happened next reminded Officer Crawley of scenes from two movies: *Twister* and *Independence Day*. "We actually saw cars flying through the air. The computer animators out in Hollywood really got it right, before we saw it all flying at us for real."

Crawley thought he also saw steel "I-beams" flying toward him; but the Tower's exterior beams were squared, and only the aluminum cladding resembled an *I*. The beams, according to Crawley, "were coming at us end over end like toothpicks. We saw air-conditioning ducts. We saw parts of buildings and papers and debris, all in a dust ball and coming at us. [Then, ahead of the cloud], I saw a man pitched to the ground." He was running in the street and at first Crawley thought the man was simply diving and sliding toward him—"like he was sliding into second base"—but the man slid over 50 or 60 feet of concrete (some 18 meters), indicating to Crawley that some sort of clear-air precursor wave was at work—something like a boundary layer of turbulent air, just ahead of the cloud itself.

Before the sliding man reached him, "a couple of other cops and two firemen made it behind the car and the pillars. One wasn't covered totally [in the shadow of the pillar], and he was cut practically in half by a piece of cloud-propelled debris."

After the cloud had passed, another movie scene bubbled up from Sean Crawley's subconscious: the opening sequence of a postapocalyptic landscape in the first *Terminator* film. It looked exactly like that fictional future, except that he could not see as far through the dust, and except for the bodies. Mercifully, the dust had softened the features of death. The de-gloved and the mangled looked indistinguishable from heaps of dust-covered insulation, until Crawley noticed faces in the insulation.

No, *Terminator* did not capture this, did not hint at the silence of apocalypse. The fog of dust muffled every sound, like a thick midwinter snowstorm. Stumbling through the fog, searching for survivors, Captain Crawley saw a portrait looming ahead, and he smiled, grimly. It was the sort of thing only Salvador Dalí would have dropped onto this landscape: a movie poster of Arnold Schwarzenegger. This time, the action hero was wearing a fireman's uniform. A caption on the poster read:

"His family was killed by terrorists. Now it's time for revenge." The title of the film was *Collateral Damage*. The patent attorney who walked up behind Crawley also had to restrain an ironic grin. Somewhere far off to their left, the dust was not quite thick enough to muffle, totally, the steady thud of people who had only ninety minutes earlier been discussing the next season of *Survivor* over coffee and doughnuts, and who now were deciding between burning to death or jumping. Eastward, there was the steady thud-thud-thud of collateral damage from the North Tower (correction, the attorney thought: Those poor souls raining from above are direct, *targeted* damage)—and just ahead, out of the mists, had come this giant sand-blasted portrait: Arnold Schwarzenegger glaring out from a world in firestorm and dust, as if he could somehow save humanity from this real-life *Terminator* landscape. The universe did not seem to have many more ironies to throw at New York that day. Officer Crawley and the attorney just had to agree with Voltaire: God was a comedian playing to an audience that was too afraid to laugh.

Seen from a quarter-mile up, from the Harbor Unit Scuba and Air Sea Rescue helicopter, the South Tower surge cloud had shed most of its velocity, but now it was more than a mile wide, and still spreading. From above, in sunlight, the top of the cloud was white and deceptively peaceful. "All of lower Manhattan and parts of Brooklyn were covered in a giant, cottonlike dust cloud," Steven Bienkowski would report. He skimmed low over the North Tower, and though more than an hour had passed since the detonation of Flight 11, the people were still falling. His automatic digital cameras recorded a pastry chef from Windows on the World blessing himself with a sign of the cross and then leaping. Simultaneously, a cell-phone caller from inside pleaded for help, reporting that a section of the restaurant floor had given way and that people were burning to death. Eighty percent of the North Tower roof was obscured by smoke, but in the occasional clear spots, the rescue team could see no hints that anyone had made it up the stairwell and into open air. Toward the end, the jumpers appeared to be increasing in numbers, but now that the South Tower cloud had formed, giving the impression that Manhattan herself lay in state in a white shroud, the horror was lessened ever so slightly for Bienkowski's team, because they could no longer see people striking the ground. They simply disappeared, "almost peacefully," into a white cloud.

At 10:10 A.M., Pat Brown radioed a Mayday from the forty-fourth floor. Minutes later, Steven Bienkowski noticed that the top twenty-five floors of the North Tower appeared to be tilting, and he realized with a start that a second collapse column had become inevitable.

TEN MINUTES AHEAD of the Brown Mayday, fireman Errol Anderson, like so many other people, was unable to outpace the first cloud. His experience of its passover had turned out to be less dramatic than Crawley's and Cullen's, but it was no less revealing of collapse-column and surge-cloud behavior. A sixth of a mile due east of the South Tower collapse column, at the same radius that proved lethal to people near Sean Crawley and Pat Cullen, Errol Anderson noticed that the first surge cloud, when it reached him at Broadway and Cortland, was actually "quite gentle," barely qualifying as a momentarily intense wind. It was able to carry paper, bits of gravel, and cottonlike debris. Anderson did not believe it was strong enough even to knock a cat down. Probably, the difference between the Crawley and Anderson experiences was due to the center of 4 World Trade Center absorbing (or air-bagging) most of the South Tower's eastward collapse column. An unmistakable reminder of the forces absorbed by Number 4 was placed in the subway. The collapse column sliced away all but the northernmost 50 feet (15 meters) of the nine-story building and forced it underground. It also launched a piece of steel through Church Street, about 450 feet east of Robert Vargas's position in an arc that must have gone right over his head. Like a bunker-busting missile, it stabbed through the street above the Cortland train station, through a set of subway tracks, and embedded itself in the track bed of the N and R trains.

Beyond Vargas's shock cocoons and the zones of severe surge-cloud destruction witnessed by Vallebuona, Morabito, Cullen, and Crawley, news cameras captured the ominous, "man-eating" cloud. The video archive, like the newsreel footage of the *Hindenburg* crashing to Earth more than six decades earlier, was at once spectacular and hideous, at once strangely beautiful and profane. But the surge cloud put visions of a mere dirigible in flames in the little leagues—and still, what the news cameras caught was only a *dying* surge with its strength all but fractionally spent. The award-winning scenes filmed from Chambers Street, Broadway, and Park Row captured the cloud more than a third of a mile (0.5 kilometer) from its point of origin; and by that time, its mass and force had already been absorbed via multiple air-baggings and deflections by tall buildings. Almost all surviving images caught the cloud too weak to flip an ambulance, propel a beam, or de-glove the cameraman.

The maximum velocity recorded by the cameras was down to the range of 40 miles (66 kilometers) per hour, and generally below 15 miles (25 kilometers) per hour. The Port Authority and New York Police Departments had sent videographers much deeper into the crime scene, and they were within the higher velocities of the death cloud when the South Tower surged; though their bodies were eventually identified, none of their "footage" was ever recovered. It seemed as if there were a Darwinian process at work on film and magnetic tape that morning: survival of the most distant.

At a radius 300 feet (90 meters) southwest of the collapse column's core, just a few steps north of the South Bridge but outside the shadow of the pillar that had shielded Tom Vallebuona, the NYPD's Teri Tobin was blasted 200 feet (60 meters) west by the surge. She survived with only a few broken bones, but something in the cloud had cracked her bullet-resistant helmet in two. Only steps from her starting point, 10 House's Michael Salka was saved by a fireman who had been immobilized by chest pains in the South Tower stairwell, about twenty minutes before the collapse. At moment Zero, Salka had carried the man into an ambulance near the South Bridge, and then the surge struck and flipped the vehicle on its side. Outside the ambulance, fireman Kevin Shea was blasted in a southerly direction, acquiring a retrograde amnesia as he flew—which would render him unable to pinpoint his starting position. Nonetheless, fellow firefighter Joe Falco had been standing near Shea and the ambulance when the blast struck, and he found Shea lying on his back, about 50 feet past the place where a Greek Orthodox church had stood only minutes before. Falco estimated Kevin Shea's flight at 150 feet (45 meters). Falco's own flight had ended 100 feet (30 meters) south of his starting point. He discovered that he had landed inside part of a room from the South Tower. A piece of the building had actually been splashed outside, and Falco ended up inside of it.

On Liberty Street, approximately 375 feet (113 meters) south of the collapse core, fireman Keith Ruby was tossed 100 to 150 feet. The precursor wave performed the life-saving service of clearing the broad glass panes of the Bankers Trust Building from his flight path—which aimed him through the lobby and crashed him into a coffee shop.

Outward and outward . . . The air flowed liquid. Eleven hundred feet (0.33 kilometer) southwest of the South Tower core, the cloud, as it passed, completely obscured the grounds of the Battery Park City Marina with computers, telephones, the contents of file cabinets, shoes, handbags, torn law books, aluminum cladding, and a traffic light. Five hundred feet (150 meters) southeast of the core, cars along Greenwich Street were flung south of O'Hara's restaurant and telescoped under one another. At this same location, the "One Way" sign on the corner of Albany and Greenwich Streets was bent completely around its pole, as one might bend a piece of tinfoil around a pencil.

Eight hundred feet (240 meters) east of the column's core, Liberty Park had been located just barely south of 4 World Trade Center's air-bag shadow. The South Tower's southeast corner therefore had a direct line of fire, down Liberty Street and into the park—where dozens of trees, each standing more than 30 feet tall, were mowed down and uprooted . . . Thirteen hundred feet (390 meters) south along West Street, a stand of trees opposite the Brooklyn Battery Tunnel was split and uprooted, and a sheet metal sign billowed southward like a canvas sail, creating a permanent fossil impression of the wind from the north . . . The surge cloud shotgunned between the buildings of Washington Street in much the same manner as it had fire-hosed Robert Vargas up the north corridor. Steel beams from the south face were propelled 700 feet (210 meters) south to Carlisle Street. The "Washington Canyon" surge traveled undiminished, as if sustained between the prongs of a giant tuning fork . . . Fourteen hundred feet (nearly 0.5 kilometer) from its starting point, it shot into the Brooklyn Battery Tunnel. From the other side, firefighter Keith Young reported that the cloud entered the tunnel with such mass and force that it exited explosively in

Brooklyn, giving rise to an initial report that a powerful "secondary" terrorist bomb had been detonated inside the tunnel.

Nearly a mile northwest of Keith Young's position, fifteen minutes
after Zero, thirteen minutes before the North Tower collapse, Sergeant
Vargas and Lieutenant Blake McLouglin were trying to exit their shock
cocoons. McLouglin's team could not believe the intensity of the
destruction they encountered in every direction, beyond a small radius
in which not even a cup of water had been spilled. Their progress southward along the Marriott-Vista's ground floor was blocked by the steel
frame of the health club's swimming pool—which McLouglin knew was
supposed to be located twenty-one floors overhead. "*This* can't be
good," he told himself. North, east, and west had proved just as impenetrable. Finally, they went *down;* and they were picking their way slowly
underground, toward the North Tower, when someone made radio contact from the outside and urged them to hurry. There was a car in the
basement—a car from the street above—barely recognizable any longer
as a car, because it was scarcely wider than McLouglin's fist.

"How did we survive this?" McLouglin asked. "Jeez! Someone tell
me what the hell happened here."

SHOCK COCOONS WERE always a puzzle. They seemed to accompany
all explosive events. The battleship *Arkansas* was floating only 900 feet
(270 meters) from the 20.3-kiloton Test Baker atomic bomb on July 25,
1946. On the deck, metering devices recorded pressures soaring, during
one part of a second, toward 3 tons per square inch before the machines
ceased transmitting. During the next three seconds, the ship was flipped
over and driven down through 180 feet (54 meters) of water, then
smeared across the seafloor like a stepped-upon insect. Yet here and
there the shock fronts diverged, or were absorbed, or both. Five decades
later, divers found the glass cover for a battle light undamaged on the
inverted ceiling, and the lightbulb inside was also undamaged. Shock
cocoons were like that: capricious and strange. They appeared miraculously in the midst of utter disintegration, where one least expected
them, as if signaling to us, again and again, that sometimes the safest
place to be during an explosion was closest to its center.

AT 10:15 A.M., five minutes after Pat Brown's Mayday, Sergeant Vargas, that day's luckiest man on Earth, had just been rescued from his shock cocoon by a fellow Port Authority police officer named Eddie Finnegan. Vargas's rescuer, who had seen the destruction above, found it difficult to believe that anyone had survived in this corner of the concourse. People a lot farther from the collapse column than Vargas had been crushed or blasted apart. Vargas asked what had happened, and when Finnegan told him, he returned a dazed expression. It was unimaginable that the entire South Tower had disappeared into the earth, just inches from his face. Of course, it had to be true. His senses told him so: Victoria's Secret, Banana Republic, and the Krispy Kreme Doughnut shop were a dark cavern whose floor smelled like a slaughterhouse. He followed Finnegan over a pile of rubble—touching, as he climbed, folded clothing, tinfoil gum wrappers, something sharp and wet—and all the while he prayed that Eddie Finnegan's flashlight would hold out.

Most of the passageways to the surface were hopelessly blocked. The sublevels were a maze even when they had been fully intact and well lighted, but fortunately the World Trade Center was Finnegan's post. He knew the territory. Sweeping his search beam along the ejecta of ruined stores, analyzing the contents and trying to form from the artifacts a picture of who had been selling what, and where, Finnegan navigated a path over and around collapse zones.

The bodies were everywhere, more than Vargas had expected to see. By 10:20 A.M., they were climbing over the buried dead, and the half-buried dead, and finally over the still-moving dead. A man let out a scream, and Vargas screamed back. What he discovered, when Finnegan aimed his light, made no sense. It might actually have been laughable, if it were not so horrible.

They traced the shriek in the night to a wall, and they realized that the shrieker was actually encased in a concrete wall—blasted somehow, into a hollow space inside the World Trade Center foundation. Vargas slapped his hand along the concrete, hoping to find a way to let the man out.

"Help me!" the stranger wailed.

"You'll be okay," Vargas said. "Just hang on. Stay with us." And he continued slapping the wall, but he knew that there was no way of rescuing the man without heavy equipment.

"Bobby, we gotta go," Finnegan said. "There's no time."

Up to this moment, they had been headed north. They were located one story below and several paces east of the Golden Sphere sculpture—which put them within 250 feet (45 meters) of the North Tower's east face.

"What's your hurry?" Vargas demanded.

"We're getting too near that other Tower," came the reply. "You'll understand what I mean, when the other Tower comes down."

Vargas marked the location in his memory, and told the stranger, "Buddy, we'll be back. We're going to get some help. I'll be back."

Minutes later, Finnegan led Vargas onto Vesey Street. And then the North Tower downblasted and Vargas found himself once again trying to outrun a surge cloud. If an Olympic sprinter were running beside him, Vargas imagined that he would have given that Olympian a run for his medal. Yet every step he took, the cloud appeared to be gaining on him by five. Finnegan dodged under an awning, led him indoors; and they watched the surge flow north, depositing dust and paper 6 inches deep at Church and Chambers Streets, a third of a mile (0.5 kilometer) from the North Tower core. And Vargas knew, as he saw the cloud pass, that the man inside the wall was dead.

FIREFIGHTER KEITH RUBY had come back to consciousness amid squashed doughnuts and the scent of coffee, nearly 150 feet south of his starting point on Liberty Street.

Paul Mallery and Sean O'Malley, as they tended to Ruby's broken femur in the Bankers Trust coffee shop, guessed that the one-story wall of debris outside had acted, in combination with the new canyon on Liberty Street (which plunged to a depth beyond what O'Malley had been able to see from its edge), as a new kind of dam. At a radius of 900 feet, the second surge cloud arrived as a hair-ruffling wind and a wall of darkness. At approximately this same radius, on West Street, Tom Vallebuona thought that the blast from the second surge was worse than the first, even though the North Tower was much farther away. This time he was not cocooned behind a pillar. And this time, he observed, the wind appeared to gain strength from the dust it was picking up from the first collapse. This time, he turned and ran—and the cloud slapped him in the back and pitched him to the ground; and he thought, "Didn't I just go through this already?"

At a radius 500 feet beyond Vallebuona and O'Malley (420 meters south of the core at Rector and Greenwich Streets), an artist from the Perillo complex looked back to see the North Tower surge cloud confined between buildings and shotgunning toward him: "We saw people being knocked over. On television, [the surge] looked like a cloud of smoke. But it was [computer] monitors and desks and chairs, flying through the air—and pieces of metal."

At a radius of 1,000 feet (300 meters) east of the North Tower core, on Vesey Street, a PAPD rescuer ducked inside his car as the second cloud approached, and he felt the air itself lift the police car's wheels off the ground and implode its windows. A set of steel columns from the North Tower's outer "basket" landed less than 70 feet (21 meters) away, in the intersection of Church and Vesey Streets.

Blake McLouglin's team, saved by a premonition and a phone call, had just emerged onto West Street, at a radius 400 to 500 feet (120 to 150 meters) south, when the North Tower core imploded. The top twenty-five stories accelerated rapidly during the first three seconds: What sounded, at the start, like the individual slam of floor upon floor, clapped faster and faster to upward of ten slaps per second, until each slap blended *undetectably* in the collapse column din. McLouglin and his men began to sprint south as fast as Vargas and his imagined Olympian; but mere muscle and bone could not carry them away fast enough. "Blake's Seven" survived the surge, "by miracle, again," but they saw other firemen, including some who had moved in from safe distances to rescue them from the Marriott. They saw them uplifted by the cloud, never to be seen alive again.

Firefighter John Morabito and Detective Roger Parrino were trapped within this same lethal radius, but they dove, instinctively, to the southeast curb of West and Vesey Streets—where the entire center of 6 World Trade Center air-bagged the North Tower surge, and spared them. In the seconds before the North Tower fell, Morabito had watched the top of the structure shift and bend toward the northwest—had seen it actually bending down toward him—with the huge white antenna standing, amazingly, still in place.

"And then," he recalled, "I started running. I heard the rumble and I just saw it going in on itself. And then I dove to the curb and just laid down." Parrino and at least three other survivors dove in beside him.

What Parrino saw, during the first three seconds of collapse, were huge sheets of flame kicking out directly overhead, then bellying down toward him, with the top of the Tower no longer visible. He understood, at that moment, that he was just one of many people, that day, to be getting the duck's-eye view of a shotgun blast. Like most of the others, he expected nothing but death. More than twenty floors had landed on the fire, then kicked it outdoors. Then the fire was sucked back toward the center of the storm, and the black waterfall emerged in its place, and arched toward him. The air blast followed, and Parrino fell to the curb just as Number 6 absorbed a shock measurable on seismographs as far away as Columbia University's Geological Observatory in Lisbon, New Hampshire.

"I've been in hurricanes," Parrino reported, "and that's what it felt like. Big things were flying [past] me. In the Marine Corps, they taught me to put my feet toward the explosion and my head away from the explosion. But I couldn't remember what the Marine Corps told me to do with my hands." At first he covered his genitals, thought about it for a second, then decided that his head contained a more vital organ in need of extra cover. Outside of Number 6's air-bag shadow, yet within sight of Parrino, a car flipped upside down into the air, and fire trucks 400 feet northwest of his position (120 meters away and beyond Parrino's view) were being battered as if tidal-waved or atomic-bombed on their southeast sides. He saw steel beams landing nearby, and he found it funny that, at six feet tall and 240 pounds, he was trying to hide behind a 6-inch curb. And then: "All of a sudden, I felt like I was covered in blankets—twenty blankets, and super soft, and actually basically very comfortable, and warm."

John Morabito nearly choked to death on the blanket of dust. After he cleared his throat and his eyes and regained some composure, he

Shock cocoons of September 11. The first of more than fifty Ground Zero flags was raised on a splinter from the North Tower's antenna. Intact, it had speared the earth near the central plaza's Golden Globe. Beneath this spot, Robert Vargas, two other Port Authority police officers, and a squirrel survived in Herculaneum-style shock cocoons.

located a section of the North Tower's antenna, embedded more than 20 feet in the street, but still standing. It was there that the firemen raised the first of more than four dozen Ground Zero flags (among them a red, white, and blue Russian flag that, always beside an American flag, made many visits to Zero, 10 House, and O'Hara's—and which was given to the crew of *Keldysh* in recognition of their kindness in the aftermath of the attacks).

According to Morabito, the antenna, "just kind of sank straight in at the moment of collapse, and teetered over at the last second." After the first flag raising (or the second, or the third), John Morabito led a team of volunteers into the subways, hoping to find survivors. On his first expedition, he found nobody, dead or alive; but he did find, at the end of a shattered track bed that opened into a cave, indications that while everything near the perimeter of the North Tower had been jetted out, everything near the center had been kept near the center. He had a difficult time believing that within such chaos, he could encounter such order: "The first thing I noticed was that all the little drainage stones that used to be spread over the roof, at the feet of the antenna, were now in the subway. As the Tower opened up, and splashed out over the city, in every direction, the roof went straight into the subway. All of that gravel, rather than being pushed out with the exterior beams, and the glass, and the stacks of papers sitting on windowsills—all of that gravel was blasted straight down. It was underground, and it had been on the roof."

The one absolute in a Pompeiian event, whether at the foot of the North Tower or on the foothills of Vesuvius, is that gravel in the basement will be the least of nature's astonishments.

FDNY battalion commander Richard Picciotto and fifteen other people survived several stories above John Morabito's gravel bed, in the North Tower shock cocoon known as Stairwell B. They were cocooned, quite literally, in the very core of the collapse column. The last two Ground Zero survivors were likewise found in the North Tower cocoon.

Genelle Guzman was a Port Authority worker from New Jersey. Descending Stairwell B with a dozen other would-be evacuees, she was nine stories above Picciotto, on Floor 13, when she heard what came to her as the sound of cannon shots coming closer, building quickly to tornado-like gusts inside the stairwell. Guzman held on to a rail—held on with a death grip until everything started falling—"crumbling faster and heavier." If anyone could match Robert Vargas's luck that day, it was Genelle Guzman. Possibly, the precise angle of a steel girder or a spur of concrete is what created the shock cocoon, only a few stories above Guzman's head. But as the offices of Marsh and McLennan and the two decks of Windows on the World passed Guzman, her portion of the cocoon did not hold. It broke away with her in it, and she somehow dropped seven stories in a remnant of the well—which shattered on a bed of rubble six stories above street level.

Even in the best of free-fall conditions (if such as "best" exists), 50 percent of the population will be killed by a fall of three stories and 99 percent by a fall of seven stories (with only 2 percent of the survivors living more than two hours). The men and women in the stairwell with Guzman had disappeared, and she found herself pinned between two concrete pillars, under the steel frame of the stairs. On the afternoon of September 12, twenty-seven hours after she went underground, a fireman found her.[4]

Genelle Guzman survived with surprisingly minor injuries; she married later that year, and saw her thirtieth birthday. The last survivor was located about the time of Guzman's birthday, but he was of less certain age, and he was named Scrat. Twelve stories below Guzman's sixth-floor landing spot, in John Morabito's subway gravel field, a recovery worker named David Scott (a marine who worked for building security at Battery Park City) discovered a squirrel whose entire coat was singed and whose tail and ears were badly burned. The animal was understandably

---

[4] If any Tower One survivor was luckier than Genelle Guzman, that day, it was Port Authority engineer Pasquale Buzzelli, one of Guzman's coworkers from the sixty-fourth floor. He was located somewhere above Guzman in the disintegrating upper layers of the Stairwell B shock cocoon—as many as *nine* floors above Guzman's position, Buzzelli believes, but no one can be sure: "I felt the walls next to me crack and buckle—then free fall, and the walls seemed to separate and move away [from me]." When he regained his bearings, he discovered that he had "kind of surfed the cloud down" and pitched up against the uppermost remnant of the stairwell, "sitting as if in an armchair, feet dangling over the edge." No one has explained the physics that saved him.

frightened, and he ran away from his would-be rescuer every time the marine came near. Scott guessed that the squirrel had come down from the tree-lined gardens around the Golden Sphere—which were, in their day, frequented by birds and squirrels. The largest garden had stood directly above the subway, on the southeast corner of 6 World Trade Center; and it made sense to David Scott that when the first plane struck, the commotion and the falling debris would have sent all the birds flying, and all the squirrels scurrying underground. Most of the squirrels in the Sphere garden—indeed, all but this one—had probably perished.

"His wounds were showing signs of infection—and he was starving to death, too, when I found him," Scott reported. "I left food for him in the tunnel, but he wouldn't let me near, and the heavy equipment was bound to kill him, when the demolition teams came through. After surviving the blast, the fires, and everything coming down—*for him to die there*—NO, I had to get him out."

It was not easy. At one point, twenty recovery workers—most of them Teamsters, marines, members of the National Guard—were giving their every spare moment, on a job that did not produce many spare moments, to rescuing a squirrel. It became a mission for them, a strange diversion in a strange hellscape. In the weeks previous to the discovery of Scrat, the best that any searcher could hope to find in the dust was a filling from a tooth, a fragment of a Band-Aid with DNA, or a clue to the identity of an unknown child. Weeks after Genelle Guzman left the hospital and the last hope of finding a soul alive had faded, David Scott found someone (or something) that everyone in the crater could root for, and even pray for. He was only a squirrel, and in the eyes of many he wasn't much; but he was all they had, and he was enough.

For two months, Scrat outran and outsmarted his rescuers (who by then included hundreds of recovery workers who were keeping the heavy equipment in stand-off mode, away from Building Number 6). Finally, in the late winter of 2002, David Scott surfaced with a Hava-hart trap, and little Scrat inside.

"I set him free near the marina in Battery Park City," Scott recalls. "I watched his hair grow back during the spring. I see him now and then. He has a new family, and he's doing well."

TIME will have its say . . .

One of the brightest engineer-scientists I know anywhere on the planet also knows how to make a good movie now and then. My friend once said that for all their power as metaphor and parable, such cataclysms as Thera, Pompeii, and the *Titanic* were ultimately the story of human beings, some of whom have been forgotten even in name.

"Forensic precision can yield only a certain kind of truth," my friend had said, "because archaeology is about people—what they built, how they lived and died, their hopes and dreams and the complex pageantry of their lives."

I thought I understood, after reading Justa's documents—her hopes and struggles for freedom . . . I thought I understood, after coming to know the last *Titanic* survivors, and hearing their stories, what it must have meant to them. And I did not have a clue. Not a clue. Only in New York, on a dark midsummer afternoon with the wound still fresh in the earth, had I truly begun to understand. And then, of course, I sometimes wished I had not.

Time . . .

My oldest child, Amber, had only recently turned seven when she visited Saint Paul's and the Family Room for the first time, on May 25, 2002. She placed roses beneath the photographs of Cousin Donna, and Pat Brown, and Stephen Jay Gould standing atop his Burgess shales, with his beloved fossil *Pikaia*. On that day, a stranger stood for a very long time before a picture of her brother. After the woman had left, Amber walked over to the picture, studied it, then came back to me and recited the brother's name: "Robert Chin." She said that our family never knew him, and that for this reason we must try to keep his name alive.

You may discover that children are often a lot smarter than grownups, if only you listen to them. Ever since Amber, every time I have gone to Zero, I have brought back with me the name of someone I never knew. By the winter of 2003, a half-dozen other family members were doing the same thing. We do not need church houses of oak and stone or memorials of granite and steel to keep our faith with the dead. No, not if we remember them in our hearts.

Clarities born of atrocity. At 1 Liberty Plaza, one family, among thousands, places roses in New York's hall of souls. In the decade of Vesuvius, the author of the Gnostic Gospel of Thomas tried to teach the world that one does not need memorials of iron and stone, or even a chapel, to keep a faith with the dead. Rather: *Split open a piece of wood, and my name is there. Turn over the stone, and you will find me there.* More than 1,900 years later, a seven-year-old girl who had lost a cousin in the September 11 attacks saw the name of Robert Chin in the Family Room and said that he was not a member of her family, or anyone she had ever known, and that for this reason she would remember his name and keep his memory alive. Ever since, "carrying in our hearts the names of people we did not know" has been a Family Room tradition. After 1,900 years, Thomas the Doubter spoke suddenly more clearly. Children, it seems, are open to clarities against which most adults have hardened their hearts and made themselves immune.

What was it that Thomas the Doubter—in the seventy-seventh paragraph of his (mid-first-century) Nile River Gospel—had quoted Jesus as saying? "Split a piece of wood, and I am there. Lift up the stone, and you will find me there."

As I write, family members and city planners are arguing, loudly and at great length, about the shape that tomorrow's memorials and buildings shall take. But Justa and "Paddy" Brown, William Murdoch and Robert Chin, would probably tell us, if something of them could still speak, that keeping a faith with them is not about architects erecting towers of thought and steel.

(*Split a piece of wood, and I am there . . .*)

The picture in the rosewood frame is all that is left of Harry Ramos, an investment banker and one of the minority of "civilians" who died *below* the North Tower fires. But his friends Michael and Hong keep his memory (or his spirit, call it what you will) alive. Michael says, "If you looked for the definition of the word *mensch* in the dictionary, it would say, 'See Harry Ramos.'" According to his friends, Harry helped his coworkers to evacuate from the eighty-seventh floor. Harry and Hong deliberately lagged behind, making sure everyone else was down the stairs ahead of them. Somewhere around the fortieth floor, they came across a very heavyset and apparently asthmatic man who could descend no farther, and who had crashed to the steps heaving and sobbing. After the roar of the South Tower collapse column passed through them, Harry and Hong were able to stir the heavyset man to further action, but somewhere above the thirtieth floor, he fell again and could not catch his breath. Shortly afterward, a fireman came upon them and shouted that there was not a moment left to spare, that they must get out—NOW! "If this man won't get up," the fireman said, "then you two need to get the hell out of here!"

Hong got scared, after the fireman hurriedly handed them the bottle of water he had been carrying and continued running up the stairs (*up the stairs*) on his mission of warning.

"Come on, Harry," Hong said. "Let's go."

Harry told Hong to go down ahead of him, ordered him down the stairs. "I'll get the man moving," Harry assured him. "Or I'll stay with him just a little while longer."

"How long is a little while?" Hong asked.

"We'll see," Harry replied. "We'll see."

(*Lift up the stone, and you will find me there . . .*)

They found Pamela Chu's wallet perfectly intact in the dust, not very far from the spot where a wall of Egyptian pink granite had actually become the dust. She was thirty-one years old when the North

Tower fell. Her mother had worried about fires in such tall buildings, after Pamela's promotion to Cantor Fitzgerald's North Tower offices; and Pamela had shown her the multiple stairwell exits and the sprinklers, and then reminded her that the building had already survived a 1993 terrorist bombing and proved itself unbreakable. "And if worse should ever come to worst," she had assured her, "helicopters will rescue people from the roof of the Tower."

Pamela had put off marriage and even romance in favor of her career, telling her mother that she was still young, and that there would always be time later. And the question that Pamela teaches me—when I visit the Family Room and look upon photographs of all those hundreds of kind faces staring out from the memorial wall, is that if we possessed a magic wand and we could give those people just one more day in their lives, to choose between being with family and friends or at their jobs, how many of them do you suppose would wish that they could have spent just one more day in the office?

Time . . .

Rome, the House of Mica, the *Valkyrie* Mark III . . . Past, present, future . . . The Chinese say that if you want to create something new, you must learn to love something old . . .

I have seen a photograph of the Ground Zero Cross, when they first found it on the morning of September 12, standing atop the mound of Tower One, above the prisons of Genelle Guzman and Scrat. The whole area was shrouded in thick fumes, and as the firemen approached from the west, the smoke parted in the east and allowed shafts of sunlight to slant down upon the crossbeams, illuminating them bloodred. As the photographer told it, twenty firemen knelt and wept. This, as the Russians told it, was the third September cross. The first two, on the morning of the attacks, were being returned whence they came: to the portion of the *Titanic*'s deck occupied by Boat 8, to the place where John Hume played his violin and helped his fellow bandsmen to calm the crowds on the port side. For some reason, much that happened during that expedition seemed to be leading me to the *Titanic*'s violinist.

On September 29, 2001, as a plane carried me from the forensic archaeology of the *Titanic* toward the forensic archaeology of the World

Trade Center, I penned a letter to Mary and to my "little rodenté" (Read: rug rats, children).

"In the worst of times," I wrote, "I used to view hope as the end of acceptance and the beginning of worry. In the worst of times I used to recall that the most dreaded and most cunning of all the ancient demons let loose from Pandora's box, the last of them, the one Pandora had almost slammed the lid on, was the one who, at first glance, came disguised as an angel. Her name was Hope.

"My children, my Mary—I wrote about the demon Hope in a novel called *Dust* and I was wrong—I hope.

"I found a new view of hope today in the most unexpected of all places—in the cemetery at Halifax, at the grave of a man named John Law Hume (Jock, to his friends). He was one of the *Titanic*'s bandsmen, the violinist, and shortly after the impact he was seen [running along the deck with his precious instrument, where he stumbled against the ship's architect, Thomas Andrews, not caring the least about any minor damage to the violin. It][5] was clear that he knew he would not be needing it for very long. And yet early in that catastrophe—and throughout that night—men like John Hume, carpenter Charles Hutchinson, Thomas Andrews, baker Charles Joughin, and the men who stood by the engines, far below [could be found, on that last night of another old world, in another century]. They were not officers, or hired leaders, but, rather, extraordinarily brave people, amongst the everymen. John Hume was one of them—helping to keep the crowds calm and [to] prevent panic of the sort that had occurred on the *Arctic*—[which was] surely within every sailor's memory: a sinking that had ended [at the last lifeboat] with ax fights on the deck.

"To the left of John Hume's grave [was] a line of [stone] markers numbered 213 . . . 214 . . . 215 . . . just a number and a date ('died April 15, 1912') . . . The unidentified anonymous dead. And my thoughts [were with all of tomorrow's] anonymous markers [for] the unidentified

---

[5] Brackets mark places in my original letter that were made unintelligible by gaps, muddled grammar, and illegible handwriting. Since it is my handwriting, I have taken the liberty of interpreting what I think the author of the letter "meant" to say, and I have bracketed the edits accordingly.

under the Towers today. And then Mike [the robot-designer] Cameron came up behind me, and told me of the photo he'd seen, taken by one of the Tower survivors, [of] firemen running up [the stairs as he was running down]. Mike said [one of the firemen] had an [expression of resolve on his face, an] expression such as men have when they know the road ahead is filled with peril, but they will move ahead anyway, saving whatever they may save. There is no doubt that he, being a fireman, knew that the beams might sag under the incredible temperatures above. But he climbed up, and stayed in the danger anyway.

"Between [the Halifax markers of violinist John] Hume and [ship's carpenter] Hutchinson, there must have been others, amongst those [numbered,] nameless graves, who acted similarly, helping wherever they could, asking nothing for themselves. We'll never know their stories.

"But Hume—to me he came to represent all of them. (Or rather, they came to represent his tradition: the extraordinary amidst the ordinary.) There'll be a monument in Shanksville one day. Hume was there, too—because there is not a doubt in my mind that the [violinist] would have behaved as the men who brought that plane down behaved— Hope sprang up, and cut short the terror. (Look to the helicopter crews, over and around the Towers—who, when news that a third plane might be on the way, and that they should be prepared to stop it in the only way possible, radioed back an expressionless "Affirmative." Look to them as ordinary policemen and cameramen, and John Hume was there, too.)

"It does not matter who is [officially] in charge at the time—the Smiths and the Lightollers, the Bushes and the Cheneys—it's the Humes and the Patrick Browns who come forth in the worst of times, come forth by the scores, seemingly out of the woodwork. There are Lincolns and Washingtons among us today, as we move from the old world into the frightening and the unpredictable. But they're not always in the White House or in charge of the military—they're [more often] sitting right next to us—and not even they, yet, know who they are. But I know they exist and I suspect I might even have just sailed with [some] of them—and such people, because they exist, give me hope that our civilization shall prevail and excel.

"John Hume, Mr. Parr and Mr. Sloan, the men who took back the plane over Shanksville, Mr. Andrews and Mr. Joughin, 'New York's bravest,' William McMaster Murdoch and Mr. Hutchinson, 'New York's finest'—they are hope. They are the future.

"They have always lived amongst us—as far back as civilization goes—from Normandy to [Pliny the Elder] and Cincinnatus. There are more John Humes in the world than there are Saddam Husseins and Bin Ladens. There have to be. There have to be.

"It's very late for me and I've been unable to sleep more than sometimes a couple of hours a night and I'm sure this is muddled and in need of some kind of rewriting, but at least I'm getting the basic idea down.

"Mike [the engineer] came to me at the cemetery, sounding very [bleak about the future. I told him what I have just told you, and he replied that] the guy in the seat next to you could just as likely be the next terrorist—but I, the one they call 'Dr. Doom and Gloom,' refused to believe that the evil ones so outnumber the good. I've got to believe that most people are basically good. I've got to. If not, then there is no hope.

"I'm very tired and the plane is coming near landing. I'll be with you soon for that big hug. Love—your Daddy, your Charlie."

TIME will have its say . . .

The first investigations of downblast and surge at the World Trade Center were, on one level, potentially life saving, and on another level, just another science project. The physics of collapse column, downblast, and ground surge operated in many different processes, ranging from cometary dinosaur-killers to civilization-disrupting volcanoes to the meteorologist's aircraft-downing "microburst-and-down surge," in which a trillion raindrops trailing a trillion slipstreams will suddenly produce collapse columns four or five Twin Tower diameters across, downblasting and surging along the ground seemingly out of nowhere, with hurricane-force winds.

"Just another science project," someone had said. Wasn't that how the *Titanic* expeditions had begun? I should have known better.

It's never just a science project, when you touch the lives of human beings who lived and breathed that science . . . Robert Chin . . . Harry Ramos . . . Pamela Chu . . .

Call it shock, call it what you will. Call it ghosts of the imagination. At Saint Paul's, you began to hear stories. EMS medic James McCloskey said he was excavating in the still-fresh ejecta blanket of the South Tower when he and three other rescue workers discovered a woman who had been caught in the surge. "And as we uncovered her," McCloskey said, "we, all four, noticed—it looked like what a child might use—like glitter. I don't know if it was some kind of gas that had gotten into her, or electricity, or what. Mostly *or what*, I would guess. This glitter, this light—it just came off of the lady. It rose up about four feet into the air and dissipated. And we all looked at each other, the four of us, and we all realized, this lady is in a better place . . ." A patent attorney claimed he saw a figure walk down a hallway in his office and disappear . . . One of Scrat's rescuers said he saw a man walking toward him in a blue suit—a man who seemed to evaporate, suddenly, as he came within arm's length . . . And I met a minister who said the attorney and the rescuers were merely seeing what they imagined they wanted to see, because there was no afterlife and, as far as he knew, no God, either—"Nothing!" His God, he said, went down with all those people, went down with the Towers.

I wondered. Dio Cassius had said that people imagined ghostly apparitions in the smoke of Vesuvius. Pliny the Younger had written, "[S]till more imagined there were no gods left, and that the universe was plunged into eternal darkness forevermore." Wiser men than I have said that the more things change, the more they remain the same.

At Saint Paul's, I met several ministers and a priest who, in the post–9/11 haze, were having crises of faith. And I saw at least one agnostic who was having a crisis of doubt. But most of all I met some of the finest and bravest people I have ever encountered. The John Humes of this world were immediately apparent, in every direction. They've mostly disappeared back into the woodwork, now. And I hear people complain about how New Yorkers are back to leaning on their horns and cursing at each other in traffic.

But perhaps that is as it ought to be: back again to normal. The John Humes will come out again, if they are needed. And it's enough for me to know that they are near us, though we don't always see them there. It's enough for me to know that Pat and Donna and "little Stevie" who loved the dinosaurs, live on in my memories, and that Jack Hume lives everywhere. I'm much more confident, today, that a hundred Septembers from now, our civilization will still be here—still a little territorial and still a little flawed, perhaps, but still good.

(Time . . .)

Not everyone believes electronic civilization shall endure. The philosopher and science fiction writer George Zebrowski points out that we will be the thirteenth major civilization to fall. And he adds that the one thing we have in common with the other twelve is that, even as the end loomed before them, they still believed they had all the time in the world.

(Time . . .)

To fall when we are so near to slowing and even reversing the human aging process, when we are within mere decades of self-replicating robotics and interstellar flight—what could be more tragic?

(Time will have its say . . .)

I, for one, cling to the hope that the groundswell of any population is what determines its direction, as a civilization. On the *Keldysh* and at Zero, I have learned to believe that there are enough John Humes, Pat Browns, and Harry Ramoses around to keep our world afloat. The Athenians and the Herculaneans believed that future generations would acquire the knowledge necessary to tame Pandora's last demon, the one they had named Hope. They assigned to us the duty of transforming the monster into an angel. But what if they had it backward? What if their so-called human folly of hope (the end of accepting one's fate, the beginning of desire and worry) had really been a virtue all along? What if we really can build a future that our ancestors would have looked upon with pride and wonder? What if the combined accomplishments of all human civilizations up to this moment are but the twilight before the dawn, the hopes and dreams—both wondrous and perilous—of a species only now about to become truly adult?

What if?

Time will have its say. It always does.

SAINT PAUL'S CHAPEL, NEW YORK

JANUARY 26, 2003

ACKNOWLEDGMENTS

This is going to be rather long—and I hope I can mention all the major helpers on this project (or series of projects), without forgetting anyone. The paths to discovery do not get much longer or stranger than this . . . A child who could not read simple sentences, or interpret what people were saying (or even the meanings of expressions on their faces) . . . And yet the child, through his sheer love of science, and paintings, and symphonies, followed a path that led somehow from an inability to read, to the writing of books . . . And then, the "difficult child" followed a path from entomology and paleontology to the *Voyager* space probes at Io, Europa, and Ganymede . . . from Europa to the *Titanic* . . . from the *Titanic* to Thera, and back again to *Titanic* . . . to the volcanic seams that run along the ocean floors . . . from the hydrothermal vents to Europa again, and to Vesuvius . . . from Vesuvius to Ground Zero, Manhattan.

First and foremost, I thank my first great teachers: Mom, Dad, Adelle Dobie, Barbara and Dennis Harris, Agnes Saunders, and Ed McGunnigle. All of them were an improbable blessing. In those days, most people did not question experts who said the forever daydreaming little boy who wrote odd stories but who could not read ("The Clock That Ran Counterclockwise" sticks most in Mrs. Harris's mind), should be classified as "unteachable" and removed permanently from the public school system. My greatest stroke of good luck—my teachers—turned out to be rarer and more valuable than all the green or red diamonds in the world. None of them believed what the experts had said about a "ride the shock wave," school-hating boy who loved Darwin and Beethoven but who could not pass even the simplest IQ tests. To this day, no one really knows what went wrong. Some had said I was somewhere in the spectrum of autism, and this may be at least partly true (as suggested by such traits as a near-total inability to lie, except in such odd circumstances as the so-called "Minbari lie": as when protecting someone honorable or innocent from harm). To this day, my beginnings are a mystery to me, just as Stephen Jay Gould (one of my later teachers) was a mystery to himself; for we both grew up with many of the same quirks, and we both embraced science as a search for truth. Every one of my first teachers, all those years ago, broke the rules and questioned the opinions of authorities—who, for example, had said, "That child should be given up on." Thank you—Mom, Dad, Mr. and Mrs. Harris, Mrs. Saunders, and Ed McGunnigle. Breaking the rules meant a lot to me.

FOR WIDE-RANGING CONVERSATIONS, guidance, joint expedition work, joint research projects, and interviews spanning almost three decades—from New York to New Zealand, from the *Titanic* to Titan, from fossil lake beds to beds of dust mites, onto the high seas and deep under them—I am grateful to: Walter Lord, Stephen Jay Gould, Isaac Asimov, Frank Lombardi (AMNH), Edward I. Coher and John Strong (L.I.U.), Bill MacQuitty, Father Bob McGuire and Rabbi Zuscha Friedman (salt of the Earth), Jim Powell (Brookhaven National Laboratory), Cyril Ponnamperuma, Sir Arthur C. Clarke (University of Moratura, Sri Lanka), Claire Edwin Folsome and Alan Wilson (founders, Extinct DNA Study Group), Gerard R. Case and Donald Baird (Princeton), Father Mervyn Fernando (Subhodi Institute, Sri Lanka), Jesse A. Stoff (Solstice), Bill Schutt (American Museum of Natural History/L.I.U. and friend to Stoffy vampire bats), Roy Cullimore, Lori Johnston, Mark Newman (Droycon Bio./Sonar, and friends to bacterial slimes), Fred Haise, George Skurla (Northrop/Grumman), Det. John Murphy (NYPD), General Tom Stafford (USAF/NASA), Scott Carpenter (NASA/U.S. Navy Deep Submergence), Michael Foale (NASA/CCCP), Kevin McMahon (Warner Brothers), Rip MacKenzie, Tony Jordan, and THE Don Peterson . . .

Aboard the *Melville* and the *Atlantis II:* Bob Ballard, Cindy Lee van Dover, Tom Dettweiler, Ralph Hollis, David Sanders, John Salsig, Paul Tibbets, Will Sellers, Kirk McGeorge (Woods Hole Oceanographic Institute), Haraldur Sigurddson (U.R.I.), Jean Franchteau, Roger Hekinian . . .

Aboard the *Ocean Voyager* and at the IP-3 Laboratory: Michel Navatril, Roy Cullimore (again, a kindhearted slime-dweller), George Tulloch, Matt Tulloch, Bill Broad, Captain Paul Henry Narnageolet, and Stephane Pennec . . .

Aboard the *Keldysh:* Jim and Mike Cameron (friends to the ancestral Europa probe robots . . . and to ancestral Terminators), John David Cameron (USMC), Anatoly Sagalevich and his entire crew (who truly have become this family's *ohana*), Genya Cherniev and Victor, Viola, Lidia, "Doc," Sergi, Georgi and his incomparable biology team, our *Mir* cowboys and Lev ("the Levitator") . . . and Andrew Wright, John Bruno, Lewis Abernathy, Ed Marsh (for possessing all the social graces we scientist types sometimes lack), Don Lynch (for figuring out what paleontologists use for birth control: our personalities), John Broadwater, Ralph White, Mike Atkins, Doc Singleman, Vince Pace— Ken Marschall and Bill Paxton (for convincing me to start painting again). . . . My thanks also to those who found and forwarded messages in bottles, launched from *Keldysh* at *Titanic*. Out of some forty to fifty messages sent between September 3–24, 2001: Frank Fulker and dog "Buddy" (message launched 9/3/01, found on East Preston Beach, West Sussex, England, 3/30/02); the Ripley family (launched 9/6/01, found in England about April 5, 2002); Susan Lamy and family (launched 9/7/01, found by dog on isle of Jersey, Channel Islands, 3/20/02); Blair Maxwell (launched 9/7/01, found Isle of Islay, Argyushire, Scotland, about 10/17/02); Michael Walsh (launched 9/22/01, found in Waterford, Ireland, 4/10/02); Rayna Howe (launched 9/22/01, found on beach of Redhill, Veryan Bay, Surrey, England, 9/3/02).

In the field and in the lab: Jim Powell (because he's worth mentioning at least twice), the Cameron brothers (ditto), Bill Schutt (L.I.U.), Hiroshi Takahashi (Brookhaven National Laboratory), Pierre Noyes (Stanford Linear Accelerator), Ed Bishop (and Dee, too), Daniel Stanley (Smithsonian Institution), Peter Kuniholm, Lynn Margulis, Carl Sagan (Cornell), Benoit B. Mandelbrot (New York), Stephen Hawking (Cambridge), Francis Crick (the Salk Institute), Greg Benford, Luis and Walter Alvarez (Berkeley), Hans Goedicke (Johns Hopkins University), George Zebrowski, Pamela Sargent (SFWA), Philip and Michael Betancourt (University of Pennsylvania), Burton Rudman and Ed Porez

(Archaeological Institute of America), Rabbi Yeduda Getz, the Reverend Jill Potter, Benjamin and Amahai Mazar, Trude and Moshe Dothan (Israeli archaeology/Bronze Age), Nanno and Mrs. Spyridon Marinatos (Athens/Thera), Michele Cozzolino, Carlo Illario (Herculaneum), Mary Lee Young (for excavating the smallest victims), Joshua Stoff (Cradle of Aviation Museum and follower of Roman shipwrecks), Holly McClure and Ruben Thunderbird (friends to Twisted Hair and other prophets), Steve Carey, Steve Sparks (University of Rhode Island), Frank Andrews (New Zealand National Observatory), Merv Loper (Victoria University), Sir Charles Flemming (DSIR, New Zealand), Charles Sheffield, Eugene Shoemaker, Michael Rampino (NASA), Pat Vickers Ritch (Oz) . . .

In the crater of Zero: Doug McClean (FDNY history), Haraldur Sigurdsson, the Reverend Milton Williams (Saint Paul's), Suk Tan Chin (sister of Robert Chin), Don Scala (PAPD), Paul Mallery (FDNY), Bartender Mike (O'Hara's Restaurant and Pub), Jim McNally, Jimmy Bruno, Hank Lombardi, Matt Carini, Gene Kelty, Brian Armstrong, Mike Harris, Gene Rice (FDNY), "Ellie" (from Zero to Keldysh), Olinda Cedeno, Keith Young (FDNY), Jerry Routolo (Windows on the World photographer/archivist), Tom Vallebouna (FDNY), Ronald Spadafora (FDNY), Rhonda Schearer (archivist/historian), Sean Crawley (NYPD), Blake McLouglin (FDNY), Roger Parrino (NYPD), Richard Meo (FDNY), Ed Gutch (PAPD), Timothy O'Neill (NYPD), the Lee Young family, Felix Limardo, Russ Galen and Mary Perillo ("civilians"), Sean O'Malley (FDNY), Sean McCloskey (NYPD/NYC Medical Examiner's Office), James McCloskey (FDNY and Saint Paul's), John Morabito (FDNY), Aaron Greenstein (PAPD), Vinnie Dunne (FDNY), Robert Vargas (PAPD), Genelle Guzman (Port Authority), Paul Hoffman (Patlaw), Richard Picciotto (FDNY), Stephanie Clarke, Hanna and Sharon McAvinue (in memory of Donna Clarke), Lt. Devona (PAPD), Pat Cullen, Thomas von Essen, Pete Hayden, Earl Anderson, Greg MaCagnone, Kevin Shea, John Salka and Joe Falco (FDNY), Michael Penna (Rescue 1), Spencer Kobren, Tim Pearson (NYPD), K. Escoffrey (FDNY), Stephen Bienowski (NYPD), Jay Jonas (FDNY), "Cisco" (at J&R Music World, under WTC), Michael Jacobs, David Scott (USMC), Teri Tobin (NYPD), and Henry "Hank" Lallave (PAPD: who, on 9-11-02, gave me his WTC lapel pin, "To keep you safe, in all the dark places you must go." (The pin has since traveled in *Mir-1* to the Atlantis fracture zone and the hydrothermal formation known as "Lost City.")

IN THE SLAVE DRIVER and friends of this project category, I thank my agent, Russ Galen (yes, he's a slave driver, but I'm a workaholic so it's a perfect match), Jennifer Brehl, Kate Nintzel, Andrea Molitor, Maureen Clark, James Cameron, Rae Sanchini, Andrew Wright, Kevin McMahon, Adam Handlesman, Ed Bishop, Arthur C. Clarke, Rip MacKenzie, Paul Mallery, Rhonda Shearer (for the FDNY and for Stephen Jay Gould), Charles Petit, Doug McClean, and Orion Resources.

CONDEMNATIONS: You know who you are.

I WOULD LIKE TO GIVE a special and heartfelt thank-you to Disney Studios, and to the team behind *Lilo and Stitch,* for having created and released that film in the midst of forensic physics and forensic archaeology at Zero. If not for that cartoon, and for my children, I do not know that I would ever have laughed again. I needed warmth and laughter, then, more than words can describe.

And a final thank-you to Pat Brown, wherever you are . . .
Ohana.

SELECTED BIBLIOGRAPHY

Adkins, L., and R. A. Adkins. *Handbook to Life in Ancient Rome.* Oxford: Oxford University Press, 1994.

Alvarez, W. (and Luis). *T. rex and the Crater of Doom.* Princeton, NJ: Princeton University Press, 1997.

Aurelius, M. *Meditations.* Translated by M. Staniforth. New York: Penguin, 1964.

Berry, P. *The Christian Inscription at Pompeii.* London: Edwin Mellen Press, 1995.

Bietak, M. "Minoan Wall-Paintings Unearthed at Ancient Avaris." *Egyptian Archaeology* 2 (1992): 26–28.

Birley, A. *Septimus Severus: The African Emperor.* New Haven, CT: Yale University Press, 1989.

Bisel, Sara C., with Jane Bisel and Shelley Tanaka. *The Secrets of Vesuvius.* Toronto: Madison Press, 1990.

Cameron, J., et al. *Ghosts of the Abyss.* Video. Disney / IMAX, 2004.

Cameron, J., et al. *Volcanoes of the Deep* and *X-Treme Life Expeditions* Disney / Earthship, 2004.

Carey, S. N., and H. Sigurddson. "The Eruption of Vesuvius in AD 79: II Variations in Column Height and Discharge Rate." *Bulletin of the Geological Society of America* 99 (1986): 303–314.

Castleden, R. *Minoans.* New York: Routledge Press, 1994.

Cioni, R., et al. "Pompeii Debris Yields Calamity Clues." *Journal of Geophysical Research* (February 2004); and summarized in *Science News,* Vol 165 (March 13, 2004), p 174.

Clarke, A. B., et al. "Transient Dynamics of Vulcanian Explosions and Column Collapse." *Nature,* February 21, 2002, 897–901.

Connolly, P. *Pompeii.* Oxford: Oxford University Press, 2000.

Deiss, J. J. *Herculaneum: Italy's Buried Treasure.* New York: Harper, 1985.

Delgado, J. P., et al. *The Archaeology of the Atomic Bomb.* Southwest Cultural Resources Center Professional Papers, no. 37. Santa Fe, NM: Southwest Cultural Resources Center, 1991.

Dio, Cassius. *Roman History.* Translated by E. Cary. Cambridge, MA: Harvard University Press, 1917.

Fagan, B. *The Little Ice Age.* New York: Basic Books, 2000.

Fernando, M. *In Spirit and in Truth: An Exploration of Buddhist / Christian and East / West Crosscurrents.* Sri Lanka: Vishva Lekha, 2001.

Foss, C. *Roman Historical Coins.* London: Trafalgar Press, 1990.

Franklin, B. "Meteorological Imaginations [Light Conductivity] and Conjectures." In vol. 2 of *Memoirs of the Literary and Philosophical Society of Manchester,* 373–377. 2d ed. London: T. Caldwell in the Strand, 1789.

Gibbon, E. *The Decline and Fall of the Roman Empire.* New York: Heritage Press, 1946.

Gigante, M., and D. Obbink. *Philodemus in Italy: The Books of Herculaneum*. Ann Arbor: University of Michigan Press, 1998.

Giuliani, R. W. *Leadership*. New York: Hyperion, 2002.

Glad, C. E. Paul. *Philodemus: Adaptability in Epicurean and Early Christian Psychagogy*. New York: E. J. Brill, 1995.

Gould, S. J. *Ever Since Darwin*. New York: W. W. Norton, 1977.

———. *The Structure of Evolutionary Theory*. Cambridge, MA: Harvard University Press, 2002.

Grant, M. *Cities of Vesuvius: Pompeii and Herculaneum*. London: Phoenix Press, 1971.

Greenhut, Z., and R. Reich. "The Tomb of Caiaphas." *Biblical Archaeology Review* 18 (1992): 28–57.

Grudd, H., et al. "Trees May Hold Secret of Atlantis." *Geophysical Research Letters*, September 15, 2000.

Harrington, C. R., ed. *The Year Without a Summer: World Climate in 1816*. ???: Canadian Museum of Nature, 1992.

Jashemski, W. F. *The Gardens of Pompeii, Herculaneum, and the Villas Destroyed by Vesuvius*. New Rochelle, NY: Caratzas Brothers, 1979.

Jones, B. W. *The Emperor Titus*. London: Croom Helm, 1984.

Josephus, F. *The New Complete Works of Josephus*. Translated by W. Whiston, with commentary by P. L. Maier. Grand Rapids, MI: Kregel Press, 1999.

Kerr, R. A. "A Volcanic Crisis for Ancient Life?" *Science*, October 6, 1995.

Keys, D. *Catastrophe [AD 535]: An Investigation into the Origins of the Modern World*. New York: Ballantine Books, 2000.

Lawrence, R. *Roman Pompeii*. New York: Routledge, 1994.

Lemaire, A., et al. "Ossuary of James." *Biblical Archaeology Review*, 2003–2004. (To date, *BAR* records, and shall continue to record, a detailed running account of scientific analysis and debates surrounding the James inscription.)

Lynch, Don, and Ken Marschall. *Ghosts of the Abyss*. Toronto: Madison Press, 2003.

Maier, P. M., trans. *Eusebius—The Church History: A New Translation with Commentary*. Grand Rapids, MI: Kregel Press, 1999.

Mastrolorenzo, G., et al. "Herculaneum Victims of Vesuvius in AD 79," *Nature*, April 12, 2001.

McAllister, T., ed. *World Trade Center Building Performance Study: Data Collection, Preliminary Observations, and Recommendations*. FEMA report 403, September 2002.

McClure, H. *Twisted Hair*. New York: R.J. Communications LLC, 2002.

Nicol, D. M. *A Biographical Dictionary of the Byzantine Empire*. London: Seaby, 1991.

Pang, K. D. "The Legacies of Eruption." *The Sciences* 31 (1991): 30–35.

Pellegrino, C. R. *Return to Sodom and Gomorrah: Bible Stories from Archaeologists*. New York: HarperCollins, 1994.

———. *Ghosts of the Titanic*. New York: William Morrow, 2000.

———. *Unearthing Atlantis*. 3rd ed. New York: HarperCollins, 2001.

Platon, N. Zakros. *The Rediscovery of a Lost Palace of Ancient Crete*. New York: Scribners, 1971.

Pliny. *Letters and Panegyricus*. Translated by Radice and Loeb. Cambridge, MA: Harvard University Press, 1969.

Quinn, P. J. *Dusk to Dawn: Survivor Accounts of the Last Night on the Titanic*. Hollis, NH: Fantail Press, 1999.

Raven, S. *Rome in Africa*. New York: Routledge, 1993.

Ritch, T., and P. V. Ritch. *Dinosaurs of Darkness*. Bloomington: Indiana University Press, 2000.

Robinson, J. M., ed. *The Nag Hammadi Library*. New York: HarperCollins, 1990.

Scarre, C. *Chronicle of the Roman Emperors*. London: Thames and Hudson, 1995.

Shaw, B. D., trans. and ed. *Spartacus and the Slave Wars: Roman Documents*. New York: Bedford / St. Martins, 2001.

Sigurdsson, H., ed., et al. *Encyclopedia of Volcanoes*. Orlando, FL: Academic Press, 1999.

———. *Melting the Earth: The History of Ideas on Volcanic Eruptions*. London: Oxford University Press, 1999.

———. *Volcanoes and the Environment: Exploring the Earth System*. Orlando, FL: Academic Press, 2003.

Sigurdsson, H., S. N. Carey, et al. "The Eruption of Vesuvius in AD 79." *National Geographic Research* 1 (1985): 332–387.

Smith, D. *Report from Ground Zero: The Story of the Rescue Efforts at the World Trade Center*. New York: Viking, 2002.

Stanley, D., and H. Cheng. "Cores of Santorini (Thera) Ash Layer in the Nile Delta." *Science*, 1987, 499–500.

Stewart, J. B. *Heart of a Soldier: A Story of Love, Heroism, and September 11th*. New York: Simon & Schuster, 2002.

Stuiver, M., and P. D. Oqay. "Changes in Atmospheric Carbon-14 Attributed to a Variable Sun." *Science*, January 4, 1980, 11.

Suetonius, G. *The Twelve Caesars*. Translated by Robert Graves. London: Penguin, 1957, 1979. See also Graves's novelizations, *I Claudius* and *Claudius the God,* and the incomparable BBC miniseries of the same title.

Sullivan, W. "Rio Artifacts May Indicate Roman Visit." *New York Times,* October 10, 1982.

Van Dover, C. L. *The Ecology of Deep-Sea Hydrothermal Vents*. Princeton, NJ: Princeton University Press, 2000.

Wallace-Hadrill, A. *Houses and Society in Pompeii and Herculaneum*. Princeton, NJ: Princeton University Press, 1994.

Ward, P. D. "The Permian Extinction." *Science,* June 6, 2002.

Zanker, P. *Pompeii: Public and Private Life*. Cambridge, MA: Harvard University Press, 1998.

INDEX

BOOKS BY CHARLES PELLEGRINO

GHOSTS OF VESUVIUS

ISBN 0-06-075100-2 (trade paperback) • Non Fiction
As one of the world's only experts on downblast and surge physics,
Pellegrino was invited to Ground Zero to examine the site and
compare it to Vesuvius. In doing so, he offers us a glimpse into the
final moments of our own "American Vesuvius."

DUST

ISBN 0-380-78742-3 (mass market paperback) • Fiction
In an idyllic Long Island community, paleobiologist Richard
Sinclair is one of the first to suspect that the environment has
begun to wage bloody, terrifying war on humanity.

GHOSTS OF THE TITANIC

ISBN 0-380-72472-3 (mass market paperback) • History
The most vivid and compelling re-creation yet of the doomed liner's
horrific final moments—and never-before-revealed truths about the
tragic leviathan's history, fate, and breathtaking legacy.

HER NAME, TITANIC

ISBN 0-380-70892-2 (mass market paperback) • History
In 1912, the ocean liner struck an iceberg. Seventy-three years later,
a group of scientists set sail on a mission that uncovered shocking
secrets buried two miles below the ocean's surface.

RETURN TO SODOM AND GOMORRAH

ISBN 0-380-72633-5 (trade paperback) • History
Dr. Charles Pellegrino, "the real Indiana Jones," takes us on a
remarkable journey from the Nile to the Tigris-Euphrates
rivers—crossing time, legend, and ancient lands to explore
the unsolved mysteries of the Old Testament.

UNEARTHING ATLANTIS

ISBN 0-380-81044-1 (mass market paperback) • History
Pellegrino reanimates an astounding lost civilization and re-creates
with explosive power the apocalyptic cataclysm that destroyed their
remarkable island metropolis.